Pushing the Indians Out

Early Movers & Shakers in
Western North Carolina (and Tennessee Territory)

Part 1. Descendants

Part 2. Early NC Land Grants

Appendix: Revolutionary War Patriots
Buried in Western North Carolina

by Charles R. Haller

July, 2014

First Edition	July 2014
Author	Charles R. Haller
Cover Illustration	Ralph Parker
Cover design	Bart Smith
Proof Readers	Marie Hoffman, Sabrina Haller
InDesign Editor	Diana Wade
Tech Support	Alexandra Wagner

Haller, Charles R., 1931-

Pushing the Indians Out

Includes Index

ISBN 978-0-9703748-2-0

1. Pioneer Cemeteries. 2. Early Genealogy. 3. Pre-1800 Maps. 4. Early Surveying. 5. Indians

6. Land Grants - Western North Carolina. 7. Land Grants, Tennessee. 8. Speculators.

9. Revolutionary War.

About the Cover

Beginning in the mid 1700s, the Conestoga Wagon was a primary mode of transportation for families migrating southward from eastern Pennsylvania along the Appalachian Mountains. This wagon style was designed to ford rivers, many of which drained eastward. Equally important for travel to hostile lands were the Pennsylvania rifles.

The front cover of this book is a reproduction of a gouache by Ralph Parker from a restored Conestoga wagon now located at the Clarence (NY) Historical Museum. Mr. Parker lives in Missouri City, TX. He maintains an active website showing many of his other paintings, for all of which he maintains a copyright. The cover is used with his permission.

Contents

Introduction   1

Mysteries of Upland Pioneer Cemeteries   3

Genealogy & Land Grants   6

What's in a Name?   9

Deciphering the 1790 Census   11

Coxes in a Nutshell   13

Quandries of the Penns   16

George Washington, Speculator or Opportunist?   18

North Carolina In the Beginning   20

Early Explorers and Mapmakers   22

Native Americans in Western North Carolina   26

North Carolina Land Entries   29

Speaking of Surveyors   34

Speculators in Western North Carolina   38

Thars Gold in Them Thar Hills   41

Lesser Speculators in Western North Carolina   43

What Happened to the Speculation Lands of Western North Carolina?   44

Speculators in Tennessee Territory   47

Deed Mapping   51

Recording Land Entries   52

Cheap Land   53

Summary   54

Acknowledgments   56

Explanation of Appendix I - Revolutionary War   58

Selected Land Grant References: 61

Western North Carolina (Military) Companies in 1790 Census   65

Part I: Descendants   66

Part II: Early Western North Carolina Land Grants   177

Subject Index - Introductory Part   285

Introduction

When I was editor of *A Lot of Bunkum,* quarterly of the Old Buncombe County Genealogical Society, in the years from 2003 through 2010, I began a series of simplified charts called "Descendants of [*individual's name*]." These genealogical road maps generally outline a prominent pioneer family in Western North Carolina and their subsequent generations. Notable individuals of generations four and five are sometimes included on these charts. Eventually, these charts totaled 57. Many "First Families," Revolutionary War patriots, and other pioneers from Western North Carolina comprise the list. In this book, I present the entire series of updated descendant charts (part I) with all new, matching state land grants (part II). Not only do the Descendant Charts show names of key individuals and their spouses in a lineage the charts also relate these individuals to their burial places.

In this publication, we ask the following questions:

- Who were the movers and shakers in early Western North Carolina?

- What role did the military play in early Western North Carolina?

- What role did native Indians play?

- What role did the lawyers play?

- What role did the Blacks play?

- Who lived where? And when?

- Who migrated where? And when? And why?

- What are the complexities of early pioneer cemeteries?

- What were the two most important events of land acquisition?

- Who acquired land? Who speculated on land?

- Where are the land record indexes located?

- Why were land grants valued in pounds and shillings until 1820?

- What little known facts do the land records hold?

- How is the 1790 Census evaluated

- How did land grants in Tennessee differ from western North Carolina

1

Mysteries of Upland Pioneer Cemeteries

The author inspected virtually all of the older cemeteries in Buncombe County as well as key cemeteries in Henderson, Transylvania, Burke, and McDowell Counties. These counties are in the Blue Ridge Physiographic Province, i.e., the Appalachian Mountains that trend across the state from a southwest to a northeast direction. Tombstone rock types were noted to determine which tombstones were original and which likely were much later emplacements thus bringing into question the actual burial place.

Today, Buncombe County cemeteries include one large public cemetery and eleven large commercial cemeteries, all of recent origin. The county total is more than four hundred. Many small older cemeteries are on private land; many of these are overgrown with tall blackberry bushes, poison ivy, brush, and trees.

The spine of the Appalachian Mountains is composed of high grade metamorphic rocks, commonly referred to as gneiss, but often, inaccurately, as schist. Bands of garnet and other semi-precious minerals may be present at certain outcrops, as well as iron ore.

In the simplest of terms, rock types give an important clue as to the history of the cemetery. Generally speaking, local metamorphic rocks, being mainly gneiss, were used to mark the earliest graves. These "fieldstones" usually have no markings, but occasionally did have a few crudely chiseled letters. In Western North Carolina; gneisses were used from the 1760s to about the 1860s.

Low grade metamorphic rocks occur in the Piedmont. The term "soapstone" is sometimes encountered in the description of gravestones. Actually soapstone is a low grade metamorphic rock, being related to common talc. It is relatively soft and thus easy to carve. "Soapstone" is rarely, if ever, encountered in the cemeteries of western North Carolina. Daniel W. Patterson's recent book *The True Image* contains good examples of soapstone gravestones from the Piedmont of central North Carolina.

White marbles, a type of low grade metamorphic rock, usually imported from Europe, appeared as early as 1820 in western North Carolina, or in rare cases before (i.e., Quaker Meadows Cemetery, Burke Co., a late 1700s cemetery), and were used until about 1900. They were relatively easy to carve with hand tools, as compared to gneisses. Consequently they normally had names and dates and sometimes short text.

In the early 1900s, William O. Wolfe, a well-know Asheville gravestone provider, imported nine or so marble angels which were carved in Italy. These angels are scattered in a variety of cemeteries in western North Carolina.

While grave markers rank among the most reliable records of vital information, a word of caution is advised. For instance, military marbles for Revolutionary War soldiers were not commonly provided by the Government until 1918. Thus many military marbles were set long after the fact, and often are in the wrong place. A case in point is the military marble for Lt. Samuel Patton (1761-1851), a Revolutionary War veteran, now located at Riverside Cemetery in Asheville. The cemetery was not opened until about 1885. Today, most military marbles come from Vermont.

From about 1885 to 1900 or so, the remains of many former citizens of Asheville, Buncombe County's main city, were moved to Riverside Cemetery, a large public cemetery. For example, many of the prominent James Patton family, having been buried in the Episcopal Churchyard on Church Street, were moved.

The First Presbyterian Cemetery in the same Church Street vicinity, Asheville, was eventually built over, much to the dismay of some congregation members. About four Baird family members were moved to Riverside, but the tombstones of four Bairds are still to be found in a crawl space under the church. The 28 extant tombstones at the church suggest up to 50 others may be there including two infant Woodfins, and William Henry Hardy, a noted Civil War casualty.

Today, the crawl space under First Presbyterian is blanketed with up to one quarter inch of suffocating red clay dust. Pioneer Zebulon Baird, who died in 1824, is represented by a flattened marble in the crawl space, as is his wife, Hannah Baird, who died in 1849. The matching Italian marbles weigh more than 400 lbs. each.

Across Church Street, another large cemetery was covered over by the Central Methodist Church. Access to this cemetery is not possible and the records indicate only that David Coleman was moved to Riverside Cemetery, but another three Colemans, several Merrimons, and possibly 100 others may still be there.

Gray marbles, mostly imported from northern Georgia, were used in Western North Carolina from about 1870 to 1920. The blemishes in this type of low grade metamorphic rock discouraged their use. Inscriptions may be hard to read and to photograph because of the inherent blemishes. They are subject to cracking during harsh winters.

Sedimentary rocks common in the northern United States, such as limestone, sandstone, and shale are virtually unknown in Western North Carolina cemeteries. In modern times, sedimentary rocks have tended to deteriorate so that markings are difficult to decipher.

Fortunately, in 1938-1939, the Works Progress Administration (WPA), in an attempt to provide employment during that difficult era, hired people to survey cemeteries. In Buncombe Co., 21 cemeteries, including the large Riverside cemetery, were surveyed. Some of the gravestones recorded at that time are no longer legible.

Igneous rocks, such as red and gray granites, transported from mines in Vermont, New Hampshire, Brazil, and other localities, proliferated in the late 1800s with the introduction of railroads and mechanical engraving tools. In the 1900s, they became the dominant type because of their durability.

The number of unmarked fieldstones, such as in the isolated Capt. William Moore cemetery, was an important clue to the history of settlement of an area. The Capt. William Moore Cemetery in Enka is one of the oldest preserved cemeteries in Buncombe Co., dating probably from the 1780s or 1790s. It contains early, imported marbles showing the names of 11 individuals from the Moore and related Candler families. In addition it contains some 65 fieldstones with no names. We can only speculate who the 65 fieldstones represent. Fortunately, in 1982, the many descendants of William Moore made a determined effort to renovate and maintain the unused cemetery.

Similarly, the abandoned and overgrown Ashworth cemetery in Fairview with its 24 or so fieldstones also leads to speculation as to who is buried there. In recent years, a plaque along the nearest road, a quarter mile distant, refers only to John Ashworth, Sr. (1735-1805) and John Ashworth, Jr. (1775-1827).

2

Genealogy & Land Grants

In the years since 2003, considerable time was spent in untangling the complicated genealogy and related state land grants of the early Davidson families, and also the complex records of the various branches of the pioneering McDowell families, the latter being mostly somehow related.

The various unrelated Patton families and their land records in Western North Carolina presented another challenging problem. At least three groups of unrelated Pattons are to be found in Western North Carolina which I tentatively call the Asheville group, the Biltmore group, and the Swannanoa group according to their geographic center of location as indicated by their cemetery records.

Further, much time was spent compiling genealogical and land records of pioneers William Moore, and of Abraham Reynolds, among many others.

Other notable early families include that of William Gudger and his wife Martha "Patsy" Young. The couple had eight children and 83 grandchildren. Although most of the grandchildren remained in Buncombe Co., some scattered to Alabama and to Tennessee. A multitude of the current native population of Buncombe County claim descent from the Gudgers.

The Robert Love family of Haywood Co. is another noteworthy pioneering family. Robert Love and his wife Mary Ann Dillard had 12 children and 85 grandchildren. Some children remained in Haywood Co.; others scattered to South Carolina, Tennessee, and to various parts of western North Carolina.

In mid-2010, while compiling the descendant chart for the Zachariah Candler family, I became interested in Zachariah's obsession with accumulating land grants issued by the State of North Carolina. In the years 1800 to 1841, this remarkable individual entered 81 state grants comprising 21,915 acres. At first, Candler's land records appeared to be chaotic, but in late 2010, I stumbled across three series of master indexes to early North Carolina state land grants.

These indexes were:
(a) reconstructed land grant files at the Burke County Public Library,
(b) a 1930s WPA land grant card file at the U.S. Forestry Service in Asheville, and
(c) land grants in the MARS program via Internet of the NC State Archives, Raleigh.

Copies of selected land grant records at the Register of Deeds, Buncombe Co., also were an aid to interpretation of some land records, bearing in mind that nearly all these early records were handwritten B/W copies.

Hand-written copies of deeds at the Buncombe County Register of Deeds probably stem from the early 1900s when Foster A. Sondley, a noted Asheville lawyer was active in untangling land records. The hand-written deed records, however, contain many omissions, especially among early deeds with a few deeds transcribed erroneously.

In 1888 when New York financier George W. Vanderbilt began buying property in western North Carolina, he helped sustain employment for Asheville's lawyers. A noted photograph dating from 1898, taken in Asheville, western North Carolina's largest city, shows an active lawyers association with 30 lawyers being present. Work on land titles acquired by Vanderbilt proved to be a much needed financial source especially welcome during the recession of 1893-1896.

By 1909, Vanderbilt's platoon of lawyers and clerks would cobble together approximately 125,000 acres from nearly 600 parcels. Some of Vanderbilt's purchases cost $0.27 per acre; some cost considerably more. A long time holdout, Theodore Graham reportedly sold Vanderbilt his 156 acres of tillable land, with its ramshackle improvements, for $359.21, or $2.30 per acre.

In 1895, Vanderbilt completed Biltmore House, the largest private home in America, located just south of Asheville, being some 178,000 sq. ft. He spent about $10 million on the house and estate.

From 1917 to 1921, the widow Edith Stuyvesant Dresser Vanderbilt sold 80,000 acres in eight lots to the Federal Government. The property was included in the Pisgah National Forest. Spot checks of sale prices range from $5.00 to $7.00 per acre.

Life-long bachelor Foster A. Sondley used his legal contacts to speculate in properties, grabbing up good deals when they arose. From 1886 to 1922, his name appears on 40 grantee records. Most properties were in downtown Asheville. From 1902 to 1912, the eccentric Sondley bought over 770 acres in upper Haw Creek, where he built a two story native stone house with a library room large enough to accommodate 32,918 local history books and a large egg shell collection that he received as partial payment for his work on an estate settlement. The house, still in good condition with its exotic copper gutters, and one acre of ground, sold in the 1990s for well into the six figures. See Descendants of Harriet Elizabeth Alexander for further information.

Eventually, I learned that Waightstill Avery, Burke County's top frontier lawyer, exceeded Zachariah Candler in his pursuit of acquiring early land grants. From 1778 to 1818, Avery acquired 117 blocks in Burke Co. and 34 blocks in Buncombe Co. The acreage totaled about 30,335 acres. Avery also had four grants in eastern Tennessee, totaling 660 acres. In the 1780s, Avery served as an attorney in Jonesborough, TN, a straight line distance of about 55 miles from his home in Morganton, NC, across the grain of the Appalachian Mountains; Avery traveled by horseback over the primitive Watauga Trail about two days each way. Probably his clients settled their legal fees in part with land.

In this paper, the land records concern first and foremost Burke Co., and to a lesser extent, Rutherford Co., areas that initially once covered nearly all of Western North Carolina. In 1792, with the formation of Buncombe Co. from Burke and from Rutherford, another set of land grants came into existence.

For readers not familiar with the key MARS program at the NC State Archives, typed summaries of individual grants may be accessed on the Internet through a series of call numbers. For instance, the call number for Buncombe Co. is S.108.513, that for Burke Co. is S.108.541, and for Rutherford Co., S.108.1030. Unfortunately, grants are listed primarily under a series of file numbers (and not grant number) which show considerable disorder.

Some files are missing. Many recorded grants likely were preempted by an earlier grant, but few court records exist to clarify the situation. The above newer, sparsely settled counties are distinct from the older counties defined in the next paragraph.

Further, many family names common to Western North Carolina are to be found in the MARS land records of Anson Co., S.108.399; Iredell Co., S.108.742; Mecklenburg Co., S.108.835; and Rowan Co., S.108.1016, etc. Colonial grants in these older areas likely were fixed and apparently not subject to recall. However, copies of many pre-Revolutionary War grants are not in the State Archives.

For instance, if we search S.108.637 in the MARS program, we find Jacob Blount, head of the prominent Blount family of North Carolina who got a grant of 240 acres in 1757 in Craven Co., NC. Further, we find on page 562-563 in vol. 1 of *The John Gray Blount Papers*, a list of 20 grants in Craven Co. received by Jacob Blount as well as eight grants in Pitt Co. His total acreage was 6,318. These grants, being pre-Revolutionary War, evidently stem from the older Granville series of land grants.

In Western North Carolina, permanent North Carolina state land grant entries date from early 1778. Generally speaking, I followed grants to individuals listed in my descendant charts up until about the 1820s, or in the case of Zachariah Candler from his first entry in 1800 until his demise in the mid 1840s.

By collating the three sets of master indexes for Burke, Rutherford, and Buncombe Counties, I was able to coordinate a reasonably accurate set of land grants for Zachariah Candler, and eventually for 62 or so groups of Western North Carolina families. As in any work covering a massive amount of data, much of it handwritten, inevitable typos creep in; these typos and matters of interpretation are thought to be minimal.

3

What's in a Name?

The handwritten land records show much variation in the spelling of family names. The problem is two-fold. Assuming the record taker was literate, he may not have understood how the name was pronounced, or may not have been familiar with possible spellings, a point especially true for non-English names. Also, the illiterate or semi-literate name-giver may not have known precisely how to spell his or her own name. Modern transcribers have similar problems with foreign names, especially German names and Irish names.

One example involves the family name of Abraham Reynolds, i.e., Randels, Runnells, and Reynolds. Why was Reynolds' name spelled on official land records in at least three different ways? Was this a corrupted foreign name such as the case with Adam Biffel, who was of German ancestry?

Noteworthy pioneers and permanent settlers from Western North Carolina included:

Alexander	Davidson (2x)	Justice	Reynolds
Ashworth	Deaver	Killian	Rice
Baird	Eller	Kuykendall	Sams
Biffel	Fletcher	Lance	Smith
Brank	Foster	Lane	Stroup
Brevard	Gash	Love	Swain
Brittain	Gillaspie	Lytle	Thrash
Bryson	Greenlee	Maney	Vance
Burton	Gudger	McDowell (3x)	Webb
Candler	Hawkins	Mclean	Whitaker
Carland	Henry	Merrill	Whitson
Carson	Hemphill	Mills	Woodfin
Cathey	Hoodenpile	Moore	Worley
Chunn	Hughey	Patton (3x)	Young
Clayton	Israel	Penland	
Craig	Jarrett	Ragsdale	

Of the above names, those of Scots-Irish origin, mostly Presbyterian, predominate. These names include: Alexander, Carson, Cathey, Chunn, Davidson, Gillaspie, Greenlee, Hemphill, Henry, McDowell, McGimpsey/McGimsey, McLean, McPeters, Moore, Patton, and Vance. Associated names include Erwin/Irwin, Moffitt, Tate, and many others. A 2002 book by Hugh Dussek (*Pre-Revolutionary History*, etc.) goes into great detail about the early preponderance of Presbyterians among the Scots-Irish of Mecklenburg Co., and the Highland Scots of Cumberland Co., both counties being in North Carolina.

Names of German origin include Biffel, Brank, Creasman, Eller, Killian, Lentz/Lance, Stroup, Thrash, and Weaver (Weber in German). German names listed in Appendix l, but not included in this land study include Corn, Messer, Shook, Siler, and Wetzel. Other German names in western North Carolina are Beard, Clontz, Hildebrand, and Shuford. The Germans were mostly Lutherans and German Reformed.

Dutch names include Hoodenpile and Kuykendall/Kijkendahl, both being recorded in many variations. The Dutch and the Germans together comprised a very small, scattered minority of pioneers in Western North Carolina.

Geographic names also show some tricky variations. While the French Broad River, the predominant river in Western North Carolina, mostly kept its name uniformly, smaller rivers and tributaries such as the Indian names Catawba, Swannanoa, and Hominy Valley are often misspelled. Moreover, some minor tributaries changed names. For instance, Sweeten Creek of central Buncombe Co. originally was referred to as Flat Creek, not to be confused with Flat (or Flatt) Creek of northern Buncombe Co.

4

Deciphering the 1790 Census

General Daniel Morgan was a principal officer in the Revolutionary War and is remembered especially for leading the vital 1781 Battle of Cowpens in northern South Carolina. His name is reflected in the 1790 North Carolina census with its Morgan District that contains four counties, namely Burke Co. and Wilkes Co., both being organized in 1777, as well as Lincoln Co. and Rutherford Co., the latter two dating from 1779. The four counties were subdivided by "Companies" (i.e., militia units)

The 1790 North Carolina Census is a primary source of information. With the exception of family name Greenlee, the above names are listed in it, either as residents of Burke Co., Morgan district, or as residents of Rutherford Co., Morgan District. Burke County contained thirteen "Companies", i.e., subdivisions, while Rutherford County contained fourteen "Companies." No printed map has been located to show the geographic relationship of the twenty-seven "Companies" even though an intensive search of U.S. libraries and map collections was made.

However, taking clues from members of the Burke County Genealogical Society in Morganton and from the Old Tryon County Genealogical Society (Rutherford) in Forest City, in conjunction with early land records, we were able to conjure up a joint opinion as to the general location of the twenty-seven Companies.

In 1974, historian C. Kenyon Withrow produced a sketch map for Rutherford County. His map explanation is worth repeating:

> *Rutherford County, North Carolina.* Showing the main water courses most often noted as reference points in early land records. Numbers indicate the general location of the fourteen Militia Companies as shown on the 1790 Census. These companies had no set boundaries, but consisted generally of the more densely settled areas along a particular creek or creeks and the adjacent areas.

The reader is directed to the tabulation of population statistics at the end of this introductory section. In 1790, the population of Burke Co. was 7,546 with the average household containing 6.02 persons. By comparison, the population of Rutherford Co. totaled 7,152 with the average household being 6.06 persons. Males slightly outnumbered females. Each county had additional slaves, adding 597 in the case of Burke Co. Urban areas, generally located along relatively flat areas along creeks and rivers, tended to have greater population density compared to hilly and rocky, wilderness areas.

By cluster analysis of families, it is possible to extrapolate in general modern day terms locations of most of the various "Companies" (military districts) of the 1790 North Carolina Census. Thus, the geographic locations of nine "Companies" in old Burke Co. are as follows:

> First Company - now southern McDowell Co. (Pleasant Gardens) & northern Rutherford Co. (in part)
> Third Company—now midwest Burke Co.
> Fourth Company—now northwestern Burke Co. & northeastern McDowell Co. (in part)
> Sixth Company—now southwestern Burke Co. & southeastern McDowell Co.
> Seventh Company—now Quaker Meadows area of Burke Co.
> Tenth Company—now Yancey Co. (also part of ?Mitchell & Avery Cos.)
> Eleventh Company—now Buncombe Co.
> Twelfth Company—now Madison Co.
> Thirteen Company—now Morganton area of Burke Co.

Geographic locations of five "Companies" in old Rutherford Co. are:

> Second Company—now Polk County
> Tenth Company—near Forest City, Rutherford Co.
> Twelfth Company—now Polk Co.
> Thirteenth Company—now Buncombe Co.
> Fourteenth Company—now Henderson Co.

The First Company of Burke Co., which much later became part of McDowell Co., is an example of cluster analysis. Here, we find family names such as Carson, Cathey, Davidson, Dobson, Hemphill, McDowell, McPeters, and Patten/Patton, all living along the Catawba River in the vicinity of Pleasant Gardens.

The Seventh Company of Burke Co. occurred in the area which became famous as Quaker Meadows. Family names such as Erwin and McDowell, stand out among the other early inhabitants. The famous landmark Quaker Meadows Cemetery, on the north side of the Catawba River, dates at least as early as 1767.

The Eleventh Company of Burke Co., which in 1792 became part of north and west Buncombe Co., is an another example of cluster analysis. In this area, we find the (often misspelled) family names notably Alexander, Beefle/Bufle, Brittain, Cunigam/Cunningham, Davison/Davidson, Deever/Deaver, Gudger, Killian, Patten/Patton, Ragsdil/Ragsdale, Rice, Vance, Weaver, Whitson, and Young. These names for the most part also are shown on the 1800 NC Census for Buncombe Co.

The Thirteenth Company of Rutherford Co., which in 1792 also became part of Buncombe Co., contains another cluster of familiar family names such as Davidson, Fletcher, Forster/Foster, Gash, and Smith. This Company was a relatively small outlier population-wise, geographically isolated, at the lower end of the Swannanoa River.

The Fourteenth Company of Rutherford Co., which in 1792 also became part of Buncombe Co. (and in 1838 a part of Henderson Co.), contains the family names Brittain, Kikendal/Kuykendal, Springfield, Woodfin, and the like, all names of pioneers who settled in a small area near the junction of the French Broad River and Mills River.

5

Coxes in a Nutshell

In 1629, Charles I (reigned 1625-1648) gave "Carolana" to his Attorney General, Sir Robert Heath. Heath died in 1648, but in 1638 had conveyed title to "Carolana" to the Dukes of Norfolk, various members of which had additional noble titles. In general, this tract covered most of what was to become the southern part of the United States—everything south of Virginia, and a north border on an imaginary line extending 3,000 miles to the Pacific.

In 1684 and 1686, Dr. Daniel Coxe, who never went to America, had acquired extensive acreage in West Jersey and in East Jersey. In 1707, Coxe sold 4,500 acres in West Jersey to the William Penn group.

By 1696, Dr. Daniel Coxe claimed he had acquired title to "Carolana," evidently from the 6th or 7th Duke of Norfolk. As late as 1719, the seven man Board of Trade in London agreed that Dr. Coxe had title to Carolana, however murky. At this time, Dr. Coxe had agreed to stop his claim west of the Mississippi River. Evidently then King George I (reigned 1714-1727) and his Privy Council did not confirm the decision of the Board of Trade.

By 1698 and 1700, Dr. Coxe attempted to establish colonies in West Jersey, Carolana, and Virginia, but none succeeded. In the meantime, the Carolana charter went unrealized and was declared invalid.

The next generation, Col. Daniel Coxe, lived in America from 1702 to 1716 and then returned to London where he persisted with the claim for Carolana by publishing a 1722 book complete with map. At an unknown date, Col. Coxe returned to America.

Records now show a vast amount of confusion over who had rights to what is now North and South Carolina and Georgia. Coxe's 1722 book was accompanied by an unauthored and undated map with the bold label "Carolana" extending along the Gulf Coast to a point considerably west of the Meschachoe (Mississippi River), and the label "Carolina" indicating a smaller province along the Atlantic coast.

Dr. Coxe died in England in 1730 and his son Col. Coxe died in New Jersey in 1739. The Coxe family continued the Carolana claim until 1769 when the family reportedly surrendered it to the Crown in return for 100,000 acres in New York.

Third generation English-American Tench Coxe (1755-1824) inherited from his ancestors an introduction into the trans-Atlantic merchant world and in land speculation. Family holdings included various businesses in Philadelphia and provided necessary operating capital. After the

Revolutionary War, Tench Coxe had a checkered career in American politics, being associated with presidents Washington, Adams, Jefferson, and Madison. He was especially conversant with Alexander Hamilton. In spite of these political connections, Cox became known as "Mister Facing Bothways." In the early stages of the war, he was a Tory, but later adopted a Patriot stance. In politics after the war, he was initially a Federalist, but then became a Republican, and even later attempted to form a third party.

Not only did Tench Cox serve in several second level, appointed government positions, but in the period 1787 to 1823, he took it upon himself as advisor to the public, and to virtually anyone who would listen to his ideas about the new Constitution, the Bill of Rights, domestic manufacturing, and the right to bear arms. Tench Coxe publicized these matters favorably by word of mouth, by means of letters, and by having them printed in Philadelphia newspapers. Mostly the public did not listen. In 1794, he promoted these ideas in a book *A View of the United States of America.*

In the early 1790s, Tench Coxe began speculating in land, acquiring some 350,000 acres in Pennsylvania. About 200,00 acres did not have clear title. Later, he turned his attention to North Carolina.

In 1794, William J. Polk, from a distinguished Mecklenburg County lineage, had acquired 21,202 acres in North Carolina's Mecklenburg Co. In 1798, Tench Coxe arranged to buy the acreage, but then backtracked on his offer. Polk sued and won the case in 1804.

In 1795, James Greenlee and his partners Lewis Beard and William W. Erwin acquired some 83,740 acres in Rutherford territory of Western North Carolina; the acreage seeped southward along the Broad, Green, and N. Pacolet Rivers to the border of South Carolina. The trio, along with 15 other investors, had formed the Rutherford Land Company.

By 1796, the Rutherford Land Co. assigned some 35 blocks to Philadelphian Tench Coxe. After a period of negotiations, Coxe who initially agreed on nine cents an acre cash, settled on credit terms of ten cents an acre. In the MARS program and in the UNCA Special Collections for Rutherford Co., the Coxe holdings eventually totaled over 357,952 acres. These were recorded generally under Rutherford Co. grant numbers 1001 to 1061. One large block of 36,494 acres was also recorded in Buncombe Co. under grant number 250. Copies of at least four grants in the UNCA collections apparently do not exist in the NC State Archives. Further some Coxe grant numbers duplicate the numbers of grants to other people.

Tench Coxe believed he could double his money with resale of his North Carolina holdings in a few years operating under the name of Speculation Land Co. However, Coxe's financing fell apart by 1796 at which time he owed $65,700. He was saved partly from debtor's prison only by loans from his father and his brother, Philadelphia merchant Daniel W. Coxe, who jointly contributed $6,600. In 1798, Coxe arranged another loan of $8,242 to satisfy the most pressing creditors. Tench Coxe also devised a legal maneuver of putting all his land investments into a trust under the authority of three accomplishes who blocked any hostile takeover; this technique eventually was overturned by the courts.

In 1798, Tench Coxe exaggerated his claim to rights of 900,000 acres of which some 400,000 were in North Carolina, 350,000 were in Pennsylvania, and some 50,000 acres in Virginia, and untold acres in New York. About 200,000 acres of the land in Pennsylvania did not have clear title. Coxe also had smaller properties in rural and urban Delaware and Maryland. Coxe attempted to form a "stock company" with acreage shares set at $1.00 each. There were few takers.

For less than a year, 1800 to 1801, Tench Coxe had the Pennsylvania State post of Secretary of the Pennsylvania Land Office. The office had been relocated at the tail end of the sixty-two mile, 1795 Philadelphia and Lancaster Turnpike. Although Tench Coxe considered this an inferior government office, in a backwoods location, he used the time to straighten out his holdings in the chaotic Pennsylvania Land Office and to consolidate his claim of 90,000 acres in Luzerne and surrounding counties. Three decades later, the claims fortuitously proved to be in the middle of the anthracite coal district whose mining activities his grandchildren utilized to rebuild the Coxe family fortunes.

Moreover, in the period 1807 to 1810, Tench Coxe's son and agent, Tench Coxe II, did contract to sell 80,000 acres of the North Carolina acreage at prices reportedly ranging between 25 and 32 cents per acre. When the younger Tench died in 1813, his brother Francis Sidney Coxe continued to promote the Rutherford Land Co.

6

Quandries of the Penns

The quest for land in America by early land speculators was set also by the example of Quaker William Penn. In the years 1677 to 1681 some 1,400 English Quakers did travel to America and settled mainly in West Jersey. Prior to formal acquisition of land in America, from 1671 to 1686, Penn made three evangelistic land trips to Holland and Germany to recruit Pietists and convince people to migrate to America. In Europe, he traveled by horse drawn postal carriage. Penn's first trip covered nearly 800 overland miles.

In 1680, Penn and eleven associates purchased the province of East Jersey and stimulated further migration to that area. In 1681, Penn gained rights to the province of Pennsylvania, or some 28.8 million acres, as a credit against large loans Penn's father made to the King of England, who was then Charles II (reigned 1660-1685). In 1681, Penn traveled about southern England to sell land in America. He sold about 300,000 acres to some 250 individual purchasers who were mainly Quaker merchants, tradesmen, and prosperous farmers from the vicinity of London and Bristol. Penn sold some blocks of 5,000 acres priced at 100 pounds each; these blocks were free from Indian encumbrance.

Nearly from the beginning, Penn had to negotiate additional purchases of lands from the local Delaware Indians. Because of language problems, Penn soon found out that the Indians considered the land grants a type of rental and demanded periodic repayments. Only a small fraction of the Penn land was free from controversy and this was nearly all in the very southeast corner of his territory. In 1682, Penn arranged an agreement with the Delaware Indians which supposedly was confirmed in 1686. The Shawnee Indians of the Cumberland Valley long withheld their agreement for encroachment in another part of Pennsylvania. The Indians who could neither read or write English, nor understand complicated legal or technical documents and maps, much later disputed the agreements. Eventually, a total of eleven treaties were signed with the Indians in Pennsylvania; these treaties drug out over a century, from 1682 to 1784.

William Penn traveled to America himself in 1682, and again in 1699, staying each time somewhat over a year. By the end of 1684, an estimated 7,000 persons were in the Delaware and southeastern Pennsylvania colonies. They concentrated in the lower part of the Delaware River valley. This constituted the first big surge of migrants in the area beyond Philadelphia.

Eventually, Penn sold shares to about 600 investors and plots totaling some 750,000 acres to emigrants. Transportation in Europe and across the Atlantic, payments to Indians, development of infrastructure, hiring of property managers, and the like eventually led Penn into debt, and in 1708 resulted in a term in debtor's prison. An agent, Philip Ford, mortgaged 300,000 acres for 6,000 pounds. Somehow Penn eventually raised 7,000 pounds to clear up the debt.

William Penn had two wives and sixteen children. When he died in 1718 his diminished liquid assets were divided among the survivors with rights to the Pennsylvania lands going to three male heirs of the second marriage in return for monetary considerations to the children of the first marriage. At this time, only about 10% of Pennsylvania was free from Indian claims.

After Hannah Penn of the second marriage died in 1725, brothers John, Thomas, and Richard inherited the rights and debts to lands in Pennsylvania. In 1726, the Pennsylvania Land Office estimated that 100,00 squatters were occupying the Penn proprietary lands.

After 1730 the brothers struggled in English courts to hold the remaining unsold acreage by paying minimal taxes which they did nearly until the Revolutionary War. John Penn was the principal proprietor of Pennsylvania from 1730 to 1746, and Thomas Penn was the principal proprietor from 1746 to 1775. In 1737, the native Indians peacefully disputed the Penn "Walking Purchase" claim, but in 1755, became aggressive, killing a number of settlers. Military and then diplomatic action led to to a temporary settlement only in 1762, but hostilities flared again in 1764. In a 1768 treaty, the Indians demanded compensation of 10,000 pounds.

Until some 325 miles of the Mason-Dixon Line were surveyed from 1763 to 1767, the Penn brothers also waged an ongoing battle with the Calvert family in a Pennsylvania, Maryland, and Delaware border dispute. This MD/PA boundary dispute was not formally settled until 1780.

Moreover, from 1763 to 1776, Connecticut claimed land rights to much of the Wyoming Valley in northeast Pennsylvania. This agreement was settled also in 1780 at which time, through a complicated process, Connecticut acquired rights to land in the Western Reserve.

At the end of the Revolutionary War in 1783, some 24 million acres claimed by the Penns remained unsold. In taking over this land, the U.S. government allotted 130,000 pounds compensation to the Penn heirs, payable over a four year period. The Penns were also allowed to keep private estates and proprietary manors. Estimates are that the Penns had grossed 688,486 pounds, but had failed to collect 118,569 pounds. The Penns also made claims for compensation to the English government and were allotted a small annual stipend of 4,000 pounds.

In 1792, the Pennsylvania Assembly, in order to pay Revolutionary War military expenses, promoted a new law which dedicated "Depreciation Lands," "Donation Lands (unclaimed military bonus lands)," and some 24 million acres of the old Penn grant to make a new offering. The price was reduced from $0.80 to $0.20 per acre. By that time, much of the land was overrun by squatters, many of whom filed claims.

7

George Washington, Speculator or Opportunist?

For another example of prominent claimants, in 1789 when George Washington became the first president of the United States, his family had control of some 69,000 acres along the rivers of northern Virginia, West Virginia, and Ohio.

After the French and Indian War ended in 1763, Washington began accumulating land warrants issued to soldiers. In 1772, Virginia Governor Dunmore finally honored Washington's claim for 10,990 acres located along the Kanawa River (now in West Virginia). In 1684, Washington made a 680 mile horseback tour of this property and found it occupied by a number of squatters. He eventually got a Pennsylvania Court to issue eviction notices.

Until surveyor William Crawford was killed by the Indians in 1782, he was Washington's principal agent in selecting promising military bounty warrants held by other soldiers which Washington bought at a steep discount due to the uncertainty of ever being granted. Washington paid surveyors fees and registration fees and also granted Crawford a negotiated interest in the land.

In 1787, Washington was granted another 32,000 acres located along the Ohio River, west of the Allegheny Mountains, in Virginia's extended western territory. The 1772 acreage included a Crown grant for his military service in the French and Indian War, and the 1787 grant was for service in the Revolutionary War. Washington's desire for even more acreage in the Mississippi River Valley never came to fruition.

By the mid-1700s, the development of plantations with slave labor in Virginia was in full force. In 1759, Washington had married widow Martha Dandrige Curtis, heir to to a substantial estate. When Washington died in 1799, the family had 316 slaves scattered over five farms at Mt. Vernon.

In 1753, four Virginians proposed to get land grants covering the forbidden land of the "Dismal Swamp," an area covering some 324,000 acres, in coastal lowlands, located on the Virginia and North Carolina border. A seven year period of survey and settlement expired with no significant accomplishment.

In 1763, a new group including Washington and eleven other Virginians with one or two of the 1753 group, had the bright idea to drain the Dismal Swamp with the production of hemp as its main goal. The Dismal Swamp Co. developed a 10-year plan composed of 4,000 pounds capital with 10 slaves initially being expanded to 300 slaves. Work on digging a 22 mile canal began in 1764. In 1770, the group applied for all ungranted land in Norfolk Co., VA, and also for land in four counties of North Carolina. Evidently land grants from the Norfolk (VA) Land office were substantial, but the Virginia group apparently was never able to get grants in North Carolina.

The canal project languished with the intervention of the Revolutionary War and lack of necessary funds, men, and equipment. The slave staff was however kept in place as per the settlement agreement and continued to produce a substantial amount of shingles from local forests.

The Dismal Swamp Canal Co. was reorganized in 1790 with its main goal being an eight foot deep canal that was finally completed in 1814. Heavy labor by slaves accomplished the job. The company began paying steady dividends only in 1810.

In 1795, Washington sold his full original share of the company to Henry Lee on credit. Lee inherited part of the worthless notes of Robert Morris, went bankrupt himself about 1801, and went to debtors prison for a short period in 1809. In 1810, Lee turned his interest back to the Washington heirs who reaped a dividend profit of $2,000 in 1811.

8

North Carolina In the Beginning

In 1663, Charles II (reigned 1660-1685) had issued a new charter to a group of eight English noblemen whose heirs maintained rights until 1729 when all quit the claim in exchange for 22,500 pounds except the heirs of Sir George Carteret, Lord Granville who maintained his eighth share of the claim, being the northern part of North Carolina. Sir George Carteret had died in 1680; by 1729, John Carteret, Lord Granville became the principal heir. In 1729, the population of the two Carolinas was estimated at 36,000 souls, which included whites plus black and Indian slaves. See Herman R. Friis, 1940.

Almost all recent publications and websites accepted without question that the 1663 charter of "Carolana" superseded the 1629 charter. A good example of this acceptance includes the recent book by David La Vere, 2013, listed in the bibliography. Nor does the 1961 book by Duane Meyer consider the 1629 claim. Strangely, the website "North Carolina Maps—Timeline" also does not mention the Coxe claims discussed earlier.

The 1663 "Carolana" charter extended from 36 degrees N. Latitude south to 31 degrees N. Latitude and theoretically extended from the Atlantic coast to French claims along the Mississippi River. In 1665, the northern boundary was expanded to 36 degrees 30 minutes N. Latitude (approximate VA/NC boundary) and the southern boundary to 29 degrees N. latitude (approximate St. Augustine, FL). This extension included all of North Carolina, South Carolina, Georgia, and about half of Florida.

From 1663 to 1729, the Carolinas were governed by an ongoing series of individuals, a few being proprietors. William Berkeley, governor of Virginia from 1642 to 1652, and from 1660 to 1677, was the only proprietor to live in America. The governors did not live in either of the Carolinas, but sent deputy governors to face the rigors of nearly primitive living conditions. What was to become North Carolina was occupied by settlers who mostly struggled to survive. Nearly three decades later did the plantation owners with their slaves move into these coastal areas; thus, North Carolina contrasted highly with the more populous plantation society of Virginia.

A few hardy traders entered the coastal area around Albemarle Sound in the 1660s. The isolated area was marked by lack of any form of local government, and for that matter, had neither church buildings nor schools.

Until John Lawson laid out Bath in 1706, and New Berne in 1711, no concentrated settlements in the northern coastal plain (outer coastal plain) of North Carolina existed. In 1710, some few hundred English or German Quakers or Pietists settled in the Albemarle area and eventually along the Pamlico and Neuse Rivers of the coastal, northern part of North Carolina. Considering all the hazards, most likely the attrition rate during the first few decades of arrival ranged to 50% or more.

North Carolina languished from 1729 to 1775 under a series of five Royal governors. During this period, the governor mediated the often conflicting interests of the King, who approved all legal actions, and the local North Carolina Assembly, who provided funds to the governor. The five governors did little for the local economy or infrastructure. The five Royal governors were George Burrington, Gabriel Johnston, Arthur Dobbs, William Tyron, and Josiah Martin. Early North Carolina counties were named after Johnston, Dobbs, and Tryon. These counties likely corresponded to land holdings.

Later pioneers to the southern part of North Carolina were Highland Scots and English who began migrating there in the 1680's and settled in the coastal, lower parts of the Cape Fear River (inner coastal plain). Over the next few decades, they continued to settle up the river for over 120 miles, thereby putting pressure on the Catawba Indians, a relatively peaceful tribe. The famous Moore family of the Charleston area contributed four brothers to the Cape Fear River area who took up some 48,000 acres. Their acreage is signified by the well-know Revolutionary War battle of Moore's Creek Bridge which occurred February 1776.

As mentioned earlier, eight proprietors held rights to North Carolina after 1663. In the following decades, most died by 1680, one or two were ousted, and one or two sold their rights to others. After 1729, only the Granville group remained. From 1729 to 1778, the Granville heirs had a claim for a 60 mile wide strip across northern North Carolina, that is, the populated portion containing Albemarle Sound and the lower Neuse River. Maps of the time, however, do not outline Granville's claim.

In the period 1747 to 1760, the Granville heirs attracted 170 families, mainly Scots-Irish, to the North Carolina Piedmont area (then Rowan Country) south of the Yadkin River. These settlers took 265 blocks totaling more than 150,000 acres. The Great Wagon Road from Philadelphia more or less bisected the area. The Great Wagon Road trended southward before splitting into three branches south of the Yadkin River. See, for instance, Robert W. Ramsey, 1964.

9

Early Explorers and Mapmakers

Until the early 1800s, the land in the eastern part of America was overlapped in part by English claims, by part French claims, and by part Spanish claims. All these nebulous claims were periodically subject to renegotiation as outlined in the various editions of *A Diplomatic History of the United States*.

When the Dutch East Indies Company was founded in 1602, and the Dutch West Indies Company in 1621, and thereafter Amsterdam became the center of modern banking, the Dutch rapidly discovered an urgent need for vastly improved world maps. Dutch mapmakers who predominated from about 1581 to 1689 made rapid strides in this area and learned how to produce high quality maps on copper plate, a technique which persisted over the next two or three centuries. Famous Dutch mapmakers included Willem Janszoon Blaue, Claes Janz. Visscher, Jan Jansson, and Jodocus Hondius. These family names carried on for the two or three generations.

The French school, which dominated from 1648 to about 1718, included Nicholas Sanson, Alexis Hubert Jaillot, and Guillaume Del'Isle. These family groups produced especially clean maps, and over time updated and recycled the indispensible copper plates. On occasion, the copper plates were sold outside the family.

The German school, dating from about 1702 to 1744, was characterized by Johann Baptist Homann and Georg Matthes Sutter, and their next generation heirs.

The following paragraphs concentrate on only a few noteworthy mapmakers who contributed to development of maps over what is now the eastern part of the United States. Of course, mapmakers pirated earlier mapmakers and generally added some updates. An extended discussion of early American maps is contained in the eight books by William P. Cumming dating from 1958 to 1988.

Juan Ponce de Leon had sailed along the East Coast in 1513. Thus, Spain claimed rights to Florida Territory and westward extensions from 1513 to 1736 and from 1783 until 1819. The northern boundary of Florida Territory generally was considered to be 31 degrees N. latitude.

The name "Carolina" appeared as early as 1657 on a pioneering map of the Cape Hatteras area by Nicholas Comberford of London. Although Comberford never went to America, he apparently got his information from Capt. Francis Yeardley, a native of Virginia. The Comberford map shows the residence of Nathaniel Batts, an early explorer and trader. Strangely, this map and subsequent English maps are oriented in an West-East direction, west being at the top of the page. Yeardley stated that he bought the area "with three great rivers" for 200 pounds from the Tuscarora Indians "in the name of England." Since his father, George Yeardley, was colonial governor of Virginia from 1619 to 1627, his claim likely had some merit.

In 1664, James Joseph Moxon produced a pioneering map of the coastal area which also used the term "Carolina." This label was in very small print. This map is oriented in a West-East direction and printed in London.

John Ogilby's map of 1673 generally followed that of Moxon, being rather primitive in showing only the coastal area of the Carolina and is also oriented in a West-East direction. This map runs inland as far as "The Apalathean Mountains." The Olgilby map is know as the "First Lords Proprietors Map," and it does not delineate the proprietory boundaries although it does show the names of Craven Co., Berkely Co., Clarendon Co., and Albemarle Co. An original copy of the map is priced on the Internet at $22,500.

In 1673, Frenchman Louis Jolliet descended the Mississippi River to near the southern boundary of what is now Arkansas. In 1682, La Salle descended the Mississippi to its mouth. By 1713, French King Louis XIV (reigned 1643-1715) could claim French rights to a vast territory including eastern Canada and virtually all of the Midwest.

About 1682, Jean Baptiste Louis Franquelin made a pioneering map of French claims along the Mississippi Valley soon after the La Salle expedition. Franquelin's 1684 map refers to "La Louisiane." His 1688 map uses the label "Contree de La Louisiane" and overlaps it with a smaller "La Floride," the latter referring to Spanish claims.

The French formally held these rights from 1682 to 1762. Spain held the rights of the Mississippi territory from 1762 to 1800, and France again from 1800 to 1803.

Joel Gascoyne's 1682 map of the Carolinas is similar to John Ogilby's 1673 map, but is more advanced. Gascoyne adds a number of rivers and also the names of some land owners. His map received the informal title of the "Second Lords Proprietors map," but also does not show proprietory boundaries. Like many early English maps, it is strangely oriented in a W-E direction.

About 1700, noted French cartographer Guillaume Del'Isle produced a vastly improved map under the title *L'Amerique Septentrionale* (map of Central and North America). Evidently, a later version of the Del'Isle map formed the basis of the 1722 Daniel Coxe "Carolana" map. The Del'Isle map is oriented in the proper North-South direction.

In 1733, Edward Moseley published his "New and Correct Map on the Province of North Carolina." The map shows parts of Virginia and also South Carolina. He does not use the term North Carolina, but substitutes the word "Clarendon Co." Moseley's map improves on the coastal area. Moseley's map is oriented North-South as are nearly all later maps of the area.

A 1737 map of the Carolinas published by the famous German geographer Johann Baptist Homann is notable for its general location of all the major rivers. In the upper left hand corner, printed notes remark that the Col. (John) Barnwell (of the South Carolina militia), defeated the Indians in the Bath Province of coastal North Carolina in 1712, while Col. (Charles) Craven defeated the Indians in Granville Province in 1716. In 1712, the "Indians" were the various branches of the Southern Tuscarora living along the lower part of the Neuse River in northern North Carolina. In 1716, the "Indians" were the Yamassees living along the Ashley River in the northern part of South Carolina. The Homann map also shows 10 "Charaky" villages in the Middle Towns and 30 villages in the Overhill Towns. Homann had died in 1724; the 1737 map printed by the Homann heirs was an improved version of Homann's 1714 map. Actually, Col. James Moore, Jr., in 1713, brought another large army to northern North Carolina from South Carolina to do battle with the Tuscarora and succeeded in destroying a major Indian fort and killing many. Thereafter, the Tuscarora began to migrate to the wilds of New York.

About 1747, noted English mapmaker Emanuel Bowen published a large series of maps, one of which had a pompous title of *A New and Accurate Map of the Province of North and South Carolina*, etc. This version is interesting for including many Indian location names. More importantly, it shows the western border of North Carolina as extending only to "Charokee" territory which occupied the Appalachians of what became Western North Carolina and Tennessee. Bowen was cartographer for King George II (reigned 1727-1760).

A 1755 map by the Virginian John Mitchell shows a settlement area in northwestern South Carolina deserted by the Cherokees. The 1755 map, *A Map of the British Colonies in America*, is an improved version of Mitchell's 1751 map. The map and its editions up to 1781 have been described as "the most important map in American colonial history." It was used at the 1783 Paris Peace Conference to delineate British, French, and American territorial boundaries. United States territory extended to the Mississippi River. The map was printed in London.

John Collet's 1770 map of eastern North Carolina is noted for its inclusion of most of the major rivers and their tributaries and a preliminary, eastern part of the boundary between North and South Carolina. Some copies of the Collet map have a faint red line at 35.5 degrees N. Latitude which may indicate the south boundary of the Granville proprietory holdings. This increasingly detailed map was printed in London. It shows, for instance, Fort Dobbs, whose archaeological remains are located just north of current Statesville.

In 1775, Henry Mouzon produced a similar, but somewhat more detailed map. The Mouzon map was published in London in a book titled *The American Atlas*. An original copy is on the internet market for $22,500.

An unauthored 1779 map shows for the first time the general location of the North Carolina coastal counties, but no county boundaries. It was probably a governmental or a military map.

Another noteworthy map by Thomas Hutchins was dated 1778, and included Virginia, Pennsylvania, Maryland, and North Carolina, the latter being mainly what is now Tennessee. From 1785 to 1789, Hutchins was geographer general of the United States and had a leading role in formulating the New England Survey System (grants surveyed en masse) that was adopted by the Northwest Ordinance of 1787. The New England System contrasted with the Southern Survey System (grants surveyed piecemeal; "metes and bounds," or acres and boundaries) in use south of the Ohio River.

A 1784 map of the United States, produced by goldsmith, engraver, and counterfeiter Abel Buell reportedly was the first map printed in the United States. It shows Virginia, North Carolina, South Carolina and Georgia each extending westward to the Mississippi River. By the time the map was printed, it was obsolete. In 2010, a copy of this undistinguished map sold at at auction for the astronomical sum of two million dollars. The Buell map actually was copied in part from John Foster's 1677 woodcut *Map of New England*, and from the other maps mentioned above.

The 1790 U.S Census, North Carolina portion, features Benjamin Tanner's 1796 map of North Carolina. North Carolina's eight districts contained 34 counties. In 1790, North Carolina's total population was 393,751 of which about 25.5% were black slaves. Strangely, Tanner's map does not specifically show the "Dismal Swamp" located along the Virginia/North Carolina coastal border. This map has a number of quaint spellings such as "Apalachean, Macklenburg, and

Nuse."

Also in 1796, Assistant Postmaster General Abraham Bradley, Jr., with two assistants, published the first version of Bradley's *Map of the United States.* This semi-schematic map shows post-roads in the eastern part of the United States as well as distances between post offices. As an example, the road from Raleigh, NC to Morganton, NC has ten stops over a distance of 250 miles. Some glaring errors occur. On the map, Buncombe Co. is erroneously located west of Burke Co., adjacent to the border with "Tennasse." Moreover, the Catawba River is featured, but the important French Broad River of Western North Carolina is not shown.

Thanks to modern technology, it is possible to google "North Carolina Maps" and get descriptions of many early maps of North and South Carolina. Although a few low quality maps appeared before 1750, maps thereafter appeared rapidly with increasing accuracy.

10

Native Americans in Western North Carolina

Overall, the Cherokee Indians became a dominant tribe and had hunting grounds extending over a vast rectangular area roughly 330 miles by 400 miles, in stages covering all of what became Tennesse and Kentucky as well as parts of six other states, including western North Carolina and the northwest corner of South Carolina. The best crude estimate is that the Cherokee nation never comprised more than 50,000 individuals. Many were caught in the yellow fever epidemic of 1699.

In the period 1721 to 1835, thirty-five ill-defined treaties were negotiated with the Cherokees. Each largely unilateral treaty, generally preceded by military conflict, ended with the Cherokees being forced progressively westward. In doing so, the Cherokees pushed against the Creeks in the south, and the Chickasaws in the west.

Beginning in 1753, the English decided to control the Cherokees by a series of isolated outposts which included Fort Prince George (SC), Fort Loudon (TN), Fort Ninety-Six (SC), and Fort Long Cane Creek (SC). The forts were minimally staffed with 100 or 200 soldiers who maintained defensive positions and guardedly ventured outside the fort. The four forts eventually were abandoned, Fort Loudon in 1760, and Fort Prince George also in 1760. The English were defeated by the Americans at Fort Ninety-Six in 1781.

During the later stages of the French and Indian Wars (1754-1763), conflicts centering around the Great Lakes gradually moved southward. In 1759, South Carolina Governor William H. Lyttleton initiated militia actions against the Cherokees with little success. In 1760, his successor, William Bull II called on the regular British army. Col. Archibald Montgomery brought about 1,100 men and combined these with 400 local forces. Montgomery moved his forces to South Carolina and on to Fort Prince George in Georgia and into southwest North Carolina, destroying Indian villages. His next goal was to relieve the tiny British garrison at Fort Loudoun. When he reached Echoe, also spelled Etchoe (near Franklin, NC), he encountered stiff resistance and had to abort the expedition. Later in 1760, Col. James Grant, with some 2,800 men overcame the Cherokee at the second Battle of Echoe.

In these two conflicts in western North Carolina, the English achieved a limited victory with relatively few casualties. However, they eventually abandoned the wilderness only to return in 1780 for yet another, much larger problematic venture against the Americans. In the meantime, the Cherokees reoccupied most of their former homelands as King George II (reigned 1727-1760) had, following the French and Indian Wars, issued a directive that no land grants were to be issued west of the Appalachians.

At the same time South Carolina Governor Lyttleton was attempting to contain the Indians in the South, North Carolina Governor Dobbs was marshaling Rowan County militia to fight the French and Indians in the Great Lakes area. Thus the Carolinas were fighting on two fronts.

In 1756, Dobbs, organized a survey of the "Militia and Taxable Persons." The survey included the 22 counties then existing in the eastern part of North Carolina. His survey showed 12,931 militia in a total population of 25,865. Blacks accounted for about 30% of the total.

From his relatively secure residence in New Bern, Dobbs authorized the construction of Fort Dobbs, the remains of which are located near Statesville. The log fort, about 40 x 53 feet, was built in 1756 and abandoned in 1766. It never contained more than about 50 men and functioned mainly as a commissary.

In early 1767, Governor William Tryon, the fourth Royal governor of North Carolina, accompanied a militia expedition of about 100 Rowan Co. and Mecklenburg Co. militia into Cherokee wilderness of Western North Carolina to determine the boundary between Indian hunting grounds and land granted to white settlers. Almost surely, Tryon visited Joseph McDowell and his clan who had settled in the 1750s in the forbidden area northwest of the Catawba River. The Tryon expedition lasted 27 days and covered some 800 miles.

Although the boundary is shown on the 1747 map by Emanuel Bowen, Tryon authorized two surveyors to remap the North Carolina portion of a line which extended south into South Carolina and north into Virginia. When the Cherokees tried to push the boundary eastward, Tryon compromised with goods to be picked up by the Indians in Salisbury.

In August 1776, South Carolina militia under Col. Andrew Williamson led a force of some 1,100 men against the Cherokee Lower Towns in South Carolina. He destroyed a number of towns.

During the Cherokee Wars of September 1776, Gen. Griffith Rutherford of the Salisbury militia led a force into Western North Carolina, through the eastern heart of the Cherokee nation. Rutherford's army was supplemented by other militia from South Carolina and various parts of North Carolina and what became Tennessee so that over time, reportedly "several thousand" men on on foot and horseback participated. The matter of logistics of feeding men and horses in a mountainous terrain with no roads put considerable constraint on actual numbers of the effective fighting force which may have been around 2,000 men. Rutherford's supply train was composed of about 375 drivers and some 1,400 horses.

Rutherford's War Trace ran about 120 miles along the intermontaine areas of Appalachia from northeast to southwest and extended over the south half of western North Carolina. The Cherokees were overwhelmed by the larger, concentrated and better armed militia forces. Rutherford's armies destroyed some 50 Middle Towns. Many warriors were killed and numerous families displaced.

In October 1776, local North Carolina and Virginia militia under Col. William Christian and Maj. Evan Shelby raided Cherokee Overhill villages, west of the Appalachian Mountains, with notable success. With the three conflicts of 1776, the main Cherokee encampments were pushed into the northwest corner of Georgia. Much later, in 1838, they were to form the nucleus of the "Trail of Tears" which resulted in their removal some 700 miles overland, to Oklahoma.

A 1777 treaty with Cherokees allowed white settlers to finalize settlement along the strip that led to the formation of Burke Co. (1777) and Rutherford Co. (1779). Wilkes Co. was formed also in 1777, and Lincoln Co. in 1779. These counties were all in western North Carolina.

The travels of the militia through Western North Carolina gave the officers under Gen. Rutherford an excellent opportunity to explore the land and scout out promising, relatively flat valley tracts of land for speculation and for settlement. In 1778 settlers rushed to claim tracts.

The 1776 militia expeditions resulted in:

(a) militia experience in mobilizing and in communicating for later Revolutionary War battles,

(b) they secured the western flank of North Carolina from a likely hostile enemy,

(c) they pushed pioneer border settlements westward, and

(d) the militia began to establish law and order in the wilderness.

As noted below, General Rutherford and two sons were rewarded for the Cherokee and other Revolutionary War campaigns with nearly 40,000 acres of land in what later was middle and western Tennessee. The middle Tennessee acreage later became part of the North Carolina Military Reservation, being part of the old Transylvania Land Co. claim, dating from 1775 originally promoted by Richard Henderson and others. The military reservation was a block 55 x 130 miles which later became part of the old Davidson Co., centering around Nashville. These military land grants date from 1784.

About 1809, some 1,000 Cherokees voluntarily moved to a settlement in Arkansas.

In 1819, another treaty with the Cherokees covered the westernmost corner of North Carolina with some 3,000 Indians being displaced west of the Mississippi River. The settlement allowed the formation of the remaining North Carolina counties which today total 100.

In 1824, John C. Calhoun who was variously Secretary of War and Senator from South Carolina, formulated a bill for removing the Five Civilized Tribes (Cherokee, Chickasaw, Choctaw, Creek, and Seminole) from Southeastern United States to reservations in Arkansas Territory and Indian Territory (mainly Oklahoma and some parts of Kansas). When Andrew Jackson became president in 1829, he promoted a stronger bill which was adopted by a slim majority in 1830. The bill affected about 74,000 Native Americans and some 4,500 slaves.

In 1837, at the time of the resettlement of the Cherokees to Oklahoma they numbered roughly 21,500, not including about 1,000 who remained on the Qualla Reservation in western North Carolina. At the time, the Cherokee removal group had some 2,000 (mostly black) slaves. Mostly the Indians treated docile Blacks as non-belligerents and as prized property. It does not take much imagination to determine where the Cherokees acquired the slaves.

11

North Carolina Land Entries

Land entries in what is now North Carolina are usually classified under four basic types, namely:

(a) Proprietary, approx. 1663-1729,

(b) Crown (Royal Colonies), approx. 1729-1776,

(c) Granville (a 60 mile strip across northern NC), approx. 1744-1763 (later Carteret heirs, 1763-1778),

(d) North Carolina State, the latter beginning in 1778 and extending to modern times. This paper concerns State land grants in western North Carolina and by extension into the large territory that in 1796 became Tennessee.

In issues of *A Lot of Bunkum* from 1992, Dr. Kenneth D. Israel provided a series of comments he took from an old handwritten book, namely *Burke County Land Entries (1778-1795)* [Secretary of State file 949]. One of the most important comments dealt with (colonial) land grants before April 14, 1778. These grants "were declared to be utterly void, and of no Force or effect." This was the first notable land decree affecting Western North Carolina. Israel abstracted many key land grants of Western North Carolina.

This major event in 1778 took away land holder claims in Western North Carolina, whether official or not. The dim records indicate that Revolutionary War patriots, mainly officers, rushed to reclaim previous grants and generally were successful.

At this time, Col. George Davidson, Sr., General William Lee Davidson, and General Ephraim Davidson claimed land in Old Burke Co., but did not forsake their substantial residences in Mecklenburg and Iredell Cos. for the wilderness of Western North Carolina.

In Western North Carolina, Land Offices were established in 1777 and began operation in 1778; these included land offices in Old Burke County and in Old Rutherford County. By 1800, some 7,000 permanent land entries were recorded in Western North Carolina. Nearly half of the state land entries recorded for Old Burke County are dated between 1778 and 1800. From January 1778 to 1785, Charles McDowell (or McDowal) was an entry taker. In 1785, Dr. Joseph Dobson took over and served as entry taker until his death in 1791. Thomas Davidson served as entry taker in Burke Co. during 1793 and 1794, and evidently was an entry taker also in Buncombe Co. He was accused of predating entries and of other irregularities, specifically grant number 175, a block of 50,000 acres. Davidson was followed by Joseph Henry.

It was an era when North Carolina state legislators met for three or four weeks a year, and schools, if they existed at all, operated only a few months a year. In eastern North Carolina, schools were first established in the villages of New Bern and in Edenton. Currently very little is known about this history.

In western North Carolina, the earliest schools included the Morgan Academy in Burke Co. organized by Presbyterian minister James Templeton and lawyer Waightstill Avery about 1783, and the Union Hill (later Newton Academy) in Buncombe Co. organized by Robert Henry about 1794; after a few years, Henry got educator and Presbyterian minister George Newton from up north. And these schools were at the grade school level. The initial educators at both schools and nearly all the educators listed below apparently had some connection to the College of New Jersey (now Princeton University). The college was founded in 1746 in New Jersey by a Presbyterian group and moved to the Princeton location about 1756. See Descendants of William Tennent.

In other parts of North Carolina, early educators included James Tate (Wilmington, 1760), David Ker (Raleigh, 1760), David Caldwell (Guilford Co., 1767), Henry Patillo (c.1765, Granville Co.), Joseph Alexander, Hezekiah Balch, and Ephraim Brevard (Queens College, Charlotte, 1768), John Bar (Rowan Co., 1774), and James Hall (Iredell Co., 1774). In the same era, Crowfield Academy was organized in Rowan Co., and Zion-Parnassus Academy in Iredell Co.

Somewhat later, Joseph Alexander was active also in forming two other schools in Newberry Co., SC, and in York Co., SC. Thus, education in the Carolinas, even at the elementary level, was very spotty.

The Queens College mentioned had a contorted history – it soon became Queens Museum, later Liberty Hall Academy, and in 1784, rechartered and moved to Salisbury. While Queens College was in Charlotte, it's three instructors and 20 rooms provided one of the most advanced schools in 18th century North Carolina. The educators from the north soon replaced Latin and Greek with reading and math as being more satisfactory for frontier students.

The University of North Carolina at Chapel Hill, was chartered in 1785 but admitted its first students only in 1795. David Ker, apparently no relation to David Ker above, was its first president, but remained only a year or so when he was replaced by Joseph Caldwell.

About 1820 when Asheville resident David L. Swain entered the University of North Carolina at Chapel Hill, he traveled horseback about 220 miles. Swain later had a distinguished career as a lawyer, governor of North Carolina, and as president of the University.

In Tennessee, Thomas Benton Craighead began Davidson Academy in 1785, located north of what is now Nashville. Earlier, In 1784, Samuel Doak began St. Martins Academy in Washington Co. (TN). In 1794, Hezekial Balch began an academy in Greeneville, (TN). These men doubled as Presbyterian ministers. Thus law and order influence by the preachers and the teachers was relatively late arriving in the Appalachians. About 1814, George Newton was enticed to leave Asheville, NC and establish an academy in Bedford Co., TN, another frontier area.

In the late 1700s, most of the North Carolina legislators were from coastal areas in the East where a moderate degree of civilization existed. Legislators here were generally from the eastern planter aristocracy which was dominated by English and Scots who mostly adhered to the Anglican church.

In the West, mental, spiritual, and physical lawlessness prevailed until the Revolutionary War.

Communication was by word of mouth and at best, piecemeal. Frontier pioneers were quick to settle the slightest personal grievance with fists and more likely with guns. Kangaroo courts and hangings were the law of the land. Theory of law often did not match reality. Many western North Carolina and Tennessee lawyers, such as Andrew Jackson, Waightstill Avery, and Thomas Hart Benton, were largely self-trained and rapidly acquired practical experience in pioneer, log-cabin courts.

Recorders of deeds and other public documents were chosen from among relatively few literates, individuals who often were preoccupied with other activities. In those days of horseback transportation, meager roads and overgrown trails, and few public office buildings, the cumbersome three- or four-tiered numbering system and the coordinated preservation of deed records in a central location was at best semi-chaotic. The older deeds remain in this state. Some deed records dating after 1778 are still missing. Some grant numbers were duplicated.

In 1775, Richard Henderson formed the Transylvania Land Company (also called the Henderson Company, and later the Louisa Company) and formulated an agreement with the Cherokee for 20 million acres in future Kentucky and north central Tennessee under the Treaty of Sycamore Shoals. Henderson was backed by local politicians Thomas Hart and Jesse Benton, and the explorer Daniel Boone. A dissident Cherokee, Dragging Canoe objected vehemently. Lord Dunmore, royal governor of Virginia, ruled that the treaty was invalid. North Carolina authorities objected also. As compensation, much later, in 1795, the Transylvania Company received 400,000 acres, via grants 637 and 714, near the Cumberland Gap, in Powell's Valley in another part of what was to become eastern Tennessee.

In 1776, Richard Caswell became the first American colonial governor of North Carolina. Caswell, a lawyer and surveyor by training, who fought in several Revolutionary War battles in North and South Carolina, eventually was commissioned as a major general of North Carolina militia. Caswell was governor from 1776 to 1780. The great land rush in North Carolina and Tennessee territory took place during Caswell's first term of office.

About 1778 or 1779, North Carolina began granting of lands now located in the Watauga area of eastern Tennessee; John Carter, a resident of Washington, Co. (TN) became the local entry taker. These grants included general purchase grants as well as warrants or grants for military and other services. Grants normally sold at 50 shillings per 100 acres; ten years later, picked over land was offered at 40 shillings per acre.

In late 1779, James Robertson and John Donelson migrated from the Watauga area westward deep into Cherokee territory to the Cumberland River area, a distance of some 200 miles. Their party of several hundred individuals including 30 or more slaves, located at a spot which later formed Nashville, TN. By doing so, they distanced themselves from increasing Revolutionary War conflicts in the Carolinas and went to the more hostile Indian country, treaty or no treaty, land grant or no land grant. Records show that 244 men signed The Cumberland Compact, a generalized agreement governing the colony; attrition was rapid so that within a decade less than half remained.

In 1782, a large Military Reservation was reserved in the Cumberland area (now central Tennessee) even though a number of pioneers had already settled there, and thus were required to file preemption claims. Preemption claims were usually handled by Col. Samuel Barton at a

Nashville office. Generally, preempters, or squatters, were limited to a claim of 640 acres.

In the years 1783 to 1797, military bounty warrants were issued mainly through the Martin Armstrong Land Office located at Hillsboro, NC. The Armstrong office issued over 5,000 military bounty warrants.

During the period 1778 to 1797, Stockley Donelson entered nearly one million acres in Tennessee. In 1783, Stockley Donelson and his brother John, Jr., applied for appointments as surveyors in the western part of North Carolina, that is, the area that later became Tennessee. His father, militia Col. John Donelson was a surveyor in Virginia who settled about 1773 in the Watauga area, and in 1779 in the north central, Cumberland Valley of what became Tennessee. About 1783 Stockley became surveyor for Sullivan Co., and eventually North Carolina surveyor general for the eastern district of Tennessee; he had close family ties to politicians Andrew Jackson and John Glasgow. In 1790, Stockley was named Lieutenant Colonel Commandant in the militia for Hawkins Co. Stockley Donelson died in 1805. In the handwritten land records, the family name was variously spelled Donaldson, Donalson, Donelson, etc. This spelling variation persists in the multi-volume, printed version of *Colonial and State Records of North Carolina.*

In some cases, Donelson had various partners, most notably the speculator William Tyrrell. Whether Donelson had government or private or credit financing for the grants is not currently known. Some of the Donelson acreage was granted at 25 shillings per 100 acres.

In 1783 and 1784, Col. William J. Polk was surveyor general for the middle district of Tennessee and used this position to enter more than 55,000 acres in Tennessee. William J. Polk was a distant cousin to James K. Polk, destined to become president of the United States. Samuel Polk, father of James K. Polk, was an early land speculator in North Carolina's Mecklenburg Co.

In 1783 to 1785, speculator John Gray Blount entered 183 blocks totaling 383,400 acres in what became Tennessee; note also his entries in Buncombe Co., NC below. John Gray Blount was associated with brothers Thomas Blount and William Blount.

In Tennessee Territory, we find the names of many of those Revolutionary War veterans who earlier received grants or warrants in Western North Carolina, as for instance, George Cathey, Ephraim Davidson, George Davidson, James Davidson, William Davidson, William Lee Davidson heirs, William Gudger, Ephraim McLean, William Moore, Samuel Murray, Elijah Patton, Robert Patton, Samuel Patton, Daniel Smith, and David Vance. The reader is referred to a 2000 book by Irene Griffey cited in the reference list.

In 1784, General Nathanael Greene, head of the Southern Army, received warrants from North Carolina for 25,000 acres located on the Duck River of the middle Tennessee District. Whether or not the warrants were converted to a grant is not known. About the same time, South Carolina gave him Boone's Barony, an estate outside Charleston, SC comprising some 3,800 acres; Greene soon sold this to meet military debts incurred as a loan from Robert Morris. Greene also received Mulberry Groove Plantation, an estate near Savannah, GA comprising some 2,700 acres. The grants from South Carolina and from Georgia were confiscated Tory property. When Greene died in 1786, his wife and five children continued to live on the Georgia property. The latter property with its slaves, partly cultivated in rice, was valued roughly at $21,000.

In 1788 and 1789, General Griffith Rutherford received warrants on some 13,000 acres in six tracts located mainly in western Tennessee Territory. A military bounty warrant had to be converted to an entry and go through the grant process. His son, Henry Rutherford, who was a deputy surveyor, received more than 20,000 acres, and another son, John Rutherford, 5,000 acres. Most of this acreage was granted in the years 1784 to 1786.

Other militia officers who received warrants for land in Tennessee Territory included Col. William Campbell, nine blocks, 2,244 acres; Capt. William Lenoir; Maj. Joseph McDowell, four blocks, 3,657 acres; and Col. John Shelby, three blocks, 2,026 acres. William Lenoir, together with speculator William T. Lewis, claimed one block of 3,500 acres, located in Green Co.

As the years went by, many warrants in Tennessee Territory were not entered and reverted either to the North Carolina legislature or to the Tennessee legislature, which ceded the warrants to universities and colleges who in turn sold the warrants in order to finance their operations. For instance, in 1835, the University of North Carolina received $14,400 for 25,000 acres of land in Tennessee.

When French General Lafayette visited the United States in 1824, he received many honors in recognition of his extraordinary services to the American cause at the time of the Revolutionary War. One award included a township grant, some 23,000 acres, which Lafayette chose near Tallahassee, FL.

12

Speaking of Surveyors

As a matter of general interest, the various States have two radically different systems of land surveys. One system is called the "Southern System" and the other loosely called the "New England System. About 20 states were surveyed using the southern system and the remaining 30 states were surveyed using the public lands system of rectangular blocks.

Land grants in the South, including North Carolina, were unordered. An individual determined a higher quality tract, usually along a river bottom, and put in a claim for so many acres, usually less than 1,000. One boundary was usually fixed along a river or a creek. Surveying extended out from this geographic location and thus enclosed an area often of irregular shape and size.

The Land Ordinance of 1785, which was introduced for "public lands," that is, unsettled territories north of the Ohio River, provided for a rectangular system of six mile square townships, subdivided into blocks of 640 acres, more or less. A reference point on the Ohio River was determined laboriously by head geographer Thomas Hutchins using astronomic equipment. From this point true north-south lines called principal meridians were laid out, and east-west lines, called base lines, were established. In recent times, a resurvey of Hutchins fixed reference point has determined that it has a latitudinal error of about 2,550 feet, or nearly one half mile.

The following discussion relates principally to the Southern System.

Surveyors of land entries were usually agents acting for others and were required to be somewhat literate and have above average mathematical skills. Often, surveyors brought sellers and buyers together thereby earning a commission. Surveyors were a hardy lot, having to camp out, deal with harsh weather, and above all fend off attacks by Indians. In his 2011 paper, Miles S. Philbeck mentions the names of nine surveyors working in Tryon Co. (Rutherford Co.) during the period of 1752 to 1765.

John McNitt Alexander, working in Rutherford Co. in 1765, was the most prominent surveyor in that area. Later, Alexander had an active career in North Carolina politics and, by fable, was a principal of the 25 or so signers of the 1775 *Mecklenburg Declaration of Independence*. During the years 1763 to 1768, John McKnitt Alexander, used his talents as surveyor to enter 38 blocks in Mecklenburg Co. totaling 8,428 acres. Most blocks were along the Catawba River and its tributaries. In 1780, Alexander used his surveying experience to enter jointly some 27 land grants in Old Burke Co. Alexander held a variety of public offices including Registrar of Deeds in Mecklenburg Co. from 1775 to 1808.

Few surveyor's names in other parts of western North Carolina are currently available, but mention of early surveyor and agent names include Francis Alexander, Robert Henry, John Strother, and Robert Tate, and later Zachariah Candler and Robert Love.

At times, Strother and Love were in the employ of John Gray Blount and other non-resident speculators. In 1799, Henry and Strother were associated in the survey of the Tennessee/North Carolina boundary. Other surveyors' names likely are available from the surveying reports in the NC State Archives.

Early land grants were surveyed using the most primitive of instruments, most notably a surveyors (magnetic) compass and a Gunter's chain (66 feet). Englishman Edmund Gunter devised his measuring chain in 1620. Later instruments included a circumferentor (a mounted magnetic compass), a zenith sector for measuring star positions, a sextant for determining latitude, a theodolite for measuring horizontal and vertical planes, a vernier or nonius compass, and various types of quadrants used to tell time.

Surveyors attempted to convert sloping ground to horizontal distances with only modest success. The dumpy level, adopted for sloping ground, required a cumberson tripod, and was not in common use until after the 1830s. In wooded, mountainous land, the system was very inaccurate. Compass readings, which fluctuated with temperature during the day, may have been in error by one degree, or at best, by one half degree. Buried deposits of iron ore especially affected magnetic compass readings, as did certain types of partially buried igneous monoliths.

In their unique 2009 study of early land grants in central Tennessee, the authors Douglas Drake, et al, compiled and plotted data for 1,500 blocks; their resultant maps average a "7 degree northeastern tilt." According an arbitrary statement by the authors, the entire central Tennessee survey area was not corrected for magnetic declination by the 18th century surveyors.

To complicate matters even more, magnetic declination, which measures the angle between the North Pole, or axis of the Earth's rotation, and the Magnetic Pole, changes over time and with location. According to a 2013 NOAA website, for instance, magnetic declination for Raleigh, NC in 1785 was 1 degree, 52 minutes East. In 1790, it was 2 degrees, 2 minutes East, and in 1800, it was 2 degrees, 13 minutes East. As another example, in Charlotte, NC, the 1785 magnetic declination was 3 degrees, 6 minutes East; in 1790, it was 3 degrees, 17 minutes East; and in 1800, it was 3 degrees, 32 minutes East.

Slope inclines required special mathematical skill and time to convert to horizontal distances. Heavy underbrush often obscured the line of sight. Moreover, human error played a big part in false mathematical recordings. One surveyor reported an arbitrary correction of 3% for the sag of the Gunters chain when crossing rivers.

Generally, surveyors notched trees to indicate property boundaries. In extreme cases, these marks had a life expectancy of up to 80 years. When boundary marks disappeared or when surveyor's determinations were in question, it was a matter of either resurveying or else going to court. If adjacent landowners could not comprise, the alternatives were usually long drawn out, expensive court settlements.

The Province of Carolina was so designated in 1629. These southern colonies came under proprietary control in 1663. Surveyors began in 1665 to divide the lowlands into squares and rectangles. By 1712, the north and south areas had developed separate local governments .

North Carolina and South Carolina formally split and became royal colonies in 1729. Each functioned separately under royal governors. At that time 15 North Carolina coastal counties were in existence and had the advanced forms of organized local government, but nebulous county boundaries.

In 1710, a proposal was made to survey the Virginia/North Carolina border. This proposal languished until 1727 and 1728, when William Mayo and Alexander Irvin struggled to complete the survey. The survey began at the north end of the Currituck Island, supposedly at 36 degrees, 31 minutes. This first survey group finally traversed 15 mile of lagoons, across some 20 miles of "Dismal Swamp," eventually reached some 242 miles from the coast, at the western edge of the Piedmont.

In 1747, Joshua Fry and Peter Jefferson extended the VA/NC line westward across the Appalachians for about 90 miles; Fry and Jefferson determined that boundary markers were located about 12 miles too far north. And in 1749, William Churton added another 90 miles. These extensions covered much of what became the border of Tennessee and Kentucky.

In 1729, seven of the eight proprietors gave up their rights to land covering North and South Carolina and received 17,500 pounds compensation from the Crown. Shortly thereafter, prominent English merchant Henry McCulloch bought 1.25 million acres scattered in the Piedmont from the Neuse River in the north to Cape Fear River, and on to the Pee Dee River in the south.

In 1745, McCulloch sold 200,000 acres in the western part to Arthur Dobbs, later to become the fourth Royal governor. Dobbs requested the Surveyor General, Matthew Rowan, to begin surveys of his land. However, by 1767, Dobbs had not fulfilled settlement requirements and the holdings were declared invalid. The former Dobbs Co., NC south of the Neuse River generally represents the extent of the Dobb's holdings; this county was split and renamed in 1791.

From 1735 to 1815, six attempts were made to formalize the boundary between North Carolina and South Carolina. In fact, the Joint Boundary Commission only in 2013 completed a technical resurvey of the 334 mile boundary. The administrative part of straightening out property tax complications of land owners has yet to be completed. Imagine being told that your property taxes had increased because the State line had changed. Or worse, that the nebulous birth place of Andrew Jackson was in North Carolina rather than in South Carolina.

Although North Carolina existed as an independent American colony from 1776, it was formally designated a state only in 1789. At this time, 50 counties in North Carolina, each with their individually established sovereign power, were problematically merged into a cohesive whole.

After the Granville Land Office opened in Edenton, NC, about 1744, William Churton became its most prominent surveyor. Among other large projects, Churton conducted the survey of the Unitas Fratrum (Moravian brotherhood) beginning around 1753. This project eventually encompassed 98,985 acres in the area now surrounding Winston-Salem. Churton died in 1767 while he was in the middle of the project to map the southern boundary of the Granville lands even though Granville himself had died in 1763; note the 1992 publication by W. N. Watt.

As payment for his service, Churton was granted some 11,000 or 12,000 acres, which he sold and which then were known as the Metcalf lands until being sold again to the Moravians. Churton also received four acres which later formed a part of Hillsborough, NC. Churton's name also appears on a large numbers of pre-Revolutionary War land grants now filed in Rowan Co. and Iredell Co. records in the NC State Archives.

For decades, boundaries remained problematic. Adjacent land owners often compromised as to the location of the common boundary. Thus, 200 miles of the Mason-Dixon line, dividing Pennsylvania and Maryland was not resolved until the years 1763 to 1768. Even later, in 1783 to 1784, Thomas Hutchins resurveyed part of the boundary.

About 1774, John Sevier settled on land along the Watauga River and later the Nolichucky River in what he thought was Kentucky, only to find out eventually he lived in what became Tennessee. The western extension of the VA-NC territorial boundary was remapped in 1779 and 1780 by surveyors Daniel Smith and Dr. Thomas Walker.

In 1796, when a census determined that Tennessee had some 60,000 inhabitants, the territory went through the same difficult process of forming a state especially since the bulk of its population was located in its eastern district and most of the western third was still nominally Indian territory.

In 1798, Jonathon Price and John Strother, surveying in western North Carolina, began the first actual regional survey of Buncombe, Burke, and Rutherford Counties. Their work was incorporated into an 1808 map, being the first detailed printed map of the area. The Price-Strother map shows general locations of Gen. Joseph McDowell's and other McDowell residences. The somewhat obsolete 1808 map shows the town of Moriston (Morriston) which had been renamed Asheville about 1796.

In 1811, Andrew Ellicott established a reference point at 35 degrees north latitude for later work on the boundary between North Carolina and Georgia. His reference point was at the corner of North Carolina, South Carolina, and Georgia. Modern surveys conclude Ellicott's determination was accurate within a "few hundred feet." In 1811, Ellicott found errors of 18 miles in North Carolina's favor. In 1817 and 1826, when surveyors, using Ellicott's reference point to extend the line between Tennessee and Georgia, they determined the boundary was actually a half mile south. As a consequence, the North Carolina and Georgia line shows a boundary jog 661 yards south.

In 1828, when Henry S. Tanner published a *New Pocket Atlas of the United States with the Roads and Distances Designed for Travelers*, modern map making in the eastern part of the United States was initiated. Tanner was preceded by an older brother, Benjamin Tanner, also a map maker.

About 1830, Americans were able to manufacture brass, a primary component of surveying instruments and gradually ceased importing expensive foreign instruments. After the mid-1800s, engineer's transits (sometimes called transit theodolites, being slightly more accurate) were used.

In the 1960s, electronic distance meters, and later, the GPS and modern geodetic devices, gave rise to a host of resurveys which will be ongoing for some decades.

As a matter of considerable interest, in 2013, the American Land Title Association reported that its members found defects or "clouds" in the title of 35% of title searches. Many clouds reflect primitive surveying techniques used in the original land grants.

13

Speculators in Western North Carolina

While the average militia soldier normally received his choice of land from state governments rather than the federal government, he often had to compete with wholesale land speculation by individuals using borrowed money. When the markets crashed, as in 1796, debtor's prisons filled with speculators. The principal centers for "land mania" were Philadelphia, and New York, and to a lessor extent Hartford, and Boston.

The first permanent NC grant for Old Burke Co. was recorded in 1780, being that for speculator John McKnitt Alexander, resident in Mecklenburg Co. Alexander had Senator William Sharpe as his partner; together they took some 27 early land grants in Old Burke County. Others joined in the land grab rush.

Robert Tate and William Tate each took some 200 early land grants in Burke Co. Robert Tate lived in York Co., PA, while William Tate established residence in Morganton and is buried at Quaker Meadows. Before and after her marriage to William Tate, Mary Bowman, daughter of John Bowman, received a number of grants in her own name. She was a virtually unique woman in entering land grants in Western North Carolina. In the 1790's, the two Tate brothers also speculated on land in South Carolina which they later conveyed to financier Robert Morris.

Beginning in 1778, Joseph Dobson Sr. and Jr., entered some 142 grants in Burke Co. and some 93 land grants in what became Buncombe Co. The two Dobsons lived along the Catawba River near the current boundary of McDowell Co. and Burke Co. The elder Dobson was a long time recorder of deeds.

In 1794 to 1795, another upheaval occurred. Land speculators were allowed to apply and receive enormous blocks of land in Western North Carolina with scant regard for pre-existing landholders. These tracts blanketed multiple small existing tracts and generated much anxiety and likely legal action. Evidently, legislators in North Carolina had followed the example of South Carolina who had in 1793 allowed the existence of "excessive grants" in the extreme northwest corner of the South Carolina.

This was the second major decree evidently resulting from legislative action in Raleigh. Large scale speculation was to center around Buncombe and Rutherford Counties.

Thus, Philadelphia financier and land speculator Robert Morris contracted with the Tate brothers for 198 grants totaling about 70,400 acres lying mostly in what much later was to become McDowell Co. Evidently these blocks, consisting uniformly of 640 acres, overlapped in part many earlier grants.

In the same era, other big time, mostly non-resident speculators, or their agents active in Western North Carolina, included David Allison, John Gray Blount, William Cathcart, Jacob Eshleman, Daniel Huger, John Holdiman, George Lattimer, John Strother, and William Stedeman. These individuals may be labeled as compulsive gamblers.

A tentative list of their main speculative holdings in the area of Old Buncombe Co., as reported by historian Albert B. Pruitt, 1989, is as follows:

>   David Allison, 250,240 acres, grant 251 (probable proxy for William Blount)
>   John Gray Blount, 506,240 acres, grants 252, 253
>   William Cathcart, 133,080 acres, grants 220, 224, 225
>   Thomas Davidson & Mark Mitchell, 50,000 acres, grant 175
>   Stockley Donelson, 60,400 acres, mainly in TN
>   Benjamin Hall, James McEntire, & William Walker, Jr., 29,640 acres, grant 193
>   John Holdiman & Jacob Eshleman, 200,960 acres, grant 279
>   Daniel Huger, 80,000 acres, grants 194, 195
>   George Lattimer, 50,660 acres, grant 230

If the reader is confused about the precise location of blocks acquired by these large land holders, key index maps are in the publications of George H. Smathers, 1938, and especially in Albert B. Pruitt, 1989. For detailed geographic locations of the rivers and tiny streams in Blue Ridge Physiographic Province, the reader is directed to the following series of modern watershed maps printed by the North Carolina Department of Water and Air Resources:

>   - Upper Broad River Basin 01 , scale 1:500,000; (Rutherford Co.,settled by 1751)
>   - Upper Catawba River Basin-1, ditto; (Burke Co. settled by 1758)
>   - French Broad River Basin 05, ditto; (Buncombe Co. settled by 1782)

In November 1796, non-resident John Gray Blount received grant no. 253 covering 320,640 acres which contained 67 pre-existing grants totaling 13,735 acres. Much of this large Blount block lay in what is now Buncombe, Madison, and Yancey counties. At the time, 131 entries were in progress for much smaller grants by other parties. Although these 131 smaller entries were excluded from the claim of Blount, few were actually finalized. Grants that were already in existence before the large Blount claim surely were honored by pre-emption claims although the record of such is meager.

For example, the village of Morristown (later Asheville) was settled by John Burton in 1794 and thus excluded. The Burton location, in Buncombe Co. grant 63 of 400 acres, comprised some 40 lots that were valued at $2.50 per lot. Most likely, it was a matter of never-ending conflict of claims between large-scale speculators and ordinary resident land holders who were obligated to file pre-emption claims. Frontier lawyers and judges were kept busy.

In 1797, John Holdiman and Jacob Eshleman acquired some 200,960 acres from William Tate, the land being located along the Tuckasegee and Nantahala Rivers. This Buncombe Co. grant was no. 279.

In the late 1700's and the early 1800s, road infrastructure was still a disaster. For instance, the Hickory Nut Gap Turnpike, essentially a dirt (or mud) road, connecting Asheville with Rutherfordton, dates from about 1815. In the same general area of western North Carolina, the primitive Oconaluftee Valley Turnpike, connected Tennessee to South Carolina.

Although in 1796, South Carolina's Governor Arnold Vanderhorst and Tennessee's Governor John Sevier supported an improved road from Greenville, SC to Greeneville, TN, a distance of some 120 miles, the improvement did not materialize until much later. The road that became the Buncombe Turnpike, completed in 1827, extended in North Carolina across Madison, Buncombe, and Henderson Counties. During the lengthy planning process, Zachariah Candler and Samuel Chunn lobbied hard to have the road altered to go by their property.

What the non-resident speculators in the Appalachians hoped to do with their large blocks is a matter of speculation. Virtually no roads existed, much less railroads. Consequently the hope for rapid expansion of the white population failed to materialize. Moreover immigration from Europe was long depressed during the three major international conflicts between 1776 and 1814, as was European investment in general. Some likely dreamed of finding vast deposits of gold in the mountains. In many cases, grants languished well beyond the death of the original owner and were passed on to heirs or reverted to the state for for lack of survey or non payment of taxes.

14

Thars Gold in Them Thar Hills

Since time immortal, people have been fascinated by the cry of "gold." And so it was in the early exploration of the Appalachians. The early American colonies had no uniform currency; therefore gold was the ultimate medium of exchange.

The Spanish were among the earliest of the explorers to the Americas. Hernando De Soto was among the earliest to eastern North America. His inland expedition, about 1540, traveled north from Florida, along the eastern edge of the Appalachians evidently as far north as current Burke Co., NC before heading westward into what is now Tennessee and on to the Mississippi River where he died. Evidently De Soto made contact with the Mississippian Mound Builder culture, tribes of native Americans who were precursors to the Cherokees. De Soto's small army likely was composed of Spanish, Portuguese, Moroccans, and other eastern Mediterraneans.

Some twenty years later, in 1567 to 1568, the Spaniard Juan Pardo led another expedition of about 120 men. Pardo established a base at Santa Elena on an island in Beaufort Co., SC, and traveled inland over much of the same Appalachian territory as De Soto. Eventually Pardo reached Joara, a large native American settlement located near the current city of Morganton, Burke Co., NC. Pardo built a stockade near Joara as well as forts at five other localities, mistakenly spreading his men among the various localities.

Pardo organized small groups of native Americans near Joara and the combined forces began to attack distant native Americans in the search for food, supplies including gold, and slaves including women. The attacks were ill-fated however. Pardo's men were wiped out.

If De Soto's men or Pardo's men encountered any traces of gold in the Appalachians, no firm evidence has been presented. However, Foster A. Sondley in his 1930's *History of Buncombe County* speculates that native Americans knew about such occurrences even though fairly extensive archaeological excavations at Joara have yet to confirm this. Incidentally, Sondley's book was published in two stages posthumously after extensive editing by noted educator Alonzo Carlton Reynolds.

In following years, the Cherokees were intrigued by glistening minerals such as mica which occurs commonly in the Appalachians. Sheets of mica were traded by the Cherokees with tribes living in the Ohio Valley. The chemical stability of mica as compared to gold is very poor; it is of relatively little value.

In the period of 1778 to 1817 when pioneer lawyer Waightstill Avery entered 117 blocks for

21,170 acres around Grandfather Mountain, he must have dreamed of finding the Mother Lode in Western North Carolina. Avery, who was the holder of 24 slaves in Burke Co., used this labor source in attempting to mine for gold. They did in fact operate three small mines in the vicinity of Grandfather Mountain.

Waightstill Avery's grandson, Alphonso Calhoun Avery, inherited his grandfather's passion for mountainous land possession, and in the years 1872 to 1873, entered 18,323 acres in 38 blocks on his own, all in the same general area. What he intended to do with this mountainous terrain in the depression era of the post-Civil War remains a partial mystery. A relative, Walter Waightstill Lenoir evidently inherited the main interest in the Avery property. In 1888, a group of investors from Wilmington, NC bought an interest.

Modern records show that gold is now known from 26 counties in North Carolina. Most occurrences are relatively minor, being in stream beds of the Piedmont. Few occurrences were of mint quantity. In fact, it was not until 1799 that significant interest in North Carolina gold occurred. A son of a German immigrant Johannes Reid (John Reed) stumbled on an alluvial 17 pound gold nugget in Cabarrus Co., NC. Only in 1803 did Reed and partners begin actively searching out other gold. In 1828, they found another 28 pound nugget, also alluvial. The Charlotte Mint existed from 1837 to 1861. In 1834, the U.S. fixed gold at $20.67 per ounce where it remained until 1933.

It was not until 1828 that Benjamin Parks found traces of gold in a stream bed near Dahlonega, GA that another fairly substantial occurrence of gold was recorded. This led to the seventh land lottery in Georgia, being the 1832 Gold Land Lottery. By 1832, when noted South Carolina politician John C. Calhoun paid $6,000 for the Obarr mine however, much of the readily accessible placer gold at Dahlonega had already been produced. Most of the gold at Dahlonega was in solid rock and required heavy, physical labor, mainly slave, to mine.

In 1834, the authorities in Dahlonega decided they needed a new courthouse and contracted with a local resident to build one for $7,000 and they provided a down payment of $2,000. The nameless builder absconded with the deposit. In 1836, the job was turned over to master builder Ephraim Clayton who lived 150 miles away, across the grain of the Appalachians, in Asheville, NC. Clayton built the courthouse, then waited years for Lumpkin Co., GA to settle the account, and in 1855 finally sued.

In 1831, another German immigrant Christopher Bechtler settled in Rutherfordton and began minting gold coins. Placer (surface deposits) mining as well as vein (underground mines) mining had increased substantially in the central Piedmont in a 100 mile trend extending from Greensboro southwest to Charlotte (1837 population - 717) and nearby Kings Mountain. Lesser amounts of gold were taken from placer mines in the Appalachians and elsewhere. By the time Christopher died in 1842, the independent Bechtler Mint had processed over $3 million worth of coin and bullion and thereby materially enhanced the local, basically farming economy. Another crude gauge of gold production was sketchy records of gold shipment to the Federal mint at Philadelphia. At a peak in 1834, North Carolina shipped about $380,000 and Georgia shipped about $415,000.

15

Lesser Speculators in Western North Carolina

Lesser speculators included lawyer Waightstill Avery. Avery's Western North Carolina grants, recorded in Burke, Buncombe, and Rutherford Counties numbered 172 grants, and totaled 36,555 acres; they were entered between 1788 and 1818. In an 1818 list of taxable property for Burke County, Avery still retained 13,001 acres in that county; evidently he had either sold 23,554 acres, had given them to his heirs, or lost them in court cases. In 1790, Avery had 24 slaves, but by 1800 had only 5 slaves.

About 1793, the brothers Zebulon Baird and Bedent Baird went to Buncombe Co. and began a joint mercantile business which lasted until about 1805. In 1794, the brothers independently began applying for land grants with Zebulon eventually accumulating 1,450 acres and Bedent a mere 650 acres. Zebulon died intestate in 1824. In 1827, Bedent attempted to claim joint interest in Zebulon's property. Zebulon's heirs hired rising star lawyer David Lowery Swain. The case languished in court until 1837 when Zebulon's heirs prevailed. By that time, Swain had completed his term as governor of North Carolina and become head of the University of North Carolina all the while maintaining his legal practice in western North Carolina.

In the years 1795 to 1800, Felix Walker, a notable politician from Rutherford Co. decided to apply for some 14 blocks (Buncombe grant 468, etc. - now Jackson Co., NC). This acreage in mostly mountainous terrain, totaled over 10,000 acres. About the same time, Burke Co. lawyer Waightstill Avery applied for overlapping acreage. The matter resided in court for ten years. Although Walker's claim was finally determined valid, he incurred large court costs, thus negating much of the value of the claim.

Zachariah Candler's NC land grants, all recorded in Buncombe Co., numbered 81 grants and totaled 21,915 acres; they were entered between 1800 and 1841. In comparison to many other speculators, Candler lived in the area of his holdings, moving progressively down the French Broad River with each stage of new acquisitions.

Land grants continued in North Carolina well into the 1900s although at a very diminished pace. A late North Carolina State grant in Burke Co. in 1936, no. 6399, was that for George McNealey.

In Old Buncombe Co., the Land Office also recorded thousands of land entries. In Buncombe Co., the first North Carolina grant recorded was dated 1792, being that for Gabriel Ragsdale. Grant numbers beyond 5,000 become very erratic. The last grant number used in Buncombe Co., dated January, 1927, was no. 19,032, this being for W. M. Joyce involving 3/4 acre on N. Hominy Cr.

16

What Happened to the Speculation Lands
of Western North Carolina?

Speculation on land anywhere in America proved to be a very risky business, mainly because large blocks invariably were financed on credit and incurred upfront entrance fees plus surveyors and other relatively minor costs as well as ongoing taxes. While the financial atmosphere may have been relatively favorable at time of purchase, emerging recessions, deflation, devaluation of currency, epidemics, and other uncontrollable local events took their toll.

In the early days when men went bankrupt, they usually went to debtor's prison. Such was the case of noted financier Robert Morris of Philadelphia and his partners John Nicholson and James Greenleaf, who as key partners in the North American Land Co. and at least three lesser companies, had vast tracts scattered over the Pennsylvania, Virginia, North Carolina, South Carolina, Kentucky, and Georgia (actually Georgia territory) as well as various lots in the District of Columbia. By 1795, their North American Land Company totaled some six million acres with clear "title" to about 4.5 million acres. Most of their land applications were secured by promissory notes to previous holders. In many areas, the partners bought warrants at 25% of their face value and thus known purchase prices ranged only from about 12 cents to about 25 cents per acre.

Nicholson apparently was the chief promoter in the group. His impeachment trial in 1794 recorded that he used dubious middlemen and fictitious names to exceed acreage limits. And obviously he bribed state surveyor generals, clerks in the Land Office, and on occasion, judges of the district court.

In 1795, Morris and Nicholson attempted to have an initial public offering and valued their 6,000,000 acres at fifty cents a share. They hoped to raise $3 million capital by issuing stock by offering 30,000 shares of 200 acres each. Shares were valued at $100. With the onset of a minor financial crisis in the U.S. in 1796, few takers appeared. A Congressional committee determined in 1795 that Morris owed the government alone some $93,000.

In the years 1797 to 1799, all three, Morris, Nicholson and Greenleaf went to infamous Prune Street Jail, a Philadelphia debtor prison.

Nicholson died intestate in prison in 1801. After years of litigation, his heirs finally received title to 8,949 acres in Northumberland Co., PA.

Morris was in prison 41 months and died in 1806. As determined by a bankruptcy court in

1801, Morris and Nicholson owed some 61 creditors about 3 million dollars. An active market developed in the trading of their promissory notes which however were devalued at less than 10 cents on the dollar.

Greenleaf spent about a year in prison and somehow, with the help of the first United States bankruptcy law, managed to settle bills of about $9 million. After that, he spent a long period developing property in Washington, D.C. and in fighting court cases ranging from the years 1802 to 1835.

In the 1790s, Willliam Duer and Alexander Macomb both went to prison for over speculation in land deals and various securities. Duer was one of the first to go to debtor's prison, languishing there from 1791 to 1799.

Another noteworthy case was that of William Blount whose land interests ranged across western North Carolina, Tennessee, and Alabama. Blount did not go to prison, but his political and financial wealth rapidly diminished when he was impeached from the U.S. Senate in 1797.

Many other factors contributing to depressed land values included supply and demand. For instance, Georgia established a system of eight land lotteries, ranging from 1805 to 1833. Government prices for lottery offerings were fixed, but the value of existing grants temporarily declined with each new offering. In 1832, a gold land lottery took place in north Georgia.

After the Louisiana Purchase was settled in 1803, a vast new and fertile area was eventually opened for settlers. Alabama and Mississippi achieved formal status in 1817 and thereby attracted migrants. By 1819, other states, including Florida and Maine were opening lands to purchasers and contributed to excess supply.

When Missouri became a state in 1820, numerous residents in Buncombe Co. and Rutherford Co. were enticed to migrate westward, some 800 miles along dirt roads and across several large rivers, to this promising territory. In 1829, a proposal was considered by the U.S. Senate to limit new land offerings. Senator Thomas Hart Benton of Missouri, originally a native of Durham Co., NC, naturally objected vehemently. Benton further proposed reducing the price of government offerings which in the beginning were fixed at $1.25 per acre.

Other examples of failure to meet financial obligations in western North Carolina are recorded. In 1798, James Hughey, as sheriff of Buncombe Co., confiscated 16,000 acres along Jenkins Cr. for non-payment of taxes and fees. Samuel Lusk, as Buncombe Co. sheriff from 1799 to 1803, confiscated large portions of the Blount lands (220,640 acres) as well as the Allison lands (104,420 acres). In 1804, David Vance was one of two trustees of Newton Academy given true and lawful (power of) attorney over 20,000 (confiscated) acres at Swannanoa/Cane Creek, this being former Blount lands.

In 1811 and again in 1813, the next Buncombe County sheriff, John Longmire, with the approval of David Stone, governor of North Carolina, took over lands in a reverse grant which went back to the State; these were in blocks of 19,000 and 10,000 acres, respectively.

After John Gray Blount died in 1833, his heirs scrambled to dispose of his large claims and they hired Robert and James B. Love as agents. The value of land dropped when a major recession occurred from 1837 to 1843. In 1839 and 1840, William B. Westall attempted to buy some 13,000 acres of the Blount holdings, this being around the area of Mt. Mitchell (now Yancey Co.). Initially, Westall's partners were Moses Evans, and later Asheville's top lawyer, Nicholas W. Woodfin, evidently the mortgage holder. In 1842, when Westall failed to pay incurred fees of a mere $52.53, the property was acquired by John W. McElroy, who defaulted to Woodfin and his partner, former governor David L. Swain. In 1867, Woodfin and Swain, both then in dire financial straits, sold the property, the sale bringing only $1,250. Overall, it was a very meager return on investment in a post war period.

In 1838, Zachariah Candler devised a working agreement with Robert Love and his son, James B. Love, to sell 150,000 acres which Love had acquired for $4,400. This acquisition embraced 100,000 acres of the old John Gray Blount grant 253 (originally 320,640 acres) and 50,000 acres of the old David Allison grant 251 (originally 250,240 acres). The acreage corresponded to about 40% of modern day Buncombe Co.

In many places, Candler's personal grants overlapped those of the original Blount grants. In 1839, Candler bought some 6,000 acres from the Blount heirs for $1,000, or about 16 cents an acre.

The master card index of land grants at the U.S. Forestry Service in Asheville records many apparent overlaps in applications for the same property. In the light of sparse records, how this was resolved is open to speculation - was it settled out of court or in court? See also Pruitt, A. B., 1993a and 1993b.

In 1800, Thomas McEntire as sheriff of Burke Co. confiscated 124,000 acres in 83 grants for unpaid taxes (see MARS grant nos. 1932 thru 2128, Burke Co.)

In 1840, politician William Holland Thomas bought 33,000 acres from the heirs of speculator William Cathcart for $1,200. From 1840 to 1856, Thomas accumulated about 148,000 acres from various other speculators, part of which was subsidized by entitlements to the Ocanaluftee tribe of the Cherokees, and which eventually comprised the Qualla Boundary (reservation), an area of 52,864 acres. In 1856, Thomas sold 30,000 acres to James R. Love for $7,300. The purchase by Love was ill-timed as property values in the South plummeted during the Civil War.

17

Speculators in Tennessee Territory

Eighteenth century land acquisition in western North Carolina was relatively placid compared to the land rush in what became Tennessee. After 1770, settlers poured into Tennessee and created a frenzy of activity. By 1783, compulsive gamblers David Allison, John Gray Blount, and Stockley Donelson were actively seeking land in both North Carolina and Tennessee. These big speculators were relying on population pressure and economic growth to spur enormous increases in land values. Few considered the buffer zones provided by hostile Indian tribes and instead relied on the Federal Government to bail them out.

About 1778, a rush of pioneers living in Tennessee Territory began staking land claims. From the massive land data compilation provided by Griffey, 2000, we can summarize some of the larger speculators in Tennessee, namely:

David Allison, 39,765 acres, 9 blocks,mainly Middle District
Martin Armstrong, 134,473 acres, 96 blocks, mainly Eastern District
John Armstrong, 18,228 acres, 10 blocks, mainly Middle District
Samuel Barton, 28,354 acres, 47 blocks, mainly Middle District
Redmon D. Barry, 32,194 acres, 53 blocks, Middle District
John Gray Blount, 380,396 acres, 183 blocks, mainly Western District
Landon Carter, 52,154 acres, 76 blocks, Middle & Western districts
Stockley Donelson, 944,271 acres, 406 blocks, mainly East District
George Doherty, 27,100 acres, 11 blocks, mainly Western District
Richard Fenner, 25,980 acres, 30 blocks, mainly Middle District
James George, 106,000 acres, 2 blocks, Tennessee River area
Edward Harris, 76,216 acres, 101 blocks, mainly Eastern District
Robert Hays, 120,068 acres, 55 blocks, mainly Eastern District
Menucan Hunt, 106,000 acres, 22 blocks, mainly Western District
Robert King, 50,060 acres, 97 blocks,Eastern District
Thomas King, 50,826 acres, 62 blocks, mainly Eastern District
related King family, 100,324 acres, 110 blocks, mostly Eastern District
William T. Lewis, 74,771 acres, 52 blocks, mainly Middle District
Nicholas Long, 29,734 acres, 19 blocks, all districts
Hardy Murfree, 40,900 acres, 29 blocks, Middle and Western Districts

John Nichols, 25,710 acres, 39 blocks, Middle District
Thomas Polk, 57,191 acres, 13 blocks, mainly Middle District
William J. Polk, 55,618 acres, 23 blocks, mainly Middle District
John Rice, 135,046 acres, 82 blocks, scattered - all districts
Elijah Robertson, 42,251 acres, 49 blocks, mainly Middle District
James Robertson, 49,715 acres, 93 blocks, mainly Middle District
John Rutledge, 67,500 acres, 15 blocks, Middle District
John Sevier, Sr., 84,192 acres, 13 blocks, mainly Eastern District
John Sevier, Jr., 41,630 acres, 6 blocks, Eastern district
Benjamin Smith, 103,418 acres, 27 blocks, Western District
Duncan Stewart, 36,728 acres, 44 blocks, Middle and Eastern District
William Tyrrell, 39,227 acres, 44 blocks, Middle and Eastern Districts
Thomas Wade, 25,000 acres, 5 blocks, Middle District
Robert Weadley, 25,454 acres, 40 blocks, Middle District

The individuals listed above had various partners and in turn were partners on other blocks. For instance, William Tyrrell was a key partner of Stockley Donelson; in turn Tyrrell shared 121,634 acres with Donelson. Donelson likely had other silent partners among his relatives. Thomas Blount was a key partner of John Gray Blount, etc. To complicate the records, "Martin" and various partners applied for an additional 42 blocks totaling 26,528 acres - this was probably Martin Armstrong who headed the Hillsboro Land Office from about 1783 to 1797.

Individual blocks taken by more than one family member include the following families: Armstrong, Blount, Donelson, King, Polk, Robertson, Rutledge, and Sevier. A good example above is that of John Sevier, Sr., and his son, John Sevier, Jr. Family names are recorded under more than one spelling. A good example: James Robertson/Robeson/Robinson.

In the pioneer environment, rules and regulations were informal and were seldom enforced. Among the large speculators, blocks of 5,000 acres were common; a few blocks were 20,000 acres or more. Corruption was rife, the use of legal loopholes was common; forged warrants, bribery, fictious names and altered dates appeared. Unsecured loans, delayed payments, and illegal credit prevailed. The mysterious duo of Martin Armstrong and Stockley Donelson evidently were at the center of much of this questionable activity.

When John Rice was killed near Memphis in 1792, lawyer and future president Andrew Jackson and his partner John Overton bought 50,000 acres of the Rice land. In 1795, Jackson went to Philadelphia to peddle this land and received an offer for $0.20 an acre from speculator David Allison who gave only notes in payment. The notes soon became due; in 1797, Allison declared bankruptcy. Jackson was held liable for the notes which he in turn had used to purchase mercantile goods. Complicating the picture, Allison went to debtor's prison where in died in 1798.

In 1794, lawyer Andrew Jackson was an agent for the sale of 85,000 acres held by John Gray Blount and brother Thomas Blount held on the Duck River (TN). The initial sale was to David Allison who mortgaged the property to Norton Pryor, Philadelphia merchant. In 1801, Pryor foreclosed. The case got very complicated in 1808 when Andrew Jackson bought the property, but found out the sale to Pyror was invalid and the value of the land had increased. Again, Jackson was held liable.

Thomas Hart Benton, who migrated from North Carolina to Tennessee about 1801, became a largely self-taught lawyer, like many of his contemporaries. Much of his practice dealt with establishing and settling land claims. In 1809, Benton became one of 12 Senators in the Tennessee legislature. Politicians spent considerable time debating the rights of squatters and whether or not they were liable for damages to property they illegally occupied.

The rush to grab land in Tennessee provided many opportunities for fraud. Two much publicized cases were the Mussel Shoals Land Fraud and the Glasgow Land Fraud cases.

Mussel Shoals was in South Carolina Territory (now Muscle Shoals, in Alabama) along the Tennessee River. In 1786, early principals at Mussel Shoals operated under the name Tennessee Company and included Wade Hampton I and John Sevier. The application to the South Carolina legislature, through the Ninety-Six District land office, was for 238,920 acres and was initially approved in January 1786. However, South Carolina gave up its western (Alabama, Mississippi) claim in 1787. Thereafter, Hampton was not involved in further attempts to get land outside of South Carolina. He did, however, continue to act as a land broker for speculator Robert Morris and others in South Carolina.

In 1789, an eleven member group composed of William Blount, his brothers John Gray Blount and Reading Blount, Richard Caswell, Griffith Rutherford, John Donelson, Joseph Martin, Anthony Bledsoe, Martin Armstrong, James Glasgow, and John Sevier applied to the Georgia legislature for territory at Mussel Shoals. When John Donelson was killed in 1785, presumably his son Stockley Donelson became involved. The applicants were nearly all prominent politicians and/or ranking military officers.

Later principals, forming the Tennessee Company, with its quest for an expanded 3.5 million acres, included Zachariah Cox, Thomas Gilbert, and John Strother.

The Tennessee Company renewed interest in 1789, and again in 1795, but offered promissory notes for about $46,785, and not specie. The Georgia legislature initially approved the request in 1795, but after much adverse public comment, rejected the matter the following year. In 1796, the Federal Government finally ruled that the land in question was native American land and the application was invalid. In 1798, Georgia ceded the lands to the Federal Government. The matter arose in the Supreme Court again in 1810 who ruled that only the Federal Government could act.

The Tennessee Company was just one of three or four diverse companies to file for land in what became Alabama and Mississippi in the period 1783 to 1796. The various claims generally went under the term "Yazoo Land Fraud." Total acreage of the four Yazoo claims was on the order of some 20 million acres.

In 1789, the companies were the Georgia Co., the Virginia Yazoo Co., and the Tennessee Co.; at this time, total purchase offering was $207,000. By 1794, the companies were the Georgia Co., the Georgia-Mississippi Co., the Upper Mississippi Co., and the Tennessee Co., and the purchase offering for the expanded area was increased to $500,000. This latter purchase offering was thus 2.5 cents per acre. By 1818, waves of smaller, secondary buyer's and squatter's tracts were occupied; the Federal Government was obligated to pay $4.28 million to settle claims.

For comparison, in 1803, when President Thomas Jefferson oversaw the purchase of the Louisiana Purchase by the United States from France, the area comprised some 530 million acres and the negotiated sale price was $15 million. English banks led by Baring Bank provided massive loans. The basic purchase price was thus slightly more than 2.8 cents per acre. However, interest on the principal added $8,529,000 and squatter's claims added another $3,728,000 for an overall cost of some 27 million dollars. This bargain turned into the bread basket of the United States.

Principals in the 1789 Glasgow Land Fraud, which involved mainly land in the Military Reservation of north central Tennessee are as listed below. Glasgow was Secretary of State of North Carolina from 1777 to 1798. The main beneficiaries of the land fraud were James Glasgow and others listed below. The benefit to Thomas Butcher, Nathan Lassiter, Samuel Sanford, and Joseph Terrebee was minor.

James Glasgow	Joshua Hadley	Moses Shelby
John Bonds	Nathan Lassiter	Benjamin Sheppard
Thomas Butcher	John McNees	John Sheppard
Joshua Davis	Mann Phillips	Joseph Terrebee
Wynn Dixon	Arthur Pierce	William Terrell
Stockley Donelson	John Price	Willoughby Williams
William Faircloth	Samuel Samford	

In another interesting case, John Sevier, who held warrants for his service in the Revolutionary War east of the Appalachians in North Carolina, asked to have these warrants transferred to land west of the Appalachians. At the same time, he requested that future grants be rated at ten pounds per 100 acres, a twenty-fold increase.

John Sevier led a multi-faceted life. He was a principal commander at the critical Revolutionary War battle of Kings Mountain in 1780. He served as governor of the unofficial State of Franklin, an area which later formed most of eastern Tennessee. At the end of this quasi-official term as governor, Sevier was indicted for treason and jailed in Burke Co., but soon released through his multiple personal contacts, notably Robert Love, a military acquaintance.

In his active career, Sevier participated in some thirty violent battles with the Cherokees, the Creek, and other Indian tribes, that is, roughly from 1756 to 1795. The most notable of these Indian conflicts occurred in 1780, 1781, 1782, 1786, 1789, and 1793. In his 1894 book The Winning of the West, Theodore Roosevelt said Sevier "was the most renowned Indian fighter of the Southeast". For 70 years, John Sevier lived a charmed life.

Sevier was governor of Tennessee from 1796 to 1801. Always in a near state of hyper activity, Siever married twice, fathered 18 children, and had at least 112 grandchildren. In the early Virginia land records, the ancestor ????? Sevier has his name recorded as Sevear, Seveyor, Sevier, and Sevare.

About 1795, a census of the residents of Tennessee Territory finally qualified the area to apply for State status. At that time, the population was on the order to 65,300 of which about 90% lived in the Eastern District. The residents of the remainder of Tennessee numbered roughly 7,000, nearly all of these being in the old Mero District, latter being expanded and called the Middle District. John Sevier was the first official governor of Tennessee.

18

Deed Mapping

In recent years, electronic *Deed Mapper* plots have been organized in various parts of Western North Carolina to consolidate data from page-sized sheets of original paper copies of the post Revolutionary War North Carolina land grants. These included the current work of Dorinda J. Whitley in northern Buncombe Co.; Dr. Robert McNeely in central Burke Co.; and Wendell Kirkham for parts of Catawba, Caldwell, and Alexander Counties.

McNeely's records, published in 2011 in book form, are available at the Burke County Public Library. In his work, McNeely plotted some 2,200 early land grants. Wendell Kirkham's *Deed Mapper* records are at the Patrick Beaver Library in Hickory.

In 1964, Robert W. Ramsey published a 6 x 9 page-sized map show 265 pre-Revolutionary War blocks, south of the Yadkin River, in the northern part of North Carolina.

William Doub Bennett published a similar mapping survey showing 41 post-Revolutionary War land grants in central McDowell Co. This was in the February, 1981 issue of the *North Carolina Genealogical Society Journal*. The Ramsey and Bennett land grant plots apparently were done with old-fashioned manual drafting. Blocks do not show any apparent "tilt."

In 2009, Douglas Drake, Jack Masters, and Bill Puryear, using *Maptech Terrain Navigator*, 2001 version, completed a large study of the area around Nashville, TN and plotted some 1500 early land grants by using overlays of USGS topographic maps, 7.5 minutes supplemented with interpretation of aerial photos. This technique shows about 7 degree block tilt arbitrarily assuming correction for magnetic deviation.

NOAA's projections of magnetic deviation date to the year 1750 for cities on the East Coast, namely Boston, New York, Philadelphia, Baltimore, Norfolk, and Charleston. They also show show Knoxville at the 1750 date. No deviations for Nashville, Memphis, and New Orleans are available before 1800, and for St. Louis only in 1820.

Working with either *Deed Mapper* or with *Maptech Terrain Navigator* is akin to working a Chinese puzzle with at least half of the pieces missing, and is very time consuming.

19

Recording Land Entries

Early land entries in Western North Carolina are recorded in various ways:
  - First, some early record books show applications for tracts that were later declared void.
  - Second, after April, 1778, records were in the form of an individual entry on page-sized single sheets.
  - Third, this was followed by a warrant for a survey.
  - Fourth, by the actual grant itself, i.e., the critical grant date.

The first three records were handwritten with the fourth, the actual grant being partially printed. Any one of the three or four types of records may have been gathered years ago by the NC State Archives and generally catalogued under a file number, not a grant number. In many cases, deeds were hand copied with some alteration, and filed in the various county courthouses. For a few tracts, all four record types have been lost. Some original North Carolina deeds unfortunately were retained by private parties. For example, some deeds to Tench Coxe were never filed with North Carolina land offices.

The important date of entry was followed by the date of actual granting. In rare cases, the lapse in time was a matter of days, but more often it was a matter of some years.

In North Carolina, the oldest known land grant in the State Archives is one from Carteret County, dating 1681.

20

Cheap Land

In 1775, the United States and the individual thirteen states began issuing "Continental Currency" which was tied to Spanish currency, and eventually came to be known as the dollar. Continental Currency varied according to State. In North Carolina, the dollar's value in state currency was 8 shillings.

Thus, 50 shillings, a common value for a 100 acre land grant, was about $6.25, or about $0.62 per acre; or conversely, one pound (20 shillings) was $2.50. But the dollar continued to depreciate, so that by the end of the American Revolution in 1783, it was worth only $0.65, or less than 2/3 of its original value in 1775.

Currency peculiarities are recorded in the early land grants in Western North Carolina. Before 1820, cost of the grant was designated in North Carolina currency, being pounds and shillings. In 1820 and later, some uniformity in monetary matters between the States was established so that the cost of state land grants was designated in dollars.

As an example, from 1800 to 1819, Zachariah Candler paid 50 shillings per 100 acres for land in Western North Carolina; after 1820, he paid $10 per 100 acres, or $0.10 per acre.

As another example, from 1800 to 1807, Abraham Reynolds paid 50 shillings per 100 acres. After 1820, he paid $10 per 100 acres, and in 1838, he paid only $5 per (apparently mountainous) 100 acres, or $0.05 per acre. Other relatively minor costs associated with a grant included surveyor's fees, filing the grant, recording the grant, and affixing an official seal.

Just think, a nickel an acre, even if it was only hilly red clay and rocks! Individuals who later donated an acre of ground for a church or a rural cemetery did not have much investment.

Thus when documents of early North Carolina land grants show a price above 25 or 50 shillings per 100 acres, they are probably fraudulent documents.

Until Tennessee was established as a state in 1796, its land grants generally were regulated by North Carolina. Over the period 1778 to 1797, Stockley Donelson, who was credited with some 950,000 acres in land grant entries in Tennessee, had a fair investment for the time. Like most gamblers, he was obsessed with constant buying and presumably periodic selling.

21

Summary

In this paper, we consider records from pioneer cemeteries, early census records, family histories, and military activities. Generally speaking, land records far antedate cemetery records and census records. The study of treaties with the native Cherokees, beginning in 1721 and ending in 1835, also helps to understand how westward and northwestward movement of white pioneers progressed.

In the wilderness areas of western North Carolina and what became Tennessee, early North Carolina land records provide by far the best evidence of the movement and settlement of pioneers. In the study of the various records, evidence is cited for much misinformation regarding the history of North Carolina and its western extension into what is now Tennessee.

Fortunately, access to and analysis of these land records and primitive surveyors records, which provide a mass of data, steadily improves. The records help to delineate pioneer settlers desire to obtain cheap land. The shenanigans of non-resident speculators from Philadelphia and New York as well point out ongoing land fraud activities.

In the early 1660s and 1680s small clusters of pioneering groups, mainly English settlers, settled along the coasts of North and South Carolina. These groups generally did not migrate inland and encroach upon the native population of Western North Carolina.

Beginning about 1740 or so, masses of migrants, dominated by Scots-Irish, traveled south from Pennsylvania and Virginia, along the Great Wagon Road, a dirt road. Even earlier, lesser numbers of migrants traveled northwestward up the Broad River Basin in South Carolina. The two groups intermingled in western North Carolina and encroached upon the natives of Western North Carolina and Tennessee.

Although in 1763 King George III (reigned 1760-1820) made some military service grants, they were mainly confined to the northern part of what became the United States. Grant size ranged from 50 to 5,000 acres, depending upon rank.

In the late 1770s, Burke County, Rutherford County, Lincoln County, and Wilkes County were formed, and then later Buncombe County with the rest of western North Carolina following in stages. In these areas, after the Revolutionary War, the granting of lands was more or less orderly.

By the early 1770s, a flood of entrepreneurs, mostly from Virginia, went to Eastern Tennessee, and shortly thereafter to north central Tennessee. After 1783, North Carolinians and others who served in the Revolutionary War were compensated with land warrants in western North

Carolina and its territorial extension into what is now Tennessee. Some exercised this option and some did not. In some cases, the heirs of veterans exercised the option. Overall, the granting of land in Tennessee with its multitude of squatters and numerous unethical politicians was chaotic and created ongoing friction with the Indians.

Land speculation in North Carolina and in Tennessee was rampant from about 1784 to 1796. The land speculation bubble burst in 1796, being stimulated by the world wide downturn in economies.

In general, land grant policies of the United States did not always correspond to that of the individual States, which in themselves varied widely, especially in the South. The literature is full of outdated information regarding governmental policies vs. actual events, especially in Tennessee. Until late in the 1800s, communications were such that State policies often acted independently of Federal policies.

Very few pioneers in Buncombe Co. migrated from Georgia, i.e., Candler and Lane. Pioneers to Buncombe Co. from Mecklenburg Co. and Lincoln Co. included Avery, Henry, and Stroup. Pioneers from Tryon/Rutherford Co. included Mills, Kuykendall, and possibly also the Carson, Cathey, and Clayton families.

By 1820, descendants of pioneers from western North Carolina anticipated opening of land in Missouri. Some of these are recorded in the following descendant chart/cemetery records, as for instance Cathey and Gash. Shortly thereafter, others migrated to Alabama, to Texas, and to various points west as shown on the accompanying genealogy charts.

Acknowledgements

The writer collated master indices of the early land grant records from three sources, namely those in the reconstructed files at the Burke County Public Library, Genealogy Section; the U.S. Forestry Service in Asheville; and the MARS program via internet of the NC State Archives, Raleigh. Each source contains some variation from the others. Full use was made of the master indices for Buncombe, Burke, and Rutherford Counties in the MARS program.

Reconstructed land grant records at the Burke County Public Library, Genealogy Room, and at the neighboring History Museum of Burke County were invaluable. Many volunteers worked hard to compile these records: individuals included Dr. Emmett R. White, Nathan Johnson, Betsy Dodd Pittman, Sandra West, Helen Morgan, Gale Benfield, and Dr. Robert McNealy (recently published).

Copies of land grant records at the Register of Deeds, Buncombe County Courthouse were also a key to interpretation of the records. Many of these early records are now available online.

A 1930s 4" x 8" alphanumeric land grant card file at the U.S. Forestry Service in Asheville proved indispensable in the initial organization of a nearly complete master index of permanent land grants in Old Burke and Old Buncombe Counties. Evidently this was a WPA project whose compiler's name is unknown. The author thanks Rodney Snedeker for granting free access to these files.

Working independently from ancient records in the NC State Archives, Elizabeth Warren Huggins and Margaret M. Hofmann put abstracts of many land grant records from North Carolina in print. Huggins' four volumes date from 1977 to 1987 and are readily available in public libraries. Hofmann's ten volumes date from 1979 to 1998 and likewise are readily available. All volumes are indexed.

Analysis of the genealogy of the very complex Davidson families of North and South Carolina relies first and foremost upon the pioneering (self-published) work of Robert S. Hand, 1991. John Lisle and Holt Felmet contributed unpublished data on the Davidson family. Splitting of the Buncombe County Davidsons into the Bee Tree Davidsons and the Gum Springs Davidsons follows that of Foster A. Sondley in his 1930 *History of Buncombe County*.

Betty Jo McDowell Garrett is commended for straightening out the genealogy of the prominent McDowell families of Burke and McDowell Counties. Ruth Dilling helped on the Ashworth and Murray families of Buncombe Co. The writer is indebted to Asheville authors Lou Harshaw and Helen Wykle for editing and content tips. Ray Elingburg provided moral support and good conversation.

Clues to data contained in cemeteries of western North Carolina were provided by Gwen Bodford, Evie Brush, Elaine Dillinger, Dottie Ervin, Jan Lawrence, Julia Reynolds Nowlin, Anne Swann, and Peggy Silvers.

I would be remiss without mentioning historian Foster A. Sondley's most lucid publication, his 1922 book of 200 pages that is titled simply *Asheville and Buncombe County*. In this book, Sondley shows a sketch map of Asheville initially dating from about 1798 (with later revisions). Sondley also lists 28 lot holders in Morrisville (later Asheville), the majority dating from 1794 and 1795.

Ronald A. Lee and Del Dorr of the Tennessee State Library & Archives kindly provided information on early Tennessee land grants.

The author spent a number of memorable days exploring, and receiving advice, on older cemeteries with local historians Bill Alexander, Ruth Dilling, L. Holt Felmet, and Dr. Kenneth D. Israel. And in one case, the author was a witness in the moving of an abandoned cemetery (Thomas Jones Burying Ground), with about 36 graves, to a nearby active church cemetery.

Libraries and their staff who collectively provided the backbone for these studies include: Pack Memorial Library in Asheville, Old Buncombe County Genealogical Society, Henderson County Public Library, Henderson County Historical and Genealogical Society, Old Tryon County Genealogical Society, Burke County Public Library, Burke County Geological Society, Hickory Public Library, McDowell County Public Library, Gaston Public Library, Charlotte Mecklenburg Public Library, Salisbury Public Library, Davidson College Library, Ramsey Library, Special Collections at UNC, Asheville, the Carson House Museum and also the Vance Museum.

Laura Gaskin, Zoe Rhine, and Ann Wright of the North Carolina Room in the Pack Memorial Library, Asheville, were very helpful in answering numerous questions.

The Old Buncombe County Genealogical Society, having the largest genealogical library in western North Carolina, and being operated by a volunteer staff, is especially commended. Ruth Dilling, Sandy Samz, and Christine McNab were especially helpful in locating research materials. Marie Hoffman and Sabrina Haller kindly proof read the manuscript and provided other technical help.

Explanation of Appendix I - Revolutionary War

Appendix I is titled "Revolutionary War Patriots Buried in Western North Carolina." First published in *A Lot of Bunkum* in 2004, this chart went through many revisions as data came to light and now contains the names of 216 Revolutionary War participants plus many wives. Nine immigrants are on the list.

Credit is given to an article by an anonymous source published in *A Lot of Bunkum*, vol. 26, no.4, p.20-22. Concerning the 1835 pension roll, the article lists 30 Revolutionary War veterans from Buncombe Co., 39 veterans from Burke Co., 13 veterans from Macon Co., and 2 veterans from Yancey Co.

In 1915, Marshall D. Haywood wrote an important article (in *North Carolina Booklet*) in which he states that perhaps 5,997 North Carolinians served in the Continental Army during the Revolutionary War. More importantly, North Carolinians in the militia totaled about 26,822, or over four times that of the regular army. During the Revolutionary War, the militia in Burke County totaled about 730 men, and included one Colonel, one Lt. Colonel, 2 Majors, and 13 Captains.

We can infer that virtually every able-bodied man living in Western North Carolina during the late 1700s was in the militia. But it was one matter to serve in the militia against marauding bands of Indians, and quite another matter to fight a full scale conflict against the King's men. Thus we read in the *Tryon Co. NC Minutes of the Court of Pleas and Quarter Sessions, 1769-1779*, a list of 119 men from what became Rutherford Co. They were subject to "Cases of Confisticated Property" and were involved in court proceedings against suspected Tories. Most were later exonerated.

Of the 119 men, the prominent Col. Ambrose Mills was not exonerated and subsequently he was hung in 1780 along with eight others, mostly officers. On the other hand, his son William Mills, who waffled between the "Rebels" and the "Tories", after hiding out for some time, managed to escape punishment, and actually between 1785 and 1794, added to his land holdings in Rutherford Co.

A similar list of 84 suspected Tories for Burke Co. is on file in the North Carolina State Archives. Apparently, none of the men on this list suffered severe consequences other than ostracism by their neighbors. How many were put on the list by disgruntled neighbors, relatives, and jilted lady friends is difficult to evaluate.

In a noted case, in late 1781, Captain William Neill and Capt. James Davidson of Burke Co. brought charges against their commanding officer Col. Charles McDowell (QM) of the Burke Co. militia. The charges against McDowell were several, including sympathy towards Tories in the area. After a lengthy court martial and testimony from a large number of witnesses, McDowell was relieved of duty and replaced by his cousin Joseph McDowell (PG).

Questions have been raised about individuals who were referred to as Generals. Various titles were conferred upon those in the Continental Army (most important), those who commanded a Militia District, and finally those who served in the Militia. In addition, well-known individuals commonly had honorary titles. For instance, when President Andrew Jackson and Missouri Senator Thomas Hart Benton addressed each other, they became General Jackson and Colonel

Benton as both had military service in the War of 1812.

Griffith Rutherford and William Lee Davidson began their careers in local militias, but evidently were raised to the formal rank of Brigadier General in the Continental army. On the other hand, Ephraim Davidson, Thomas Love, and Joseph McDowell (QM) acquired the unofficial title of "General" through their prominence in the local militias of Iredell Co., Haywood Co., and Burke Co., respectively. The distinction of titles is reflected in Tennessee territory land grants, as for instance, G. Rutherford and heirs, 39,574 acres; W.L. Davidson heirs, 16,900 acres; Ephraim Davidson, none; Thomas Love, 1,740 acres; and Joseph McDowell, 3,017 acres.

Other officers who were awarded land from North Carolina in the Tennessee Territory military district include: John B. Ashe, Reading Blount, John Butler, Richard Caswell, James Gorham, James Moore, Hardy Murfree, Abner Nash, Francis Nash, William Polk, Evan Shelby, Isaac Shelby, Jethro Sumner, and James Williams. Nathanael Greene and John Sevier were discussed earlier.

As an example, in her 1992 book, page 168, Helen Marsh records the following:

George Davidson, heir of William Davidson, Lt. Col., Cont. Line, 5760 acres, Davidson Co.,

Military Warrant 254, Je 28, 1785, Mar 14 1786 (NC 31 - Tennessee territory)

(*editor's note* -note rank, date, and NC land grant number).

William L. Davidson is listed also as a Lt. Col. in a 1789 list of officers, NC Line, in vol. 1. p. 559, of the *John Gray Blount Papers*.

On page 60, Marsh records the following:

Ephraim McLean, Commission Guard, 320 acres, Davidson Co., (NC 16 - Tennessee territory)

In his 1903 book titled *Historical Register of Officers of the Continental Army, 1775 to 1783*, Francis B. Heitman lists the following officers: Col. "Waitstill" Avery (militia), Capt. George Davidson, Lt. Thomas Davidson, Lt. Col. William Lee Davidson (also Brig. Gen., militia), Col. Charles McDowell (militia), Brig. Gen. Joseph McDowell, Sr. (militia), Capt. Joseph McDowell (militia), Brig. Gen. Griffith Rutherford (militia), Maj. John Rutherford (militia), Capt. David Vance (militia), Commissary John Webb, and Capt. James "Withrow" (militia). After the War, many attained higher rank in the militia.

Officers from western North Carolina not mentioned in the Heitman book and who thus held obscure rank in the militia included: William Addington, Daniel Bryson, John Carson, James Cowden, James Davidson, William Davidson (2X), Alexander Erwin, William W. Erwin, Alfred Gaither, Isham Harris, Sr., Thomas Hemphill, Joseph Henry, James Jennings, Abraham Kuykendall, Robert Love, Thomas Lytle, Sr., Robert Patton, Samuel Patton, William H. Rice, Edmund Sams, Daniel Smith, and William Walton, Sr.

Among the men of lesser rank who eventually settled in western North Carolina and who served in the northern campaign and thus Continental soldiers were: James Alexander, Phillip Brittain, Lambert Clayton, Theodorus Felmet, Thomas Foster, James Jennings, John Lanning, and Samuel Patton.

In recent years, Will Graves processed some 19,000 Virginia pension applications for men who served in the southern campaign. These are accessed through Google and the entry "Southern Campaign Revolutionary War Pensions.

Cemetery assistance was received from the Abraham Kuykendahl Chapter of the DAR, specifically Frances Reese and Evie Brush, and from the Edward Buncombe Chapter of the DAR, specifically Elaine Dellinger and Gwen Bodford.

In the genealogy section of this book, we also find many, but not all men who served in the Confederate army during the Civil War. They are designated by the letters CSA. For instance, the Henry Stevens, Sr. family had eight brothers who served in the CSA. All eight brothers survived the Civil War.

The Civil War struck disaster upon land holders and slave owners in Western North Carolina. For instance, the two largest slave owners in Western North Carolina, namely William F. McKesson (174 slaves, Burke Co.) and Nicholas W. Woodfin (122 slaves, Buncombe Co.) saw their net value decreased 75 to 80% between 1860 and 1870 because of loss of slaves, worthless Confederate bonds, and strongly diminished land values. Before the war, these concentrations of black labor were used mainly in gold mining and in railroad bed construction. McKesson and Woodfin were brothers-in-law having married McDowell sisters.

Key to Designations

A minimal number of abbreviations are used in the descendant charts. Thus, CSA means Confederate States of America, RW refers to patriotic service in the Revolutionary War. An MD is a medical doctor and Rev. is a minister. PG refers to Pleasant Gardens in McDowell Co., while QM refers to Quaker Meadows in Burke Co.

In the Descendant Charts, cemeteries located in Buncombe Co. are not bracketed. Cemeteries outside Buncombe Co. normally are referred to by county or state location and usually are bracketed.

On the Land Grant charts, "n/a" reflects data or records that were not found; possibly some of the missing details could be located with further intensive research, particularly through the NC State Archives, and perusal of the complete sets of entry, survey, and grant files.

In Appendix I, normal state abbreviations are used. Foreign country abbreviations include England, Germany, and Ireland. Among military records, Pvt. is a Private, Lt. is a Lieutenant, Capt. is a Captain, Maj. is a Major, Col. is a Colonel, Gen. is a General, etc.

Selected Land Grant References:

Anonymous, 1805, *Yazoo Land Company. House of Representatives Document 110. Eighth Congress*, Second Session: Signal Mountain, TN, Mountain Press, reprint, n. d., 41 p.

Anonymous, 2009, *Manual of Surveying Instructions, for the Survey of the Public Lands of the United States*: Denver, CO, US Bureau of Land Management, Wyoming State Office, 494 p.

Barksdale, Kevin T., 2009, *The Lost State of Franklin*: Lexington, KY, Univ. Press Kentucky, 283 p.

Bedini, Silvio A., 2001, *With Compass and Chain. Early American Suveyors and Their Instruments*: Frederick, MD, Prof. Surveyors Publ. Co., 774 p.

Bennett, William D., 1981, Josiah Brandon's Burke County, NC 1777-1800: Raleigh, NC, *North Carolina Gen. Soc. Jour.*, vol. VIII, no. 1, p. 2-11, maps
_____, 1982, Early Settlements on the Upper Catawba: *ibid*, vol. VIII, no. 3, p. 130-140

Bridwell, Ronald E., 1980, *The South's Wealthiest Planter. Wade Hampton I of South Carolina, (1754-1835)*: Columbia, SC, Univ. South Carolina, Ph.D. thesis, 832 p.

Cadle, Farris W., 1991, *Georgia Land Surveying History and Law*: Athens, GA, Univ. Georgia Press, 583 p., maps

Chernow, Barbara Ann, 1978, *Robert Morris, Land Speculator*, 1790-1801: NY, Arno Press, 249 p.

Coxe, Daniel, 1722, *A Description of the English Province of Carolana*, etc.: London, B. Crouse, 122 p., map.

DenBoer, Gordon, 1998, North Carolina. *Atlas of Historical County Boundaries:* New York, Charles Schribner's Sons, 434 p., maps (other states in this indispensable series include CT, IA, KY, MA, MN, NH, PA, RI, SC, VE, and WI)

Drake, Douglas, Jack Masters, & Bill Puryear, 2009, *Founding of the Cumberland Settlements. The First Atlas, 1779-1804*: Gallatin, TN, Warioto Press, 236 p., maps. (part of a series of 3 oversize vols. + supplements)

Fossett, Mildred B., 1976, *History of McDowell County*: Marion, NC, McDowell County American Bicentennial Commission, 239 p. (especially map on p. 235 showing settlers 1758-1790)

Friis, Herman R., 1940, *A Series of Population Maps of the Colonies and the United States, 1625-1790*: New York, American Geogr. Soc., Publ. no. 3, 46 p., maps

Griffey, Irene M., 1989, *The Preempters. Middle Tennessee's First Settlers*: Clarksville, TN, privately publ., 65 p.

_____, 2000, *Earliest Tennessee Land Records & Earliest Tennessee Land History*: Baltimore, MD, Clearfield Co., 505 p. (documents roughly 7,000 landowners)

Haller, Charles R., 2003, The New York Speculation Lands, 1795-1920: Asheville, NC, *A Lot of Bunkum*, vol. 24, no. 2, p. 22-23

_____, 2010, Early Land Speculators in WNC: Asheville, NC, *A Lot of Bunkum*, vol. 31, no. 1, p.17-19.

Hofmann, Margaret M., 1979, *Province of North Carolina, 1663-1729. Abstracts of Land Patents:* Weldon, NC, Roanoke News Co., 384 p.

_____, 1982, *Colony of North Carolina, 1735-1764. Abstracts of Land Patents.* , Vol. 1: *ibid*, 650 p.

_____ , 1984, *ibid*, 1765-1775, Vol. 2: ibid, 857 p.

_____, 1986, *Granville District, Abstracts of Land Patents*, 1748-1763, , Vol. 1: Weldon, NC, ibid, 199 p. (nothing in WNC in this 5 vol. series; but Rowan Co., vols. 3 & 5)

_____, 1987, *ibid*, Vol. 2: *ibid*, 415 p.

_____, 1989, *ibid*, Vol. 3: *ibid*, 163 p.

_____, 1993, *ibid*, Vol. 4: *ibid*, 416 p.

_____, 1995, *ibid*, Vol. 5: *ibid*, 463 p.

_____, 1998, *North Carolina, Abstracts of State Grants, 1778-1780, Vol. 1*: Ann Arbor, MI, Print-Tech, Inc., 267 p. (Burke Co., p. 3-26; Rowan Co., p. 35-40)

_____, 2003, *ibid, Vol. 2, 1778-1780: ibid,* 294 p. (not WNC, but Rowan Co., p. 67-75 & 197-201; Tyron Co., p. 156-161)

Holcomb, Brent, 1980, *North Carolina Land Grants in South Carolina*: Greenville, SC, A Press, 184 p.

Huggins, Edith W., 1977, *Burke Co., North Carolina Land Records. Vol. 1, 1778*: Raleigh, Carolina Copy Center, 187 p.

_____, 1981, *ibid, Vol. 2*, 1779-1790, (also) Miscellaneous Records 1777-1800: ibid, 224 p.

_____, 1987, *ibid, Vol. 3*, 1751-1809: (also) Misc. Records): ibid,167 p. + index

_____, 1987, *ibid, Vol. 4*, 1755-1821, (also) Misc. Records: ibid, 159 p. + index

Jurgelski, Bill, 2002, The Robert Love Survey Map. Important Link of Macon County Past: Franklin, NC, *Echoes*, vol . 15, no, 1, p. 4-7 and 82, (1820 survey map)

Jones, Otis A., ed., 2006, *Following in their Footsteps. Land Surveying in North Carolina*: Chapel Hill, Chapel Hill Press, 266 p.

Jordan, Cora, and Emily Doskou, 2008, *Neighbor Law, Fences, Trees, Boundaries and Noise*; Berkeley, CA, Nolo, 412 p.

Koon, Sue H., 1974, *Rutherford County, North Carolina 1790 Census and 1782 Tax List*:

Spindale, NC, Genealogical Society of Old Tryon County, 38p.

La Vere, David, 2013, *The Tuscarora War. Indians, Settlers, and the Fight for the Carolina Colonies*: Chapel Hill, UNC Press, 262 p.

Linklater, Andro, 2002, *Measuring America. How an Untamed Wilderness Shaped the United States and Fulfilled the Promise of Democracy*: NY, Walker & Co., 310 p.
_____, 2013, *Owning the Earth. The Transforming History of Land Ownership*: NY, Bloomsbury, 482 p.

Marsh, Helen C. & Timothy R. Marsh, 1992, *Land Deed Genealogy of Davidson Co., TN (1783-1792)*: Greenville ,SC, Southern Historical Press, Vol. 1, 283 p.

McIlvenna, Noeleen, 2009, *A Very Mutinous People: the Struggle for North Carolina, 1660-1713*: Chapel Hill, UNC Press, 212 p.

McNab, Christine C., & W. Henry McNab, 2008, The Blount Lands of Buncombe County and other Areas of North Carolina: Asheville, NC, *A Lot of Bunkum*, vol. 29, no. 1, p. 4-8, map

McNab,W. Henry, 2010, Speculation Lands and the Green River Plantation: Asheville, NC, *A Lot of Bunkum*, vol. 31, no. 2, p. 6-7 (family of Tench Francis Coxe)

McNeeley, Robert L., 2011, *Land Grants of Greater Burke County, North Carolina. Burke, McDowell, Caldwell, Alexander, and Catawba Counties (Upper Catawba River Watershed)*: Salt Lake City, UT, Family Heritage Publ., 148 p. maps.

Meyer, Duane, 1961, *The Highland Scots of North Carolina, 1732-1776*: Chapel Hill, UNC Press, 218 p., illus.

Nugent, Nell Marion,et al, 1934-1999, *Cavaliers and Pioneers Abstracts of Virginia Land Patents and Grants, 1623-1800:* Richmond, VA, Dietz Print, et at, 8 vols.

Patton, Sadie S., 1955, *Buncombe to Mecklenburg - Speculation Lands*: Hendersonville, NC, Western North Carolina Hist. Assoc., 47 p.

Philbeck, Miles S. , 1984, *Upper Broad River Basin Pioneers, 1750-1760*: Wilson, NC, privately printed, 185 p.
_____, 2011, The First Landowners in the Broad River Basin in Present-day North Carolina: Forest City, NC, *Bull. Geol. Soc. Old Tryon Co.*, vol. 39, no. 4, p. 152-184

Pruitt, Albert B., 1988, *Glasgow Land Fraud Papers, 1783-1800: North Carolina Revolutionary War Bounty Land in Tennessee:* n.p., n.p., 541 irregular numbered pages
_____, 1989a, *Abstracts of Land Entries: Buncombe Co., NC 1794-1796*: Whitakers, NC,privately publ., 168 p. , 2nd ed., maps
_____, 1989b, *Abstracts of Land Entries. Rutherford Co., NC, 1779-1795: ibid*, 192 p., map

_____. 1989c, ibid, 1795-1803: *ibid*, 184 p.

_____, 1993a, *Petitions for Land Grant Suspension in North Carolina,1776-1836. Pt. 1: ibid*, 146 p.

_____, 1993b, ibid, Pt. 2: *ibid*, 247p.

_____, 1996, *Tennessee Land Entries. Military Bounty Land, Martin Armstrong Office.* (7 vols.): Whitakers, NC, privately publ.- the Pruitt series of early land records comprise 66 volumes for North Carolina and 10 volumes for Tennessee. All are privately published.

Ramsey, Robert W., 1964, *Carolina Cradle. Settlement of the Northwest Carolina Frontier, 1747-1762*: Chapel Hill, Univ. North Carolina Press, 251 p.

Sakolski, Aaron M., 1932, *The Great American Land Bubble*: New York, Johnson Reprint Co., 373 p., 1966 reprint

Salley, Alexander S., 1910-1915, *Warrants for Lands in South Carolina, 1672-1711*: Columbia, SC, Univ. South Carolina Press 1973 reprint, 724 p.

Smathers, George H., 1938, *History of Land Titles in Western North Carolina*: Asheville, NC, Miller Printing Co., 148 p. + suppl. 10 p., map.

Walker, Emily B., 1987, *North Carolina Land Grants in the Western District (Tennessee), etc., Vols. A-B, 1788-1796*: South Fulton, TN, privately publ., 41 p.

Warner, Deborah J., 2005, True North - And Why it Mattered in Eighteenth-Century America: Philadelphia, *Proc. American Philosophical Soc.*, vol. 149, no. 1, p. 372-385

Watt, William N., 1992, *The Granville District*: Tayorsville, NC, privately publ., 131 p.,maps
   - sets northern boundary at 36 degrees, 30 minutes N.Lat.
   - sets southern boundary at 35 degrees, 40 minutes N. Lat.

Western North Carolina (Military) Companies in 1790 Census

Burke Co. (est. 1777)

(Military) Company	Family Heads	General Location	Males 16+	Males <16	Total Females	Family Total	Total/ Heads	Total Others	Total Slaves
1st	113	PG	167	219	354	740	6.55	n/a	91
2nd	80	Burke/Caldwell	90	148	263	501	6.26	n/a	23
3rd	83	midwest Burke	120	155	246	521	6.28	7	76
4th	81	NW Burke, etc.	99	129	203	431	5.32	n/a	10
5th	85	U.Burke, etc.	123	146	271	540	6.35	n/a	51
6th	98	W.Burke	141	172	306	619	6.32	2	59
7th	99	QM, etc	124	153	276	553	5.59	n/a	87
8th	113	Caldwell/Alex.	150	183	323	656	5.81	n/a	27
9th	114	Caldwell	147	187	379	713	6.25	n/a	26
10th	74	Yancey/ Mitchell	99	126	213	438	4.42	n/a	21
11th	88	Buncombe-part	132	118	260	510	5.8	n/a	41
12th	73	Madison	94	155	217	466	6.38	n/a	15
13th	153	Morganton	211	219	428	858	5.61	n/a	70
	1,254		1,697	2,110	3,739	7,546	6.02	9	597

Rutherford (est. 1779)

(Military) Company	Family Heads	General Location	Males 16+	Males <16	Total Females	Family Total	Total/ Heads	Total Others	Total Slaves
1st	76		105	109	218	432	5.68	n/a	76
2nd	84	Polk Co.	110	147	230	487	5.8	n/a	80
3rd	54		70	110	146	326	6.03	n/a	60
4th	54		70	99	166	335	6.2	n/a	24
5th	100		121	163	291	575	5.75	n/a	28
6th	102		127	191	319	637	6.25	n/a	44
7th	74		111	138	230	479	6.47	n/a	35
8th	75		106	148	246	500	6.67	2	20
9th	98		119	167	285	571	5.83	n/a	11
10th	85	(Forest Ciity)	114	165	259	538	6.33	n/a	60
11th	142		186	285	428	899	6.33	n/a	51
12th	105	?Polk Co.	140	209	297	646	6.05	n/a	39
13th	62	Buncombe-part*	93	93	163	349	5.63	n/a	9
14th	70	Henderson Co.	108	85	185	378	5.4	n/a	8
	1,181		1,580	2,109	3,463	7,152	6.06	2	545

* lower end of Swannanoa (Biltmore)

Buncombe Co. in 1800 Census

Family Heads	Location	Males 16+	Males <16	Females	Family Total	Total/ Heads	Others	Slaves
899	Old Buncombe	1,257	1,515	2,659	5,431	6.02	34	347

Burke Co. in 1800 Census

1,421	Burke-revised	2,120	2,492	4,378	8,990	6.33	52	826

Part I: Descendants

1. John Alexander (1732-1795)
2. Harriet Elizabeth Alexander (1816-1897)
3. John Ashworth, Sr. (1735-1805)
4. Waightstill Avery (1741-1821)
5. Zebulon Baird (1764-1824) & Bedent Baird (1766-1839)
6. Narcissa Beck (1824-1907)
7. Robert Brank, Sr. (c.1745-1785)
8. Jean Brevard (c.1685-c.1735)
9. Joseph Brittain (n.d.)

10. Lt. Col. William Candler (n.d.)
11. Daniel Candler (c.1745-c.1825)
12. Zachariah Candler (c.1773-1845)
13. John Carson (1752-1841)
14. James Cathey (c.1685-c.1751)
15. Lambert Clayton (1755-1828) & Sarah Davidson (1759-1843)
16. William Coleman (1785-1874)
17. Dr. Daniel Coxe (1640-1730)
18. William Davison/Davidson (c. 1684-1723)
19. Maj. William Davidson (1736-1814), aka Bee Tree Davidsons
20. Samuel Davidson (c.1705-c.1790), aka Gum Spring Davidsons
21. William Forester, Sr. (c. 1725-____)
22. Ann Dennis (c.1732-c.1812) (Gash, Gudger, Whitson)
23. William Gudger, Sr. (1752-1833)

24. Dr. James Freeman Epps Hardy (1802-1882)
25. Robert Henry (1765-1863)
26. James Hughey (c.1777-____)
27. Andreas Killian, Sr. (1702-1788)
28. Carolyn Lane (1761-1842)
29. Samuel Bell Love (____-1781)
30. David Lowry, Jr. (n.d.)
31. Capt. Thomas Lytle (1750-1835)

32. Ephraim McDowell (1672-1755+)
33. Capt. Joseph McDowell (c.1715-1771)
34. Hunting John McDowell (c.1717-1796)
35. Dr. Joseph Lewis McDowell (1812-1875)
-- McDowells in Government
36. John McLean (c.1700-____)
37. Branch H. Merrimon (1802-1881)
38. William Mills (c.1650-____)
39. William Moore (c.1726-1812)
40. Samuel Murray, Sr. (1739-1817)
41. James Patton (1756-1845), the Asheville Pattons
42. William Patton (c.1742-1818), the Biltmore Pattons
43. Robert Patton (1741-1832), the Swannanoa Pattons
44. John Penland (c.1706-1776)
45. William Dinwoodie Rankin (1804-1879)
46. Abraham Reynolds, Sr. (c.1768-1848)
47. Joseph Marion Rice, Sr. (1761-1850)

48. Daniel Smith (1757-1824)
49. Henry Stevens, Sr. (c.1750-c.1801)
50. Charles Edward Tennent, Sr. (1812-1881)
51. Samuel Vance (c.1691-c.1778)
52. William Brittain Westall (1805-1882)
53. Mary Whitaker (1798-1872)
54. William Whitson (1750-1806)
55. John Woodfin (n.d.)
56. Francis S. Worley (c.1755-____)
57. James Young, Sr. (n.d.)

Descendants of John Alexander

Name	Cemetery
1. John Alexander (1732-1795)	
+ Rachel Davidson, b. ca. 1730	
2. James Alexander (1756-1844) **RW**	Piney Grove
+ Rhoda Cunningham (1763-1848) (11 child.)	Piney Grove
3. John C. Alexander (1783-1857)	Bethesda U.M.
+ Jane Patton (1787-1874)	
4. James Washington Alexander (1808-1859)	
+ Mary ____	
4. George Newton Alexander (1813-1890)	Berea Baptist
+ Mary Jane Stradley (1821-1916)	Berea Baptist
4. John Patton Alexander (1826-____)	
4. William M. Alexander (1829-____)	
4. Robert W. Alexander (1836-____)	
3. Rhoda C. Alexander (1785-1881) (no child.)	
+ William McDaniel	
3. William Davidson Alexander (1st) (1788-____) (no child.)	
3. George Couples Alexander (1790-1880) (9 child.)	Piney Grove
+ Elizabeth Heath Foster (1799-1884)	Piney Grove
4. George W. Alexander?	
4. Sophronia Alexander (1820-1899)	
+ Calvin Patton (____-____) **CSA**	
4. James H. Alexander (1823-1891)	
+ Mary E. White (1824-1884)	
4. Orra Alexander (1826-1870)	
4. Thomas Foster Alexander (1828-____)	
4. Salina Alexander (1830-____)	
4. George Newton Alexander (1833-____)	
+ Mary ____	
4. Rhoda E. Alexander (1831-1891)	
+ Thomas L. White (1846-1924)	
4. William R. Alexander (1840-1922) **CSA**	Piney Grove
+ Mary Gash (1847-1934)	Piney Grove
3. James Mitchel Alexander (1793-1858)	Alexanders Chapel
+ Nancy Foster (1797-1862) (6 child.)	Alexanders Chapel
4. Harriet Elizabeth Alexander (1816-1897) (6 child.)	Alexanders Chapel
+ 1st Elisha Ray (1810-1844)	
+ 2nd Richard Sondley II (1800-1858)	
4. Alfred M. Alexander (1819-1889)	Alexanders Chapel
+ Susan Coffin (1818-1870)	Alexanders Chapel
4. Mary Eliza Alexander (1821-1861)	Alexanders Chapel
+ Rev. Jackson S. Burnett (1820-1893)	Alexanders Chapel
4. Orra A. Alexander (1824-1859)	

Name	Cemetery
3. William Davidson Alexander (2nd) (1800-1877)	Piney Grove
+ Leah Burgin (1804-1842) (7 child.)	Piney Grove
3. Humphrey Newton Alexander (1803-1847)	
+ Mary Foster	
3. Elizabeth Alexander (1806-____)	
+ Joseph A. McIntire	

Editor's notes:

According to an old, undated article in the *Asheville Citizen Times* by local historian Joyce Parris, John Alexander was a Revolutionary War veteran from Lincoln Co. Later, Nancy Manning, op. cit., determined that he was born in Rowan Co. and moved to Lincoln Co., before coming to what is now Buncombe Co.

James Alexander appears on the 1790 NC census, Morgan District, Burke Co., Eleventh Company (now Buncombe Co.,) with 4 males and 2 females. On the 1800 census, he is listed with 5 males and 4 females.

George Cunigam, RW, probable brother of Rhoda Cunningham, wife of James Alexander, is on the 1790 NC Census, Burke Co., Morgan District, Eleventh Company, with 2 males and 7 females. On the 1800 NC Census, Buncombe Co., the family of George Cunningham has 5 males and 5 females.

Although a firm connection between the numerous Alexanders of Mecklenburg Co. and those of Buncombe Co. has not been made, the probabilities are high. Norris W. Preyer's 1987 book *Hezekiah Alexander and the Revolution in the Back Country* (of Mecklenburg Co.) is a good basic reference.

Selected References:

Haller, Charles R., 2006, From Alexanders Hotel to Alexanders Hotel: Asheville, NC, *A Lot of Bunkum*, vol. 23, no. 3, p. 5-6

Manning, Nancy, 2005, First Families of Old Buncombe. James Alexander: Asheville, NC, *A Lot of Bunkum*, vol. 26, no. 3, p.30-32

Modified from *A Lot of Bunkum*, vol. 27, no. 2 (2006)

Descendants of Harriet Elizabeth Alexander

Name	Cemetery
1. Harriet Elizabeth Alexander (1816-1897) (6 child.)	Alexanders Chapel
+ 1st Elisha Ray (1810-1844)	Alexanders Chapel
2. John Edwin Ruthven Ray (1833-1920)	Riverside
+ Mary Stringfield (1835-1906)	Riverside
3. Edwin Lloyd Ray (1874-1939)	Riverside
2. Frances Ann Elizabeth Ray (1836-1923)	?Riverside
+ Goodson McDaniel Roberts (1828-1904)	Riverside
3. Harry H. Roberts (1867-____)	
2. James Mitchel Ray (1838-1923)	Riverside
+ Alice Caldwell (1849-1914) (5 child.)	Riverside
3. Wayne Sondley Ray (1865- 1936)	
2. Susan Elizabeth Ray (1840-1860)	
2. Josephine E. Ray (1843 - 1934) (5 child.)	Riverside
+ David Thompson Millard (1838-1896)	Riverside
3. Herbert Richard Millard (1874-1933)	Riverside
+ Katherine Erwin (1899-1983)	Riverside
3. Charlton Connally Millard (1877-1948)	Calvary Episcopal
+ Grace Lipscombe	Calvary Episcopal
3. Harriett Millard (1879-1885)	
3. Dallam Millard (1881-1888)	Riverside
3. David Ralph Millard (1882-1965)	Riverside
+ Florence N. Hamilton (1892-1977)	Riverside
4. David Ralph Millard, Jr. (1919-____)	

*****

+ 2nd Richard Sondley II (1800-1858)	
2. Foster Alexander Sondley (1857-1931) **Author**	Alexanders Chapel

Editor's notes:

According to historian Joyce Ray Lea, many Ray descendants went to Henry Co., TN.

As noted below, an intensive article about the unique life of lawyer, author, and historian Foster A. Sondley occurs in *A Lot of Bunkum*. In brief, his "1930" *History of Buncombe County* was published in stages, in 1933 and 1937, thus long after his death and was extensively edited, mainly by noted educator Alonzo C. Reynolds.

Sondley's personal library included 32,5128 non-fiction books and articles which eventually formed the backbone of the Pack Memorial Library in Asheville.

The eccentric bachelor Sondley was rumored to have fathered two children, one by his long time white secretary, Virginia Belle Masters, and one by a nameless black maid.

Selected References

Haller, Charles R., 2008, Was Sondley's History Altered: Asheville, NC, *A Lot of Bunkum*, vol. 29, no. 2, p. 4-11, 15

-Foster A. Sondley is listed in the *Dictionary of North Carolina Biography*.

Descendants of John Ashworth, Sr.

Name	Cemetery
1. John Ashworth, Sr. (1735-1805)	(Buncombe Co.)
+ Nancy Ann Wood (1745-1833) (7 child.)	(Buncombe Co.)
2. Alse Ashworth (1763-____) (11 child.)	
+ George Hill	
2. Nancy Ashworth (1769-1835)	
+ James Bridges	
2. Mary "Polly" Ashworth (1773-1865) (12 child.)	(Buncombe Co.)
+ John Williams (1775-1848)	
2. John Ashworth, Jr. (1775-1827)	
+ Celia Nettles (1798-1778) (14 child.)	
2. Sarah Ashworth (1780-____) (6 child.)	
+ John McBrayer	
2. Susannah Ashworth (1782-____) (6 child.)	
+ Jonathan Withrow	
2. Elizabeth Ashworth (1785-____)	
+ William Merrill	

Editor's Notes

The abandoned and overgrown Ashworth Cemetery in Fairview, eastern Buncombe Co., with its 24 or so fieldstones, leads to speculation as to who is buried there. In recent years, a plaque along the nearest road, some quarter mile distant, refers only to John Ashworth, Sr. (1735-1805), and to John Ashworth, Jr. (1775-1827).

The descendant chart above is condensed from a recent compilation by Ruth Dilling, long-time OBCGS member and an Ashworth descendant.

Census Records

Jos. Ashworth is on the 1790 NC Census, Morgan District, Rutherford Co., Eleventh Company, with 3 males and 1 female.

Jno. Ashworth is on the 1790 NC Census, Morgan District, Rutherford Co., Thirteenth Company, with 2 males, 5 females, and 3 slaves.

John J. Ashworth, Jr. is on the 1800 NC Census, Buncombe Co., with 2 males and 1 female.

Descendants of Waightstill Avery

Name	Cemetery
1. Waightstill Avery, (1741-1821) **RW**	(Morganton)
+ Leah Probart Franck (____-1832)(4 child.)	(Morganton)
2. Isaac Thomas Avery (1785-1864)	
+ Harriet Eloise Erwin (1795-1858)(16 child.)	
3. William Waightstill Avery (1816-1864) twin, **CSA**	1st Presby.*
+ Mary Corinna Morehead (1825-1897)(5 child.)	1st Presby.*
3. Clarke Moulton Avery (1819-1864) **CSA**	1st Presby.*
+ Elizabeth Tilghman Walton (____-____)(4 child.)	
3. Thomas Lenoir Avery (1821-1852)	(Marysville, CA)
3. Leah Adelaide Avery (1822-1897)	Forest Hill
3. Isaac Erwin Avery (1828-1863) **CSA**	(Gettysburg)
3. Mary Ann M. Avery (1831-1890)	
+ Joseph F. Chambers	
3. Harriet Justina Avery (1833-____)	
+ Pinkney B. Chambers (____-____) **CSA**	
3. Alphonso Calhoun Avery (1835-1913) **CSA**	Forest Hill
+ 1st Susan W. Morrison (1838-1886)(7 child.)	Forest Hill
+ 2nd Sarah Love Thomas (____-____)(4 child.)	
3. Laura Mira Avery (1837-1912)	
3. Willoughby Francis Avery (1843-1876) **CSA**	1st Presby.*
+ 1st Martha Caroline Jones (____-1868)(1 child.)	
+ 2nd Laura Atkinson (____-____)(1 child.)	

Editor's Notes

The note "1st Presby." signifies the First Presbyterian Church Cemetery in Morganton, Burke Co., NC

Waightstill Avery, born in 1741 in Connecticut, graduated from the College of New Jersey in 1766. Thereafter, he read law in Maryland, and went to North Carolina in 1769. In 1771, he was one of the organizers of Queens College, located on the northeast side of Charlotte.

Waightstill Avery was a signer of the 1775 Mecklenburg Declaration of Independence. From 1777 to 1779, he was the first Attorney General of North Carolina and later held other state offices . Avery settled in Burke Co. about 1786 and entered the first of many land grants in 1788 on the French Broad River. In Morganton, Avery had the largest law library in western North Carolina.

Selected References

Avery, A(lphonso) C(alhoun), 1913, *History of the Presbyterian Churches at Quaker Meadows and Morganton from the year 1780 to 1913*: Raleigh, NC Edwards & Broughton, 109 p.

The Dictionary of North Carolina Biography has short articles on Alphonso Calhoun Avery, Clark Moulton Avery, Isaac Erwin Avery, Waightstill Avery, William Waightstill Avery, and Willoughby Francis Avery.

Descendants of Zebulon Baird

Name	Cemetery
1. Zebulon Baird (1764-1824) **RW (1)**	First Presbyterian
+ Hannah Erwin (or Irwin) (1779-1849)	First Presbyterian
2. Elmira Margaret Baird (1802-1878) (8 child.)	(Madison Co.)
+ David Vance, Jr.(1792-1644)	(Madison Co.)
2. John N. W. Baird (1804-)	(Missouri)
+ Lancy Wilson (Missouri)	
2. James E. Baird (c. 1805-1885)	(Mississippi)
+ Isabella Narcissa Walker	(Mississippi)
2. Andrew N. Baird (c. 1807-c. 1849)	
2. Joseph C. Baird (1812-1888)	Alexander Chapel
+ Rebecca (unknown) (1831-1894)	Alexander Chapel
2. Sarah Ann Baird (1816-1881)	Riverside
+ Baccus Jarret Smith (1804-1886)	Riverside
2. Adolphus Erwin Baird (1820-1878) **CSA**	Riverside
+ Loretta Hunter (1823-1905) (5 boys, 6 girls)	Riverside
2. Mary Adelaide Baird (1824-1879)	Riverside
– never married	

Descendants of Bedent Baird

Name	Cemetery
1. Bedent Baird (1766-1839) **(2)**	Old Weaverville
+ Mary Ann Welch (or Welsh) (c.1784-c.1868)	Old Weaverville
2. Israel Baird (1800-1848)	First Presbyterian
+ Mary Ann Tate (1805-1877) (11 child.)	First Presbyterian
2. Margaret O'Riley Baird (1802-1892) **(3)**	Refuge **(2)**
+ Samuel Smith Refuge	
2. William R. Baird (1804-1883)	Old Weaverville
+ Christina L. Weaver (1823-1861)	Old Weaverville
2. John Baird (1807-	
2. James Madison Baird (1809-1878)	(Mississippi)
+ Elizabeth T. Rupert?	(Mississippi)
2. Jane Elizabeth Baird (1810-1900) (8 child.)	Old Weaverville
+ Montraville Michael Weaver (1808-1882) **(4)**	Old Weaverville

Footnotes

1. Zebulon Baird and his nephew, Israel Baird, and their wives are buried under the First Presbyterian Church of Asheville.

2. "Refuge" is more properly called the Christian Church of Refuge, Jupiter. Margaret R. Smith has an engraved marker there, but her husband, Samuel Smith, apparently is represented only by an un-engraved fieldstone.

3. Bedent Baird, his son William R. Baird, a Mason, and their wives were members of the M.E. Church South as shown by their tombstones.

4. Montraville Weaver was a Methodist minister, a first trustee of Alexander Chapel, and large landholder.

Census Records

Zebulon Baird appears on the 1790 NC Census, Morgan district, Wilkes Co., First Company with 7 males and 5 females. He is listed on the 1800 NC Census, Buncombe Co., with 2 males and 2 females.

Bedent Baird is shown on the 1800 NC Census, Buncombe Co., with 2 males, 1 female, and 2 slaves.

Selected Reference

Haller, Charles R., 2006, Bedent Baird vs. Zebulon Baird Heirs: Asheville, NC, *A Lot of Bunkum*, Vol. 27, no. 4, p. 4-7 and 8-9

Descendants of Narcissa Beck (1824-1907), immigrant4

Name	Cemetery
1. Narcissa Beck (1827-1907) (15 child.)	Beulah Baptist
+ Kinston Middleton (1818-1885)	Beulah Baptist
2. Anberry Middleton (1841-1926)	Beulah Baptist
+ James F. Revis, Sr., **CSA** (1837-1880)	Beulah Baptist
2. Mary Middleton (1843-1924) (17 child.)	Beulah Baptist
+ Robert Franklin Orr, **CSA** (1835-1914)	Beulah Baptist
3. Joseph Sherman Orr (1862-1882)	Beulah Baptist
3. Anberry Orr (1865-1940)	Oakdale
+ William Alexander Morris, Rev. (1859-1941)	Oakdale
3. Arlena Orr (1867-____)	
3. Caldonis N. Orr (1867-____)	
3. Robert Kinson Orr (1869-1939)	Oakdale
3. Jason Martin Orr (1870-____)	
3. Ruth Jane Orr (1872-1873)	Beulah Baptist
3. Benjamin Franklin Orr (1874-1939)	Beulah Baptist
3. Virginia Orr (1876-1879)	Beulah Baptist
3. Julia Adeline Orr (1877-1878)	Beulah Baptist
3. Leona L. Orr (1879-____)	
3. Morris Newton Orr (1880-1942)	Oakdale
3. Victoria Iona Ōrr (1882-____)	
3. Narcissus Orr (1883-1950)	Beulah Baptist
+ J. Luther Mace (1883-1950	Beulah Baptist
3. infant son (1885)	Beulah Baptist
3. Nora Fay Orr (1888-1892)	Beulah Baptist
3. Henry Orr (1890-____)	
2. Ellen Middleton (1844-____)	
+ D. B. F. Corn	
2. James Wesley Middleton (1845-____)	
+ Martha King	
2. Nancy Middleton (1846-____)	
+ Peter Stallings	
2. Elizabeth Middleton (1847-____)	
2. Susan Middleton (1849-____)	
+ Benjamin King	
2. Christopher Middleton (1850-____)	
2. Edward Drayton Middleton (1852-____)	
+ 1st Sophronia Felona Huggins (1847-1897)	Beulah Baptist
+ 2nd Philomena Huggins	
2. Benjamin Beck Middleton (1853-1926)	Beulah Baptist
+ Sarah Adeline Huggins (1858-1940)	Beulah Baptist
2. Joseph Alonza Middleton (1856-____)	
+ 1st Julia Corn: + 2nd Jane Orr	

Name	Cemetery
2. Naomi Rebecca Middleton (1857-1936)	Beulah Baptist
+ William Edney Huggins (1848-1907)	Beulah Baptist
2. Ruth Catherine Middleton (1860-1929)	Tracey Grove Bapt.
+ Boyd McCrary (1855-1944)	Tracey Grove Bapt.
2. Lucy D. Middleton (1861-____)	Lanning-Pittilo
+ John N. B.Lanning (1860-1952)	Lanning-Pittilo
2. John Baxter Middleton (1864-1939)	Hooper Creek Bapt.
+ Matilda King (1869-1944)	Hooper Creek Bapt.

Modified from *A Lot of Bunkum*, vol. 28, no. 4, p. 10 (2007)

Biffel-Eller-Weaver Notes
The Reems Creek Contingent

Selected References

Eller, J. Gerald, 1998, *John Jacob Eller and his Descendants*: Fernandina Beach, Fl., Wolfe Publ., 806 p.

Osborne, Josephine, and Wanda Peak Teague, 1984, The Tribe of Jacob: *A Supplement, 1862-1984*: (Weaverville, NC), Bonnie Bone Publ., 170 p.

Ray, Susie Roberts, 2003, What Happened to Joseph Eller's Estate?: Asheville, NC, *A Lot of Bunkum*, vol. 24, no. 2, p. 4-9

Robertson, Blanche R., 1997, The Water Powered Mills of Reems Creek: in *May We All Remember Well. Vol. I*: Asheville, NC, Brunk Enterprises, p. 82-96.

Robertson, Blanche R., & Norma D. Morgan, 2011, *Reems Creek Township Cemeteries*: Asheville, NC, World Comm., 332 p. + index 114 p. (45 cemeteries)

Weaver, Pearl N., 1962, *The Tribe of Jacob. The Descendants of Rev. Jacob Weaver of Reems Cr., NC, 1786-1868*: Weaverville, NC, n.p., 146 p.

White, Emmett R., 1998, Jacob Biffle in *Revolutionary Soldiers of Western North Carolina, Burke Co., Vol. II*, p. 35-36: Greenville, SC, Southern Historical Press

Some Census Records

Adam Bufle, 1790 NC Census, Burke Co., Morgan District, Eleventh Company (now Buncombe Co.), 1 male, 1 female

Adam Biffle, 1800 NC Census, Buncombe Co., 1 male, 1 female, 1 slave

Jacob Beefle, 1790 NC Census, Burke Co., Morgan District, Eleventh Company (now Buncombe Co.) 2 males, 2 females

Jacob Biffle, 1800 NC Census, Buncombe Co., 3 males, 3 females

Jno. Bufle, 1790 NC Census, Burke Co., Morgan District, Eleventh Company (now Buncombe Co.) 2 males, 2 females

John Biffle, 1800 NC Census, Buncombe Co., 3 males, 5 females

Jacob Eller, 1790 NC Census, Rowan Co., Salisbury District, 2 males, 2 females.

Jacob Ellor, 1800 NC Census, Buncombe Co., 4 males, 7 females.

John Weaver, 1790 NC Census, Burke Co., Morgan District, Eleventh Company (now Buncombe Co.) 2 males, 3 females, 1 slave

John Weaver, 1800 NC Census, Buncombe Co., 4 males, 6 females, 4 slaves

Other Notes

Adam Biffle reportedly was born 1728 at Kontwig, a small village near Zweibrucken, southern Germany. He died in 1804. He married Catherine Henkel who was born 1735 in PA; she died before 1810. The couple was buried on the north shore of Lake Louise, Weaverville, NC. Adam Biffle built a grist mill in Reems Creek before 1793. One daughter, Elizabeth Biffle (b. 1757), married John Weaver (b. 1763) who was in the area that became Buncombe Co. by 1786.

In 1753, John Jacob Eller, Sr. went from Montgomery Co., PA to what is now Sullivan Co., TN. His oldest son, John Jacob Eller, Jr. was born there about 1754. Another daughter of Adam Biffle, Mary Biffle, married John Jacob Eller, Jr. who was in Buncombe Co. before 1800.

The Biffles, Ellers, and Weavers formed a loose knit German community near Weaverville, mainly along the southern end of Reems Creek. They were to be joined later by Waggoners and others of German background.

Descendants of Robert Brank, Sr.

<u>Name</u>	<u>Cemetery</u>
1. Robert Brank, Sr. (c.1724-1785) **RW** (1)	(?Burke Co., NC)
+ Jean _____ (____-____) (6 child.)	(?Burke Co., NC)
2. Peter Brank, Jr. (1742-1780) **RW**	(?Buncombe Co., NC)
+ Rebecca Alexander (1745-1825)	
2. Elizabeth Brank (1748-1825) (10 child.)	(Burke Co., NC)
+ Robert Penland (c.1744-c.1828) **RW**	(Burke Co., NC)
2. Pricilla Brank (1756-1836) (8 child.)	Vance
+ Capt. David Vance (1745-1813) **RW**	Vance
2. Rachel Brank (____-____) (9 child.)	Wm. Brittain
+ William Brittain (1762-1846) **RW**	Wm. Brittain
2. Jane Brank (Kentucky)	
+ Robert Henry (Kentucky)	
2. Robert Brank, Jr. (1757-1846) **RW** (2)	(Garrard Co., KY)
+ Margaret McLean (1761-1837) (9 child.) (3)	(Garrard Co., KY)

Footnotes

(1) Robert Brank, Sr. was on a 1770 list of taxables for settlers along the Catawba River above the Horse Ford.

(2) In April, 1795, Robert Brank (Jr.) bought lot no. 39 in the village of Morrisville from John Burton.

Robert Brank, Jr. is on the1800 census for Buncombe Co., with 1 male, 2 females, 3 slaves.

(3) Margaret McLean was the daughter of Ephraim McLean, RW veteran, and Elizabeth Davidson.

Selected References

Anonymous, 1982, *Abstracts of the Brank, Burgin, and Penland Families*: Morganton, NC, privately publ., ca. 50 p. (copy in Burke County Public Library

White, Emmett R., 1984, *Revolutionary War Soldiers of Western North Carolina. Vol. 1, Burke Co.*: Easley, SC, Southern Historical Press, 318 p.

_____, 1998, *ibid*, Vol. II: *ibid*, 352 p.

Descendants of Jean Brevard

Name	**Cemetery**
1. Jean Brevard (c.1685-c.1735)	(Maryland)
+ Katherine McKnitt (c.1689-c.1724) (6 child.) widow	(Maryland)
2. Adam Brevard (c. 1712-1783) **RW**	(Maryland)
+ Mary McKnitt (c.1713-____) (3 child.)	
2. John Brevard, Sr. (c.1715-1790) **RW**	(Centre Presbyt.)
+ Jane McWhorter (1726-1800) (12 child.)	(Centre Presbyt.)
3. Capt. Ephraim Brevard (1744-c.1781) **MD, RW**	(Mecklenburg Co., NC)
+ Martha Polk (____-____) (1 child.)	(Charlotte, NC)
4. Martha Brevard	
+ _____ Dickerson	
3. Joseph Brevard I____-____) **RW**	
3. Lt. Col. Hugh Brevard (c.1746-1781) **RW**	(Burke Co. NC)
+ Jane Young	
3. Mary Brevard (1748-1824)	(Kentucky)
+ Gen. William Lee Davidson (1746-1781) **RW**	(Mecklenburg Co., NC)
3. Capt. John Brevard, Jr. (1751-1826)	(Smith Co., TN)
+ Hannah Thompson	
3. Benjamin Brevard	
3. Adam Brevard (1753-1829) **RW**	
+ Sarah Maria Winslow (1758-1822)	
. Capt. Alexander Brevard (1755-1829) **RW**	(Machpelah Presbyt.)
+ Rebecca Davidson (1762-1824)	(Machpelah Presbyt.)
4. Robert Alfred Brevard (1799-1879)	
+ Sarah Harriet Davidson(____-1829) (3 child.)	
3. Nancy Brevard (1757-c.1780)	
+ John Davidson (c.1750-c.1780)	
3. Robert Brevard (1763-1847) **RW**	(C.G. Co., MO)
+ Nancy _____	
3. Jane Brevard (1765-1833)	
+ Ephraim Davidson (1762-1842)	
3. Benjamin Brevard (1761-____)	
+ Jane Simonton	
2. Benjamin Brevard (c.1717-c.1793)	(Maryland)
+ Rebecca Alexander?	
2. Robert Brevard (1718-1800)	(Iredell Co., NC)
+ Sarah Craig	
2. Elizabeth Brevard (c.1722-1835)	(Iredell Co., NC)
+ James Huggins, Jr.	
2. Zebulon Brevard, Sr. (1724-1798)	(Iredell Co., NC)
+ Ann Templeton	
2. Thomas Brevard (1726-____)	
+ Hannah Creiger	

Editor's Notes:

In 1775, John Brevard and Hugh Brevard were mentioned in connection with a Safety Committee in Salisbury, Rowan Co., NC.

On May 20, 1775, Ephraim Brevard was one of the 27 signers of the Mecklenburg Declaration of Independence. In September 177, Brevard, an MD, accompanied Gen. Rutherford on his

Cherokee expedition in western North Carolina.

Census Records

The following appear on the 1790 NC census, Salisbury District, Iredell Co.:

Adam Brevard, 3 males, 3 females, 5 slaves

Alexander Brevard, 4 males, 5 females, 12 slaves

Benjamin Brevard, 1 male, 3 females, 5 slaves

John Brevard, 3 males, 3 females, 5 slaves

Robert Brevard, 2 males, 4 females, 8 slaves

Selected References

King, Victor C.,1956, *Life and Times of the 27 Signers of the Mecklenburg Declaration of Independence of May 20, 1775*: Charlotte, NC, privately publ. (Anderson Press), 225 p + index

Hand, Robert S.,1991, *Those members of the Brevard Family who descended from John/Jean Brevard* (etc.): Chadds Ford, PA, privately printed, 224p.

White, Emmett R., 1998, *Revolutionary War Soldiers of Western North Carolina, Vol. II, Burke Co.*: Easley, SC, Southern Historical Press, 352 p.

Descendants of Joseph Brittain

Name	Cemetery
1. Joseph Brittain (c.1723-c.1773) **(1)**	(Rowan Co.)
+ 1st Mary _____ (3 child.)	
2. Mary Brittain	
+ _____ Elrod	
2. James Brittain (c. 1750-1831+) **RW (2)**	(Henderson Co., NC)
+ Delilah Springfield (c.1765-1816+) (14 child.)	(Henderson Co., NC)
2. Phoebe Brittain	

*****

+ 2nd Jemima (c.1730-c.1795) (6 child.)	
2. Joseph Brittain (1756-1823) **RW**	(Tennessee)
+ Dorothy Horner	
2. Phillip Brittain (c.1760-c.1830) **RW**	(Bedford Co., TN)
+ Mary _____ (3 child.)	
2. William Brittain (1762-1846) **RW (3)**	Wm. Brittain
+ Rachel Brank (c.1763-1847) (9 child.)	Wm. Brittain
2. Benjamin Brittain (?Guilford Co.)	
+ Comfort Dunnegan	
2. Aaron Brittain (?Haywood Co.)	
2. Samuel Brittain (?Burke Co.)	

Footnotes

(1) The supposition that Joseph Brittain married twice is derived from the 2001 publication of Ann Brittain McCormick, et al.

(2) According to Dr. Kenneth D. Israel, the grave of James Brittain was moved years ago from what became a home site in the Mills River Valley eastward to the Mills River Presbyterian Church cemetery.

(3) William Brittain is buried in a tiny, isolated cemetery westward of Brittains Cove Presbyterian Church (Dula Springs) in northern Buncombe Co.

Census Records

Aron Brittain is on the 1790 NC Census, Burke Co., Morgan District, First Company, with 1 male and 2 females.

Aaron Briton is on the 1800 NC Census, Burke Co., with 4 males and 3 females.

Jas. Brittain is on the 1790 NC Census, Rutherford Co., Morgan District, Fourteenth Company (now Henderson Co.) with 3 males, 4 females

James Brittain (Sr.) is on the 1800 NC Census, Buncombe Co., (now Henderson Co.) with 5 males and 6 females.

In April, 1795, James Brittain bought lot 14 in Morrisville (later Asheville) from John Burton.

Jumima Brittu is on the 1790 NC Census, Burke Co., Morgan District, Thirteenth Company with 2 males and 1 female.

Phillip Brittn is on the 1790 Census, Burke Co., Morgan District, Thirteenth Company, with 2 males and 5 females.

Philip Briton is on the 1800 NC census, Burke Co., with 3 males and 2 females.

Phillip Brittain is on a list of taxable property, Capt. Miller's Company (Burke Co.) for 1806 and 1807.

Samuel Briton is on the 1800 NC Census, Burke Co., with 1 male and 1 female.

William Brittain is on the 1790 NC Census, Burke Co., Morgan District, Eleventh Company (now Buncombe Co.) with 3 males, 2 females

William Brittain is on the 1800 NC Census, Buncombe Co., with 6 males, 4 females, 1 slave

Selected References

Cawyer, Shirley B., 1988, *The Genealogical Study of James Brittain of Buncombe Co., NC*: Stephensville, TX, privately printed, 617 p.

McCormick, Ann Brittain and Ed McCormick, 2001, *The Mont Brittain Family of Mills River*: Sanford, NC, John-Beverly Publ., 214 p.

Styles, Marshall, L., 2010a, *Western North Carolina's Revolutionary War Patriot Soldiers. A Collection of the Records. Vol. 2, Philip Brittain Pension File S39243*: Simpsonville, SC, privately publ., 50 p.

_____, 2010b, ibid. Vol. 3, William Brittain Pension File S8100, *ibid*, 114p.

White, Emmett R., 1984, *Revolutionary War Soldiers of Western North Carolina. Vol. I, Burke Co.*: Easley, SC, Southern Historical Press, 318 p. (William Brittain)

_____, 1998, *ibid*, Vol. II: ibid, 352 p. (James & Philip Brittain)

Descendants of Lt. Col. William Candler of Callan Castle, Ireland

<u>Name</u>   <u>Cemetery</u>

1. William Candler
   + Anne _____
   2. Thomas Candler
   + Jane Tuite
      3. Daniel Candler (c.1700-1765), to Bedford Co., VA c.1735
      + Hannah _____ (c.1700-c.1800) (7 child.)
         4. John Candler, Sr. (c.1730-1802)
         + 1st Nancy Oliver (c.1730-_____)
         + 2nd Penelope Guthrie Johnson (1739-1815)
         4. Elizabeth Candler (c.1733-1791+)
         + John Caffrey (c.1722-1790)
         4. Col. William Candler (1736-1784), to Georgia 1769, **RW**
         + Elizabeth Anthony (1747-1803) (11 child.)
            5. Mary Candler (1761-_____)
            + Ignatius Few, **RW**
            5. Henry Candler (c.1762-_____), **RW**
            + 1st Nancy Oliver
            + 2nd Elizabeth Reid
            5. John Candler, **RW**
            5. Joseph Candler, **RW**
            5. Daniel Candler (1779-1816)
            + Sarah Slaughter (_____-_____) (7 child.)
               6. Samuel Charles Candler (1809-1873)
               + Martha B. Beall (_____-_____) (11 child.)
                  7. Asa Griggs Candler (1851-1929) **Mr. Coca Cola**
                  + Lucy Elizabeth Howard (_____-_____) (5 child.)
         4. Ellenor Candler (c. 1739-1790)
         + Byrum Ballard (1740-1817)
         4. Henry Candler, c. 1742, d. young
         4. Thomas Candler, c. 1744, d. young
         4. Zedekiah Candler (c.1745-c.1825)
         + Anna Moorman (1756-1804) (8 child.)
            5. Zachariah Candler (c.1733-1844)
            + 1st Rachel Thornhill, no child.
            + 2nd Rhoda Pelham, no child.
            + 3rd Mary "Polly" Boone (1784-1857) (6 child.)
            5. John T. Candler

Selected References:

Bockstruck, Lloyd D., 1996, *Revolutionary War Bounty Land Grants*: Baltimore, Genealogical Publ., 608 p.

Henry Candler, GA, 1784, 250 acres

Henry Candler, GA, 1784, 250 acres

Joseph Candler, GA, private, 1785, 640 acres

William Candler, Jr., GA, 1784, 250 acres

William Candler, Sr., GA, Col. 1784, 1000 acres

Candler, Allen D., 1902, *Colonel William Candler of Georgia. His Ancestry and Progeny*: Atlanta, GA, Franklin Printing, 189 p.

Graham, Elizabeth Candler & Ralph Roberts, 1992, *The Real Ones, Four Generations of the First Family of Coca-Cola*: Fort Lee, NY, Barricade Books, 344 p.

Marsh, Ed., 2000 Website

Descendants of Daniel Candler of Bedford Co., VA

<u>Name</u>   <u>Cemetery</u>

1. Zedekiah Candler (c.1745-c.1825) **(1)**
   + Anna Moorman (1756-1804) (8 child.)
   2. Zachariah Candler (c.1773-1844) + 3x **(2)**
   + 3rd Mary "Polly" Boone (1784-1857) (6 child.)
      3. James Madison Candler (c.1800-1880+)
      3. George Washington Candler (1808-1862) + 2x **(3)**
      + Rebecca Evaline Moore (1814-1853) (7 child.)
         4. William Gaston Candler (1834-1934) + 2x **(4)**
         + 1st Lucinda Matilda Gudger (1834-1889) (4 child.)
            5. Edgar W. Candler (1857-1926)
            + 1st Mabrye Morgan (1883-1911) (4 child.)
               6. Coke Candler (1907-1989)
               + Catherine Haynes West (3 child.)
               + 2nd Sue Smith (1861-1913)
               + 3rd Rose Henry (1870-1952)
            5. Otis Bell Candler (1860-1914)
            + Annie Demaris Clayton (1858-1934) (3 child.)
               6. Eloise Candler (1886-1983)
               + Arthur Ponder Willis (1880-1951) **MD**
                  7. Arthur Willis Candler (1910-1983) **MD**
                  + Madith Rutherford (1904-1983)
            5. Bonnie E. Candler (1868-1907) (3 child.)
            + Claudius B. Gudger
            + 2nd Letha M. Summey (1874-1948)
         4. Margrette E. Candler (1836-1913)
         + Thomas Jefferson Harkins (1832-1914)
            5. Herschel S. Harkins (1854-1911) **Mayor (5)**
            + Sarah J. E. Jones (1859-1941) (8 child.)
               6. Thomas Joshua Harkins (1879-1968)
               + Roxy Seevers (1876-1972)
         4. Mary Jane "Mollie" Candler (1839-1916) (1 child.)
         + Virgil S. Lusk (1836-1929) **CSA, Mayor (6)**
            5. Mamie E. Lusk (1869-1943)
            + Samuel J. Pegram (1858-1925)
         4. Thomas Jefferson Candler (1841-1924) **CSA**
         + Hester Eugenia Jones (5 child.)
         4. Charles Zachariah Candler (1843-1864) **CSA**
         4. James Madison Candler (1846-1914) **MD (7)**
         + Mary Elvira Mahoney (____-____) (7 child.)
         4. Rachel Elizabeth Candler (1849-1874)
         + Meredith Owenby
      3. Polly Myra Candler
      + Perman Courtney
   3. Eliza Candler
   + John A. Netherton
   3. Thomas Jefferson Candler, c. 1802-p. 1839 - left 6 child. **(8)**
   + unknown
      4. Zachariah M. Candler
   3. Lucinda Candler

Complex Candler Marriages

Name	Cemetery
Zachariah Moorman Candler (1773-1845), m.	
c. 1791 - Rachel Thornhill, no child.	
c. 1793 - Rhoda Pelham, no child.	
c. 1806 - Mary "Polly" Boone (6 child.)	
George Washington Candler (1808-1862), m.	Capt. Wm. Moore
c. 1832 - Rebecca Evaline Moore (1814- 1853) (8 child.)	Capt. Wm. Moor
1865 - Emaline Davis (1 child.)	
William Gaston Candler (1834-1934), m.	Samuel B. Gudger
1856 - Lucinda M. Gudger (1834-1889) (4 child.)	Samuel B. Gudger
1895 - Letha M. Summey (1874-1948)	Samuel B. Gudger
Edgar W. Candler (1857-1936), m.	Samuel B. Gudger
1905 - Mabrye Morgan (1883-1911) (4 child.)	Samuel B. Gudger
1913 - Sue Smith (1861-1913)	
1916 - Rose Henry (1876-1957)	Samuel B. Gudger

Footnotes

(1) According to one author, Zedekiah Candler (c.1745-c.1825) had some 5,000 acres near Lynchburg, VA, which he named Kilkenny, and he called his home Callan. He also had some 30 slaves. After his marriage to Anna Moorman, the couple reportedly lived continuously in Bedford Co., VA.

(2) Zachariah Candler (c. 1773-1844) married three times. His third wife, Mary "Polly" Boon(e) descends from Ratliff Boon (1755-1815) and his wife Nancy Harriss (no connection to Daniel Boone).

In 1798, Zachariah Candler went to Buncombe Co. and the next year, he began to establish a reputation as a real estate broker, constantly buying and selling. The following is a summary of his dealings taken from extant Deed Books. He got one plot of 5,278 acres from Burdit Sams, one plot of 3,630 acres from John Strother, and another plot of 3,000 acres from John Wood. By far the largest acquisition is a 1838 deed for 150,000 acres which he received from Robert Love and James B. Love for which he paid $1,400; a plot that embraced 100,000 acres of the old John G. Blount grant 253, which was originally 320,640 acres, and 50,000 acres of the old David Alison grant 251, originally 250,240 acres dating 1796.

Index to Deed Books - Grantee records for Zachariah Candler, total about 164 transactions of which 81 were N.C. grants.
page C-372, 11 plots, 1805-1809
page C-373, 53 plots, 1799-1818
page C-374, 59 plots, 1811-1833
page C-375, 41 plots, 1819-1849
Index to Deed Books – Grantor records for Zachariah Candler, total about 183 transactions:
page 571-C, 7 plots, 1804-1813
page 572-C, 59 plots, 1816-1829, the largest being 3,262 acres granted to Thomas Moore
page 573-C, 59 plots, 1829-1831, the largest being 3,000 acres granted to Samuel Chunn
page 574-C, 58 plots, 1826-1857, the largest being 5,000 acres granted to William H. Moore;

also 20,000 acres granted to Samuel W. Davidson and James W. Patton; also 5,000 acres granted to James W. Alexander. After Zachariah died in 1845, sales transactions were completed by his son George Washington Candler (1808-1862), a lawyer. For instance, in 1845, Davidson & Patton paid his heirs $700 for about 20,000 acres.

Some notable transactions in the copies of the deeds include:

Book 7/89 and F/117, 3,000 acres in 8 tracts from John Strother, 11/1/1799

Book 11/152, 5,278 acres from Burdit Sams, 9/13/1817, French Broad River

Book 16/470, 3,000 acres on Hominy Creek, from John Woods, 5/5/1825

Book 21/546, 150,000 acres French Broad from Robert Love, et. al., 11/21/1838

(3) George Washington Candler (1808-1862) was a prominent early attorney. In 1851 to 1852, he was located at Sulphur Springs. His son, William Gaston Candler (1834-1934), also an attorney and land speculator, had an office in Asheville. His son, Edgar W. Candler (1857-1936) also was a lawyer. Rumors persist that William Gaston Candler had a number of extramarital affairs, but documented support of this statement is minimal.

(4) Among his varied interests, William Gaston Candler operated a store and mill which became known as Candler Town. His house, built about 1856, was located on Hwy 151, just east of the junction with SR 3449.

(5) Herschell Springfield Harkins (1854-1910) m. Sarah Jane Elizabeth Jones (1859-1941). He was a noted lawman and mayor of Asheville, 1887 to 1889. The couple is buried at Riverside. His son, Thomas Joshua Harkins (1879-1968) was an attorney and prominent Mason in Asheville; he married Roxy Seevers. The latter couple is buried at Calvary Episcopal.

(6) Virgil Stuart Lusk (1836-1929) m. Mary Jane Candler (1839-1916). Lusk was a lawyer and politician and mayor of Asheville 1882-1884. The couple is buried at Riverside.

(7) Descendants of James Madison Candler (c.1800-1880+) resided in Jackson Co., NC. James Madison Candler reportedly went to Arkansas in the late 1840s.

(8) Thomas Jefferson Candler (c. 1802-c. 1839) was killed in the Second Seminole War, 1835-1843. Some descendants resided in Madison Co., NC.

Selected References

Haller, Charles R., 2010, In Pursuit of Zachariah Candler: Asheville, NC, *A Lot of Bunkum*, vol. 31, no. 3, p. 4-11, 13

Sams, Sandra, 2007, William Gaston Candler, 1834-1934. His Ancestry and Family: Asheville, NC, *A Lot of Bunkum*, vol. 28, no. 3, p. 11-17.

Descendants of Zachariah Candler

Name	Cemetery
1. Zachariah Candler (c.1773-1845) + 3x	(Madison Co.?)
+ 3rd Mary "Polly" Boon (1784-1867) (7 child.)	
2. Zachariah Candler, Jr. (c.1801-1837?)	(Madison Co.?)
2. Thomas Jefferson Candler (c.1802-c.1839) (6 child.)	(Florida)
+ unknown	
. Charles N. P. Candler (1823-1884) **CSA, MD**	Leicester Epis.
+ Eliza I. Henry (1822-1915) +3x	Cedar Hill
3. Zachariah Marion Candler (1828-1911) **CSA**	(Madison Co)
+ Margaret M. Hawkins (1831-1912) (10 child.)	(Madison Co.)
4. James Frank Candler (1866-1925)	(Madison Co.)
4. Marion Candler (1869-1892)	(Madison Co.)
4. William Henry Candler (1872-____)	
3. James Madison Candler (____-____) **CSA**	
3. George Washington Candler	
3. Thomas Jefferson Candler (1836-____) **CSA**	
+ Mary A. Davis (1842-____) (13 child.)	
4. Bascombe C. Candler (1883-____)	
3. Eliza M. Candler (1844-1920+)	(Madison Co.?)
+ Jackson Cody	
2. George Washington Candler (1808-1862) + 2x	Capt. Wm. Moore
+ 1st Rebecca Evaline Moore (1814-1853) (7 child.)	Capt. Wm. Moore
3. William Gaston Candler (1834-1934) **CSA**, + 2x	Samuel B. Gudger
+ 1st Lucinda Matilda Gudger (1834-1889) (4 child.)	Samuel B. Gudger
4. Edgar W. Candler (1857-1936)	Samuel B. Gudger
+ 1st Mabrye Morgan (1883-1911) (4 child.)	Samuel B. Gudger
5. Coke Candler (1907-1989)	Samuel B.Gudger
+ Catherine H. West (1909-1993) (3 ch.)	Samuel B. Gudger
+ 2nd Sue Smith (1861-1913)	
+ 3rd Rose Henry (1870-1957)	Samuel B. Gudger
4. Otis Bell Candler (1860-1914)	Samuel B. Gudger
+ Annie Demaris Clayton (1858-1934) (3 child.)	Samuel B. Gudger
5. William Washington Candler (1892-1990)	Samuel B. Gudger
+ Madith Rutherford (1914-1983)	Samuel B. Gudger
5. Lane Gladstone Candler (____-1954)	Samuel B. Gudger
5. Eloise Candler (1886-1983)	Samuel B. Gudger
+ Arthur Ponder Willis (1880-1951) **MD**	Samuel B. Gudger
6. Arthur W. Candler (1910-1983) **MD**	Samuel B. **Gudger**
+ Madith Rutherford (1904-1983)	Samuel B. Gudger
4. Bonnie E. Candler (1868-1907) (3 child.)	Samuel B. Gudger
+ Claudius B. Gudger (1874-1950)	Samuel B. Gudger
+ 2nd Letha Mae Summey (1874-1948)	Samuel B. Gudger
3. Margrette E. Candler (1836-1913)	Harkins/Candler
+ Thomas Jefferson Harkins (1832-1914)	Harkins/Candler
4. Herschel S. Harkins (1854-1911) **Mayor**	Riverside
+ Sarah J. E. Jones (1859-1941) (8 child.)	Riverside
5. Thomas Joshua Harkins (1879-1968)	Calvary
+ Roxy Seevers (1876-1972)	Calvary
3. Mary Jane "Mollie" Candler (1839-1916) (1 child.)	Riverside
+ Virgil S. Lusk (1836-1929) **CSA, Mayor**	Riverside

Name	Cemetery
4. Mary Elizabeth "Mamie" Lusk (1869-1943) (2 child.)	Riverside
+ Samuel J. Pegram (1858-1925)	Riverside
5. Mary Stuart Pegram (1901-1977)	
5. Samuel J. Pegram II (1902-1956)	Riverside
3. Thomas Jefferson Candler (1841-1924) **CSA**	Oak Forest
+ Hester Eugenia Jones (1846-1921+) (6 child.)	Oak Forest?
3. Charles Zachariah Candler (1843-1862) **CSA**	(Virginia)
3. James Madison Candler (1846-1915) **CSA, MD**	(Jackson Co.)
+ Mary Elvira Mahoney (1849-1919) (7 child.)	(Jackson Co.)
3. Rachel Elizabeth Candler (1849-1874)	(Haywood Co.?)
+ Merritt J. Owenby (1852-1910+)	(Haywood Co.?)
+ 2nd Emeline Davis	
3. Ellen R. Candler (1861-____)	
+ William A. Long (1855-____)	
2. James Madison Candler (c.1812-1880+)	(Arkansas)
+ Mary A. ____ (1814-____) (7 child.)	
2. Polly Mira Candler (c.1813-1845+)	(Alabama?)
+ 1st Perman Courtney	
+ 2nd John Cannon (c.1812-____)	(Alabama?)
2. Lucinda Candler (c.1813-1850)	(Madison Co.?)
2. Eliza Candler (c.1815-1845+) (10 child.)	
+ John A. Netherton (1809-____)	
3. Thomas Jefferson Netherton (1838-1863)	(Mississippi)
3. James A. Netherton (1842-____) **CSA**	

Editor's Notes

Zachariah Candler appears neither in the 1790 NC Census nor in the 1800 NC Census.
Modified from *A Lot of Bunkum* , vol. 31, no. 3 (2010)

Descendants of John Carson, 1773 immigrant from Ireland

Name	Cemetery
1. John Carson (1752-1841) **RW (1)**	?Round Hill
+ 1ˢᵗ Rachel Matilda McDowell (1756-1795) (7 child.)	?Round Hill
2. Jason Carson (____-1830) **War of 1812**	(Mississippi)
+ Mary Camden (____-____) (7 child.)	
2. James Carson	
2. Joseph McDowell Carson (1778-1860) **MD**	(Polk Co.)
+ Rebekah Wilson (1790-1840) (10 child.)	(Polk Co.)
3. Tench Coxe Carson (1810-1861)	(South Carolina)
+ Martha Adeline McBee (1816-1870) (4 child.)	(South Carolina)
3. John Hazzard Carson (1814-1865)	(South Carolina)
+ June Moore (1825-1896) (2 child.)	(South Carolina)
3. Ruth Margaret Carson (1817-1870)	(Polk Co.)
+ James G. Weaver (1819-____)	
3. Joseph McDowell Carson, Jr. (1822-1859)	(Polk Co.)
3. John Montezuma Carson (1824-1861) **CSA**	(Polk Co.)
3. Catherine R. Carson (1828-1896) (8 child.)	(South Carolina)
+ Thomas S. Duffy	(South Carolina)
2. Rebecca Carson (1785-____)	
+ Thomas McIntire	
2. John W. Carson (____-1836) **War of 1812**	(Tennessee)
+ unknown	
2. Charles Carson (____-1850)	
+ Margaret Wilson	
2. Sally (Sarah) Carson (1788-1840) (6 child.)	(Texas)
+ William Davidson Smith ((1784-c.1840)	(Texas)
*****	
+ 2ⁿᵈ Mary Moffitt McDowell (1768-1852) (5 child.)	Round Hill?
2. Samuel Price Carson (1798-1838) **(2)**	(Arkansas)
+ Sarah Catherine Wilson (1810-1882) (1 child.)	
3. Rachel Rebecca Carson (1834-1895)	
+ Joseph McDowell Whitson, Jr. (1821-1885)	
2. Matilda M. Carson (1799-1824)	
+ Jason Carson Wilson	
2. William Moffitt Carson (1801-1863)	Carsons Chapel
+ 1ˢᵗ Almyra T. Wilson (____-1844) (7 child.)	
+ 2ⁿᵈ Sarah C. W. Carson (1810-1882) (1 child.)	
2. George M. Carson (1804-1863)	
2. Jonathan Logan Carson (1807-1866)	
+ Mary Sturdivant Presnell (1812-1907) (2 dau.)	(Marion, NC)

Footnotes:

(1) John Carson is listed in the 1790 NC Census, Burke Co., Morgan District, First Company (now McDowell Co. and part of Rutherford Co.) with 7 males, 2 females, 12 slaves.

(2) Samuel Price Carson fathered an illegitimate daughter, Emily, by Emma Trout. In 1827, Carson was the center of a much cited duel with Robert Brank Vance.

Selected References

Haller, Charles R., & Betty Jo McDowell Garrett, 2009, McDowell-Carson Family Notes: Asheville, NC, *A Lot of Bunkum*, vol. 30, no. 2, p. 18-31

White, Emmett R., 1984, John Carson in: *Revolutionary Soldiers of Western North Carolina, Vol. 1, Burke Co.*, p. 35-36: Easley, SC, Southern Historical Press

Descendants of James Cathey, immigrant

Name	Cemetery
1. James Cathey (c.1685-c.1757) **(1)**	
+ Ann _____ (____-c.1761) (7 child.)	(Rowan Co., NC)
2. John Cathey (c.1709-c.1764)	
+ Jean _____ (____-____) (7 child.)	
2. William Cathey (c. 1711-1746)	(Augusta Co., VA)
2. Elizabeth Cathey (c. 1713-___)	
+ _____ Bashford	
2. Andrew Cathey (c. 1715-____)	(Berkeley Co., SC)
+ Rebecca _____ (____-____) (5 child.)	
3. William Cathey (c.1741-1812) **(2)**	(?Haywood Co., NC)
3. George Cathey (c.1743-____)	
. George Cathey, Sr. (c.1717-c.1789)	(Burke Co., NC)
+ Margaret _____ (c.1715-____) (4 child.)	(Burke Co., NC)
3. Ann Cathey (1739-c.1774) (7 child.) 1st wife	(Rowan Co., NC)
+ William Moore, Sr. (c.1726-1812)**RW (3a)**	(Buncombe Co., NC)
3. Margaret Cathey (1744-____)	(Iredell Co., NC)
+ John Moffitt (c.1745-____)	(?Mecklenburg Co., NC)
3. James Cathey (c.1746-1791)**RW (4)**	Rowan Co.
+ Jane Rutherford	
3. Capt. George Cathey, Jr. (c.1747-1840)**RW (5)**	(Pettis Co., MO)
+ Margaret Chamberlain (c.1755-1830) (10 child.)	(Missouri)
4. Maj. William Cathey (1777-1864)	(Haywood Co., NC)
+ Catherine Turner (1771-1851) (1 child.)	(Haywood Co., NC)
5. Col. Joseph Cathey (1803-1874)	(Haywood Co., NC)
+ Nancy Alice Hyatt (1808-1879) (9 child.)	(Haywood Co., NC)
4. Ann Cathey (1782-1867) (10 child.)	
+ William H. Moore (1772-1852) **(3b)**	
2. Margaret Cathey (c.1719-____)	(Mercer Co., KY)
+ Samuel Coburn(Mercer Co., KY)	
2. Ann Cathey (c. 1721-____) (2 child.) + 3x?	
+ William Brandon (1726-1785)	(Rowan Co., NC)

*****

1. George Cathey, Sr. (c.1690-1767) **(6)**	(Rowan Co., NC)
+ Jean _____ (c.1692-1777) (7 child.)	(Rowan Co., NC)
2. Andrew Cathey (c.1721-1786)	(Mecklenburg Co., NC)
+ 1st Martha _____	
+ 2nd Rebecca Armstrong	
2. George Cathey, Jr. (c.1724-1801)	(Mecklenburg Co., NC)
+ Frances Henry (c.1724-1798) (10 child.)	(Mecklenburg Co., NC)
2. John Cathey (c.1725-1788)	(Mecklenburg Co., NC)
+ Mary Henry	
2. Eleanor Cathey (1726-____)	

Name	Cemetery
+ 1st John Toole	
+ 2nd _____ Williams	
2. Margaret Cathey (c.1735-____)	(Mecklenburg Co., NC)
+ Alexander Wallace	
+ 2nd Thomas Braly	
2. Archibald Cathey (c.1737-1777)	(Mecklenburg Co., NC)
2. Esther Cathey (c.1742-1825) +3x	(Mecklenburg Co., NC)

*****

1. John Cathey (____-1743)
1. Sarah Cathey (____-____)
   + Samuel Givens

Footnotes

(1) James Cathey reportedly immigrated about 1717 from Ulster with brothers George and John. James married Ann _____. The couple had seven children.

James Cathey has been traced from Cecil Co., MD about 1719 to Chester Co., PA, and in the spring of 1749 to "The Irish Settlement," south of the Yadkin River in North Carolina. At the later time, principals included James Cathey, his son George Cathey, Sr., George Cathey, Jr., Alexander Cathey, and Andrew Cathey.

The famous Thyatira Presbyterian church, dating from about 1750, was constructed on the elder George Cathey's land. Headstones date from 1755. The location, originally in Anson Co., now in Rowan Co., is about 10 miles west of Salisbury on Highway 150. Rowan Co. was formed in 1753 from Anson Co.

(2) In 1779, William Cathey (c.1741-1812) got Burke Co. land grants 45 and 95. The former location of Cathey's Fort dating from about 1776, now in McDowell Co., near the junction of Turkey Cove Creek and the Catawba River, marked the location.

(3a) & (3b) William Moore, Sr. (c.1726-1812,) and his grandson, William H. Moore (1772-1852), both of whom married Ann Catheys, are discussed in detail in another paper.

(4) James Cathey was born in Anson (later Rowan) Co., NC about 1746. He married Jane Rutherford. During the Revolutionary War, he served as a Capt. in the militia; his family records are sparse.

(5) George Cathey, Jr. , was born in Anson Co. (later Rowan Co.), NC about 1747 and died In Pettis Co., MO about 1840. He married (about 1776) Margaret Chamberlain. The couple had 10 children. He was in Old Burke County by 1769; in 1779, he obtained Burke Co. grant no. 90, which was located on the Catawba River, below Pleasant Gardens.

The records for this George Cathey are contained in pension file S16699 and in DAR records. During the Revolutionary War, he held the rank of Pvt., Lt., and eventually Capt., the latter while serving under Cols. McDowell, Campbell, Shelby, and Sevier.

(6) Another George Cathey, Sr., (c.1690-1767) married Jean _____ (c.1692-1777), both being buried at Thyriata Presbyterian; he was an immigrant brother. This couple had seven children, a portion of whom are shown above. Of these seven children, Andrew and George, Jr. are buried at Steele Creek Presbyterian, Mecklenburg Co.

Selected Census Records

George Cathey is on the 1790 NC Census, Burke Co., Morgan District, 1st Company, with 5 males, 4 females, and 5 slaves.

Geo. Cathey (Sr.) is on the 1800 NC Census, Buncombe Co. with 5 males, and 5 females.

Geo. Cathey is on the 1800 NC Census, Buncombe Co., with 1 male.

Marget Cathey is on the 1790 Census, burke Co., Morgan District, 1st Company, with 1 male and 4 females.

Wm. Cathey is on the 1790 NC Census, Burke Co., Morgan District, 1st Company, with 7 males, 5 females, and 5 slaves.

William Cathey is on the 1800 NC Census, Buncombe Co. with 7 males, and 4 females.

William J. (Jr.) Cathery is on the 1800 NC Census, Buncombe Co. with 1 male, 1 female, and 1 slave.

Selected References

Cathey, Boyt H., 1993, *Cathey Family History and Genealogy*: Franklin, NC, Genealogy Publ. Service., 579 p.

Ramsey, Robert W., 1964, *Carolina Cradle. Settlement of the Northwest Carolina Frontier, 1747-1762*: Chapel Hill, NC, Univ. North Carolina Press, 251 p.

White, Emmet R., 1984, *Revolutionary War Soldiers of Western North Carolina. Vol. I, Burke Co.*: Easley, SC, Southern Historical Publ., 318 p.

_____, 1998, ibid, Vol. II: *ibid*, 352 p.

Descendants of Daniel Coxe

Name	Cemetery
1. Daniel Coxe (1640-1730), **MD**	(England)
+ Rebecca Coldham (____-____)(2 child.)	
2. Daniel Coxe (1673-1739)	(New Jersey)
+1st Sarah Eckley (____-1725)(4 child.)	
3. William Coxe (1723-1801)	
+ Mary Turnbutt Francis (____-1800)(13 child.)	
4. Tench Francis Coxe (1755-1824)	(Philadelphia)
+ 1st Catherine McCall (1755-1778)(no child.)	
+ 2nd Rebecca Wells (1764-1806)(10 child.)	
5. Anne Rebecca Coxe (1783-1849)	
5. Tench Francis Coxe, Jr., (1784-1813)	(Polk Co., NC)
5. Francis Sidney Coxe (1789-1852)	(Rutherfordton)
+ Jane McBee Alexander (1804-1890)(3 child.)	
6. Tench Charles Coxe ((1824-1877)	
+ Sarah A. Stevens (1829-1896)(4 child.)	
6. Joseph J. Coxe (1835-1853)	(**R**utherfordton)
6. Franklin J. Coxe (1839-1903)	(Rutherfordton)
+ Mary Matilda Mills (1838-1914)(5 child.)	(Rutherfordton)
7. Tench Charles Coxe (1874-1926)	(Rutherfordton)
+Sarah F. Potter (1874-1960)	(Rutherfordton)
5. Alexander Sidney Coxe (1790-1821)	(Philadelphia)
5. Charles Sidney Coxe (1791-1879)	(Philadelphia)
+ Ann Maria Brinton (1801-1876)(9 child.)	(Philadelphia)
6. Brinton Coxe (1833-1892)	(New Jersey)
+ Maria M. Fisher (1847-1933)(1 child.)	(New Jersey)
6. Alexander B. Coxe (1838-1906)	(Montg. Co. PA)
+ Sophia. E. _____ (1839-1924)(2 Ch.)	(Montg. Co., PA)
6. Eckley B. Coxe (1839-1895)	
+ Sophia G. Fischer (1841-1926)	
6. Henry B. Coxe (1841-1904)	(Philadelphia)
5. Sarah Redman Coxe (1793-1809)	(Philadelphia)
5. James Sidney Coxe (1796-1822)	(Charleston, SC)
+Ellen Sullivan ____-____(no child.)	
5. Mary Rebecca Coxe (____-1855)	(Philadelphia)
5. Henry Sidney Coxe (____-1850)	
+ 1st Lucy Ann FitzHugh (____-____)(no child.)	
+ 2nd Mary A. Berry (____-____)(no child.)	
5. Edmund Sidney Coxe (1800-1861)	(Philadelphia)
2. + 2nd Mary Johnston (____-____)(3 child.)	

Selected References

Cooke, Jacob E., 1978, *Tench Coxe and the Early Republic*: Chapel Hill, UNC Press, 573 p.

Coxe, Daniel, 1722, *A Description of the English Province of Carolana*, etc.: London, B. Crouse, 122 p., map. (This was reprinted in 1726, 1727, 1741, and in 1840, the later year in both England and in the United States; the Charlotte Mecklenburg Library has a personal copy of Edmund S. Coxe.)

Coxe, Tench, 1965, *A View of the United States of America*: New York, A. M. Kelley, 513 p. (a compilation of papers written 1787 to 1794, reprint)

DuBin, Alexander, 1936, *Coxe Family*: Phila., Historical Publ. Soc, 60 p.

Haller, Charles R., 2003, The New York Speculation Lands: Asheville, NC, *A Lot of Bunkum*, vol. 24, no. 2, p. 22-23

Lattimore, Robin, Julia Hensley & Lesley M. Bush, 2003, *Across Two Centuries*: Rutherford, NC, Hilltop Publ., 208 p.

McNab, W. Henry, 2010, Speculation Lands and the Green River Plantation: Asheville, NC, *A Lot of Bunkum*, vol. 31, no. 2, p. 6-7

Wright, Robert E., & David T. Green, 2006, The Judas: Tench Coxe (1755-1824): in *Financial Founding Fathers: The Men Who Made America*: Chicago, Univ. Chicago Press, p. 38-64, 203.

Primary Sources of Coxe Family Manuscripts

Historical Society of Pennsylvania, Philadelphia (496 linear feet)

UNC Asheville, Ramsey Library, Special Collections (4 linear feet)

Descendants of Lambert Clayton & Sarah Davidson

Name	Cemetery
1. Lambert Clayton (1755-1828) **RW**	Davidson River
+ Sarah Davidson (1759-1843) (9 child.)	Davidson River
2. Jane Clayton (1783-1873) (15 child.)	Davidson River
+ John Orr (1775-1873)	Davidson River
2. John Clayton (1785-1868)	Davidson River
+ Susan (Sarah) Wetzel (1787-1872) (12 child.)	Davidson River
2. George Clayton (1788-1876)	Davidson River
+ Sallie Wetzel (1790-1888) (3 child.)	Davidson River
2. Thomas Davidson Clayton (1790-1872)	(Cecil Co., MO)
+ Rachel Dawson (1794-1868) (8 child.)	(Cecil Co., MO)
2. Nancy Ann Clayton (1793-1840) (10 child.)	Davidson River
+ George Clayton Neill (1786-1878)	Davidson River
2. Sarah S. Clayton (1798-1874) (4 child.)	Davidson River
+ James Neill (1795-1863)	Davidson River
2. Rachel Clayton (1799-1884) (10 child.)	Mills River Pres.
+ William Brittain (1798-1867)	Mills River Pres.
2. Henrietta Clayton (1802-____) (8 child.)	
+ Elijah Young (c. 1800-____)	
2. Ephraim Clayton (1804-1892)	Clayton Cem.
+ Nancy McElroy (1800-1882) (6 child.)	Clayton Cem.

Editor's Notes:

Davidson River Cemetery is in Transylvania County, near Brevard. Mills River Presbyterian Cemetery is in Henderson Co. The Ephraim Clayton Cemetery is in West Asheville, near the 4th Tee of the Crowne Plaza Hotel Golf Course. As noted above, Lambert Clayton and Sarah Davidson had 76 grandchildren.

Sarah Davidson apparently stems from the Iredell Davidsons.

Prior to the Civil War, Ephraim Clayton achieved fame as a master builder operating over much of western North Carolina, upstate South Carolina, and even in northern Georgia. As Lou Harshaw notes in her 1976 book *The Gold of Dahlonega*, in 1836 Clayton completed a new Courthouse at Dahlonega after an earlier contractor disappeared with building funds. Ironically, in 1855, Clayton initiated a lawsuit with city officials of Dahlonega in order to recover his costs.

Primary References

Felmet, L. Holt, Jr., 2008, Lambert Clayton & Sarah Davidson Clayton: Asheville, NC, *A Lot of Bunkum*, vol. 29, no. 1, p. 14-17

_____, 2009, A Plausible Explanation as to the Ancestry of Sarah Davidson Clayton: Asheville, NC, *A Lot of Bunkum*, vol. 30, no. 1, p. 9-14.

Green, Virginia S., 1995, *The Clayton Clique. Pt. I*: Tampa, FL, privately publ., 222 + 20 p.

Haller, Charles R., 2008, Builders of Asheville: Asheville, NC, *A Lot of Bunkum*, vol. 29, no. 1, p. 25

Hand, Robert S., 1991, *Davison/Davidson Family. The Descendants of William and Elizabeth Davison of County Armagh, Ireland*: Chadds Ford, PA, privately printed, 201 p. (2nd ed.)

Maxwell, Mary, H. R. Walker, & Robert M. Clayton, 1927, *Antecedents and Descendants in part of Lambert Clayton and his wife Sarah Davidson*: Atlanta, GA, Correll-Smith Printers, 32 p.

Montieth, Frankie (Mrs.). 1985, *Transylvania Co., NC Cemetery Survey*: Brevard, NC, privately publ., 248 + 79 + 2 p. (116 cemeteries)

Descendants of William Coleman

Name	Cemetery
1. William Coleman (1785-1874)	Coleman
+ 1st Cynthia Swain (1791-1829) (10 child.)	?Central Meth.
2. William Tiffany Coleman (1813-____)	?Central Meth.
2. Carolina Matilda Coleman (1814-1829)	?Central Meth.
2. George Swain Coleman (1816-____)	(Texas)
+ Maria Douglas (____-____)	(Texas)
2. Mary Isabella Coleman (1817-____)	(?Macon Co.)
+ Julius Thomas Siler (1825 -1866) **CSA**	(?Macon Co.)
2. John Hall Coleman (1819-____)	(Texas)
2. Althea Margaret Coleman (1821-1898) (5 child.)	Riverside
+ Milton Pinckney Penland (1813-1880)	Riverside
3. Louisa Alexandra Penland (1850-1927) (3 child.)	Riverside
+ Isaac Hutsell Bailey (1843-1936) **CSA**	Riverside
2. David Coleman (1824-1883) **CSA**	Riverside
2. Newton Coleman (1825-____) **CSA**	(?Tennessee)
2. Patience Louise Coleman (1827-____)	
+ William Rockhold (____-____)	
2. James Coleman (1829-c.1830)	?Central Meth.

*****

Name	Cemetery
+ 2nd Ann Evelyn Baird (1804-1884) (5 child.)	Coleman
2. Andrew Baird Coleman (1834-1850)	?Coleman
2. Robert Lowry Coleman (1835-1898) **CSA**	Riverside
+ Victoria Susannah Rice (1838-1919)	Riverside
2. Thaddeus Charles Coleman (1837-1896) **CSA**	Coleman
+ Mary Elizabeth Sloan (1841-1926) (4 child.)	Coleman
3. Thaddeus Weir Coleman (____-____)	
+ Jessie L. Pargaud (____-____)	
3. Sarah Lindsay Coleman (1868-1959) (2nd wife)	Riverside
+ William Sidney Porter (1862-1910)	Riverside
3. James Sloan Coleman, Sr. (1871-1900)	Coleman
+ Pearl Gladys Crawford (1873-1963)	Calvary
3. Evelyn Kalmbach Coleman (1875-1927)	(South Carolina)
+ William Coleman (1875-1924)	(South Carolina)
2. Matthew Conley Coleman (1839-1842)	?Central Meth.
2. Henry Solomon Coleman (1842-1865) **CSA**	(Virginia)

Editor's Notes

William Coleman's first land records in Buncombe Co. date from 1828.

Selected References

Gudger, Owen, 1928, *Coleman Genealogy*: unpublished mss, Asheville, NC, Sondley Collection, Pack Memorial Library, 3 p.

Haller, Charles R., 2007, Descendants of Caroline Swain: Asheville, NC, *A Lot of Bunkum*, vol. 28, no. 4, p. 18

_____, 2008, Who was David Coleman?: Asheville, NC, *A Lot of Bunkum*, vol. 29, no. 2, p. 22-24

McPherson, Jessie C., 1970, *A History of the Coleman-Sloan-Johnston Families*: Columbia, SC, privately publ., 214 p.

Thaddeus Charles Coleman is listed in the *Dictionary of North Carolina Biography*

Descendants of William Davison/Davidson
Cluster A in John B. Lisle DNA Website

<u>Name</u>   <u>Cemetery</u>

1. William Davison (c.1684-1723)
    + Elizabeth _____
            6 children (Anne, George, John, Helen, Judith,Margaret)
    2. George Davison, Sr. (c.1707-1759)   (Iredell Co., NC)
    + 1st Rachel Jones (____-____) (2 child.)
    + 2nd Margaret Ware Simmeral (____-1776+)
    (2 children by _____ Simmeral)
            (4 children by George Davidson)
        3. Capt. George Davidson, Jr. (1743-1774)
        3. Gen. William Lee Davidson (1746-1781) **RW**   (Mecklenburg Co, NC)
        + Mary Brevard (1748-1824) (7 child.)   (Kentucky)
            4. George Lee Davidson (1770-1843)   (Lowndes Co., AL)
            + Catherine Mushat (1768-1847) (7 child.)
            4. Pamela Davidson (1772-1851)   (Logan Co., KY)
            + George McLean (1767-1849)
            4. Margaret Davidson (1774-1868)   (?Lexington Co., MO)
            + **Rev.** Finis Ewing (1773-1841)
            4. John Alexander Davidson (c.1776-1822)   (Jefferson Co., MS)
            + Elizabeth Green (c.1777-1825) (5 child.)
            4. Jean Davidson (c.1777-1825)   (Jefferson Co., MS)
            + Henry Green (1767-____)
            4. Ephraim Brevard Davidson (1779-1821)   (New Madrid, MO)
            + 1st Charlotte C. Cook (1782-1809) (4 child.)
            + 2nd Mary Baker Ewing (1787-1859) (6 child.)
            4. William Lee Davidson, Jr. (1781-1862)   (Marengo Co., AL)
            + 1st Elizabeth L. Davidson (1782-1845)
            + 2nd Sarah D. Houston (1792-1871)
            [Mary Brevard + 2nd Robert Harris (1728-1794)]
        3. Samuel Davidson (c. 1748-____)

Cluster B in John B. Lisle DNA Website

Name	Cemetery
2. John Davidson, Sr. (c. 1709-1749)	(Iredell Co., NC)
+ Jane (see remarks) (1712-?) (8 child.) + 3x	
3. Col. George Davidson, Sr. (1728-1814)	(Iredell Co., NC)
+ Catharine P. Reese (1731-1814) (9 child.)	(Iredell Co., NC)
4. John Davidson, Jr. (c.1750-c.1780) **RW**	(Old Fort, NC)
+ Nancy Brevard (1757-c.1780)	(Old Fort, NC)
4. Jane/Jean Davidson (1754-1831)	
+ James Kerr (____-____)	
4. George Davidson, Jr.(1757-1813)	(Maury Co., TN)
+ Rosannah Falls _____	
4. William Davidson (c.1760-1803)	
+ Polly _____	
4. Gen. Ephraim Davidson (1762-1842) **RW**	(Iredell Co., NC)
+ Jane Brevard (1765-1833) (6 child.)	(Iredell Co., NC)
5. George S. F. Davidson (1805-1888)	(Iredell Co., NC)
4. Sarah Davidson (1765-1790)	
+ James Conner (1754-1835)	
4. Thomas Davidson (1770-1833)	
+ Agnes (Nancy) White (1772-____)	
4. Catherine Lee Davidson ((c.1774-____)	
+ George L. Davidson	
4. Ruth Penelope Davidson (b.1776-c.1815)	
+ James Caldwell (1768-____)	
3. Rachel Davidson (c.1730-____) (5 child.)	(Williamson Co., NC)
+ John Alexander (1731-1795)	
3. Thomas Davidson (c. 1733-____)	(Charleston, SC)
+ Sarah	
3. Capt. Samuel Davidson (1736-1782) twin **RW**	Oteen, NC
+ Ann Dunlop (____-____) (1 child.)	
+ Mary Smith (____-____) (2 child.)	
4. Ruth Davidson (c. 1765-1826) (6 child.)	
+ James Hazard Wilson (1763-1838)	
4. Mary Davidson (c.1767-____)	
+ Gabriel Ragsdale (1759-1797)	
3. Maj. William Davidson (1736-1814) twin **RW**	Bee Tree Comm.
+ Margaret McConnell (c.1738-1806) (10 child.)	Bee Tree Comm.
4. Mary McC. Davidson (1763-1842) (9 child.)	Newton Acad.
+ Col. Daniel Smith (1757-1824) **RW**	Newton Acad.
4. Ruth Davidson (1777-1849) (8 child.)	(Maury Co., TN)
+ Gen. Samuel H. Williams (1769-1835)	(Maury Co., TN)
4. William Mitchell Davidson (1780-1846)	(Texas)
+ Elizabeth Vance (1787-1861) (10 child.)	(Murphy, NC)
3. Elizabeth Davidson (1741-1820) (12 child.)	(Maury Co., TN)
+ Ephraim McLean (1730-1823) **RW**	(Greenville, KY)
3. Margaret "Peggy" Davidson (c. 1742-____)	
+ 1st David Alexander	
+ ? 2nd James Smith	
3. John (one-eyed) Davidson (c.1744-1825)	(Maury Co., TN)
+ 1st Ruth Clement (c.1750-1792) (7 child.)	(Burke Co., NC)

4. Ephraim Edward Davidson(1785-1850)   (Mississippi)
   + Mary "Polly" Brank (1789-1864) (9 child.)   (Mississippi)
   + 2nd Frances Bateman (1773-1832) (1 child)   (Maury Co., TN)

Editor's Notes

Cluster A

George Davison, Sr. (c. 1707-1759), William Lee Davidson's father, migrated from Northern Ireland to Pennsylvania in 1740. The family moved to Rowan (Iredell Co. after 1788) about 1748, settling on what became Davison's Cr., a branch of the Catawba River. The Centre Presbyterian Congregation was established nearby a few years later.

Cluster B

John Davidson, Sr. (c.1709-1749) immigrant from Ireland went to the lower Catawba Valley about 1748, settling near his brother George. His wife Jane Morrison Tucker was married twice previously. Jane Morrison Tucker's maiden name was Jane Margaret Legacorry. John and Jane had eight children; second generation children George, Rachel, Thomas, and twins Samuel and William were born in Ireland.

Rachel Davidson with brothers Samuel and William migrated to the Bee Tree community circa 1781 to 1782. About 1782, Capt. Samuel Davidson was murdered by the Indians near Oteen and is buried at an unknown location although a memorial granite exists nearby. In 1783, uncle Ephraim and brother John Davidson entered the 440 acre tract at Oteen, formerly claimed by brother Samuel, now deceased.

Earlier, during the Revolutionary War, Davidson's Fort (now near Old Fort, on the Upper Catawba) was the largest one of its kind in what later became McDowell Co. The fort, sometimes called Samuel Davidsons Fort, later became the property of Col. George Davidson, Sr., who became in 1778-1779 an extensive land holder.

A full list of the children of Maj. William Davidson and his wife Margaret McConnell is shown separately. The elders are buried in a lost family cemetery near the junction of Bee Tree Creek and the Swannanoa River, but not in the cemetery of the First Presbyterian Church of Swannanoa. A poor quality memorial marble, probably from Georgia, erected by the DAR in 1903 for Maj. Davidson is in front of the church.

Many fables have appeared about Ruth Davidson (1777-1849), younger daughter of Maj. William Davidson. She married Samuel Humphries Williams (1769-1835), who was in the War of 1812 and carried the title of General. The couple and some of their children are buried in Zion Presbyterian Church in Maury Co., TN.

By one older account, George Davidson (1728-1814), Ephraim McLean (1730-1823), and John (one-eyed) Davidson (c.1744-1825) all died in Knox Co., TN, but a more recent account puts the burial places in Iredell Co., NC; Maury Co., TN; and Maury Co., TN, respectively.

Selected References

Haller, Charles R., 2005, Who was William Davidson of Gum Spring?: Asheville, NC, *A Lot of Bunkum*, vol. 26, no. 2, p. 8-10

_____, 2008, Col. Hugh Harvey Davidson: Asheville, NC, *A Lot of Bunkum*, vol. 29, no. 3, p. 23-28

_____, 2009, The Many Faces of Samuel Winslow Davidson: Asheville, NC, *A Lot of Bunkum*, vol. 30, no. 4, p. 21-25

_____, 2012, Davidson Family in Western North Carolina: in press

Hand, Robert S., 1991, Davison/Davidson Family. *The Descendants of William and Elisabeth Davison of County Armagh, Ireland*: Chadds Ford, PA, privately publ., 201 p. (2nd ed.)

White, Emmett R., 1984, *Revolutionary War Soldiers of Western North Carolina. Vol. I, Burke Co.*: Easley, SC, Southern Historical Press, 318 p.

Geographic Explanation

The famous Bee Tree Community is located near the town of Swannanoa, now in eastern Buncombe Co., NC. Two of the oldest cemeteries in Buncombe Co., the Robert Patton Cemetery and Piney Grove are located nearby.

The Oteen postal district is part of East Asheville, NC

Descendants of Major William Davidson, aka Bee Tree Davidsons

Name	Cemetery
1. Maj. William Davidson (1736-1814) **RW**	Bee Tree Cr.
+ Margaret McConnell (1738-1806) (10 child.)	Bee Tree Cr.
2. Mary "Polly" Davidson (1760-1842) (9 child.)	Newton Acad.
+ Col. Daniel Smith (1757-1824) **RW**	Newton Acad.
2. John Davidson (1764-1845) **RW**	(Bedford Co.)
+ Martha Davidson (1779-1842) (9 child.)	(Bedford Co.)
2. George Davidson (1768-1837) twin	(Mississippi)
+ Sallie McWhorter (1771-____) (7 child.)	(Mississippi)
2. Judge Hugh Lawson Davidson, Sr. (1768-1841) twin	(Bedford Co.)
+ Jean "Jane" Vance (1777-1858) (12 child.)	(Bedford Co.)
2. Jane Davidson (1772-1804) ("Jean")	
2. Thomas Davidson (Kentucky)	
2. Sarah "Sallie" Davidson (1774-1836)	(Maury Co.)
+ 1st Joshua Williams (1762-1831)	(Maury Co.)
+ 2nd William Lusk	
2. Elizabeth Davidson (1775-1843)	(Williams. Co.)
+ Thomas Alexander (c.1772-1854)	(Williams. Co.)
2. Ruth Davidson (1777-1849) (8 child.)	(Maury Co.)
+ Samuel H. Williams (1769-1835) "Gen.", **War of 1812**	(Maury Co.)
2. William Mitchell Davidson (1780-1846)	(Texas)
+ Elizabeth Vance (1781-1861) (10 child.)	(Murphy, NC)
3. Hugh Harvey Davidson (1814-1889) **CSA**	(Murphy, NC)
+ 1st Lucinda Emeline Moody (1824-____) (8 child.)	
4. Samuel Winslow Davidson (1849-1915) **CSA**	
+ 1st Mary Jane Calvord (3 child.)	
+ 2nd Elizabeth Reid	
+ 2nd Mary Ann Roberts (5 child.)	
+ 3rd Ann Nelson (no child.)	
+ 4th (Mrs.) Strong (no child.)	
3. Allen Turner Davidson (1819-1905)	Riverside
+ Elizabeth Adeline Howell (1824-1917) (8/10 child.)	Riverside
4. Theodore Fulton Davidson (1845-1931) **CSA**	Riverside
+ 1st Sarah K.Alexander (1847-1887) (no child.)	Riverside
+ 2nd Sarah Lindsey Carter (1863-1934) (no child.)	Riverside
4. Ella Henrietta Davidson (1851-1939) (4 child.)	Riverside
+ Theodore Summey Morrison (1852-1926)	Riverside
4. Addie Lee Davidson (1864-1940) (6 child.)	Riverside
+ William Bethell Williamson (1862-1939)	Riverside
3. Samuel Winslow Davidson (1823-1895)	(Murphy, NC)
+ 1st Margaret J. Alexander (6 child.)	
+ 2nd Aveniell Ansley	
2. Col. Samuel Winslow Davidson (1781-1858) **War of 1812**	Piney Grove.
+ 1st Martha McRee (1781-1847) (7 child.)	Piney Grove
3. Margaret Elizabeth Davidson (1805-1878)	Newton Acad.
+ John Erwin Patton, Sr. (1805-1889)	Newton Acad.
3. James Cruser Davidson (1806-1891)	Piney Grove
+ Sarah S. Foster (1812-1890) (9 child.)	Piney Grove
4. Samuel Winslow Davidson (1841-1914) **CSA**	Piney Grove
+ Nancy Cornelia Sherrill (1843-1910)	Piney Grove

3. Rachel Adeline Davidson (1809-1849) (5 child.)	Piney Grove
+ John Burgin (1799-1884) (2nd marriage)	Piney Grove
3. William Franklin Davidson (1812-1902)	Berea Bapt.
+ Minerva E. Foster (1820-1897) (9 child.)	Berea Bapt.
3. Mary Harriet Davidson (1813-1876) (7 child.)	Piney Grove
+ Albertus Burgin (1806-1874)	Piney Grove
3. Albert Cruser Davidson (1815-1850)	Piney Grove
+ Sophronia S. Burgin (1823-1864) (5 Child.)	Piney Grove
4. Samuel Winslow Davidson (1848-1921)	Piney Grove
+ Rosanna M. Young (1852-1930) (6 child.)	Piney Grove
3. Samuel Winslow Davidson, Jr. (1819-____)	
+ 2nd Elizabeth Vance Davidson (1781-1861)	(Murphy, NC)

Editor's Notes

According to Elaine McAllister Dellinger, Historian, Ruth Davidson Chapter, NSDAR, Ruth Davidson Williams (1777-1849) is buried with her husband and five children at the Zion Presbyterian Church, Maury Co., TN.

Bedford, Maury, and Williamson Counties are in central Tennessee.

Selected References

Haller, Charles R., 2008, Col. Hugh Harvey Davidson: Asheville, NC, *A Lot of Bunkum*, vol. 29, no. 3, p. 23-28

_____, 2009, The Many Faces of Samuel Winslow Davidson: *ibid*, vol. 30, no. 4, p. 21-25

Allen Turner Davidson and Theodore S. Fulton Davidson are in the *Dictionary of North Carolina Biography*.

Descendants of Samuel Davidson - Gum Spring Davidsons
Cluster C in John B. Lisle DNA website

Name	Cemetery
1. Samuel Davidson (c.1705-c.1790) **RW**	(WNC)
+ Margaret _____	
2. James Davidson (c. 1741-1816) **RW**	(Rutherford Co., TN)
+ Mary McConnell (c.1745-c.1800) (7 child.)	
3. Rebecca Davidson (1769-___) (12 child.)	
+ William Young (1763-____)	
3. Martha Davidson (1770-1842) (8 child.)	(Bedford Co., TN)
+ John Davidson (1764-1845) **RW**	(Bedford Co., TN)
4. John Davidson, Jr. (____-____)	
3. John Davidson (c. 1774-____)	
+ Nancy _____	
3. Ruby Davidson (c.1776-____)	
+ _____ McGhee	
3. Mary Davidson	
+ _____ Johnson	
3. Sarah Davidson	
+ _____ Lusk	
3. Cynthia Davidson (c.1785-____)	
+ Nathaniel Hubbard	
2. Benjamin Davidson, Sr. (c. 1743-c.1825) **RW**	(Transylvania Co., NC)
+ Ann (Cathey/Patton?) (c.1748-1830+) (11 child.)	(?Transylvania Co., NC)
3. Rhoda Davidson (c.1771-____) (3 child.)	(Georgia)
+ Rev. Samuel Davis	(Georgia)
3. Polly Davidson (c. 1772-___) (4 child.)	(Georgia)
+ Isaac Davis	
3. Elizabeth Davidson (c.1773-1852) (6 child.)	(?Transylvania Co.,NC)
+ John Murray	
3. James Davidson (c. 1774-____)	(?Missouri)
3. Rebecca Davidson (c.1777-____) (4 child.)	(Illinois?)
+ Benjamin Gullick	
3. Sarah Davidson (c. 1779-____)	
3. Ann Davidson (c. 1780-____)	
+ David Hadden	(?Henderson Co., NC)
3. Benjamin Davidson, Jr. (c. 1781-____)	(Missouri)
+ Huldah Harriet Lane	
3. Erixina Davidson (c. 1782-____) (1 child.)	
+ James Johnston, Jr.	
3. Sophia A. Davidson (c.1784-____)	
+ George Douglas Davis	
3. Martha Davidson (c. 1785-____)	(Tennessee)
+ Joseph Gray	
2. Jesse Davidson (c. 1745-___) d. young	
2. Col. William Davidson (c.1747-c.1800) **RW**	(?Roane Co., TN)
+ unknown	
4. William Davidson, Jr. (____-____)	
4. George Davidson (____-____)	
2. Mary Davidson (c. 1749-____)	

Cluster C in North Carolina 1790 Census

11th Company, Morgan District, Burke County

    James Davidson (c.1741-____), 2 males 16+, 6 females, 3 slaves

    William Davidson (c.1747-c.1802), 4 males 16+, 2 males less than 16,
    4 females, 8 slaves

    Samuel Davidson (n.d.), 1 male, 1 female

1st Company, Morgan District, Burke County

    Benjamin Davidson (c.1743-c.1825), 2 males 16+, 1 male less than 16,
    9 females, no slaves

Cluster C in 1800 Census

Burke County

    Widow Davidson, 2 males 16+, 3 females, 6 slaves
    (?widow of Samuel Davidson)

    William Davidson, 4 males 16+, 2 slaves (?William Davidson, Jr.)

Buncombe County

    Benjamin Davidson, 2 males, 4 females, 1 slave

Editor's Notes

In 1790, Benjamin Davidson had 12 persons in his household of which 3 were males. James Davidson had 8 persons in his household of which 2 were males. William Davidson had 10 persons in his household of which 6 were males. Subsequent research in tracing the male and female descendants gave very poor results. Benjamin Davidson and his wife reportedly had 11 children (2 sons, 9 daughters). Documentation is not available to assign the number of children in the households of James and William Davidson.

We thank John B. Lisle for reporting the will of James Davidson (c.1741-c.1816) as taken from *Rutherford Co., TN Wills, Inventories, and Settlements*, Vol. III.

Selected Tennessee References

Cartwright, Betty G. C., & Lillian J. Gardner, 1958, *North Carolina Land Grants in Tennessee, 1778-1791*: Memphis, TN, Nortex Offset Publ. (Quanah, TX), 199 p.

Griffey, Irene M., 2000, *Earliest Tennessee Land Records & Earliest Tennessee Land History*: Baltimore, MD, Clearfield Co., 505 p. (Note: p. 155 refers to George Davidson, heir of Lt. Col. William Davidson)
- Note: p. 155 refers to George Davidson, heir of Gen. William (Lee) Davidson - Cluster A. This grant no. 31 was awarded 14 March 1786. It embraced 5,760 acres, on the north side of the Tennessee River, Davidson area. The General died in 1781. The heirs of General William (Lee) Davidson (Ephraim Davidson, George Davidson, Jean Davidson, and Mary Davidson-wife) altogether took some 12,260 acres, mostly located in the Western district of TN.

- The same page lists grant no. 314 for 1,000 acres, Middle District, Duck R., north side. It was granted 17 Dec. 1786. This grant apparently was made to Col. William Davidson (Cluster C) who died about 1800. Other relatives of the Col. apparently held another 4,500 acres in the Middle and Western Districts.

Pickel, Eugene M. 1981, *History of Roane County (TN) to 1870*: Kingston, TN, Rowan Co. Heritage Comm., 93 p. (no index)

Roberts, Snyder E., 1981, *Roots of Roane Co., TN, 1792-1974*: Kingston, TN, Roane Publ. Co., 181 p. + index (Note: refers to "Col. William Davidson")

Wells, Emma M., 1927, *History of Roane Co., TN (1801-1870)*: Chattanooga, TN, Lookout Publ., 353 p. (Note: p. 46 refers to "William Davidson - Capt. Thomas Coulter's Co., in 1802 Tax List"; p. 30 refers to "William Davidson - NC Regiment")

Descendants of William Forester, Sr.

Name	Cemetery
1. William Forster, Sr. (c. 1725-____)	
+ 1st Mary _____	
2. Jane (Jean) Forster (1746-1824)	
+ John Burton	
2. William Forster, Jr. (1748-1830) **RW**	Newton Acad.
+ Elizabeth Heath (1753-1827)	Newton Acad.
3. Mary Forster (1772-1826)	
3. Thomas Foster (1774-1858)	Newton Acad.
+ Orra Sams (1778-1853) (1 child.)	Newton Acad.
3. William Forster III (1776-1826)	Newton Acad.
+ Frances "Fanny" Ballew (1786-____)	Newton Acad.
3. Rebecca Forster (1779-1847) (8 child.)	Dillingham
+ Absalom Dillingham (1770-1837)	Dillingham
3. Elizabeth Forster (1782-____)	
+ John Wilson	
2. Thomas Forster (1751-1839) **RW**	Newton Acad.
+ Mary Rafferty (____-____) (no child.)	
2. Mary Forster (1753-____)	
2. Margaret Forster (1755-1839)	
+ 1st James Barnes	
+ 2nd Henry Stevens, Sr. (c.1750-c.1801)	
2. Ann Forster (1758-____)	
2. Dorcas Forster (1760-____)	
2. David Forster (1763-____)	

*****

+ 2nd Margaret _____	
2. Mary Forster	
2. John Forster	
2. Samuel Forster	

Census Records:

Wm. Foster is on the 1790 NC Census, Rutherford Co., Morgan District (now Buncombe Co.) with 3 males, 6 females, and 3 slaves.

William Forrester is on the 1800 NC Census, Buncombe Co., with 2 males, 5 females, and 6 slaves.

Descendants of Ann Dennis (Gash, Gudger, Whitson)

<u>Name</u>	<u>Cemetery</u>
1. Ann Dennis (c.1732-c.1812)	Cemetery Hill?
+ 1st _____ Johnston	
2. Reuben Johnston (____-1843)	(Transylvania Co.?)
+ 2x	

*****

+ 2nd Martin Gash (c.1740-c.1809)	Cemetery Hill?
2. Joseph Dennis Gash (1767-1805)	Cemetery Hill?
+ Denna (Demy) Woodfin (1771-1817) (5 child.)	Cemetery Hill?
3. Rachel Gash (1794-1850+) (4 child.)	(Missouri)
+ Greenlee Sams	(Missouri)
3. John B. Gash (1795-1847)	(Missouri)
+ 1st Jenny Culbertson _____ (8 child.)	
+ 2nd Leah Culbertson _____ (11 child)	
3. William M. Gash (1799-1847)	(Missouri)
+ Stacy E. Longmire (1797-1858) (8 child.)	
3. Joseph Dennis Gash, Jr. (1801-1837)	(Missouri)
+ Eula Culbertson	
3. Ebenezer Gash (1805-1872)	(Missouri)
+ Maria McReynolds & 3 others	
2. John Gash (1769-1857)	Newton Academy
+ Nancy Gudger (1777-1851) (12 child.)	Newton Academy
3. William Gudger Gash (1796-1797)	Cemetery Hill?
3. Joseph Dennis Gash (1797-1852)	(Missouri)
+ Eliza Killian (1801-1865) (8 child.)	(Missouri)
3. Naomi Young Gash (1799-____)	(Tennessee)
+ John P. Hardin	(Tennessee)
3. Martin A. Gash (1802-1850)	(Transylvania Co.)
+ Margaret Siler (1800-1850) (6 child.)	(Transylvania Co.)
3. Martha Ann Gash (1804-1885) (7 child.)	(Transylvania Co.)
+ Strawbridge Young (1799-1874)	(Transylvania Co.)
3. William Riley Gash (1807-1859)	(Henderson Co.?)
+ 1st Melinda Spann (10 child.)	
+ 2nd Winnafore Gillespie (1814-1850)	(Henderson Co.)
+ 3rd Rachel Roberts (2 child.)	
3. Alfred Raney Gash (1809-1888)	(Henderson Co.)
+ Mary Livingston (1802-1882) (8 child.)	(Henderson Co.)
3. Sarah Eliza Gash (1810-1814)	
3. Leander Sams Gash (1813-1872)	(Henderson Co.)
+ Margaret Adelaine McClain (1818-1890) (7 child.)	(Henderson Co.)
3. Burditt Stuart Gash (1816-1891)	Newton Academy
+ Elizabeth F. Weaver (1817-1888) (8 child.)	Newton Academy
3. Louisa Elizabeth Gash (1818-1890)	(Henderson Co.)
+ John Watson Erwin (1806-1888)	(Henderson Co.)
3. Rachel Catherine Gash (1821-1872)	(Transylvania Co.)
+ Overton L. Erwin (1816-1879)	(Transylvania Co.)
2. Martin A. Gash, Jr. (1773-1836)	(Missouri)
+ Mary A. Gudger (c.1779-1828) (12 child.)	(Missouri)
3. Joseph Dennis Gash (1796-1849)	(Missouri)
+ Sally Longmire (1795-1836) (10 child.)	

Name	Cemetery
3. James B. Gash (1798-1800)	(?North Carolina)
3. Martin Alley Gash (1801-1851)	(California)
+ Mary ____-____ (1 child.)	
3. Sarah B. Gash (1803-1852+)	(Missouri)
+ Daniel Bryant	
3. Martha Gash 1805-1890)	(Missouri)
+ Moses D. Bates, Sr. (1791-1857)	(Missouri)
3. Nancy M. Gash (1807-1849) (5 child.) (1st wife)	(Missouri)
+ John Newton Boulware, Sr. (1806-____)	
3. William Jefferson Gash (1809-1875)	(Missouri)
+ Mary R. McWilliams (1825-1917)	
3. Montraville Gash (1811-1835)	(Missouri)
3. John B. Gash (1814-1821)	(Missouri)
3. Rebecca C. Gash (1817-1847)	(Missouri)
3. Mary Elizabeth Gash (1820-1872)	(Missouri)
+ 2 x	
3. Moses Bates Gash (1823-1809)	(Missouri)
+ Lucinda C. Nichols (1832-1900)	

Census Records

Martin Gash is on the 1790 NC Census, Rutherford Co., Morgan district, Thirteen Company (now Buncombe Co.) with 3 males, and 1 female.

Martin Gash is on the 1800 NC Census, Buncombe Co., with 4 males and 1 female.

Selected Reference

Haller, Charles R., 2009, Who Was Martin Gash/Gass, Immigrant: Asheville, NC, *A Lot of Bunkum*, vol. 30, no. 1, p. 21-25, 27

Descendants of William Gudger, Sr. (see also Gash/Gudger/Whitson)

Name	Cemetery
1. William Gudger, Sr. (1752-1833) **RW**	?Cemetery Hill
+ Martha "Patsy" Young (1750-c.1836) (8 child.)	?Cemetery Hill
2. Stacy E. Gudger (c.1775-1839) (10 child.)	(Missouri)
+ John Longmire (c.1770-1836+)	(Missouri)
2. Nancy Gudger (1777-1851) (12 child.)	Newton Academy
+ John Gash (c.1769-1856)	Newton Academy
2. Mary A. Gudger (c.1779-1828) (12 child.)	(Missouri)
+ Martin Gash, Jr. (c.1773-1836)	(Missouri)
2. James Madison Gudger. (1782-1861)	?Gudgers Chapel
+ Anne Dillard Love (1786-1867) (10 child.)	?Gudgers Chapel
3. Robert Love Gudger (1806-1870+)	
+ 1st Mary Johnston (1813-1830)	
4. James Madison Gudger (1836-1916)	
+ 2nd Fannie J. E. Patty (7 child.)	
3. Samuel Bell Gudger (1808-1888)	Samuel B. Gudger
+ Elizabeth Siler Lowry (1810-1903) (8 child.)	Samuel B. Gudger
4. Mary Caroline Gudger (1833-1917) (7 child.)	Oak Forest Presby.
+ William Hamilton Moore (1812-1879)	Oak Forest Presby.
4. Lucinda M. Gudger (1834-1889) (4 child.)	Samuel B. Gudger
+ William Gaston Candler (1834-1934)	Samuel B. Gudger
4. James Cassius L. Gudger (1837-1914) **CSA**	(Haywood Co.)
+ Mary Goodwin Willis (1837-1891) (4 child.)	(Haywood Co.)
5. Eugene Willis Gudger (1866-1954)	(Haywood Co.)
4. David Madison Gudger (1840-1917)	Oak Forest Presby.
+ 1st Louisa J. Taylor (1847-1895)	Oak Forest Presby.
+ 2nd Bessie J. Whitlow (1862-1925) (8 child.)	Oak Forest Presby.
5. Owen H. Gudger (1880-1959)	Oak Forest Presby.
+ Nelle Murray Locke (1884-1972)	Oak Forest Presby.
4. Laura A. E. Gudger (1843-1927)	Oak Forest Presby.
+ John A. Stikeleather (1840-1912)	Oak Forest Presby.
4. Louise Emeline Gudger (1846-1865)	
4. Leonora Thomasine Gudger (1849-1879)	Samuel B. Gudger
+ James W. Rice (1836-1929)	Samuel B. Gudger
4. Eva Lane Gudger (1854-1913)	Samuel B. Gudger
+ Jasper L. Young (1848-1930)	Samuel B. Gudger
3. Lucinda Matilda Gudger (1811-1885) (12 child.)	Riverside
+ William Johnston (1807-1890)	Riverside
3. William M. Gudger (1813-1832)	
3. Joseph Jackson Gudger (1815-1890)	(Madison Co.)
+ 1st Sarah Emeline Bernard (1824-1863) (6 child.)	(Madison Co.)
4. Hezekiah Alexander Gudger (1849-1917)	Riverside
+ Jeanie Hardy Smith (1854-1943) (5 child.)	Riverside
4. James Madison Gudger, Jr. (1855-1920)	Riverside
+ Katie Y. Hawkins (2 child.)	
+ 2nd Catherine Farnsworth Clark (1825-1894)	
3. James Gallatin Gudger (1818-1903)	(Tennessee)
+ Margaret Alexander	(Tennessee)
3. Dillard Franklin Gudger (1820-1845)	Henry
+ Mary Jane Hawkins (1825-1904) +2x (9 child.)	Montmorenci Meth.

Name	Cemetery
3. Adolphus M. Gudger (1822-1902)	Gudgers Chapel
+ Eveline S. Penland (1830-1893) (5 child.)	Gudgers Chapel
3. Montraville W. Gudger (1825-____)	
+ Betty Stanfield	
3. Lorenzo P. Gudger (1828-1845+)	
+ Frances Laughridge	
2. Sarah "Sally" Gudger (c.1783-1862) (10 child.)	(Tennessee.)
+ Joseph McDowell Whitson, Sr. (1782-1861)	(Tennessee)
2. Elizabeth Gudger (c.1785-1874) (7 child.)	(Alabama)
+ Thomas Jefferson Whitson (c.1781-1870)	(Alabama)
2. William Gudger, Jr. (c.1789-1860) **War of 1812**	(Georgia)
+ Nancy Henry (1799-1870+) (10 child.)	(Georgia)
2. Joseph Young Gudger (c.1792-1869)	Piney Grove
+ Rachel E. McRee (1795-1863) (12 child.)	?Piney Grove
3. James McRee Gudger (1819-1888)	Piney Groove
+ Sarah Murray (1818-1898)	Piney Grove

Editor's Notes:

William Gudger, Sr., and Martha "Patsy" Young had eight children and 83 grandchildren. Of the grandchildren, 32 carried on the Gudger family name.

Two Gudger daughters married two Gashes and two daughters married two Whitsons.

Census Records

Martin Gash is on the 1790 NC Census, Rutherford Co., Morgan district, Thirteen Company (now Buncombe Co.) with 3 males, and 1 female.

Martin Gash is on the 1800 NC Census, Buncombe Co., with 4 males and 1 female.

Ben Gudger is on the 1790 NC Census, Burke Co., Morgan district (now Buncombe Co.) with 2 males and 1 female.

Benjamin Gudger is on the 1800 NC Census, Buncombe Co., with 3 males and 3 females.

Wm. Gudger is on the 1790 NC Census Burke Co., Morgan District, Eleventh Company with 3 males, 6 females, and 1 slave.

William Gudger is on the 1800 Census, Buncombe Co., with 4 males, 3 females, and 2 slaves.

Wm. Whitson is on the 1790 Census, Burke Co., Morgan District, Eleventh Company, with 6 males, 2 females, and 2 slaves.

William Whittson is on the 1800 NC Census, Buncombe Co., with 7 males, 3 females, and 3 slaves.

John Whittson is on the 1800 NC Census, Buncombe Co., with 1 male.

Selected References

Anonymous, 2005, William Gudger, War Pension claim W15772: Asheville, NC, *A Lot of Bunkum*, vol. 26, no. 4, p. 19

Felmet, L. Holt, Jr., 2007, Reader's Comments: William Gudger: Asheville, NC, *A Lot of Bunkum*, vol. 28, no. 3, p. 30

Haller, Charles R., 2007, Pioneer William Gudger, Sr.: Asheville, NC, *A Lot of Bunkum*, vol. 28, no. 1, p. 18-21

White, Emmett R., 1984, *Revolutionary War Soldiers of Western North Carolina. Vol. I, Burke Co.*: Easley, NC, Southern Historical Press, 318 p.

Eugene Willis Gudger, Hezekiah Alexander Gudger, and James Madison Gudger, Jr. are listed in *Dictionary of North Carolina Biography*.

Note: modified in part from Speck, Gary B., 2005, Family Pages for the Descendants of William Gudger: *website: Ancestry.com*, 110 p.

Descendants of Dr. J. F. E. Hardy

Name	Cemetery
1. James Freeman Epps Hardy (1802-1882) **MD** (1)	
+ 1st Jane Shaw Patton (1808-c.1838) (7 child.)	(?Charleston, SC)
2. James Patton Hardy (c.1825-1847) (2)	
2. Emma Hardy (1828-1924)	Riverside
+ Gilbert Boudinot Tennent (1816-1879)	Riverside
2. John Geddings Hardy (1830-1885) **MD, CSA** (3)	?Riverside
+ Anna E. _____ (c.1833-c.1894)	?Riverside
2. Charles Wesley Hardy (1832-1833)	
2. George Phillips Hardy (1803-d. young)	
2. Col. Washington Morrison Hardy (1834-____) **CSA**	
+ Mary Rebecca C. Erwin.(1825-____)	
3. Erwin T. Hardy (1865-____)	
3. Ann G. Hardy (1867-____)	
3. James E. Hardy (1869-____)	

*****

+ 2nd Cordelia Haywood Erwin (1812-c.1875) (2 child.)	
2. William Henry Hardy (1842-1861) **CSA** (4)	1st Presby. Asheville
2. Erwin E. Hardy (1849-____)	

Footnotes:

(1) Burial place of Dr. James Freeman Epps Hardy is not determined. He may be buried under the First Presbyterian Church of Asheville. His wife, Jane Shaw Patton, died at an early age and likely is buried at Charleston, SC. She descends from the Asheville Pattons.

James F. E. Hardy bought 320 acres on the Swannanoa River from Clerk & Master in Equity, Bk 19/182, 4-14-1834. He is listed in the 1830 Census, Buncombe Co., with 4 males and 2 females.

(2) James Patton Hardy was killed in the Mexican War at the siege of Pueblo.

(3) A marble marker for Dr. John Geddings Hardy was moved from an unknown location, possibly the First Presbyterian Church Cemetery, and put in a Patton plot at Riverside Cemetery in the 1890s.

(4) William Henry Hardy achieved notoriety as being the first soldier from Buncombe Co., NC to fall in the War Between the States, at the First Battle of Manassas. In 1931, the DAR placed a bronze plaque in his honor in the Buncombe County Court House.

Selected References

Haller, Charles R., 2007, The Mysterious Drs. Hardy: Asheville, NC, *A Lot of Bunkum*, vol. 28, no. 3, p. 27,p. 26-27

Matthews, Elle R., 2007, William Henry Hardy: *A Lot of Bunkum*, vol. 28, no. 2, p. 16-17

Descendants of Robert Henry
son of Thomas Henry from Ireland, wife Martha Shields

<u>Name</u>	<u>Cemetery</u>
1. Robert Henry, (1765-1863) **RW** (1)	(Clay Co.)
+ Dorcas Bell Love (1797-1857) (7 child.)	Henry/Asheville Sch.
2. Mary Louise Henry (1815-1844) 1st wife (3 child.)	Henry/Asheville Sch.
+ Reuben Deaver (1809-1852) (2)	Henry/Asheville Sch.
2. Capt. Robert Marcellus Henry (1821-1885) **CSA**	(Macon Co.)
+ Mary E._____	
2. Elizabeth Isabella Henry (1822-1915) (6 child.)	Cedar Hill Baptist
+ William B. Tidwell (1st of 3 husbands)	(?Clay Co.)
3. Mary Belle Tidwell (1841-1922)	Henry/Asheville Sch.
+ George Newton Taylor (1834-1910)	Henry/Asheville Sch.
2. Capt. William Lewis Henry (1823-1900) **CSA**	Henry/Asheville Sch.
+ Cornelia Catherine Smith (1836-1917) (13 child.)	Acton U. M.
3. Robert Pinckney Henry (1856-1911)	(Winston-Salem)
+ Minnie Alice Trogdon (4 child.)	
3. Cora Aletha Henry (1857-1858)	Henry/Asheville Sch.
3. Mary Arizona Henry (1859-1942)	Henry/Asheville Sch.
+ John B. Hyatt (1860-	
3. William Smith Henry (1861-1888)	Henry/Asheville Sch.
3. Gustavus Adolphus Henry (1863-c.1875)	?Henry/Asheville Sch.
3. Edmond Lee Henry (1865-1934)	Henry/Asheville Sch.
+ Mary E. Powell (1865-1945)	Henry/Asheville Sch.
3. Sidney Polk Henry (1867- 1891)	Henry/Asheville Sch.
3. Kate Love Henry (1868-1946)	Acton U. M.
+ E. J. Boyles	
3. Sallie L. Henry (1869-c.1875)	?Henry/Asheville Sch.
3. James T. Henry (1872-1947)	Henry/Asheville Sch.
3. Arthur L. Henry (1874-1919)	?Henry/Asheville Sch.
+ 1st Maggie Davis	
+ 2nd Mrs. Mantie Britt	
3. Walter Vance Henry (1877-1945)	Acton U. M.
+ Helen Marion Orphin (1896-1937)	Riverside
4. William Vance Henry (1913-2000)	
+ Mayburr E. Osborne (1909-	
4. Marion Henry	
3. Wade Hampton Henry (1879-1924)	Acton U.M.
+ Emma Jones	
2. Martha Ann Henry (1825-1896)	(Richland Co., SC)
+ Edgar John Arthur	(Richland Co., SC)
2. Lt. Col. James Love Henry (1835-1884) **CSA**	Riverside
+ Mollie A. _____ (3 child.)	

Footnotes:

(1) Jos. Henry is on the 1790 NC Census, Morgan District, Lincoln Co., Eleventh Company with 4 males and 3 females.

Joseph Henry is on the 1800 NC Census, Buncombe Co. with 3 males, 2 females, and 8 slaves. He was a prominent land speculator in Buncombe Co. as well as elsewhere.

Robert Henry is shown neither on the 1790 NC Census nor on the 1800 NC Census; likely he was in the household of Joseph Henry. Joseph Henry and Robert Henry jointly received NC land grants 907 and 1592 in 1801 and 1804.

Joseph Henry and Robert Henry were cousins.

(2) Reuben Deaver, proprietor of the Sulphur Springs Hotel, married 1st Mary Louise Henry who died 1844, and 2nd Mary S. Torion, born 1819. When Reuben Deaver died prematurely, the hotel was taken over by his brother-in-law William L. Henry. The hotel, which in 1849 had a capacity of 150 guests, burned in 1862.

Selected References

Clinard, Karen L., & Richard Russell, 2008, *Fear in North Carolina. The Civil War Journals and letters of the William Henry Family*: Asheville, NC, Reminiscing Books, 444 p.

Haller, Charles R., 2007, Robert Henry and His Clan: Asheville, NC, *A Lot of Bunkum*, vol. 28, no. 2, p. 7-15.

Descendants of James Hughey

Name	Cemetery
1. James Hughey, (ca. 1777-____)	
+ Ellen _____	
2. Samuel Hughey (1802-1886)	Hughey
+ Margaret Young Brank (1807-1900)	Hughey
3. Newton Robert Hughey (1834-____)	?Hughey
3. Clarissa Ann Hughey (1836-1916)	Hughey
+ Lafayette Patton (no child.)	
+ Robert A. Jones (2 child.)	
+ Silas Martin Stroup (5 child.)	
3. Julia Ann Hughey (1851-1934) unmarried	?Hughey
3. Harriett Rebecca Hughey (1845-1909)	?Hughey
+ Joseph Cordell	
3. James Marion Hughey (1847-1937)	Hughey
+ 1st Laura Timothy Morgan (1854-1927)	Hughey
4. Ida Blanche Hughey (1873-____)	
+ W. C. Craig	
4. Margaret Anna Hughey (1875-____)	
+ James Smith	
4. Arthur Lee Hughey (1877-1923)	
+ Rosa Lee Self	
4. Carrie Ellen Hughey (1879-____)	
+ G. W. Shope	
4. James Ernest Hughey, d. 1880	Hughey
4. Segernia Getrude Hughey (1882-1955)	
+ Luther Ray	
4. John Morgan Hughey (1887-1939)	Hughey
4. Walter Glen Hughey (1889-1971)	Hughey
+ Lillie Dale Keasler Hughey (1904-1949)	Hughey
5. Ruth Hughey (1921-____)	
5. James Anderson Hughey (1922-1946)	Hughey
5. Morris Whittington Hughey (1923-____)	
5. John Calvin Hughey (1928-1986)	Hughey
5. Walter Corbitt Hughey (1933-____)	
4. Ivan Goodrich Hughey (1894-1975)	
+ Ida Riddle	
4. Roy Duncan Hughey (1895-1983)	Hughey
+ Nellie Gertrude Allison (1897-1984?)	
5. James Donald Hughey (1918-____)	?Hughey
+ Iris Virginia Ray Hughey (1914-1990)	Hughey
5. William Joyce Hughey	
5. Marjorie Belle Hughey	
5. Hazel Irene Hughey	
4. Kenneth William Hughey (1897-1969)	Hughey
+ Pearl Rosie Robinson (1904-1980)	Hughey
4. Raymond Hughey (1901-1977)	Hughey
+ 2nd Cynthia Ophelia Sloan Tucker (no child.)	Hughey
3. Laura Elizabeth Hughey (1849-1908), unmarried	?Hughey
3. Christopher Alexander Hughey (1848-____)	
+ Allie Femster	

<u>Name</u>	<u>Cemetery</u>
3. Adeline Hughey (1853-1903), unmarried	?Hughey
2. Six others:	Hughey
Sallie, George, Ann, Julia, Joseph Lawrence, & James Washington	Hughey

Misc. Hughey Family Cemetery Burials:
James M. Hughey, 1880-1953
James E. Hughey, 1884-1973

Census Records:

Joseph Hughey is on the 1790 NC Census, Burke Co., Morgan District, Thirteenth Company (now the City of Morganton) with 1 male and 2 females.

Joseph Hughey is on the 1800 NC Census , Buncombe Co., with 2 males and 4 females.

James Hughey is on the 1800 NC Census, Buncombe Co. with 2 males, 2 females, and 1 slave.

Editor'sNotes

The two brothers, Joseph Hughey (born ca. 1768) and James Hughey (born ca. 1777), apparently were born in Rowan Co., NC.

In April, 1795, Joseph Hughey bought lots 5, 29, and 30 in the village of Morrisville from John Burton. Also in April, 1795, James Hughey bought lot 18 from John Burton.

Joseph Hughey was the first sheriff of Buncombe Co., NC, being sheriff from 1792 to 1797. James Hughey was sheriff in 1798 and 1799.

About 1820, Joseph Hughey migrated to Jefferson Co., IN, while James Hughey settled near Democrat, in northern Buncombe Co. A strong descendant contingent of James Hughey remained in the vicinity of Riceville, NC.

Selected References

Felmet, L. Holt, 2006, Hughey-Rice Families, Asheville, NC, *A Lot of Bunkum*, vol. 27, no. 4, p. 20-21, 23

Haller, Charles R., 2006, Hughey Family Cemetery, Bull Creek Rd., Riceville: Asheville, NC, *A Lot of Bunkum*, vol. 27, no. 3, p. 21-23

Descendants of Andreas Killian

<u>Name</u>	<u>Cemetery</u>
1. Andreas Killian, Sr. (1702-1788) **RW** (12 child.) (1)	?Newton, NC
+ 1st Margaret Fischer	
+ 3rd Mary Cline?	
2. Daniel Killian, Sr. (c.1750-c.1832) **RW** (2)	Asbury Meth.
+ 1st Osley Baker (____-____) (7 child.)	
3. John Killian (1788-1869)	(Georgia)
+ Priscilla Lee Askew (1 child.)	
3. Joseph Killian (1791-1867)	(Haywood Co.)
+ Ann Petchey (1790-1866) (4 child.)	(Haywood Co.)
3. Daniel Killian, Jr. (1793-1872)	(Georgia)
+ Mary Washan (____-____) (7 child.)	
3. Mary Killian (c.1795-____) (3 child.)	(Georgia)
+ John Smart	
3. Nancy Killian (1796-1839)	Asbury Meth.
3. William W. Killian (1800-1860)	Asbury Meth.
+ Emily McKay (1814-1908) (4 child.)	
3. George Killian (1802-1880)	(South Carolina)
+ Polly Johnson (1808-1887) (7 child.)	
+ 2nd Charlotte _____ (1764-1840) (1 child.)	
3. Lydia Killian (1805-1887)	(Alabama)
+ George W. Bell	

Footnotes:

(1) Andreas Killian migrated from Germany and arrived in Philadelphia in 1732 via the ship *Adventure*. He went to Anson Co., NC (now Lincoln Co.) about 1749. He sired 12 children: (a) namely Margaret, Leonard, and John by his 1st wife Margaret; (b) Jean, Margaret (Crate), Andrew, George, and Brine by an unknown wife; and (c) Daniel, Samuel G., Christine, and Elizabeth by his 3rd wife.

(2) Brothers Daniel Killian, Sr. and Samuel G. Killian served in the Revolutionary War.

Census Records:

Daniel Killian is on the 1790 NC Census, Burke Co., Morgan District, Eleventh Company (now Buncombe Co.) with 3 males and 1 female.

Daniel Killian is on the 1800 NC Census , Buncombe Co. with 5 males and 4 females.

Selected References

See Killian in the Land Grant Section.

Descendants of Carolyn Lane
(see also Lowery/Lowry)

Name	Cemetery
1. Carolyn Lane (1761-1842) (12 child.)	Sandy Mush Meth.
+ 1st David Lowery, Jr. (____-1787)	(Georgia)
2. Mary Lowry (1781-1819)	
+ unknown Hansen	
2. James Lowry (1783-1857)	Sandy Mush Meth.
+ 1st Esther Siler (1786-1849) (12 child.)	Sandy Mush Meth.
3. Elizabeth Siler Lowry (1819-1908) (8 child.)	Samuel B. Gudger
+ Samuel Bell Gudger (1808-1888)	Samuel B. Gudger
3. James Marion Lowry (1820-1901)	Samuel B. Gudger
+ Harriet F. McKee (1827-1915)	Samuel B. Gudger
+ 2nd Hannah E. Patton McKee (1788-1867)	Sandy Mush Meth.
2. Charles Lowry (1784-____)	
2. Patience Lowry (1787-1867)	
+ Erwin _____	
<div align="center">*****</div>	
+ 2nd George Edward Swain, Sr. (1763-1829) (1)	Newton Academy
2. Caroline Swain (1789-1792)	
2. Cynthia Swain (1791-1829) (10 child.)	Coleman
+ William Coleman (1785-1874)	Coleman
2. George Swain, Jr. (1792-1877)	
+ Frances Taylor	
2. Caroline Swain (1795-1828)	
+ John Hall	
2. Matilda Swain (1797-1858) (5 child.)	(Macon Co., NC)
+ Jacob Siler (1795-1871)	(Macon Co., NC)
2. Althea Swain (1798-1846)	(Macon Co., NC)
+ William Siler	(Macon Co., NC)
2. David Lowry Swain (1801-1868) **Gov.** (2)	(Raleigh, NC)
+ Eleanor Hope White (____-1882) (6 child.)	(Raleigh, NC)
3. Anne Caroline Swain (1829-1867)	(Raleigh, NC)
3. David Swain I (1830-1831)	(Raleigh, NC)
3. David Lowry Swain (1834-1840)	(Raleigh, NC)
3. Richard Caswell Swain (1837-1872) **MD**	(Freeport, IL)
+ 1st Susan E. Burt (____-1862)	
+2nd Margaret L. Steele (1844-1895) (2 child.)	Riverside
4. Eleanor L. Swain (1863-1947) (4 child.)	Riverside
+ 1st James S. Grant	
+ 2nd Thaddeus E. Clayton (1863-1941)	Riverside
3. Ella Swain (1842-1843)	(Raleigh, NC)
3. Eleanor Hope Swain (1843-1881) (6 child.)	(Raleigh, NC)
+ Smith Dykins Atkins (1835-1913) Gen.	(Freeport, IL)
4. Eleanor Hope Atkins (1869-____)	
+ Needham Tyndale Cobb	
2. Mary Swain (1803-1829)	Sandy Mush Meth.

Footnotes:

(1) George Swain was Postmaster at Asheville from 1807 to 1827. Col. William Davidson sold Lot 27 in Morristown (later Asheville) to George Swain in April, 1799.

(2) George's son, David Lowry Swain, was governor of North Carolina from 1832 to 1835, and president of the University of North Carolina from 1835 to 1868.

David Lowry Swain had enormous influence on the history of Western North Carolina and on the University of North Carolina. A short page on David Lowry Swain is in the 1994 *Dictionary of North Carolina Biography*. Unfortunately, no published book length biography on this important individual is available.

Census Records:

Charles Lane is listed on the 1800 NC Census, Buncombe Co., with 6 males, 2 females, and 8 slaves.

George Swain is listed on the 1800 NC Census, Buncombe Co. with 5 males, 6 females, and 3 slaves.

Selected References

Barile, Suzy, 2009, *Undaunted Heart: The True Story of a Southern Belle and a Yankee General*: Hillsborough, NC, Eno Publ., 237 p.

Haller, Charles R., 2006, Why Was Caroline Swain Buried at Sandy Mush?: Asheville, NC, *A Lot of Bunkum*, vol. 27, no. 2, p. 23-24

_____, 2007a, Descendants of David Lowry, Sr.: *ibid*, vol. 28, no. 3, p. 25

_____, 2007b, Caroline Swain Again: *ibid*, vol. 28, no. 4, p. 15-18

McNab, Christine C. & Charles R. Haller, 2010, Descendants of Caroline Lane (updated): Asheville, NC, *A Lot of Bunkum*, vol. 31, no. 1 p.26-27

Descendants of Samuel Bell Love

Name	Cemetery
<u>Name</u>	<u>Cemetery</u>
1. Samuel Bell Love (____-1781)	(Virginia)
+ Dorcas Bell (____-c.1774)(6 child.)	(Virginia)
2. Robert Love (1760-1845) **RW**	Green Hill (1)
+ Mary Ann Dillard (1767-1842) (12 child.)	Green Hill
3. Thomas Dillard Love (c.1784-1832)	
+ Anna Taylor (1794-1843) (9 child.)	
3. Anne Dillard Love (1787-1861)	?Gudgers Chapel
+ James Madison Gudger (1782-1861)	?Gudgers Chapel
3. Dillard Love (1789-1872)	(Macon Co.)
+ Margaret Young (1799-1869) (2 child.)	(Macon Co.)
3. John Bell Love (1791-1873)	(Haywood Co.)
+ Margaret E. Coman (1810-1893) (11 child.)	(Haywood Co.)
3. William Calhoun Love (1794-1838)	(Tennessee)
+ Elizabeth Jordan (1801-1838) (7 child.)	(Tennessee)
3. Winnifred Sophia Love (1796-1873) (7 child)	(South Carolina)
+ 1st Michael Moore (1791-1826)	(South Carolina)
+ 2nd James A. Miller (1800-1854)	(South Carolina)
3. Dorcas Bell Love (1797-1857) (7 child.)	Henry Cem. (2)
+ Robert Henry (1767-1863) **RW**	(Macon Co.)
3. James Robert Love (1799-1863)	Green Hill
+ Maria W. Coman (1805-1847) (8 child.)	Green Hill
4. Sarah J.B. Love (1833-1877) (3 child.)	Green Hill
+ William Holland Thomas (1805-1893) **CSA**	Green Hill
3. Martha Webb Love (1799-1819) (no child.)	Green Hill
+ William Welch (1796-1865)	
3. Sarah Bell Love (1802-1870) (8 child.)	(Tennessee)
+ Ganum Cox McBee (1799-1880)	(Tennessee)
3. Mary Ann Love (1805-1865) (10 child.)	Green Hill
+ William Welch (1796-1865)	Green Hill
3. Rebecca Love (1807-1831) (1 child.)	
+ Lorenzo Dow Patton (1804-1870)	
2. Thomas Love (1766-1844)	(Henry Co., TN)
+ Martha Dillard (1774-1832)(4 child.)	(Henry Co., TN)
3. Albert G. Love (1814-1851)	(Henry Co. TN)

Selected References

Freeman, Clyde S., 1980, *Robert Love. A Biographical Sketch*: Escondido, CA, unpubl. mss, 29 p.

Jurgelski, Bill, 2002, The Robert Love Survey Map. An Important Link to Macon County's Past: Franklin, NC, *Echoes*, vol. 15, no. 1, p. 4-7 & 82 (1820 survey map)

Footnotes:

(1) Green Hill Cemetery is in Waynesville, Haywood Co.

(2) The Henry Cemetery, variously called Sulphur Springs, Asheville Academy, etc., is in West Asheville.

Census Records:

James Love (Sr.) is on the 1790 NC Census, Stokes Co., Salisbury District, with 2 males, 7 females, and 7 slaves.

James Love (Jr.) is on the NC Census, Stokes Co., Salisbury District, with 1 male and 2 females.

Robert Love is on the 1790 Census, Rowan Co., Salisbury District, with 2 males and 6 females.

Thomas Love is on the 1790 NC Census, Stokes Co., Salisbury District, with 2 males and 3 females.

Thomas Love is on the 1800 NC Census, Buncombe Co., with 6 males, 2 females, and 7 slaves.

Editor's Notes

Robert Love entered 150 acres in 1792 in what later became Haywood Co., NC. In subsequent years, with various partners, he entered another 1,560 acres. About 1800, a tiny village, Mount Prospect developed on land owned by Love. In 1810, the village name was changed to Waynesville when Love donated land for a courthouse and jail. In earlier years, 1778 to 1783, Robert Love had entered for 974 acres of land, in 4 blocks, which was located mostly in eastern TN. Love died in Waynesville and is buried there.

In the years 1795 to 1812, a younger brother, Thomas Love entered 500 acres in the general area of Waynesville. Thomas later migrated to Macon Co., NC and still later to Henry Co., TN, where he is buried. In the period after 1778, Thomas Love entered for 5 blocks in Tennessee, totaling 1740 acres. Thomas Love is buried in Henry Co., TN.

Robert Love and his wife Mary Ann Dillard had 12 children and 85 grandchildren. A son-in-law Robert Henry and a grandson-in law, William Holland Thomas, were noted frontier lawyers and otherwise achieved noteworthy careers. The career of Robert Henry is cited in the section on the Henry family.

William Holland Thomas was the subject of several books in connection with the 1835 rescue of some 1,100 Oconaluftee Cherokees from deportation to Oklahoma and with the formation of a reservation known as the Qualla Boundary, an area currently comprising 58,854 acres in western North Carolina. In 1840, Thomas paid the heirs of speculator William Carthcart $1,200 for 33,000 acres. By the Civil War, Thomas and the tribe had accumulated 148,000 acres, which was later partly sold. The reservation was first surveyed only in 1876 and officially designated as a reservation only in 1975.

Descendants of David Lowery, Jr. (see also Lane)

Name	Cemetery
1. David Lowery, Jr. (____-1787)	(Georgia)
+ 1st Caroline Lane (1761-1842) (m. 2nd George Swain)	Sandy Mush Meth.
2. Mary Lowry (1781-1919)	
2. James Lowry (1783-1857)	Sandy Mush Meth.
+ 1st Esther Siler (1786-1849) (11 child.)	Sandy Mush Meth.
3. Caroline Lane Lowry (1805-1832) (4 child.)	Sandy Mush Meth.
+ David B. Cummings	(Missouri)
3. Margaret O'Rafferty Lowry (1808-____)	(Georgia)
+ 1st Christley Weaver	(Georgia)
+ 2nd Pierce Roberts	
3. Elizabeth Siler Lowry (1809-1809)	
3. David Richardson Lowry (1812-1861)	
+ Ann Harshaw Wiley	
3. Mathilda Swain Lowry (1814-1899)	(Macon Co.)
+ 1st James Madison Robinson (1810-1843)	
+ 2nd James K. Gray	
3. Mary Hanson Lowry (1817-1832)	Sandy Mush Meth.
3. Elizabeth Siler Lowry (1819-1908) (8 child.)	Samuel B. Gudger
+ Samuel Bell Gudger (1808-1888)	Samuel B. Gudger
4. Mary Caroline Gudger (1833-1917)	Oak Forest Presby.
+ William Hamilton Moore (1824-1879) **War of 1812**	Oak Forest Presby.
3. James Marion Lowry (1820-1901)	Samuel B. Gudger
+ Harriet F. McKee (1827-1915) (8 child.)	Samuel B. Gudger
3. Harriet Althea Lowry (1823-1903) (8 child.)	(Cherokee Co.)
+ Burton K. Dickey (1813-1885)	(Cherokee Co.)
3. Thomas Siler Lowry (1823-1849)	(Mississippi)
3. Cynthia Louise Lowry (1826-____) (4 child.)	(?Henderson Co.)
+ James Patton (1817-1854)	
3. Lorena Patience Lowry (1828-1907) (4 child.)	Montmorenci Meth.
+ Randolph Newman Henry (1826-1889)	Montmorenci Meth.
2. Charles Lowry (1784-____)	
2. Patience Lowry (1787-1867)	

*****

James Lowery+	
2nd Hannah E. McKee (1788-1867)	Sandy Mush Meth.

Census Records:

For an unknown reason, none of the above Lowery/Lowrys are apparent in either the 1790 NC Census, or in the 1800 Buncombe Co. Census.

James Lowrie is in the 1810 Buncombe Co. Census with 2 males, 3 females, and 6 slaves.

Selected References

Allen, William C., (1935) 1977, *The Annals of Haywood County, NC*: Spartanburg, SC, The Reprint Co., 714 p., reprint with new genealogical index

Porter, Leona B., 1951, *Lowry Family: in The Family of Weimar Siler*: Franklin, NC, 100th Mtg. Committee, (Silar family)188 p.

Data modified from an unpublished mss. at UNCA by Mary Gudger Moore and from *A Lot of Bunkum*, vol. 28, no. 3 (2007), and vol. 31, no. 1 (2010).

Descendants of Capt. Thomas Lytle

Name	Cemetery
1. Capt. Thomas Lytle, Sr. (1750-1835) **RW** (1)	Bethel C. S.
+ Susanah Perkins (c.1752-1840) (5 child.)	Bethel C. S.
2. John P. Lytle (1784-1861+) never married	(McDowell Co.)
2. George Lytle (1785-1858)	Bethel C. S.
+ Ann Clark (1785-1860+) (8 child.)	
3. Rebecca Lytle (1807-1865) (9 child.)	
+ Wilson Bird (1807-c.1886)	Bethel C. S.
3. Susannah Lytle (1818-1866)	
3. Millington Lytle (1809-1899)	
+ 1st Rebecca Burgin (1817-1860) (1 child.)	
4. Mary Ann Lytle (1840-1931)	Cane Creek
+ 2nd Mary Whitaker (1841-1931)+3x (3 child.)	
4. Margaret C. Lytle, (1872-1875)	Cane Creek
4. Thomas Henry Lytle (1874-____)	
4. George Whitaker Lytle (1876-____)+2x	
+ 1st Alice Sisk (5 child.)	
4. Effie Jerusho Lytle (1883-1886)	Cane Creek
3. James P. Lytle (1811-____)	
+ Margaret Clayton?	
4. John Mills Lytle (1840-1900)	
3. Littleton Lytle (1812-1897)	Sharon
+ 1st Mary W. Burgin (1813-1857) (8 child.)	Sharon
+ 2nd Minerva A. Gilliam (1838-1917) (8 child.)	Sharon
3. Thomas B. Lytle (1816-1889)	(Arkansas)
+ 1st Mary M. Lytle (____-1856)	Bethel C.S.
+ 2nd Nancy Phipps (2 child.)	
+ 3rd _____ Nancy Burgin (3 child.)	
3. John Lytle (1820-1892)	Bethel C.S.
+ Elizabeth Lytle (1823-1910) (7 child.)	Bethel C.S.
4. Milton Potillo (1845-1921)	
3. George Mills Lytle (1821-____)	
+ 1st Emily Ballew (c. 1821-c.1859) (3 child.)	
+ 2nd Amanda M. Williams (n.d.) (4 child.)	
2. Millington Lytle (c.1789-1874)	
+ Polly Potillo (1791-c.1870)	
2. Elizabeth Adeline Lytle (1796-1837) (4 child.)	Piney Grove
+ John Burgin, Jr. (1799-1884)	Piney Grove
2. Thomas Lytle, Jr. (1797-1883) (2)	Campground
+ Jennie McEntire (1797-1873?) (10 child.)	Campground
3. Joseph McEntire Lytle (1821-1862)	
+ Rachel Ann Burgin (1827-1862) (6 child.)	
4. George Logan Lytle (1859-1940)	
+ Mary Ella Gudger (1862-1946) (5 child.)	

Editor's Notes:

Thomas Little, Sr. (or Lytle) entered a land grant on the Catawba River in 1778 and apparently resided there soon thereafter. He has a monument at the Bethel-Cherry Springs Methodist cemetery, located about 5 miles south of Old Fort, McDowell Co.

Thomas Lytle, Jr. is buried in the Campground Cemetery, McDowell Co.

Selected References

Lytle, C. Roy, 1996, *Descendants of Captain Thomas Lytle*: Matthews, NC, privately printed, 299 p.

Silvers, Peggy G., 2008, *Echoes in the Mist, The Burgin Family 1623-2008*: Nebo, NC, privately printed, c. 750 p., 2nd, rev. ed.

White, Emmett R., 1984, *Revolutionary War Soldiers of Western North Carolina. Vol. I, Burke Co.*: Easley, SC, Southern Historical Press, 318 p.

Descendants of Ephraim McDowell, 1729 immigrant

Name	Cemetery
1. Ephraim McDowell, Sr. (1672-1755+)	(Virginia)
+ Margaret Irvine (1674-1728 (4 child.)	(Ireland)
2. James McDowell (c.1698-____)	
+ (unknown)	
2. Thomas McDowell (c.1699-1765)	
+ Janet Reid (1704-1787)	
2. Margaretta McDowell (c.1703-____) (5 child.)	(South Carolina)
+ James Mitchell (____-____) (1)	(South Carolina)
3. Mary Mitchell (1745-1787)	
+ James Greenlee, Jr. (1740-1813)	
3. Maj. Ephraim Mitchell (____-1792) **RW**	
2. Alexander McDowell (c.1706-____)	
2. Mary Elizabeth McDowell (1711-1809) (9 child.)	(Virginia)
+ James Greenlee (c.1707-1757)	
2. Capt. John McDowell (c.1714-1742)	(Virginia)
+ Magdalene C. Woods (c.1706-c.1797) (married 3x)	
3. Col. Samuel McDowell (1735-1817) **RW**	(Danville, KY)
+ Mary McClung (1733-1827) (12 child.)	(Danville, KY)
4. Dr. Ephraim McDowell (1771-1830) **MD**	
+ Sarah Shelby (____-____) (9 child.)	
3. James B. McDowell (1739-1771)	(Virginia)
+ Elizabeth Cloyd (c.1736-1810) (6 child.)	
4. James McDowell	
+ Sarah Preston (____-____) (3 child.)	
5. James McDowell (1796-1851)	(Virginia)
+ Susanna S. Preston (10 child.)	(Virginia)
3. Sarah Martha McDowell (1741-1811) (12 child.)	
+ George B. Moffitt (1735-1811)	
4. Margaret Moffitt (1763-1816) (6 child.)	?Quaker Meadows
+ Joseph McDowell, Jr. (1756-1801) QM	Quaker Meadows
4. Mary Moffitt (1768-1825) (10 child.)	?Round Hill
+ 1st Joseph McDowell (PG)(1758-c.1796) **RW**	?Round Hill
+ 2nd John Carson (1752-1841) **RW**	?Round Hill

Footnotes:

The line includes a number of individuals who had prominent roles in the Revolutionary War.

(1) For instance, four sons of the Mitchell family were in the War; at this time only the name of Maj. Ephraim Mitchell has been recorded.

(2) The Revolutionary War activities of Joseph McDowell QM, and Joseph McDowell PG, have been described by Emmett R. White, 1984, *op cit*. Modifed from *A Lot of Bunkum*, vol. 30, no. 2 (2009)

Descendants of Capt. Joseph McDowell, 1729 immigrant

<u>Name</u>   <u>Cemetery</u>

1. Joseph McDowell, Sr. (c.1715-1771)   Quaker Meadows
   + Virginia Margaret O'Neil (c.1719-c.1780)(7 child.)   (?Ireland)
    2. Sarah Nancy McDowell (1739-c.1800)
    + Charles Finley (1736-1816)
    2. Col. Charles McDowell (c.1743-1815) QM, **RW**   Quaker Meadows
    + Grace Greenlee Bowman (1750-1823) (7 child.)   Quaker Meadows
      3. Margaret McDowell (1783-1850+)   (Caldwell Co.)
      + William G. Dickson (1775-1855)   (Caldwell Co.)
      3. Capt. Charles McDowell, Jr. (1785-1859)   Quaker Meadows
      + Anna McDowell (1793-1859)(8 child.)   Quaker Meadows
        4. Eliza Grace McDowell (1816-1876)(5 child)   Riverside
        + Nicholas W. Woodfin (1810-1876) **CSA**   Riverside
        4. Mira Adeline McDowell (1822-1872)   Riverside
        + 1st John Wood Woodfin (1819-1863) **CSA**   Riverside
        + 2nd Rev. John S. Burnett
        4. Margaret Ann McDowell (1828-1856)(2 child.)
        + William Finley McKesson (1813-1870+) (1)
      3. Sarah Grace McDowell (1787-____)   (Transylvania Co.)
      +William Paxton ((1783-1875)   (Transylvania Co.)
      3. Athan Allen McDowell (1790-1832)   Quaker Meadows
      + Ann Ballard Gordon (1795-1859)(4 child.)   ?Quaker Meadows
      3. James R. McDowell (1792-1826)   Quaker Meadows
      3. Eliza Grace McDowell (179_-____)
      + Stanhope Erwin
      3. William McDowell (1801-1865)
      + Priscilla Wright Withers (c.1806-____)(3 child.)
    2. Elizabeth McDowell (1741-1825)(3 child.)   (Kentucky)
    + John McKinny (c.1735-1805)   (Kentucky)
    2. Hugh McDowell (1742-1772)   Quaker Meadows
    + Jane _____ (c.1742-____) (4 child.)
    2. Hannah McDowell (1747-1817)(5 child.)   (Kentucky)
    + George Chrisman (1745-1816)   (Kentucky)
    2. Jane McDowell (1750-1838)(11 child.)
    + Capt. John Brown (1738-1812)
    2. Maj. John McDowell (1751-1822)   McDowell Presbyt.
    + Hannah Keller (1755-1832)(5 child.)   McDowell Presbyt.
    2. Joseph McDowell, Jr. (1756-1801) QM, **RW**   Quaker Meadows
    + Margaret Moffitt (1763-1816)(8 child.)   (?Kentucky)
      3. Joseph Jefferson McDowell (1800-1877)   (Ohio)
      + Sarah Allen McCue (1804-1885)(6 child.)   (Kentucky)
        4. Rachel A. T. McDowell (1826-1900)(8 child.)
        + Andrew McMicken, Jr.

Editor's notes:

Revolutionary War activities of Joseph McDowell QM and Charles McDowell QM are described in Emmet R. White, 1984. Modified from *A Lot of Bunkum*, vol. 30, no. 2 (2009)

(1) By 1860, William F. McKesson was the largest holder of slaves in Burke Co. with 174 slaves that were primarily employed in gold mining and road building. At that time, his real estate was valued at $80,000 and personal property at $185,000.

Descendants of Hunting John McDowell, 1729 immigrant

Name	Cemetery
1. John McDowell (c.1717-1796) PG, **RW**	Round Hill?
+ Ann Evans Edmiston (c.1734-1814) (3 child.)	Round Hill?
2. Rachel Matilda McDowell(1756-1795) (7 child.)	Round Hill?
+ John Carson (1752-1841) (1st wife)	Round Hill?
2. Maj. Joseph McDowell (1758-c.1795) PG, **RW**	Round Hill?
+ 1st Mary Moffitt (1768-1825) (5 child.)	Round Hill?
3. George McDowell (1784-1804)	
3. John McDowell (1787-1855)	(Rutherford Co.)
+ Mary Mansfield Lewis (1790-1872) (10 child.)	?Riverside
4. Joseph Lewis McDowell (1812-1875)	
+ Louisa Jane Twitty (1824-1860) (8 child.)	
3. James Moffitt McDowell (1791-1854)	(Yancey Co.)
+ 1st Margaret C. Erwin (1801-1831) (7 child.)	(Burke Co.)
4. Mary McDowell	
4. James McDowell	
4. Joseph A. McDowell, Sr. (1821-1875) **CSA**	1st Presby.-Ash.
+ Julia Ann Patton (1827-1905) (11 child.)	
4. William Wallace McDowell (1823-1893) **CSA**	Riverside
+ Sarah Lucinda Smith (1826-1905) (10 child.)	Riverside
4. John Calhoun McDowell (1825-1876)	(Morganton)
+ Sarah Ann Erwin (1826-1903) (7 child.)	
4. Katherine A. E. McDowell (1826-1896) (2nd wife)	
+ Montraville Patton (1806-1896) **CSA**	
4. Margaret E.McDowell (1830-1860) (3 child.)	
+ John Marcus Erwin (1826-1881)	
(he m. 2nd Kate Smith)	

*****

+ 2nd Hannah Haynie (1820-1904) (5 child.)	
3. Anne McDowell (1793-1859) (6 child.)	
+ Charles McDowell, Jr. (1785-1858)	
3. Joseph McDowell, Jr. (1796-1800)	

*****

2. Anne McDowell (c.1760-1829) (10 child.)	(Tennessee)
+ William Whitson (1750-1806) **RW** (1)	?Cemetery Hill

Acknowledgements

Betty Jo McDowell Garret, of Morrisville, NC corrected many errors in the original draft of all the McDowell charts and otherwise contributed her expertise into McDowell family research.
Modified from *A Lot of Bunkum*, vol. 30, no. 2, p. 26-31 (2009)

1790 NC Census Records

Jas. McDowell is on the 1790 NC Census, Burke Co., Morgan District, 1st Company with 3 males, 2 females, and 2 slaves. PG

Jno. McDowell is on the 1790 NC Census, Burke Co., Morgan District, 1st Company with 2 males, 1 female, and 1 slave. PG

Jos. McDowell, Jr. is on the 1790 NC Census, Burke Co., Morgan District, 1st Company with 3 males, 1 female, and 9 slaves. PG

Jno. McDowell is on the 1790 NC Census, Burke Co., Morgan District, 6th Company with 4 males, 4 females, and 5 slaves.

Col. Jos. McDowell is on the 1790 NC Census, Burke Co., Morgan District, 7th Company with 2 males, 5 females, and 10 slaves. QM

Charles McDowell is on the 1790 NC Census, Burke Co., Morgan District, 7th Company with 3 males, 5 females, and 10 slaves. QM

Wm. McDowell is on the 1790 NC Census, Burke Co., Morgan District, 13th Company with 5 males and 4 females.

Editor's Notes:

(1) Revolutionary War veteran William Whitson achieved fame as Buncombe Co. Tax Collector, 1790-1806; Trustee of the Newton Academy, 1793; and Justice of the Peace, 1790-1796.

Whitson had land at the junction of Whitson's Creek (later T. W. Patton's Creek, and now Haw Creek), and the Swannanoa River.

Whitson died as the family was preparing to move to Maury Co., TN, and evidently is buried in Buncombe Co., possibly on Cemetery Hill.

The Revolutionary War activities of John McDowell PG and Joseph McDowell PG are in Emmett R. White, 1998.

Descendants of Dr. Joseph Lewis McDowell

<u>Name</u>

1. Dr. Joseph Lewis McDowell (1812-1875) **MD**
   + 1st Louise Jane Twitty (1824-1860) (8 child.)
   2. William Joseph McDowell (1853-1931)
   + Ione Vinson (1874-1954) (2 sons, 2 dau.)
      3. John William MacDowell (1892-1963)
      + Rainsford Fairbanks Dubose (1895-1981) (4 sons)
         4. McNeely Dubose MacDowell (1914-1976)
         + Dorothy Lee Kelly (1917-____)
         (she m. 2nd Henry Charles Wood)
         4. Rainsford Bayard MacDowell
         4. John Vinson MacDowell
         4. Marion St. Pierre MacDowell (1924-____)
         + 1st Pauline Johnston Oswald (1928-____) (4 dau.)
            5. Pauline Bayard MacDowell (1947-____)
            + Manuel James Rogers
            5. Julia Dubose MacDowell (1951-____)
            + Michael Holmes Fleming
            5. Beverly Oswald MacDowell (1956-____)
            + unknown
            5. Rosalie Anderson MacDowell (1958-____)
            + Paul Qualley
            + Rhett Hartzog
                              *****
         + 2nd Mary Frances Stone Steele (1935-____)
            5. Michael St. Pierre MacDowell (1967-____)
                              *****
   + 2nd Margaret Amandy Goy (1845-1872)

Editor's Notes

The above info from Dorothy Lee Kelly MacDowell, 1980, *McDowells in America*, p. 241-250.

Joseph Lewis McDowell was the son of John McDowell (1789-1855) and Mary Mansfield Lewis (1790-1872), and descendent of "Hunting John" McDowell, which see.

McDowells in Government

Burke Co., NC
1. Athan A. McDowell (1790-1832) QM,
   NC Senate 1825-1829
2. Charles McDowell (1743-1815) QM,
   NC Senate 1777-1778, 1782, 1784-1789,
   NC House of Commons 1809-1811,
   Land Entry taker, Burke Co., 1778-1785,
3. James McDowell
   NC Senate 1820, 1832
4. James R. McDowell (1792-1826) QM
   NC House of Commons 1817-1820
5. John McDowell (1751-1822)
   NC House of Commons 1792-93
6. Joseph McDowell (1758-c.1795) PG (name to McDowell Co., 1842)
   NC Council of State 1787,
   NC House of Commons 1780-1789,
   NC Senate 1790-1794,
   Assistant Marshall for NC for 1790 census,
   U.S. Representative 1793-1795
7. Joseph McDowell, Jr. (1756-1801) QM,
   NC House of Commons 1787-93,
   Elected to Continental Congress 1787 (did not attend),
   U.S. Representative 1797-1799

Highland Co., Ohio
8. Joseph Jefferson McDowell (1800-1877) son of no. 5 above
   Ohio Representative 1832,
   Ohio Senate 1833,
   U.S. Representative 1843-1847

Rutherford Co., NC
9. John McDowell (1787-1855)
   NC House of Commons 1820-1822

Descendants of John McLean, Immigrant

Name	Cemetery
1. John McLean (c.1700-____)	
+ Margaret Moore (c.1705-____)	(Logan Co., KY)
2. Charles McLean (c.1726-c.1805) **RW**	
+ Mrs. Susan Howard Allison (c.1735-1812)(3 child.)	
2. Ephraim McLean, Sr. (1730-1823) **RW**	(Muhlenberg Co. KY)
+ Elizabeth Davidson (1741-1820) (12 child.)	
3. Margaret McLean (1761-1837) (9 child.)	
+ Robert Brank, Jr. (1757-1846)	
3. Ephraim McLean, Jr. (1766-1812)	(Maury Co., TN)
+ Polly Boyd (____-____)(8 child.)	
3. George McLean (1767-1849)	(KY)
+ Pamela Davidson (1772-1851)(9 child.)	(Allensville, KY)
3. Jane McLean (1769-1847)(3 child.)	(Logan Co., KY)
+ Gen. Robert Ewing (1760-1832)	(Logan Co., KY)
3. Charles McLean (1778-1825)	(TN)
+ Sarah Vance (1780-1847) (10 child.)	(TN)

Editor's Notes

Good, but short biographies of the immigrants Charles and Ephraim McLean are in the 1937 book *History of old Tryon and Rutherford Counties, NC, 1730-1936*. These papers document the amazing travels of the brothers from Scotland, about 1748-1750, to Philadelphia, and utimately to North and South Carolina, and in later years, to Tennessee and Kentucky. Both brothers fought as privates at King's Mountain, but served as officers in the Militia.

In 1761, Ephraim McLean, Sr. (1730-1823), married Elizabeth Davidson (1741-1820), daughter of John Davidson (c.1709-1749) and Jane Morrison (c.1712-____) (Davidson Cluster B). In 1770, the brothers were commissioned Captains in the Tryon (Co.) troops.

In 1775, Ephraim McLain was shown in connection with a Safety Committee in Salisbury, Rowan Co.

In 1777, Ephraim McLean was in the House of Commons, representing Burke Co. In 1778, Ephraim McLean and Charles McLean were in the House of Commons, both representing Burke Co. Ephraim McLean occupied the same post in 1779. In 1778-1779, Ephraim McLean entered six land grants in Burke Co., NC. On the 1790 NC Census, Ephraim McLean (Jr.?) was listed in the Morgan District, Lincoln Co., Seventh Company, with 2 males, 1 female, 5 slaves.

Selected References

Emmett R. White, 1981, *Revolutionary War Soldiers of Western North Carolina. Vol. I, Burke Co*: Easley, SC, Southern Historical Press, 318 p.

Descendants of Branch H. Merrimon

Name	Cemetery
1. Branch Hamlin Merrimon (1802-1881), **Rev.- M. E.**	** (see below)
+ Mary Evelyn Paxton (1811-1849) (10 child.)	**
2. Augustus Summerfield Merrimon (1830-1892), **CSA**	(Raleigh)
+ Margaret Jane Baird (1834-1907) (8 child.)	(Raleigh)
2. Martha A. Merrimon (1832-1903)	Riverside
2. Sterling Chesterfield Merrimon (1834-1907)	(South Carolina)
+ Letitia Atonette Downey	(South Carolina)
2. Branch A. Merrimon (1836-1883), **CSA**	Riverside
2. Erasmus H. Merrimon (1839-1899), **CSA**	Riverside
+ Eliza A. _____ (1846-1923)	
2. Emory H. Merrimon (1840-1926)	
+ Rachel Augusta Hedrick (1842-1920)	(Ohio)
2. James Harvey Merrimon (1842-1921), **CSA**	Riverside
+ 1st Julia Adelaide Lynch (1845-1873) (4 sons)	Riverside
3. James Gibbon Merrimon (1866-1948)	Riverside
+ Blanche Southwick (1872-1955) (2 child.)	Christ School
3. Emory Houston Merrimon (1869-1938)	Riverside
3. Julian Lynch Merrimon (1871-1881)	
3. Branch M. Merrimon (1873-1878)	
+ 2nd Annie J. Pleasant (1853-1895) (2 dau.)	Riverside
2. Mary A. Merrimon (1844-1925)	Riverside
2. Eliza A. Merrimon (1846-1928)	Riverside
2. Jesse William Merrimon (1849-1938)	Lewis Mem.
+ Lily G. _____ (1856-1945)	Lewis Mem

Editor's notes:

The following markers in the Merrimon plot at Riverside are a mystery.
Evelyn Merrimon (1881-1966)
James H. Merrimon (1903-1969)
James Gibbon Merrimon (1896-1955)
Riverside burial records show also the following, but no markers are present:
Inez Powell Merrimon - year 2001 ashes at Riverside
2 children of A. H. Merrimon (read J. H. Merrimon & 2nd wife)
1 child of Sterling Merrimon
Emory H. Merrimon (1840-1926)
** Rev. B. H. Merrimon (1802-1881)
** Mrs. B. H. Merrimon (1811-1849)
(Blanche) Southwick Merrimon (1873-1955), wife of James Gibbon Merrimon

Riverside Cemetery plot, lot 130, section K, has been reconstituted - marble markers for Julia Adelaide Merrimon (1815-1873), her sons Julian Lynch (1871-1881), and Branch H. (1873-1878) have been moved here from another cemetery - likely Central Methodist. In 1893, a marble marker for Branch Merrimon (1836-1883) was moved to Riverside.

**The remains for his parents, the Rev. Branch H. Merrimon, M. E. minister, and his wife, Mary E. P. Merrimon, were moved here also in 1893, but no marker currently exists. The latter three burials were originally in the cemetery now below the Central Methodist Church.

The massive, 14-foot tall granite marker for Rev. Branch Hamlin Merrimon (1802-1881), his wife, and sixth son, Judge James Harvey Merrimon (1842-1921), and his 2nd wife, is a contemporary addition to the plot.

The patriarch Branch Hamlin Merrimon (1802-1881) was primarily a Methodist minister, but also a merchant. His seven sons included merchants, and later lawyers and judges, and to some extent real estate speculators. The oldest son, Augustus Summerfield Merrimon, appears as a student in the 1850 Buncombe County census records; evidently A. S. Merrimon was the first of the Merrimons to move to Asheville. His age listed at 18 was incorrect.

Augustus Summerfield Merrimon, who appears in the *Dictionary of North Carolina Biography*, had eight children as follows:

Edgar, b.1854
Branch, b.1857
Mary, b.1859
William, b.1862
Maggie, b.1865
Unnamed, b.1870
Maude Lillian, b.1874
Charles, b.?

The index to Buncombe County Deed records (*Digges Index*) includes the following grantee records - they were mostly town lots:

Branch Hamlin Merrimon, 10 x, 1834-1874
Augustus Summerfield Merrimon, 10 x, 1852-1875
James Harvey Merrimon, 23 x, 1869-1911
James Gibbon Merrimon, 29 x, 1890-1921
Chart modified from *A Lot of Bunkum*, vol. 29, no. 4, p. 24-25 (2008)

Descendants of William Mills

Name	Cemetery

1. William Mills (c. 1650-____)
  + Rachel Gilbert
  2. Gilbert Mills (c. 1670-1699+)
  + Margaret Ashmore
    3. Alexander Mills
    3. William Mills (c.1699-1766)   (Virginia)
  + Mary Walton Lavender (1703-1767+) (8 child.)
      4. Thomas Mills (1721-c.1755)
      4. Ambrose Mills (1722-1780) **TORY-RW**   (Rutherford Co.)
     1st Mourning Stone (c.1722-1755)   (South Carolina)
        5. William Mills (1746-1837) **RW**   (Henderson Co.)
       + Eleanor Morris (1746-1843) (8 child.)   (Henderson Co.)
      (she m. 2nd John Carrick)
          6. John Columbus Mills (c.1766-1843)
         + Sarah Robertson
          6. Millicent Mills (1768-1811)
         + Richard Yielding
          6. Marville E. Mills (c.1772-1848)   (Henderson Co.)
         + Mary D. Chambliss
          6. Sarah Mills (c.1775-1856) (12 child.)   (Henderson Co.)
         + Asa Edney, Rev. (1772-1842)   (Henderson Co.)
          6. Mourning Mills (c.1776-1827)   (Henderson Co.)
         + Henry C. Lewis (____-1815)   (Henderson Co.)
          6. Phalby Mills (c. 1776-____)
         + D. Myers
          6. Eleanor Mills (1777-1842)   (Henderson Co.)
          Samuel Edney, Jr.   (Henderson Co.)
          6. Elizabeth Mills (c.1778-1858)   (South Carolina)
         + George Jones   (South Carolina)
         + 2nd Anne Brown (____-____) (6 child.)
      4. Sarah Mills (1725-____) (7 child.)
  + Edward Watts
      4. William Henry Mills (1727-____)
  + Anne Welch (____-____) (9 child.)
        5. Jesse Mills (c.1762-1842) **RW**   (Rutherford Co.)
       + Sarah Garrett (1763-1843) (5 child.)   (Polk Co.)
      4. Elizabeth Mills (1729-1767+)
      4. Anna Mills (c.1731-1767+)
      4. Amelia Mills (1735-1767+)
      4. Jesse Mills (1740-1767)
      Lucy Tilman (____-____) (1 child.)

Census Records

Wm. Mills is on the 1790 NC Census, Rutherford Co., Morgan District, Twelfth Company (now ?Polk Co.) with 3 males, 6 females, and 8 slaves.

William Mills is on the 1800 NC Census, Buncombe Co. (now Henderson Co.) with 1 male, 2 females, and 20 slaves.

Selected References

Barnett, Lorene Burton Ambrose, 1979, *The Mills, Stokes and Forrester Families of Primarily Greenville Co.*, SC: Blue Ridge, SC, Faith Printing Co., 186 p.

Felmet, L. Holt, Jr., 2005 William Mills of Fruitland: Asheville, NC, *A Lot of Bunkum*, vol. 26, no. 2, p. 19-21

_____, 2008, Revolutionary War Ancestors of L. Holt Felmet, Jr.: *ibid*, vol. 29, no. 1, p. 18

Styles, Marshall L., 1995, *Colonel Ambrose Mills. A Soldier in the King's Army During the American Revolution*: Duncan, SC, privately publ., 107 p. + 5 p.

_____2010, *Western North Carolina's Revolutionary War Patriot Soldiers. A Collection of their Records. Vol. 12, Jesse Mills Pension File W7448*: Simpsonville, SC, privately publ., 82 p.

Descendants of William Moore

Name	Cemetery
1. William Moore, Sr. (c.1726-1812) **RW** (1)	Capt. Wm. Moore
+ 1st Ann Cathey (c.1739-c.1774) (7 child.)	(Rowan Co.)
2. Nancy Moore (1755-c.1812)	
+ Jonathan McPeters (1756-1846) **RW (2)**	(?Yancey Co., NC)
2. William Moore, Jr. (c.1757-1820+) (3)	
+ unknown	
3. William H. Moore (1777-1852) (4) **WAR of 1812**	(Pettis Co., MO)
+ Ann Cathey (1782-1867) (11 child.)	(Cooper Co., MO)
2. Sarah Moore (c.1756-1862) (11 child.)	(Tennessee)
+ John Montgomery	
2. Thomas Moore (c.1759-1823)	(Georgia)
2. Ann Moore (c. 1763-____)	
+ James Rutherford	
. James Moore (1768-1859)	(Catawba Co.)
+ Henrietta Sherrill (1773-1843) (13 child.)	(Catawba Co.)
2. Alice Moore (1770-1869) (10 child.)	Penland, Enka
+ John Penland (1764-1855) **RW**	Penland, Enka

*****

+ 2nd Margaret Patton (1749-1814) (7 child.) (5)	Capt. Wm. Moore
2. Samuel C. Moore (c.1776-____)	(Arkansas)
2. Charity Moore (c.1780-____)	(Missouri)
+ Jesse Ballew (Missouri)	
2. Rachel Moore (1782-1866) (10 child.)	(Macon Co.)
+ George Penland (1778-1877)	(Macon Co.)
2. Mary Moore (1786-____) (10 child.)	(?Haywood Co.)
+ Robert Penland (1779-1856)	(?Haywood Co.)
2. Elizabeth Margaret Moore (1785-1850) (5 dau.)	
+ Benjamin Tutt (1785-1830)	
2. Charles Augustus Moore (1791-1873)	Oak Forest
+ 1st Margaret Penland (1789-1828) (2 child.)	Capt. Wm. Moore
3. William Hamilton Moore (1812-1879)	Oak Forest
+ Mary C. Gudger (1833-1917) (7 child.)	Oak Forest
3. Rebecca E. Moore (1814-1853) (8 child.)	Capt. Wm. Moore
+ George W. Candler (1808-1862)	Capt. Wm. Moore
4. Margrette E. Candler (1836-1913) (11 child.)	Harkins/Candler
+ Thomas Jefferson Harkins (1832-1914)	Harkins/Candler
2nd Lucinda Killian (1809-1883) (5 child.)	Oak Forest
3. Robert P. Moore (1839-1922)	
+ Sophronia Wells (1861-____)	
4. Charles A. Moore (1851-1923)	
3. Daniel Killian Moore, Sr. (1845-1920) **CSA**	
+ Caroline Dickey (1846-1908)	
3. Charles F. Moore	(Arkansas)
3. Margaret Moore	
+ W. Julius Alexander	
2. Thomas C. Moore	(Arkansas)

Footnotes:

(1) Many studies speculate on the early generations of the Moore family with very few facts in hand. Thus first generation Capt. William Moore (1726-1812) is supposed to have married Ann Cathey (d.c.1774) as his 1st wife, however her birth date and the names of her parents are speculative and dates can only be supposed from the apparent birth dates of her children. She probably died in Salisbury, NC.

The Cathey family, led by James Cathey (c.1685-c.1757) came to America around 1717, settling at first in Cecil Co., MD. The family included wife Ann, last name unknown, and children. The Cathey family went to Augusta Co., VA by 1739. Most migrated to the Cathey's Creek, a tributary south of the Yadkin River of North Carolina about 1747. Between 1747 and 1762, heads of families in North Carolina included James Cathey, the father, his sons George, Sr. (c.1717-c.1790), and Andrew, and grandson George, Jr. (c.1747-1840), and Alexander Cathey (son of John-deceased 1743). The will of the elder James mentions granddaughters Margaret, daughter of George, and Ann, daughter of Andrew.

The 1790 North Carolina Census has the following:
6th Company, Morgan District, Burke Co. (now western Burke & McDowell Cos.)
William Moore (Sr.), 1 male 16+, 3 males less than 16, 5 females, 6 slaves
10th Company, Morgan District, Burke Co. (now Madison, Mitchell & Avery Cos.)
William Moore (Jr.), 1 male 16+, 3 males less than 16, 3 females
The 1800 NC Census, Buncombe Co. has the following:
William Moore (Sr.), 3 males, 5 females, 9 slaves
William Moore (Jr.), 5 males, 2 females
The 1800 NC Census, Burke Co. has another:
William Moore, 4 males, 3 females

The 1810 NC census lists four William "Moors" (Buncombe Co.), and one William Moore Burke (Co.)

(2) Jonathan McPeters (1756-1846) has a contemporary granite marker in the Cane River Baptist Cemetery, near Burnsville, Yancey Co. His Revolutionary War pension record is S7195.

(3) William Moore, Jr. (c.1757-1820+) evidently did not marry another Ann Cathey as sources speculate. Land records and census records indicate that he was still in Western NC as late as 1820. The current interpretation is that he died in Tennessee, possibly in Greene Co.

(4) But third generation William H. Moore (1777-1852) apparently did marry another Ann Cathey (b. 1783). The couple evidently migrated to Missouri about 1817; he died near Boonville, MO. This Ann Cathey was the daughter of Capt. George Cathey, Jr. whose Revolutionary War pension file is S16699 and whose wife was Margaret Chamberlain.

Another William H. Moore, apparent son of the above, age 53, born in North Carolina, is shown on the 1860 census for Cooper Co., Palestine TWP, MO.

(5) Capt. William Moore married about 1775 as his second wife, Margaret Patton (1749-1814). She reportedly was the daughter of Capt. Robert and Charity Patton.

The famous Capt. William Moore Cemetery in Enka contains a small number of marble gravestones for William Moore and his immediate family as well as a large number of field stones in the immediate community, probably soldiers and slaves.

Another William Moore, b.1765 in Lancaster Co., PA, married 1784 another Margaret Patton in Davidson Co., NC. He died 1835. He was a Private in the Revolutionary War, pension file W5389.

Selected References

Browder, Blanche Penland, 1975, *The Penland Family of North Carolina*: Haynesville, NC, privately publ., 182 p., rev. ed.

Cathey, Boyt Henderson, 1993, *Cathey Family History and Genealogy*: Franklin, NC, Genealogy Publ. Service, 594 p.

Haller, Charles R., 2007, Pioneer William Moore: Asheville, NC, *A Lot of Bunkum*, vol. 28, no. 1, p. 7-12

_____, 2012, Early WNC Land Entries by Capt. William Moore: *in press*

White, Emmett R., 1998, *Revolutionary War Soldiers of Western North Carolina. Vol. II, Burke Co.*: Easley, SC, Southern Historical Press, 358 p.

Descendants of Samuel Murray, immigrant

Name	Cemetery
1. Samuel Murray, Sr. (1739-1817) **RW**	(Fletcher, NC)
+ Elizabeth Rees (____-1813) (9 child.)	(Fletcher, NC)
2. William Murray (1764-1781) **RW**	(Newberry Co., SC)
2. James Isaac Murray (1769-1847)	(Tuxedo, NC)
+ 1st Margaret Dugan (1772-1840) (11 child.)	
+ 2nd Nancy Sutherlin	
2. Elizabeth Murray (1771-1793) (2 child.)	
+ John Wilson	
2. Samuel Murray, Jr. (1774-1847)	(Henderson Co., NC)
+ Elizabeth Morrow (____-____) (2 child.)	
2. Ann Murray (1776-____)	
2. Thomas Alexander Murray, Sr. (1779-1852)	(Fletcher, NC)
+ Sarah Seawood (c.1790-1881) (11 child.)	
2. John Rees Murray (1782-1815)	(Skyland, NC)
+ Flora Lance (1780-1855) (8 child.)	
2. William Murray (1783-1867)	(Catoosa Co., GA)
+ Sarah Ann Ashley (1805-1860) (1 child.)	
2. Robert Murray (1785-1857)	(Buncombe Co., NC)
+ 1st Mary Elizabeth Hawkins (1806-1844) (15 child.)	(Buncombe Co., NC)
+ 2nd Susanna Murray	

Census Records

Samuel Murry, Sr., is on the 1800 NC Census records, Buncombe Co., with 6 males, 2 females, and 3 slaves.

Samuel Murry, Jr., is on the 1800 NC Census records, Buncombe Co., with 2 males and 1 female.

Selected References

Gowing, Audrey Hawkins, 2001, *All Roads Lead to Haywood Co., NC. Vol. 1, The Hawkins-Rogers Connection*: Waynesboro, VA, Humphries Press, 447 p. (Robert Murray, p. 17-20)

O'Rourke, Donald E., 1987, Samuel Murray, Sr: in Asheville, NC, *Old Buncombe County Heritage book*, Vol. II, p. 273-274

Styles, Marshall, 2010. *Western North Carolina Revolutionary War Patriot Soldiers. vol. 13, Samuel Murray, Sr.*: Simpsonville, SC, privately publ., 54 p.

Author's Notes

The primary source of information is from a manuscript by Ruth Dilling, dated 31 May 2012.

Descendants of James Patton, 1783 immigrant
Patton Family Cluster A - the Asheville Pattons

Name	Cemetery
1. James Patton (1756-1845)	First Presbyterian
+ Ann Reynolds (1775-1827) (11 child.)	Riverside*
2. Mary Patton (c.1798-1833) (7 child.)	(?Charlotte, NC)
+ John Irwin (1787-1860)	(?Charlotte, NC)
2. James Washington Patton (1803-1861)	Riverside*
+1st Jane Clarissa Walton (1808-1837) (6 child.)	
3. James Alfred Patton (1830-1864) CSA	Riverside*
+ Anna Chapman (1832-1903) (3 child.)	Riverside
3. William Augustus Patton (1835-1863) CSA	Riverside*
+ Julia G____ (3 child.)	
+ 2nd Henrietta Kerr (1805-1890) (2 child.)	Riverside*
3. Thomas Walton Patton (1841-1907) CSA	Riverside
+ 1st Annabella B.Pearson (1843-1866) (2 child.)	Riverside*
+ 2nd Martha Bell Turner (1843-1929) (2 child.)	
4. Josie Buel Patton (1876-1933) (7 child.)	Riverside
Haywood Parker (1864-1945)	Riverside
3. Frances Louisa Patton (1843-1918)	Riverside
2. John Erwin Patton (1805-1880)	Newton Academy
+ Margaret Eliza Davidson (1805-1878) (no child.)	Newton Academy
2. Benjamin Franklin Patton (1807-1840)	(Clarkesville, GA)
+ Ann E. Gage (1816-1836)	
2. Jane Shaw Patton (1808-1838) (6 child.) (1st wife)	(?Charleston, SC)
+ Dr. James F. E. Hardy (1802-1888) **MD**	
2. Thomas Taylor Patton (1809-1861)	
+ Nancy Louiseann Walton (1811-1844) (2 child.)	
3. Clarissa Irvin Patton (1832-1897) (5 child.)	
+ John Hugh Murphy	
3. Louisa Matilda Patton (1834-1915)	
2. Sara Rosanna Patton (1811-1877) (4 child.), 2nd wife	
+ 1st Washington Morrison (1801-1836)	(Charlotte, NC)
+ 2nd Stephen Lee (1801-1879)	Riverside*
2. Ann Eleanor Patton	
+ Nicholas Perkins	
2. Elizabeth Patton	(Clarkesville, GA)
+ Dr. George D. H. Phillips	(Clarkesville, GA)
2. Julia Adelaide Patton (c.1815-1845) (4 child.)	(?Charlotte, NC)
+ Joseph Harvey Wilson	

Editor's Notes

*Patton family individuals originally were buried in the Patton plot in the lower graveyard below First Presbyterian Church, Asheville, at the site of an early Asheville library. In the 1890s, Asheville lawyer Haywood Parker organized the removal of most from the Church Street Cemetery and had them reburied at Riverside Cemetery.

In 1849, Henrietta Kerr and her sister, Elizabeth Kerr, were instrumental in forming Asheville's Trinity Episcopal Church. After about 1850, Patton family members were divided between membership in the First Presbyterian Church and the adjacent Trinity Episcopal Church.

The relationship between Frances Louisa Patton (1843-1918) and Lyman Atkinson Deal

(1877-1900), who have adjacent, identical gravestones at Riverside, is not clear.

Census Records

Jas. Patten is on the 1790 NC Census, Burke Co., Morgan District, Eleventh Company, with 1 male and 5 females.

James Patton is on the 1800 NC Census, Buncombe Co., with 2 males, 8 females, and 2 slaves. (The above James Patten/Patton evidently is not the Patton below.)

James Patton (Sr.) is on the 1810 NC Census, Buncombe Co., with 18 males, 6 females, 12 slaves, and 3 others.

James Patton, Sr., is on the 1820 NC Census, Buncombe Co., with 19 males and 8 females.

James Patton, Jr., is on the 1820 NC Census with 2 males and 2 females.

James Patton, Sr., is on the 1830 NC Census, Buncombe Co., with 4 males and 6 females.

James Patton, Jr., is on the 1830 NC Census, Buncombe Co., with 4 males and 4 females.

Land Records

In late 1797, Patton & Erwin (James Patton and brother-in-law Andrew Erwin) bought 170 acres on Flat Creek (Sweetens Creek) from James Davidson. In the same year, they bought 3 other parcels near Asheville. From 1804 to 1809, the partnership bought 12 other parcels of farm land.

In March, 1805, Patton & Erwin bought lot 4 in Asheville. An undated sketch map of Asheville published by Foster A. Sondley in 1922 shows that Patton & Erwin eventually acquired lots 4-8, 14-15, 17, 19-22, and 31-34 (with Gash) and thus had nearly half of the early city blocks.

Patton & Erwin reportedly moved permanently to Buncombe Co. only in 1807. Eventually, James Patton had interests in 39 parcels in Buncombe County. About 1814, the partnership split with Patton taking the Buncombe Co. land and Erwin taking land in Tennessee.

Selected References

Echerd, Arthur R., 1991, *James Patton Genealogy*: n.p., n.p., 27 + XXIV p.

Haller, Charles R., 2004, Pattons, Pattons, and More Pattons: Asheville, NC, *A Lot of Bunkum*, vol. 25, no. 3, p. 13-15

_____, 2007, A Conversation with Mary Parker: Asheville, NC, *ibid*, vol. 28, no. 3, p. 18-20

Patton, Thomas W., 1891, *Biography of James Patton*: Asheville, NC, n.p., 35 p. (reprint; original dates 1839)

Descendants of William Patton
Patton Family Cluster B - the Biltmore Pattons

<u>Name</u>	<u>Cemetery</u>
1. William Patton (c.1742-1818) **RW**	Newton Academy
+ Hannah Brandon (?3 child.)	
2. Lt. Samuel Patton (1761-1851) **RW** (1)	?Riverside
+ Mary Alexander Johnston (____-1845) (9 child.)	
3. William Patton	
+ Nancy ____ (9 child.)	
2. John M. Patton (1765-1834) War of 1812	Newton Academy
+ Ann Mallory (1768-1855) (12 child.)	Newton Academy
3. Elizabeth Mallory Patton (1787-1852) (3 child.)	(Georgia)
+ 1st John McClatchey II (1769-1840)	(Tennessee)
+ 2nd Devereaux Jarrett	
3. Hannah Brandon Patton (1788-____) (10 child.)	
+ 1st Col. James McKee (1780-1849)	Newton Academy
+ 2nd Col. James Lowry (1783-1857) (2nd wife)	
3. Sarah Patton (1790-____) (4 child.)	
+ Devereaux Jarrett	
3. Mallory Brandon Patton (1791-1852)	(Georgia)
+ Elizabeth Smith (1789-1867) (12 child.)	(Georgia)
3. Mary "Polly" Patton (1794-1853)	Newton Academy
+ James McConnell Smith (1787-1856)	Newton Academy
3. Robert H. Patton (1795-1863) **CSA**	(Georgia)
+ Mary Elizabeth Chunn (1799-____) (8 child.)	
3. Harriett Dorothy Patton (1798-____) (6 child.)	(Macon Co.)
+ Jesse R. Siler (1793-1876)	(Macon Co.)
3. Fidelio Patton (1800-1845)	Newton Academy
+ Minerva Williamson (____-____) (2 child.)	
3. Lucinda Patton (1802-1865) (2 child.)	Newton Academy
+ Joshua Roberts (1795-1865)	Newton Academy
3. Lorenzo Dow Patton (1804-1870?)	
3. Montraville Patton (1806-1896) **CSA** (2)	
+ 1st Maria L. Hackett (1810-1867) (7 child.)	Newton Academy
4. Mortimer Brandon Patton (1842-1854)	Newton Academy
4. Henry Patton (1844-____)	
4. Robert Patton (1846-____)	
4. Anna Maria Patton (1847-1914)	Newton Academy
4. Mary E. Patton (1849-____)	
4. Jessie M. Patton (1851-1910)	Newton Academy
+ 2nd Katherine A.E. McDowell (1826-1898)	
3. Ann Adeline Patton (1808-1844)	
2. Sarah Patton	

Census Records

Jno. Patten is on the 1790 NC Census, Burke Co., Morgan District, Eleventh Company, with 2 males, 4 females, and 2 slaves.

John Patton is on the 1800 NC Census, Buncombe Co., with 6 males, 6 females, and 15 slaves.

In Oct., 1795, John Patton acquired lots 2, 10, and 16 in Morrisville from John Burton. On Sondley's later Map of Asheville, John retained lots 2 and 7.

Samuel Patton is on the 1790 NC Census Burke Co., Morgan District, First Company with 4 males and 2 females.

Samuel Patton is on the 1800 NC Census, Burke Co., with 6 males and 4 females.

Samuel Patton is on the 1810 NC Census, Burke Co., with 1 male and 5 females.

Samuel Patton is on the 1820 NC Census, Buncombe Co., with 1 male and 4 females.

Wm. Patton is on the 1790 NC Census, Burke Co., Morgan District, First Company with 1 male and 2 females.

William Patton is on the 1810 NC Census, Burke Co., with 1 male and 2 slaves.

William Patton is on the 1820 Census, Buncombe Co., with 4 males and 1 female.

Footnotes

(1) A contemporary military marble for Lt. Samuel Patton is located in Asheville's Riverside Cemetery. This marble was put in place after 1900, and thus the question of actual burial site.

(2) Montraville Patton was a mayor of Asheville, 1866 to 1867.

Selected References

Agricola, David V., 2001, *Patton Lineages Originating in Pennsylvania Prior to the Revolution*: Cleveland, OH, privately publ., ca 150 p., 2nd ed.

Haller, Charles R., 2005, Who was Montraville Patton?: Asheville, NC, *A Lot of Bunkum*, vo. 26, no. 4, p. 4

_____, 2008, Who was Samuel Patton?: *ibid*, vol. 29, n0. 4, p. 15-17

Porter, Lenna B., 1951, *The Family of Weimar Siler, 1755-1831*: Franklin, NC, Comm. 100th Mtg. (Siler Family), 178 p. + index

Richman, Ellen E., 2005, *Biltmore Estate*: Charleston, SC, Arcadia Print., 128 p. (shows picture of large frame "house of Col. John Patton")

White, Emmett R., 1984, *Revolutionary War Soldiers of Western North Carolina. vol. 1, Burke Co*: Easley, SC, Southern Historical Press, 318 p.

Descendants of Robert Patton, 1755 immigrant
Patton Family Cluster C - the Swannanoa Pattons

Name	Cemetery
1. Robert Patton (1741-1832) (1) **RW**	(Gibson Co., TN)
+ Rebecca Cathey (c.1766-c.1828) (8 child.)	?Patton (2)
2. James Patton (c.1782-____)	(Mississippi)
2. Ann Catherine Patton (1783-____)	
+ Hance Alexander McWhorter (1772-1860)	(Gibson Co., TN)
2. George Patton (1786-1840) (3)	Patton
+ Nancy Patton (1792-1860) (11 child.)	Patton
2. Elizabeth "Betsy" Patton (1788-1860) (5 child.)	(Hood Co., Texas)
+ 1st James Patton (1786-1813) (a first cousin)	(Alabama)
3. James Calvin Patton (1833-1895+)	
3. William W. Patton (1835-c.1863) **CSA**	
3. Robert C. Patton (1837-c.1862) **CSA**	
3. Leurges W. Patton (1839-____) **CSA**	
3. Benjamin F. Patton (1841-c.1862) **CSA**	
+ 2nd David Crockett (1786-1836) **Frontiersman**	(San Antonio, TX)
3. Robert Patton Crockett (1816-____)	
+ Mathilda Porter (7+ child.)	
3. Rebecca Elvira Crockett (1818-____)	
+ 1st George Kimbro	
+ 2nd Rev. James M. Halford	
3. Matilda Crockett (1821-____)	
+ 3 x	
2. Sarah Patton (c.1790-____)	(?Georgia)
+ William Edmundson	
2. Margaret Patton (c.1794-____) (4+ child.)	(Weakley Co., TN)
+ Abner Burgin, Sr. (1789-1837)	(Gibson Co., TN)
2. Mathilda Carolina Patton (c. 1795-____)	Patton
+ Peter Trosper	
2. Rebecca Patton (c.1800-____)	
+ James Edmundson	

Footnotes:

(1) This Robert Patton is not to be confused with Robert Patton (1748-1813) who married Elizabeth Dysart (1763-1844) and who is buried in the Druscilla Church cemetery in McDowell Co.

(2) The Patton Cemetery in reference here is the one located outside and northwest of Swannanoa, NC. It is one of the oldest in Buncombe Co., and contains many early fieldstones with no names.

(3) George Patton, son of Robert, married Nancy Patton, daughter of Aaron Franklin Patton (1765-1826), and granddaughter of Mathew Leander Patton (c.1700-1778). Aaron Patton and his wife Magdaline Cunningham (c.1765-c.1835) are buried in the Patton Cemetery, Swannanoa.

Census Records

Aron Patten is on the 1790 NC Census, Burke Co., Morgan District, Eleventh Co., with 1 male and 3 females.

Aaron Patten is on the 1800 NC Census, Buncombe Co., with 3 males and 5 females.

Matthew Patten, Sr. is on the 1790 NC Census, Burke Co., Morgan District, Eleventh company with 3 males, 2 females, and 1 slave.

Matthew Patton, Jr. is on the 1800 NC Census, Buncombe Co., with 4 males and 2 females.

Robt. Patten (Sadl.) is on the 1790 NC Census, Burke Co., Morgan district, Eleventh company with 3 males, 5 females, and 2 slaves.

Robt. Patton is on the 1800 NC Census, Buncombe Co., with 3 males, 7 females, and 6 slaves.

Selected References

Haller, Charles R., 2004, Pattons, Pattons, and More Pattons: Asheville, NC, *A Lot of Bunkum*, vol. 25, no. 3, p. 13-16

Nance, Linda Patton, 2006, *Descendants of Robert Patton, Swannanoa, NC*: Wilmington, NC, privately publ., 160 p.

Thomas, Lillian B., ca. 1972, *Robert Patton, His Descendants & Brothers*: Asheville, NC, privately publ., 70 p., 2nd, rev. ed.

Widener, Helen O., & Tad Browning, 2008, *Scraps of Life. Elizabeth Patton Crockett*: Irving, TX, Pine Mountain Books, 93 p.

Whitaker, C. Bruce, 1987, Robert Patton: in *Buncombe Co. Heritage Book*, vol. 2, p. 289-290: Asheville, NC, Old Buncombe Co. Gen. Soc.

Descendants of John Penland

Name	Cemetery
1. John Penland (c.1706-1776)	
+ Jean _____ (c.1710-c.1768)	
2. Margaret Penland (1740-____)	
2. William Penland (1742-1815) **RW**	Burke Co.
+ Annis Donnal (c.1745-c.1830) (9 child.)	Burke Co.
3. James Penland (c.1765-1816)	
+ Mary "Polly" _____	
3. Anna Penland (c. 1767-____)	
3. William Penland, Jr. (c.1769-1809)	Buncombe Co.
+ Elizabeth Rachel Penland (c.1776-____)	
3. Jean Penland (c. 1771-____)	
3. George Penland (c.1780-186_)	
+ Mary Erwin (____-____) (5 child.)	
3. Peter Penland (c.1773-1835)	
3. Abraham Penland (c.1775-____)	
+ Elizabeth Gibbs (1786-1867) (11 child.)	
3. George W. Penland (c.1780-____)	
3. Alexander Penland	(Ohio)
+ Elizabeth Gibbs (1786-1867) (11 child.)	(Ohio)
3. Margaret Penland (c.1791-1873)	Capt. Wm. Moore
+ Charles Augustus Moore (1791-1873)	Oak Forest
2. Robert Penland, Sr. (c.1744-1828) **RW**	(Burke Co.)
+ Elizabeth Brank (1748-1841) (10 child.)	(Burke Co.)
3. Jane Penland (1771-1858)	(Burke Co.)
+ Samuel Alexander (1759-1842)	(Burke Co.)
3. Leah Penland (c.1773-1877)	(Burke Co.)
+ John Saulmon	
3. Eleanor Penland (c.1775-1861)	
+ Nathan Gibson	
3. George Penland (c.1778-1877) **War of 1812**	(Macon Co.)
+ Rachel Moore (1782-1866) (10 child.)	(Macon Co.)
3. Robert Penland, Jr. (c.1779-1856) **War of 1812**	(Haywood Co.)
+ Mary "Polly" Moore (1786-____) (10 child.)	(Haywood Co.)
3. Peter Penland (1782-1865)	
+ Rachel Henry (____-____)	
3. Henry Penland (c.1783-1854)	
+ Elizabeth Parks (c.1792-1888) (7 child.)	
3. Priscilla Penland	
+ _____ Wakefield	
3. Ruth Penland	
+ _____ Alexander	
3. Rachel Penland	
+ William A. Erwin (1803-1881)	(Burke Co.)

Name	Cemetery
2. George Penland (c.1753-1829) **RW**	?Vance
+ Ann Alexander (____-____) (7 child.)	?Vance
3. Robert Penland	
3. Chris Penland	
3. Elizabeth Rachel Penland	
3. Alexander Penland	
3. William Penland	
3. Jane Penland	

Census Records

According to Emmett R. White, 1998, the three brothers, William, Robert, Sr., and George Penland all served in the Revolutionary War.

George Penland is on the 1790 NC Census, Burke Co., Morgan District, Third Company with 5 males and 5 females.

George Penland is on the 1800 NC Census, Buncombe Co., with 5 males, 5 females, and 1 slave.

A contemporary granite marker for George Penland (c.1753-1829) and his wife, Ann Alexander, is in the Vance Cemetery, northern Buncombe Co.

Robt. Penland is on the 1790 NC Census, Burke Co., Morgan District, Third Company with 5 males, 6 females, and 1 slave.

Robert Penland is on the 1810 NC Census, Burke Co. with 2 males and 4 females.

Wm. Penland is on the 1790 NC Census, Burke Co., Morgan District, Third Company with 7 males, 3 females and 1 slave.

William Penland is on the 1800 NC Census, Burke Co., with 6 females, 4 females, and 1 slave.

Editor's Notes

A marble tombstone for John Penland (1764-1855), b. Pennsylvania, also a Revolutionary War veteran, and his wife Alice Moore (1770-1869), is in the Penland Cemetery, Enka. This group is not related to the other Penlands. This John Penland does not occur in the 1790 NC Census, nor in the NC 1800 Census, Buncombe Co., but he does occur on the 1810 through 1850 census of Buncombe Co. Children of John Penland and Alice Moore:

Abraham, b.1791, m. Elizabeth Jones

William, b.1797, m. Nancy Stevens

Elizabeth, b.1800, m. James Cathey

John Harvey, b.c.1800, m. Evaline Nichols

Charles Davidson, b.1804, m. 1st Elizabeth _____, m. 2nd Mary Smith

George Newton, b.c.1812, m. Nancy Jones

Likewise, Joshua Penly (i.e., Penley), William Penly, Sr., and William Penly, Jr., shown on the 1790 NC Census, Burke Co., Morgan District, Third Company may or may not be related to the Penlands. The following land grant table indicates they were isolated from the Penlands.

Selected References

Browder, Blanche P., 1975, *The Penland Family of North Carolina*: n.p., privately publ., 225 p., rev. ed.

White, Emmett R., 1998, *Penland: in Revolutionary War Soldiers of Western NC. Vol. 2, (Burke Co.)*: Greenville, SC, Southern Hist. Press, p. 248-256

Descendants of William Dinwoodie Rankin

Name	Cemetery
1. William Dinwoodie Rankin (1804-1879) **Mayor**	*Riverside
+ Elizabeth Lightfoot (1812-1908) (5 child.)	*Riverside
2. Amelia A. Rankin (1837-1922)	Riverside
+ Moses Joseph Bearden (1821-1904)	
2. David Rankin	
2. James Eugene Rankin (1845-1928) **CSA, Mayor**	Riverside
+ Fannie Cocke (1845-1922) (6 child.)	Riverside
3. Clarence Rankin (1869-1934)	Riverside
3. William Ellis Rankin (1870-1950)	Riverside
+ ?	
4. Virginia Rankin (1904-____)	
3. Arthur Eugene Rankin (1872-1931)	Riverside
+ Nancy P. Cartmell (1875-1959)	Riverside
4. Annah Rodman Rankin (1898-1975)	Riverside
4. James Eugene Rankin II (1911-1978)	Riverside
+ Mary Glenn (1916-1980)	Riverside
3. James Guy Rankin (1874-1962)	Riverside
3. Grace E. Rankin (1877-1962)	
+ Patrick Branch	
4. Frances Louise Branch (1900-1903)	
3. Edgar Leroy Rankin (1885-____)	
2. Alonzo Rankin (1847-1906)	Riverside
+ 1st Mary C. _____ (1856-____) (3 child.)	
3. Minna Rankin (1883-1939)	Riverside
3. Georgia A. Rankin (1886-1957)	Riverside
+ 2nd Caroline Pope Rankin (1859-1938)	
2. William Rankin (1860-____)	

Editor's notes:

The following markers in the Rankin plot at Riverside are not here tied to the above lineage:

Elizabeth Rankin (1883-1939)

Carroll St. John Rankin (1885-1887)

Eugene Marcus Bearden (1872-1937)

Mary Moore Bearden (1884-1975)

Hanna Moore (1898-1985)

Dorothy Allison Moore (1903-1995)

Virginia Saffold Seahorn Rankin (1865-1946)

*In 1893, W. D. Rankin was moved to Riverside from another cemetery.

The NC 1850 Census, Buncombe Co., shows William D. Rankin, 44, merchant, b. TN, 4 males and 3 females. He was mayor of Asheville from 1855 to 1857.

James Eugene Rankin was mayor of Asheville at various periods from 1872 to 1919.

The male members of the Rankin family were primarily bankers. In addition, they speculated in real estate. The Buncombe County deed records (*Digges Index*) includes the following grantee records - they were mostly town lots:

W. D. Rankin, 20 x, 1853-1878
David Rankin, 7 x, 1875-1896
James Eugene Rankin, 76 x, 1874-1923
Fannie Rankin, 12 x, 1888-1909
Arthur E. Rankin, 11x, 1889-1923
Alonzo Rankin, 32 x, 1873-1894

Modified from *A Lot of Bunkum*, vol. 29, no. 4, p. 25 (2008)

Descendants of Abraham Reynolds, Sr.

Name	Cemetery
1. Abraham Reynolds (c.1778-1848)	Abraham Reynolds
+ Mary Leazer (c.1780-1813) (12 child.)	Abraham Reynolds
2. John Reynolds, **Rev.** (1797-1876)	?Central Methodist
+ Anna Pou O'Hara (1796-1893) (4 child.)	
3. John Daniel Reynolds, **MD** (1832-1875)	
+ Theresa Elmira Shepherd (4 child.)	
4. Carl Vernon Reynolds, **MD** (1871-1963), m. 2x	Riverside
2. Catherine Reynolds (1798-	
2. Abraham Reynolds, Jr. (1799-1804)	Abraham Reynolds
2. Ann Reynolds (1801-1881) (4 child.)	(Alabama)
+ John Whitaker McAfee (1790-1880)	(Georgia
2. Samuel F. Reynolds (1802-____)	(Missouri)
_____ Jones	
2. Mary Leazer Reynolds (1804-1892) (12 child.)	
+ Thomas Jones (c.1798-c.1885)	
2. Joseph Page Reynolds, Sr. (1806-1867)	?Brick Church
+ Cornelia Atkinson (1810-1886) (9 child.)	?Brick Church
3. John Haskew Reynolds, MD (1836-1918)	Big Sandy Meth.
+ Sarah Ann Ferguson (1840-1892) (7 child.)	Big Sandy Meth.
4. Alonzo Carlton Reynolds (1870-1953) **Educator**	Green Hills
+ Nannie Elizabeth Woods (1874-1968) (9 child)	Green Hills
4. Joseph Letcher Reynolds (1879-1941) Rev.	Riverside
+ Sue Mackey (1886-1961) (6 child.)	Riverside
5. Sara C. Reynolds (1915-1989)	Green Hills
+ Brice Howard Beatty	
5. John Mackey Reynolds (1917-1996)	
+ Nancy Davis	
2. William Aaron Reynolds (1807-c.1865)	?Brick Church
+ 1st Sarah Ledford (3 child.)	
+ 2nd Mary Ann Cody, (1828-?) (7 child.)	
2. Daniel Reynolds (1809-1878)	Riverside
+ Susan Adelia Tate Baird (1826-1915) (10 child.)	Riverside
3. William Taswell Reynolds (1849-1892)	Riverside
+ Mamie Spears (1862-1939) (4 child.)	Riverside
4. Robert Rice Reynolds (1884-1963) m. 5x	Riverside
4. George Spears Reynolds (1881-1924)	Riverside
+ Hattie Marie Mitchell (1868-1953)	Riverside
5. George S. Reynolds, Jr. (1921-2003)	(Georgia)
2. Ruth Reynolds (1811-1830)	?Abraham Reynolds
2. Susanah Reynolds (1812-1865) (9 child.)	
+ Wilson Boyd	
2. Barbara Reynolds (1813-c.1865)	Alexanders Chapel
+ Walter Hill	

Editor's Notes

Abraham Reynolds apparently came to Buncombe Co. from Rowan County. An unconfirmed source states that he was the son of John Reynolds by his third wife. Much work is needed on research of Rowan Co. land and genealogical records of the Reynolds and Leazer families, as for instance in the various publications of Jo White Linn, deceased.

Between 1800 and 1838, Abraham Reynolds accumulated 1,740 acres as NC State land grants in contiguous plots along Bent Creek. He apparently left no will, but the acreage remained intact even through the Civil War and its aftermath. In 1900, George W. Vanderbilt bought four of Abraham's tracts embracing 1,140 acres through his agent J. Berkeley Cain; ninety-eight descendants of Abraham Reynolds were the grantees. Some descendants chose not to sell (about 600 acres) upon which they resided.

The NC Census Records, Buncombe Co., 1800 to 1840, indicated that Abraham Reynolds was born between 1770 and 1780; he was still living in 1840. His wife Mary was born after 1775 and was deceased by 1830.

Abraham Reynolds married Mary Leazer in Rowan Co., NC about 1795. She was the daughter of John Leazer/Lieser and his wife Barbara Lobingier. The marriage took place on Coddle Creek, an area which had a large population of German settlers.

Selected References

Beatty, Sara E., 1980, *The Genealogy of Abraham and Mary (Leazer) Reynolds*: Asheville, NC, privately printed, 180 p.

Haller, Charles R., 2006, Genealogy of the Reynolds Clan: Asheville, NC, *A Lot of Bunkum*, vol. 27, no. 2, p. 20-21

Alonzo Carlton Reynolds, a noted educator, and Robert Rice Reynolds, a politician, appear in the *Dictionary of North Carolina Biography*.

Descendants of Joseph Marion Rice, Sr.

Name	Cemetery
1. Joseph Marion Rice, Sr. (1761-1850)	Hughey Cem.
+ Margaret "Peggy" Young (c.1769-1842)	Hughey Cem.
2. Elizabeth Rice (1787-1874)	Brank Cem.
+ Robert Houston Brank (____-____)	Brank Cem.
3. Margaret Young Brank (1807-1900)	Hughey Cem.
+ Samuel Hughey (1802-1886)	Hughey Cem.
2. William Rice (1795-1871)	?Berea Baptist
+ 1st Martha Longmire, d.ca.1837 (5 child.)	?Hughey Cem.
3. James Ovaly Rice (1819-1863)	(Ringgold, GA)
+ May Elvira Wolf (1818-1872) (11 child.)	Asbury U.M.
3. John Longmire Rice (1821-1864)	
+ Martha Roseann Stephenson (1824-1902)	
4. William Francis Rice, Rev. (1847-1929)	Hughey Cem.
+ Margaret Henryetta Lindsay (1846-1925) (2 child.)	Hughey Cem.
4. Alfred Marion Rice (1849-1914)	Hughey Cem.
+ Margaret Laura Penland (1857-1933) (7 child.)	Bethel U.M.
4. John Winslow Rice (1858-1942)	Hughey Cem.
+ Lucy Swan (1863-1892)	Hughey Cem.
Mae Lillie Henderson (____-____)	
3. Margaret Rice (1830-1900)	
3. Jackson H. Rice, d. ca. 1858	(Newport, TN)
+ Rosannah Ray (____-____)	
4. Joseph Hasque Rice (1848-1927)	Bethel U.M.
+ Rhoda Carolina Shope (1853-1932) (10 child.)	Bethel U.M.
3. Sue Addy Rice (____-____)	
3. Alfred Rice, (c.837-1863)	

*****

+ 2nd Martha Mathilda West (1820-1898) (8 child.)	?Berea Baptist
3. Mary Lucinda Rice (1840-1923)	
3. Louisa Rice (1842-1871)	
3. Marcus Lafayette Rice (1843-1931)	
3. Susan Elizabeth Rice (1846-1848)	
3. Nancy Rebecca Rice (1846-1933) (twin)	
3. Eveline Carolina Rice (1848-____)	
+ John Stroup (____-____)	
3. Admiriam Judson Rice (1850-1926) unmarried	Berea Baptist
3. Sarah Hazeltine Rice (1852-1925) unmarried	Berea Baptist
2. Joseph M. Rice, Jr. (c.1803-____)	(Newport, TN)
+ Sarah A. Jones (c.1806-____) (10 child.)	
2. unknown son	

Census Records

Joseph Rice is on the 1790 NC Census, Burke Co., Morgan District, Eleventh Company (now Buncombe Co.), with 1 male and 3 females.

Joseph Rice is on the 1800 NC Census, Buncombe Co., with 4 males and 2 females.

William Rice is on the 1790 NC Census, Buncombe Co., Morgan District, Twelfth Company with 4 males and 2 females.

William Rice is on the 1800 NC Census, Buncombe Co., with 6 males and 2 females.

Selected References

Felmet, L. Holt, 2006, Hughey-Rice Families: Asheville, NC, *A Lot of Bunkam*, vol. 27, no. 4, p. 20-21

Haller, Charles R., 2006, Descendents of Joseph Marion Rice, Sr.: *ibid*, p. 22

Descendants of Daniel Smith

<u>Name</u>	<u>Cemetery</u>
1. Daniel Smith (1757-1824) RW (1)	Newton Acad.
+ Mary McConnell Davidson (1763-1842) (9 child.) (2)	Newton Acad.
2. William Davidson Smith (1784-c.1840)	(Texas)
+ Sally "Sarah" Carson (1788-1840) (6 child.)	(Texas)
2. James McConnell Smith (1787-1856)	Newton Acad.
+ Mary "Polly" Patton (1794-1853) (11 child.)	Newton Acad.
2. Elizabeth "Betsy" Smith (1789-1867) (12 child.)	(Georgia)
+ Mallory Brandon Patton (1791-1852)	(Georgia)
2. John Leander Smith (1791-1861)	(Tennessee)
+ Jane Davidson Williams (1799-1870)	(Tennessee)
2. Mary "Polly" Smith (1795-1872) (8 child.)	
+ John Hawkins (1792-1857)	Henry
2. Daniel Smith, Jr. (1798-1860)	(Tennessee)
+ Margaret Isabella McCree (1801-1880+)	
2. Nancy A. Smith (1800-____)	
+ G. William Burnett	
2. Moses Smith (1802-1892)	
+ Hannah Lane? (1802-1892)	
2. Jane D. Smith (1804-____)	
+ Alfred Fortune	

Footnotes:

(1) The relationship between Daniel Smith, Nathan Smith, and Samuel Smith on the 1800 NC Census, Buncombe Co., all being heads of households, is unknown. The three were each early holders of NC land grants.

Daniel Smith is on the 1800 NC Census, Buncombe Co., with 6 males, 5 females, and 1 slave.

(2) Mary McConnell Davidson was the daughter of Maj. William Davidson (1736-1814) and Margaret McConnell (c.1738-1806).

Selected References

McDowell, Frances A., c. 1997, *William Wallace McDowell & Sarah Lucinda Smith McDowell*: n.p., n.p. (Concord, NC; Ralph Scheurig), 190 p.

Hand, Robert A., 1991, *Davison/Davidson Family. The Descendants of William and Elisabeth Davison of County Armagh, Ireland*: Chadds Ford, PA, privately publ., 201 p. (2nd ed.)

White, Emmett R., 1984, *Revolutionary War Soldiers of Western North Carolina, Burke Co., Vol. 1*: Easley, SC, Southern Historical Press, 318 p.

Descendants of Henry Stevens, Sr.

Name	Cemetery
1. Henry Stevens Sr. (c.1750-c.1801)	
+ Margaret Foster Barnes (1755-1839) (8 child.) her 2nd +	
2. Henry Stevens, Jr. (1796-1862)	Newton Academy
+ Nancy Martin Foster (1808-1887)	Newton Academy
3. William Henry Stevens (1825-1851)	Newton Academy
+ (never married)	
3. Dr. James Mitchell Stevens (1827-1915) **CSA, MD**	Leicester Episcopal
+ Catherine C. Corpening (1834-1907) (8 child.)	Leicester Episcopal
3. Thomas Newton Stevens (1830-1901) **CSA**	Newton Academy
+ (never married)	
3 . David Marson Stevens (1832-1908) **CSA**	West Chapel
+ Mary Jane Dillingham (1834-1898) (13 child.)	West Chapel
3. Merritt Foster Stevens (1834-1911) **CSA**	Newton Academy
+ (never married)	
3. Minerva Rebecca Stevens (1837-1843)	Newton Acad.
+ (never married)	
3. Francis MacDonald Stevens (1839-1914) **CSA**	Gashes Creek Bapt.
+ 1st Sarah Jane Tweed (1839-1893) (6 child.)	Tweeds Chapel
+ 2nd Amanda Salina Brookshire (1841-1925)	Gashes Creek Bapt.
3. Jesse Smith Stevens (1842-1917) **CSA**	Riverside
+ Anna St. Clair Murry (1843-1910) (9 child.)	Riverside
3. Robert Morris Stevens (1845-1925) **CSA**	Gashes Creek Bapt.
+ 1st Louisa Camilla Sherrill (1845-1925) (2 child.)	Gashes Creek Bapt.
+ 2nd Adilla Anderson Cole	
3. Alfred Alexander Stevens (1848-1913) **CSA**	Green Hills
+ Susan Alice Whitaker (1859-1936) (11 child.)	Green Hills
3. Nancy Catherine Stevens (1850-1930)	West Chapel
+ Noble A. Penland (1847-1929)	West Chapel
3. Fannie Lucinda Stevens (1853-1881) (7 child.)	Newton Acad.
+ Marcus Layafette Reed (1853-1938)	Gashes Creek Bapt.

Selected References

Matthews, Ella R., 1957, *The Genealogy of Henry and Nancy Foster Stevens*: Asheville, NC, Stephens Press, 70 p. (see p. 54-58 for A Partial War Record of the 8 CSA brothers)

Haile, Margaret W., 1979, *Dillinghams of Big Ivy, Buncombe Co., NC*: Baltimore, MD., Gateway Press, 862 p.

Modified from *A Lot of Bunkum*, vol. 28, no. 2 (2007)

Census Records:

Henry Stevens is on the 1840 NC Census, Buncombe Co., with 7 males, 2 females, and 7 slaves.

Henry Stevens is on the 1850 NC Census, Buncombe Co., with 8 males and 3 females.

Descendants of Dr. Charles Edward Tennent

Name	Cemetery
1. Charles Edward Tennent, Sr, **MD**. (1812-1881)	Oak Forest Presby.
+ Mary Julia Fripp, (1822-1906) (10 child.)	Oak Forest Presby.
2. Sarah Eliza Tennent (1845-1919) (1 child)	Riverside
+ James S. West (1845-1913)	Riverside
2. Anna Martha Tennent (1846-1908)	(Florida)
2. Mary Edings Tennent (1850-1914) (2 child.)	Oak Forest Presby.
+ Samuel Frederick Venable (1830-1903)	Oak Forest Presby.
2. Julia Fripp Tennent (1855-1953)	Riverside
2. Charles Edward Tennent, Jr. (1856-1925)	Oak Forest Presby.
2. John Fripp Tennent (1858-1897)	Oak Forest Presby.
+ 1st Laura Belle Allensworth (1869-1955)	
+ 2nd Mary L. Simpson (1 child)	
2. James Edings Tennent (1864-1927)	(Lenoir, NC)
+ Dora L. Raby (6 child.)	(Lenoir, NC)
3. Eleanor Tennent (1899-1968)	(Tennessee)
+ Clarence D. Dickinson	(Tennessee)
3. Mary Alice Tennent (1890-____)	Riverside
3. George Raby Tennent (1892-____)	
+ Rosalie L. Moring (1 child)	
3. Charles Gaillard Tennent (1894-1979)	Riverside
+ Jessie L. Mercer 1904 -____) (5 child.)	Riverside
3. Anne Tennent 1895-____) (4 child.)	
+ 1st Charles E. Dillavou	
+ 2nd Austin T. Laycock	
3. Dorothy Julia Tennent (1898-1965) (4 child.)	(Washington, DC)
+ 1st John M. Janitschek	
+ 2nd Shelby N. Griffith	(Washington, DC)
3. William Vergereau Tennent (1863-1949)	(Kentucky)
3. Laura Belle Tennent (1869-1953)	Riverside
3. Gaillard Stoney Tennent, (1872-1955) MD.	Riverside
+ 1st Marie Louisa Westfeldt (1870-1917)	Calvary Episcop.
4. John S. Tennent (1896-____)	
+ 2nd Ora E. Carpenter (1884-1959)	Riverside

*****

1. Gilbert Boudinot Tennent (1816-1879)	Riverside
+ Emma Hardy (1820-1894) (4 child.)	Riverside
2. James Hardy Tennent (1849-1855)	(Charleston, SC)
2. Samuel Stevens Tennent (1850-1907)	(Georgia)
2. Gilbert Tennent (1852-1890) MD	Riverside
2. Jenny Tennent	

Editor's Notes

In 1718, Willliam Tennent, Sr. went from Scotland to America. A noted Presbyterian minister and pioneer educator, he is credited with founding the Log Cabin School in Bucks Co., PA in 1726. William Tennent, Sr. retired in 1742, but two sons, Gilbert Tennent and William Tennent, Jr., carried on ministerial and teaching activities.

About 1648, teaching activities were moved, and in 1756 a charter was issued to the College of New Jersey formed with 23 trustees including Gilbert Tennent and William Tennent, Jr. The college was renamed Princeton University in 1796.

As shown by the above chart, prominent members of the Tennent family eventually settled in North and South Carolina. By 1775, William Tennent, Jr. was active as a pastor at the Independent Presbyterian Church, Charleston, SC, and toured the back country of South Carolina and also the area of Charlotte, NC.

The College of New Jersey was notable for supplying trained educators and Presbyterian ministers to the frontiers of what became North Carolina and Tennessee. In the late 1700s, these pioneering educators in North Carolina included Joseph Alexander, John Bar, David Caldwell, James Hall, David Ker, George Newton, Henry Patillo, and James Tate. In Tennessee, early educators included Hezekial Balch, Thomas Benton Craighead, and Samuel Doak, and later George Newton.

Selected References

Haller, Charles R., 2004, George Newton and His Academies: Asheville, NC, *A Lot of Bunkum*, vol. 25, no. 2, p. 7

_____, 2008, Tennent Family, Buncombe Co., NC: *ibid*, vol. 29, no. 2, p. 25

Tennent, Mary A., 1971, *Light in Darkness. The Story of William Tennent, Sr.*: Greensboro, NC, Greensboro Print Co., 282 p.

McLachlan, James, 1976. *Princetonians, 1748-1768, A Biographical Dictionary*: Princeton, NJ, Princeton Univ. Press, 706 p.

Sloan, Douglas, 1971, *The Scottish Enlightenment and the American College Ideal*: NY, Columbia Univ., 298 p.

_____, 1973, *The Great Awakening and American Education, a Documentary History*: *ibid*, 270 p.

Descendants of Samuel Vance (son of Andrew)

Name	Cemetery
1. Samuel Vance, (c.1691-c.1778), immigrant	(Virginia)
+ Sarah Colville, immigrant (8 children; 5 sons, 3 dau.)	(Virginia)
2. Capt. David Vance (1745-1813) **RW**	Vance
+ Priscilla Brank (1756-1836) (8 child.)	Vance
3. Jean (Jane) Vance (1777-1858) (12 child.)	(Tennessee)
+ Hugh Lawson Davidson, Sr. (1768-1841)	(Tennessee)
3. Sarah Vance (1780-1847) (10 child.)	(Tennessee)
+ Charles McLean (1773-1825)	(Tennessee)
3. Samuel Vance (1783-1849)	(Tennessee)
+ Christina Weaver (c.1789-186-)	(Tennessee)
3. Elizabeth Vance (1787-1861)	(Cherokee Co.)
1st William Mitchell Davidson (1780-1846)	(Texas)
+ 2nd Samuel Winslow Davidson (1781-1858)	Piney Grove
3. Priscilla Vance (1789-____) (8 child.)	(Tennessee)
+ George Whitson (c.1780-1826)	(Tennessee)
3. David Vance, Jr. (1792-1844) **War of 1812**	Vance
+ Elmira Margaret Baird (1802-1878) (8 child)	?Riverside
4. Laura Henrietta Vance (1826-1900)	Riverside
+ Morgan S. Nielson (1822-1894)	Riverside
4. Robert Brank Vance (1828-1899), **CSA**	Riverside
+ 1st Harriet V. McElroy (1833-1885) (6 ch.)	Riverside
5. David Vance (1852-____)	
5. James N. Vance (1859-1926)	Riverside
5. Zebulon F. Vance (1867-____)	
5. Mary Vance (1871-____)	
+ ____ Cox	
+ 2nd Lizzie R. Cook	
4. Zebulon Baird Vance (1830-1894), **CSA, Gov.**	Riverside
+ 1st Harriet Newell Espy (1832-1878) (8 child.)	Riverside
5. Robert Espy Vance (1854-1855)	Riverside
5. Charles Noel Vance (1856-1922)	Riverside
+ Katie T. ____ (1864-____)	
5. David Mitchell Vance (1857-____)	(?Tennessee)
+ Maud Mary Watkins	
5. Zebulon Baird Vance, Jr. (1860-1924)	Riverside
+ Mary Herndon (1874-____)	
5. Thomas Malvern Vance (1862-____)	(?Washington)
+ Gertrude W. ____ (1867-____)	
+ 2nd Florence Steele Martin (1840-1924)	Riverside
4. James Noel Vance (1832-1855)	Vance
4. Ann Edgeworth Vance	(Tennessee)
+ Richard Nye Price	(Tennessee)

<u>Name</u>	<u>Cemetery</u>
4. Sarah Priscilla Vance (1838-1914)	Riverside
+ Hugh Douglas Hale	
4. David Leonidas Vance (1840-1843)	(Madison Co.)
4. Hannah Moore Vance (1842-1920)	Riverside
+ Edward W. Herndon (1839-1886) **CSA**	Riverside
3. Robert Brank Vance (1793-1827)	Vance
3. Celia Vance (1795-1879) (9 child)	(Cherokee Co.)
+ Benjamin Stringfield Brittain (1793-1864)	(Cherokee Co.)

Editor's Notes:

Most historians state that David Vance went to Rowan Co. about 1775. He is mentioned in the *Colonial Records of North Carolina*, vol. 10, 1775-1776, p. 253, which related to Salisbury, Rowan Co. Other records note that he was a Lt. in the NC Reg., Continental Line, with a commission dating from Apr. 76 to Je. 78; at this time he fought in the northern campaign.

He married Priscilla Brank about 1776. When Vance went to Burke Co. in late 1778, the couple lived one mile north of Morganton. Vance became an elder at Quaker Meadows Presbyterian Church. When he fought at Kings Mountain in Oct. 1780, he was a Captain.

Vance moved to Reems Creek about 1784, an area which became part of northern Buncombe Co. in 1792. Likely, Vance was an organizer of the Reems Creek Presbyterian Church, which dates from 1791. He continued to serve in the Militia and eventually reached the rank of Colonel.

David Vance represented Burke Co. in the NC House of Commons from 1786-87 and from 1790-92. A son, Robert B. Vance, was in the House of Representatives from Buncombe in 1823 and 1824-25. A grandson, Zebulon B. Vance was governor of North Carolina from 1862-65.

In a 1992 article in *A Lot of Bunkum*, Kenneth D. Israel recorded land entries from an old hand-written book of *Burke County Land Entries, 1778-1795* as follows:
#97, p. 33, David Vance, 100 acres, Crooked Creek (now McDowell Co.), Feb. 1778
#242, p. 81, David Vance, 300 acres west branch of Richland Creek (Haywood Co.), Feb., 1778
These entries were later declared null and void.

As shown on the accompanying chart, Vance had six permanent land entries in Burke Co. and eleven permanent land entries in Buncombe Co., as for instance:

Burke Co. entries
grant 144, entered 1778, 100 acres, Crooked Creek, now McDowell Co.
grant 1027, entered 1783, 320 acres Reems Creek, now Buncombe Co.

Buncombe Co. entry
grant 1237, entered 1803, 250 acres Reems Creek

In 1984, Emmett R. White, Sr. stated that in 1783-1784, Vance received warrants or grants for military service in the Middle District of Tennessee, on the Duck River, Stones River, and Elk River. He willed the acreage to his children, some of whom migrated there.

Deeds recorded at the Buncombe County Courthouse include 328 acres on Reems Creek, David Vance, grantee; William Dever, Sr. grantor, Bk S1-2/274 and S2-2/274, 10/ 20/1795.

In the 1790 NC Census, David Vance's household, Eleventh Company, Morgan District, Burke Co., includes 3 males, 5 females, and 3 slaves. On the 1800 NC census, Buncombe Co., the household included 5 males, 4 females, and 10 slaves.

In 1793, David Vance was on the Board of Trustees for the Newton Academy. On 9-26-1804, David Vance was one of two trustees given true and lawful (power of) attorney over 20,000 acres at Swannanoa/Cane Creek. This deed, Deed Book 10/196, was authorized by the Trustees of the General Assembly of the Presbyterian Church, Princeton, NJ. Grantors were Richard Stockton and Elias Boudinot.

David Vance's will, dated 28 August 1811, gives 620 acres on the Elk River in Tennessee to his oldest son, Samuel. It gives to sons David and Robert 898 acres on Reems Creek, in Buncombe Co. Further it gives to David and Robert 1,000 acres in Maury Co., TN. It gives 1,000 acres on the Stony River in Rutherford Co., TN to his five daughters Jean Davidson, Sarah McLean, Betsy Davidson, Priscilla Whitson, and Celia Vance. The will also mentions partial warrants for other tracts of 2,300 acres and 700 acres in Tennessee.

Some early burial records for Riverside Cemetery refer to "Asheville Cemetery," a synonymous term.

Selected References:
Avery, Alphonso C., 1913, *History of the Presbyterian Churches of Quaker Meadows and Morganton from the Year 1780 to 1813*: Raleigh, NC, Edwards & Broughton Co., 109 p.
Haller, Charles R., 2008, Vance Family of Reems Creek: Asheville, NC, *A Lot of Bunkum*, vol. 29, no. 4, p. 10-14
Moss, Bobby G., 1990, *The Patriots at Kings Mountain*: Blacksburg, SC, Scotia-Hibernia Press. 317 p.
White, Emmett R., Sr., 1984, *Revolutionary War Soldiers of Western North Carolina. Burke Co., Vol. 1*: Easley, SC, Southern Historical Press, 318 p., + index

Three members of the Vance family, Robert Brank Vance (1793-1827), Robert Brank Vance (1828-1899), and Zebulon Baird Vance (1830-1894) are in the *Dictionary of North Carolina Biography*.

Descendants of William Brittain Westall (3 wives, 20 child.)

Name	Cemetery
1.William Brittain Westall (1805-1882)	(Yancey Co.)
+ 1st unknown (____-____)(1 child.)	
+ 2nd Matilda Jane Penland (1799-1841)(6 child.)	
2. Thomas Casey Westall (1830-1903)	Riverside
+ Martha Anne Penland (1833-1897)(11 child.)	Riverside
3. Henry Addison Westall (1854-1947)	
+ 1st Laura Hill (1859-1926)(4 child.)	
+ 2nd Jane Eastwood	
3. Samuel W. B. Westall (1855-1863)	
3. Sarah Matilda Westall (1857-1877)	Riverside
3. Julia Elizabeth Westall (1860-1945) (8 child.)	Riverside
+ William Oliver Wolfe (1851-1922) + 3x	Riverside
4. Leslie E. Wolfe (1885-1886)	Riverside
4. Effie Nelson Wolfe (1887-1950)(3 child.)	(Anderson, SC)
+ Frederick Warlow Gambrell (1884-1952)	(Anderson, SC)
4. Frank Cecil Wolfe (1888-1956)	Riverside
4. Mabel Elizabeth Wolfe (1890-1958)	Riverside
+ Ralph Wheaton (1881-1973)	Riverside
4. Benjamin Harrison Wolfe (1892-1918) twin	
4. Grover Cleveland Wolfe (1892-1904) twin	Riverside
4. Frederick William Wolfe (1894-1980)	
+ Mary Burriss	
4. Thomas Clayton Wolfe (1900-1938) **Author**	Riverside
3. James Manassas Westall (1861-1943)	Riverside
+ Minnie R. White (____-____)(5 child.)	Riverside
3. William Harrison Westall (1863-1944)	Riverside
+ Emily Justice (1863-1942)(2 child.)	Riverside
3. Lee Johnson Westall (1866-1884)	Riverside
3. Thomas Crockett Westall (1870-1940)	
Una McLeod (____-____)(2 child.)	
3. Mary R. Westall (1868-1888)	Riverside
3. Harry Greeley Westall (1872-1902)	Riverside
+ Emily Justice (1863-1942)	Riverside
3. Elmer Copen Westall (1874-1941)	Riverside
+ Grace Parmalee (____-____)(1 child.)	
+ 3rd Eliza Madeline Angel (1820-1898)(13 child.)	

Selected References

Camford, Thomas W., 1998, *The Westalls and their Kin*: Port Townsend, WA, Ah Tom Publ., 392 p.

Cawyer, Shirley B., 1988, T*he Genealogical Study of James Brittain of Buncombe Co., NC*: Stephensonsville, TX, privately printed, 617 p.

Haller, Charles R., 2005, Thomas Wolfe's Father: Asheville, NC, *A Lot of Bunkum*, vol. 26, no.4, p. 13-17

Mauldin, Joanne M., 2007: *Thomas Wolfe*: Knoxville, TN, Univ. Tennesse Press, 361 p.

Young, Perry D., 2000, *The Westall Family*: Chapel Hill, NC, privately printed, 46 p.

Descendants of Mary Whitaker

<u>Name</u>	<u>Cemetery</u>
1. Mary Whitaker (1798-1872)	West Chapel
+ Jeremiah West (1795-1880+)	West Chapel
2. John Preston West, Sr. (1817-1864), **CSA**	(Spotsylvania, VA)
+ Sarah Jane Vaughan (1822-1897) (8 child.)	West Chapel
3. John Preston West, Jr. (1843-1865), **CSA**	(Richmond, VA)
3. Mary Catherine West (1841-1924)	West Chapel
+ George William Worley (1841-1924), **CSA**	West Chapel
2. Rozilla West (1820-1910)	Bethesda U.M.
+ James Mitchell Miller, **CSA**, d.1864	(Richmond, VA)
2. Jasper Newton West (1821-1904)	(Nebraska)
+ Esther Emily Cordell (1828-1904)	(Nebraska)
2. Millie West (1822-____)	
+ William M. Lewis, (1829-1862), **CSA**	
2. William Riley West (1823-1905), **CSA**	Bethesda U.M.
+ Salina E. Webb (1838-1922)	Bethesda U.M.
2. Mitchell West (1825-c.1861)	(Springfield, MO.)
2. James West (1827-1912), **CSA**	(Commerce, TX)
+ Margaret Ann E. Wilson	(Commerce, TX)
2. Alexander West (1830-1910), **CSA**	West Chapel
+ Rachel E. Penland (1840-1920)	West Chapel
2. Salina West (1831-1883)	Bethesda U.M.
+ Gabriel P. Miller, CSA, d.1864	(Petersburg. VA)
2. Noah West (1831-1861), **CSA**	West Chapel
2. Rachel Matilda West (1834-1923)	Sharon U.M.
1st Frank M. Balleu	
+ 2nd Robert Williams	Sharon U.M.
2. Harriet E. West (1836-1862)	West Chapel
2. Nancy West (1838-____)	
____ Carter	

Selected References:

Hyde, Dorothy R., 2007, Jeremiah and Mary Whitaker West: Asheville, NC, *A Lot of Bunkum*, vol. 28, no. 4, p. 25-27

Descendants of William Whitson (see also Gash)

Name	Cemetery
1. William Whitson (1750-1806)	?Cemetery Hill
+ Anne McDowell (c.1760-1829 (10 child.)	(Tennessee)
2. William Whitson, Jr. (c.1779-c.1849)	(?Arkansas)
2. George Whitson (c.1780-1826)	(Tennessee)
+ Priscilla Vance (1782-1826) (8 child.)	(Tennessee)
2. Thomas Jefferson Whitson (1781-1870)	(Alabama)
+ Elizabeth Gudger (c.1785-1874) (7 child.)	(Alabama)
2. Joseph McDowell Whitson, Sr. (1782-1861)	(Tennessee)
+ Sarah "Sally" Gudger (c.1783-1862) (10 child.)	(Tennessee)
3. Selena Whitson (1806-1880+) (2 child.)	(McDowell Co.)
+ Alney Burgin (1787-1868)	(McDowell Co.)
3. Melissa Whitson	
3. Drucilla Whitson (1811-1890)	(McDowell Co.)
+ Alney Burgin (1814-____)	(McDowell Co.)
3. Lucinda Whitson	
+ Joseph Williams	
3. Eliza Whitson, d. young	
3. Jason Carson Whitson (1817-____)	(McDowell Co.)
3. McDowell Whitson	
3. Samuel Carson Whitson (1825-1855)	(McDowell Co.)
3. George W. Whitson (1826-____) dentist	
+ Jane Roberts (1833-____) (8 child.)	
4. William Whitson (1854-____)	
4. Henry Lawrence Whitson (1855-1947)	
4. Joseph J. Whitson (c.1856-____)	
4. George M. Whitson (1860-1932)	Piney Grove
+ Minnie C. Seaver (1870-1944)	Piney Grove
4. Charles P. Whitson (1863-1927)	Piney Grove
+ Nettie Adkins Worley (1865-1962)	Piney Grove
4. Dow Gudger Whitson (c.1864-____)	
4. Samuel Whitson (c.1867-____)	
4. Sallie L. Whitson (1871-1963)	
2. Mary Whitson (1782-1860)	
+ Martin Hardin (1774-1824)	
2. John Whitson (1786-1844)	
2. James S. Whitson (1787-1841)	(Alabama)
+ Elizabeth Long	(Alabama
2. Samuel Whitson (c.1797-1871)	(Texas)
+ 3x	
2. Sarah Whitson (1800-1860)	(Tennessee)
+ John Wesley Witherspoon	(Tennessee)
2. Rebecca Whitson (c.1801-____)	(Tennessee)
+ Edmund L. Williams	(Tennessee)

Selected References

Mitchell, Ann C., 2009, *Joseph Whitson Family, 1615-2009*: Florence, AL, privately publ., 83 p.

Editor's Notes:

An old handwritten book of *Burke County Land Entries, 1778-1795* records (Secretary of State file 949) William Whitson as having received 400 acres on Ivy River, August 1783 (NC grant 1040). This area is near the present boundary of Buncombe and Madison Cos. Also in August, 1783, he got 200 acres on the east side of the French Broad River (across from the mouth of the Swannanoa) (NC grant 1076). In March, 1784, he received another 500 acres in the same area (NC grant 1128). And in April, 1784, another 640 acres on the Pigeon River in present day Haywood Co. (record missing). Except for the latter, these grants were recorded in Burke Co. and partially re-recorded in Buncombe Co.

He acquired other acreage, most notably 200 acres on the Swannanoa River on 12-9-1795 via NC State grants 214 and 218. These two grants were recorded in Buncombe Co. Ten of Whitson's early grants are shown in the table under Gash/Gudger/Whitson, which see.

In the 1790s, William Whitson held a number of local government positions in Buncombe Co. In 1792, he was a justice of the first court and was living in the district embraced by the lower Swannanoa River and Cane Creek. In 1793, he was one of twelve trustees of the Newton Academy, the others being Andrew Erwin, Daniel Smith, John Patton, Edmund Sams, James Blakely, William Foster, Sr., Thomas Foster, Jr., William Gudger, Samuel Murray, Joseph Henry, David Vance, William Brittain, George Davidson, John Davidson of Hominy, and Rev. George Newton.

When William Whitson died late in 1806, he probably was buried at Cemetery Hill, a now obliterated cemetery in the Beverly Hills area of East Asheville. At that time, the family was in the midst of moving to Maury Co., TN. His wife, Anne McDowell Whitson, a daughter Sarah Whitson Witherspoon, and four sons William, George, Thomas, and James moved their families. Daughters Mary Whitson Hardin and Rebecca Whitson Williams also migrated. Sons Joseph, John, and Samuel apparently remained behind. William Whitson's will, filed in Maury Co., TN, is dated 6 Nov. 1806.

The 1790 NC Census lists William Whitson in the Eleventh Company, Burke Co., Morgan District with 1 male over 16, 5 males under 16, 2 females and 2 slaves. In the 1800 NC Census, Buncombe Co., the household has 1 male 26-45, 2 males 16-26, 2 males 10-16, 2 males 0-10m, 1 females 26-45, 2 females 0-10, and 3 slaves.

William Whitson, Sr., sold 640 acres on Rosses Creek to Patton & Erwin via Buncombe Co. Deed Book B/55, 10/27/1806.

Anne McDowell Whitson sold some 1,140 acres in Buncombe Co. for the considerable sum of $4,500 dollars to James Patton and Andrew Erwin via Buncombe Co. Deed Book B/135, 12/15/1808. This property consisted of six parcels. The main property of 640 acres containing the former Whitson residence was located at the junction of Haw Creek, formerly Whitson's Creek, and the Swannanoa River. This main property abutted that of William Gudger.

Descendants of John Woodfin

Name	Cemetery
1. John Woodfin	
+ Mary Grady (12 child.)	
2. Nicholas Washington Woodfin (1810-1875) **CSA**	Riverside
+ Eliza Grace McDowell (1816-1876) (5 child.)	Riverside
3. Anna Mira Woodfin (1841-1917)	Riverside
3. unnamed son (1842-1842)	First Presbyterian
3. Mary Matilda Woodfin (1843-1918)	Riverside
+ Benson M. Jones	
3. unnamed son (1845-1845)	First Presbyterian
3. Mira McDowell Woodfin (1848-1929)	Riverside
+ William A. Holland	Riverside
2. Henry Grady Woodfin	
2. John Wood Woodfin (1818-1863) **CSA**	Riverside
+ Mira Adeline McDowell (1822-1872)	Riverside

*****

unknown relationship	
1. Denna Woodfin (1771-1817) (5 child.)	?Cemetery Hill
+ Joseph Dennis Gash (1767-1805)	?Cemetery Hill

Selected References:

Haller, Charles R., 2007, Nicholas W. Woodfin: Asheville, NC, *A Lot of Bunkum*, vol. 28, no. 3, p. 21-22

Census Records

Nicholas Woodfin is on the 1790 NC Census, Rutherford Co., Morgan District, Thirteen Company, with 3 males and 2 females.

Nicholas Woodfin is on the 1800 NC Census, Buncombe Co. (now Henderson co.), with 4 males and 6 females.

Tho. Woodfin is on the 1790 NC Census Rutherford Co., Morgan District, Thirteenth Company, with 3 males and 2 females.

Thomas Woodfin is on the 1800 NC Census, Buncombe co. (now Henderson Co.), with 5 males and 4 females.

Editor's Notes

Nicholas W. Woodfin became a prominent lawyer in Western North Carolina, settling legal matters from about 1835 until after the end of the Civil War. The Civil War proved especially difficult for Woodfin, who as owner of 121 slaves in 1860 was by far the largest slave holder in Buncombe Co. He held extensive land. According to the *Dictionary of North Carolina Biography*, the value of Woodfin's estate diminished precipitously from $165,000 in 1860 to $36,000 in 1870 through loss of slaves, cancellation of Confederate bonds, and decline in land values.

Descendants of Francis S. Worley

Name   **Cemetery**

1. Francis S. Worley (c.1755-c.1803, or 1810)
  + ?Mary Polly Brown
    2. Nathan Worley (1780-1870)   Lower Big Pine
    + 1st – ?Amanda Robinson (10 child.)
        3. James O. Worley (c.1800-1848)
        + Edith Jones (1799-____) (8 child.)
        3. Francis Worley (c. 1802-____)
        + Kiziah Davis (1802-____) (8 child.)
        3. Catherine Worley (1806-1858) (4 child.)
        + Allen Jones (1810-____)
        3. Priscilla Worley (1809-____)   (Missouri)
        + 1st unknown (1 child)
        + Jesse J. Reeves (1809-____) (6 child.)   (Missouri)
        3. Annice Worley (c. 1810-____) (6 child.)
        + James Berry Boyd (1798-1847)
        3. Priscilla Worley (1809-____)
        + Jesse J. Reeves
        3. Kiziah Worley (c. 1812-____) (13 child.)
        + Jonathan Surrett (c. 1811-____)
        3. Nathan Worley (c. 1814____)
        3. Esther Worley (1817-____) (7 child.)
        + William Robinson (c. 1816-____)
        3. Andrew Ervin Worley (1818-1881)   (Arkansas)
        + Cynthia Clark (1816-____) (6 child.)   (Arkansas)
            4. George William Worley (1841-1924) **CSA**   West Chapel
            + Mary Catherine West (1841-1924)   West Chapel
                            *****

    + 2nd - Susananna King (1805-1885?) (12 child.)   Lower Big Pine
        3. Mary Elizabeth Worley (1829-____)
        + William Waldroup
        3. William M. Worley (1830-1919)
        + Sarah Jane Waldroup (1835-1898) (13 child.)   Lower Big Pine
        + Jane E. Fisher (1849-____)   Lower Big Pine
        3. Margaret Worley (1831-____) (5 child.)
        + Benjamin Roberts (1826-____)
        3. Robeson Worley (1833-____)
        + Ruth Jane Davis (1835-1922) (8 child.)
        3. Julia Caroline Worley (1834-1919) (3 child.)   Fortner
        + James Roberts
        3. Ruth M. Worley (1836-____) (2 child.)
        + Daniel C. A. Davis (1833-____)
        3. Harriet Woody Worley (1837-1934) (7 child.)   Kirt Payne
        + George W. Buckner (1834-1928)   Kirt Payne

Name	Cemetery

      3. Adolphus D. Worley (1842-1928)

      + Mary Emeline Buckner (1838-1911) (4 child.)   Lower Big Pine

      3. John Worley (1843-____)

      + 1st Hannah Matilda Martin (1839-____) (6 child.)

      + 2nd Harriet Louise Teague

      3. David Worley (1845-1919)

      + 1st Susannna Davis (5 child.)

      + 2nd Elizabeth Sawyer (c.1848-1924) (1 child)   Lower Big Pine

      3. Jane Worley (1850-____) never married

      3. James Worley

    2. Catherine Worley (1781-1820)

    David Miller

    2. Joseph Worley (1784-1867)

    + 1st unknown

    + 2nd Parossella Davis (7 child.)

    2. Wiley Worley

    2. Ruth Worley

Selected References

Haller, Charles R., 2006, Descendants of Francis S. Worley: Asheville, NC, *A Lot of Bunkum*, vol. 27, no. 3, p. 20

Yates, Mrs. Jesse J., 2007, A Partial Record of George William Worley: Asheville, NC, *A Lot of Bunkum*, vol. 28, no.3, p. 22-25 (reprint)

Modified from website of Randall S. Treadway

Descendants of James Young, Sr.

<u>Name</u>   <u>Cemetery</u>

1. James Young, Sr.
  + Ann Stuart (____-____) (13 child.)
  2. John Stewart Young (1734-1827)   (?Transylvania Co.)
  + Jane Smith (1750-1841) (6 child.)   (?Transylvania Co.,)
  2. James Young (1737-____)   (Tennessee)
  + Catherine? (____-____) (4 child.)
  2. Kisia Young (1739-____)
  2. Mary Young (1741-____)
  2. Ann Young (1743-____)
  2. Joseph Young (1746-____)
  2. Stacy Young (1748-1844)   Hominy Baptist
  + John Webb (1765-c.1826) **RW** (1)   Hominy Baptist
  2. Martha "Patsy" Young (1750-1837) (8 child.)   Cemetery Hill
  + William Gudger (1752-1735)   Cemetery Hill
  2. Ann Nancy Young (1752-1845) (5 child.)   Newton Academy
  + Edmund Sams (1750-1845) RW (2)   Newton Academy
    3. Orra Sams (1778-1853) (1 child)   Newton Academy
    + Thomas Foster (1774-1858)   Newton Academy
    3. Greenlee Sams   (Missouri)
    + Rachel Gash (1794-1850+) (4 child.)   (Missouri)
    3. Burdit Sams   (Missouri)
    3. Benoni Sams   (?Henderson Co.)
    3. Edmund Sams, Jr. (1793-1881+) +3x   (?Madison Co.)
  2. Sarah Young (1755-____)   (Tennessee)
  + John McNabb   (Tennessee)
  2. Elizabeth Young (1757-____)
  2. Joseph Young (1759-____)
  2. William Young (1763-____)   (?Candler)
  + Rebecca Davidson (1769-____) (12 child.) (3)   (?Candler)
    3. Lemuel Young (1802-1889)
    + Miriam Owenby (1805-____) (6 child.)
    3. Charity Young (c.1803-1870) (7 child.)   Hominy Bapt.
    + Perminter D. Morgan (1806-1865)   Hominy Bapt.
    3. Stacy Young (1804-____) (11 child.)
    + John Owenby
    3. William Young (1810-1857)
    + Mary "Polly" Rabun (1811-1899) (9 child.)   Hominy Bapt.

Footnotes:

(1) According to Candler historians Eleanor Newcomb Rice and Kenneth D. Israel, the old John Webb cemetery (Old Baptist Church) was between old Hwy 19-23 and new Hwy 19-23, about ¼ mile north of the current Hominy Baptist Cemetery.

(2) Edmund Sams was a charter member of the Hominy Baptist Church formed circa 1812 and supervised construction of the first log church house.

(3) Rebecca Davidson reportedly was the daughter of James Davidson.

Census Records

Wm. Young is on the 1790 NC Census, Burke Co., Morgan district, Eleventh Company (now Buncombe Co.), with 2 males and 2 females.

William Young is on the 1800 NC Census, Buncombe Co., with 3 males and 3 females.

Selected References

Israel, Kenneth D., 2009, James Young, Sr. & His Wife Ann, and Their Family: Asheville, NC, *A Lot of Bunkum*: vol. 30, no.2, p.7-15

_____, 2009, William Young & Mary "Polly" Raburn Young: *ibid*, vol. 30, no. 3, p. 22-26

Part II: Early Western North Carolina Land Grants

Alexander Family (Buncombe Co., 1790-1890)

Ashworth Family (Buncombe Co., 1794-1838)

Avery Family Land Grants (Burke & Buncombe Cos., 1788-1875)

Baird Family (Buncombe Co., 1794-1838)

Baird-Beard Family (Burke Co., 1792-1825)

Biffel/Eller/Weaver (Burke & Buncombe Cos., 1780-1838)

Biffel-Eller-Weaver Notes

Brank Family (Burke & Buncombe Cos., 1778-1838)

Brevard Family (Burke & Buncombe Cos. 1778-1860)

Brittain Family (Buncombe Co., 1794-1837)

Bryson Family (Buncombe Co., 1816-1835)

Burton Family (Burke & Buncombe Cos., 1791-1805)

Zachariah Candler (Buncombe Co., 1800-1841)

Carland Family (Buncombe Co., 1826-1834)

Carson Family (Burke & Buncombe Cos., 1778-1842)

Cathey Family (Burke & Buncombe Cos.,1778-1806)

Chunn Family (Buncombe Co., 1804-1834)

Lambert Clayton (Burke & Buncombe Cos., 1794-1840)

Other Clayton Family (Buncombe Co., 1809-1868)

Craig Family (Buncombe Co., 1792-1838)

Davidson Family (Burke Co., 1778-1817)

Davidson Family (Buncombe Co., 1778-1850)

Deaver Family (Buncombe Co., 1793-1843)

Fletcher Family (Buncombe Co., 1790-1818)

Foster Family (Buncombe Co., 1791-1836)

Gash, Gudger, Whitson Family (Burke & Buncombe Cos., 1778-1840)

Gillaspie Family (Buncombe Co., 1796-1836)

Greenlee Family (Burke, Buncombe, & Rutherford Cos., 1778-1838)

Hawkins Family (Burke & Buncombe Cos., 1778-1843)

Hemphill Family (Burke & Buncombe Cos., 1778-1859)

Henry Family (Burke & Buncombe Cos., 1784-1840)

Hoodenpile Family (Burke & Buncombe Cos, 1786-1809)

Hughey Family (Buncombe Co., 1789-1834)

Israel Family (Buncombe Co., 1802-1861)

Jarrett Family (Buncombe Co., 1797-1846)

Justice Family (Buncombe Co., 1792-1838)

Killian Family (Burke & Buncombe Cos., 1778-1830)

Kuykendall Family (Rutherford & Buncombe Cos., 1779-1804)

Lance Family (Buncombe Co.,1799-1891)

Lane/Swain Family (Buncombe Co., 1791-1858)

Love Family (Burke & Buncombe Cos., 1792-1825)

Lytle Family (Burke & Buncombe Cos., 1778-1783)

Maney Family (Buncombe Co., 1793-1826)
McDowell Family (Burke & Buncombe Cos.,1778-1836)
McLean Family (Burke Co., 1778-1779)
McPeter, et al (Burke Co., 1778-1843; Buncombe Co., 1778-1853)
Merrill Family (Buncombe Co., 1793-1882)
Mills Family (Rutherford Co., 1785-1812)
Moore Family (Burke & Buncombe Cos., 1778-1829)
Murray Family (Buncombe Co., 1796-1875)
Patton Family (Burke & Buncombe Cos., 1778-1883)
Penland Family (Burke & Buncombe Cos., 1778-1903)
Ragsdale Family (Buncombe Co., 1792-1829)
Reynolds Family (Buncombe Co., 1800-1869)
Rice Family (Buncombe Co., 1794-1836)

Sams Family (Burke & Buncombe Cos., 1790-1829)
Smith Family (Buncombe Co., 1778-1844)
Stroup Family (Buncombe Co., 1829-1841)
Thrash Family (Buncombe Co., 1808-1876)
Vance Family (Burke & Buncombe Cos., 1778-1837)
Webb Family (Buncombe Co., 1797-1829)
Westall Family (Buncombe Co., 1808-1834)
Whitaker Family (Buncombe Co, 1804-1896)
Woodfin Family (Buncombe Co., 1794-1844)
Worley Family (Buncombe Co., 1796-1829)
Young Family (Buncombe Co., 1798-1873)

Alexander Family NC Land Grants

Buncombe Co.

Registered Name	Grant	Acres	Entered	Patent	Location
Avery Alexander	4305	5.5	4-9-1860	5-24-1861	FB River, W. side
Avery Alexander	4448	4	5-6-1881	1-27-1883	Cane Cr.
Avery Alexander	4449	50	5-6-1881	1-27-1893	Brush Cr. (assignee)
B. J. Alexander	11056	n/a	6-27-1890	7-15-1891	Avery Cr., Smith's Bridge
B. J. Alexander	11057	n/a	6-27-1890	7-15-1891	Reams Cr., Smith's Bridge
George C. Alexander	2182	50	8-26-1814	12-4-1815	Bee Tree Cr., (Davidson's)
George C. Alexander	2826	50	12-14-1826	11-20-1830	Swannano R., both sides
George C. Alexander	3774	150	10-7-1835	7-16-1839	Swannano R., N. side
George C. Alexander	3775	50	7-5-1837	7-16-1839	Beetree Cr., Swananoa
George C. Alexander	3811	50	10-15-1838	12-9-1840	Cole Br., Swananoa
George C. Alexander	3813	30	4-26-1839	12-9-1840	Swannanoa R., N. side
George C. Alexander	3815	50	9-18-1838	12-9-1840	Beetree Cr., E. side, Wolf Br.
James Alexander	449	100	5-20-1796	8-31-1798	Bee Tree Cr.,adj. Wm. Davidson
James Alexandria	727	50	7-21-1791	12-6-1799	Bull Cr., right fork
James Alexander	728	100	7-21-1791	12-6-1799	Grassy Br., Swanannoa
James M. Alexander	3345	70			Rims Cr., adj. his mill
James M. Alexander	3814	100	90-12-1840	12-9-1840	Bee Tree Cr., Swananoa
James Alexander	4287	57	11-25-1853	7-2-1855	N. Turkey Cr.
John Alexander	40	50	10-16-1790	1-7-1794	Swananoa, Crook Br., adj. Davidson
John Alexander	2250	100	2-9-1816	11-30-1816	branch where now lives
John Alexander	2920	50	1-30-1828	12-21-1830	Swannano, head Big Br.
M. Alexander	4326	50	1-12-1858	12-28-1858	head S. Turkey Cr.
Newton H. Alexander	3462	12	6-9-1835	12-10-1836	FB River, W. side, adj. own land
Newton H. Alexander	3463	73	12-7-1835	12-10-1836	FB River, W. side, adj. John Rogers
Newton H. Alexander	3559	32.5	12-7-1835	11-9-1837	FB River, W. side, adj. John Rogers
Newton H. Alexander	3560	40	12-7-1835	11-9-1837	FB River, W. side, adj. John Rogers
Newton Alexander	2964	100			Bee Tree Cr.
Newton H. Alexander	3310	50			FB River, W. side
Newton H. Alexander	3812	100	10-18-1837	12-9-1840	FB River, Gap Cr.
William Alexander	100	50	2-11-1794	1-19-1795	Beetree Cr., Cove Br., Swananaoa
William Alexander	858	50	10-23-1788	12-11-1800	Hommany Cr., both sides
William D. Alexander	3990	25	4-12-1841	1-21-1843	Bee Tree Cr., Swananoa
William D. Alexander	4096	50	5-13-1843	1-7-1845	Bee Tree Cr., Bull Cr.
William J. Alexander	4222	58	9-26-1853	11-7-1853	FB River, E. side, adj. Blake

Ashworth Family NC Land Grants

Buncombe Co.

Registered Name	Grant	Acres	Entered	Patent	Location
James Ashworth	1581	250	1-29-1803	12-11-1804	adj. J. Ashworth, Sr.
John Ashworth	176	50	1-24-1795	5-17-1795	Cain Cr.
John Ashworth	584	50	11-27-1796	12-24-1798	Hickory Nut Mtn.
John Ashworth	691	50	1-23-1798	12-2-1799	Walnut Cove, adj. own
John Ashworth	692	50	1-23-1798	12-2-1799	adj. own
John Ashworth	693	200	1-23-1798	12-2-1799	Clear Cr., Lorrell Spr.
John Ashworth	751	100	3-27-1796	12-17-1798	Hickory Nut, Bear Wallow
John Ashworth, Jr.	752	100	5-8-1794	12-17-1799	Flatt Cr., Broad R.
John Ashworth, Sr.	1047	50	n/a	n/a	Ashworth Cr., S. side
John Ashworth, Sr.	1050	50	n/a	n/a	Hickory Nut Mtn. gap
John Ashworth, Jr.	1397	210	1-29-1803	12-11-1804	Ashworth, Cr., adj. own
Johnson Ashworth	4280	30.25	1-11-1855	2-10-1855	Cane Cr., FB River, E. side
Joshua Ashworth	4397	42	8-27-1870	2-7-1873	Pisgah Mtn.
Johnson Ashworth	4457	23	8-14-1882	1-9-1885	Cane Cr., adj. own
Joseph Ashworth	3919	50	11-3-1838	12-29-1840	Cain Cr.
Nancy Ashworth	1538	75	n/a	n/a	Still Br., adj. Ashworth, Sr.

Avery Family NC Land Grants

Buncombe Co.

Registered Name	Grant	Acres	Entered	Patent	Location
Isaac Thomas Avery	1440	640	12-10-1804	12-10-1805	Mills R.
Isaac Thomas Avery	1444	640	12-10-1804	12-10-1805	Mills R.
Weightstill Avery	6	300	1-1-1788	1-6-1794	FB River, W. side
Waightstill Avery	41	200	7-16-1793	7-7-1794	FB River, SE side
Waightstill Avery	90	350	7-25-1792	7-7-1794	Richmond Cr.
Waightstill Avery	91	50	7-25-1792	7-7-1794	Richmond Cr.
Waightstill Avery	202	100	5-1-1792	7-22-1795	FB River, Averys Cr.
Waightstill Avery	207	200	n/a	8-22-1795	FB River, W. side
Waightstill Avery	221	200	1-24-1795	6-6-1796	FB River, Avery Cr.
Waightstill Avery	249	100	1-20-1784	11-22-1796	Jacks Cr.

Avery Family NC Land Grants

Waightstill Avery	572	1600	4-22-1795	12-24-1798	Big Cr.
Waightstill Avery	573	400	4-22-1795	12-24-1798	Big Cr.
Waightstill Avery	574	400	4-22-1795	12-24-1798	Big Cr.
Waightstill Avery	575	800	4-22-1795	12-24-1798	Big Cr.
Waightstill Avery	576	200	4-25-1795	12-24-1798	FB River, E. side
Waightstill Avery	577	200	10-23-1788	12-24-1798	Averys Cr.
Waightstill Avery	578	50	3-31-1790	12-24-1798	Caney R.
Waightstill Avery	579	320	8-1-1783	12-24-1798	Pidgeon R., Beaverdam Cr.
Waightstill Avery	580	250	n/a	12-24-1798	Ben Davidsons Cr.
Waightstill Avery	581	100	10-20-1792	10-24-1798	Pigeon R., E. fork
Waightstill Avery	582	125	4-25-1795	10-24-1798	FB River, E. side
Waightstill Avery	583	200	10-23-1788	12-24-1798	Averys Cr., Mill Shoal
Waightstill Avery	595	400	4-22-1795	12-24-1798	Tuckaseegee R., Big Cr.
Waightstill Avery	810	200	7-22-1794	9-1-1800	FB River, McDowells Cr.
Waightstill Avery	880	50	4-20-1796	12-16-1800	Pidgeon R., E. fork, Great Cove
Waightstill Avery	908	200	4-13-1790	3-14-1801	Pigeon R., E. fork, Mud Cr.
Waightstill Avery	909	400	4-25-1795	11-14-1801	Tuckaseegee R., Big Cr.
Waightstill Avery	910	150	6-1-1790	11-14-1801	Pigeon R., E. fork, Mud Cr.
Waightstill Avery	911	400	4-25-1795	11-14-1801	Tuckassejah R., Big Cr.
Waightstill Avery	912	320	4-25-1795	11-14-1801	Tuckaseegee R., Big Cr.
Waightstill Avery (1)	963	300	4-25-1795	11-14-1801	Tuckaseegee R.
Waightstill Avery	1044	150	n/a	n/a	n/a
Waightstill Avery	1586	100	7-31-1792	12-16-1806	Pigeon R., E. fork
Waightstill Avery	2132	110	4-22-1794	6-6-1796	Bald Mtn. Cr.
Waightstill Avery	2144	110	1794	6-6-1796	Bald Mtn. Cr.
Waightstill Avery	2283	400	7-11-1816	12-18-1817	Muddy Cr., Great Swamp
Waightstill Avery	2420	400	6-2-1818	9-7-1819	FB River, SW side, Glade Cr.

Footnotes - Buncombe

(1) also Robert Love - 1st

Burke Co.

A. C. Avery	6551	640	12-5-1872	12-23-1874	Linville Mtn.
A. C. Avery	6552	640	12-5-1872	12-23-1874	Linville Mtn., Padis Cr.
A. C. Avery	6553	640	12-5-1872	12-23-1874	Burke/McDowell Co. line
A. C. Avery	6554	640	12-5-1872	12-23-1874	Linville Mtn., Padies Cr.
A. C. Avery	6555	112	12-5-1872	12-23-1874	Linville Mtn., Paddys Cr.
A. C. Avery	6556	640	12-5-1872	12-23-1874	Linville Mtn. Co. line
A. C. Avery	6557	640	12-5-1872	12-23-1874	Linville Mtn.
A. C. Avery	6567	350	8-16-1873	12-30-1875	Adj. own land
A. C. Avery	6568	529	8-16-1873	12-30-1875	Adj. own land

Avery Family NC Land Grants

A. C. Avery	6569	640	8-16-1873	12-30-1875	Adj. own land
A. C. Avery	6570	615	8-16-1873	12-30-1875	near Hugh Taylors still house
A. C. Avery	6571	218	5-19-1873	12-30-1875	Shortoff Mtn.
A. C. Avery	6572	640	5-19-1873	12-30-1875	Shortoff Mtn.
A. C. Avery	6573	379	5-19-1873	12-30-1875	Shortoff Mtn., Russells Cr.
A. C. Avery	6574	116	5-19-1873	12-30-1875	Adj. own land
A. C. Avery	6575	624	5-19-1873	12-30-1875	Adj. own land
A. C. Avery	6576	529	5-19-1873	12-30-1875	Shortoff Mtn.
A. C. Avery	6577	246	5-19-1873	12-30-1875	Falls Rock
A. C. Avery	6578	400	5-19-1873	12-30-1875	Falls Rock
A. C. Avery	6579	249	8-16-1873	12-30-1875	Adj. own land
A. C. Avery	6583	643	8-16-1875	12-30-1875	Bandy Cove Mtn.
A. C. Avery	6584	640	8-16-1873	12-30-1875	Adj. own land
A. C. Avery	6585	482	8-16-1875	12-30-1875	Steel Cr.
A. C. Avery	6586	640	8-16-1873	12-30-1875	Bandy Cove Mtn.
A. C. Avery	6587	337	8-16-1873	12-30-1875	Brown Mtn., Upper Cr.
A. C. Avery	6588	320	8-16-1873	12-30-1875	Ad., own land
A. C. Avery	6589	640	8-16-1873	12-30-1875	Adj. own land
A. C. Avery	6590	480	8-16-1873	12-30-1875	Millers Mtn., W. side
A. C. Avery	6591	320	8-16-1873	12-30-1875	Brown Mtn., Upper Cr.
A. C. Avery	6592	640	8-16-1873	12-30-1875	Adj. own land
A. C. Avery	6593	640	8-16-1873	12-30-1875	Adj. own land
A. C. Avery	6594	640	8-16-1873	12-30-1875	Shortoff Mtn.
A. C. Avery	6595	320	8-16-1873	12-30-1875	Shortoff Mtn.
A. C. Avery	6596	480	8-16-1873	12-30-1875	Shortoff Mtn.
A. C. Avery	6597	187	8-16-1873	12-30-1875	Steele Cr.
A. C. Avery	6598	150	8-16-1873	12-30-1875	n/a
A. C. Avery	6599	640	8-16-1873	12-30-1875	n/a
A. C. Avery	6600	640	8-16-1873	12-30-1875	Bandy Cove Mtn.
C. M. Avery (1)	6395	21	3-1-1859	3-7-1859	Silver Cr.
C. M. Avery	6396	17	3-1-1859	3-7-1859	Silver Cr., Baileys fork
Henry Avery	3458	250	1-6-1808	12-17-1808	Johns R., Warrior fork
Isaac Avery (2)	6638	36-1/4	11-14-1877	4-18-1878	Catawba R., Conee Cr.,
James Avery	5984	100	7-22-1839	12-17-1840	Lynville R., above falls
Peter Avery	6622	57	12-1-1868	12-21-1870	Russels Cr., E. side

Avery Family NC Land Grants

Rufus Avery	6672	50	10-12-1881	3-2-1883	Catawba R.
Rufus Avery	9481	60	2-22-1889	6-12-1881	Baileys fork
Waightstill Avery	404	220	3-19-1779	10-28-1782	Swan Pond, Canoe Trap
Waightstill Avery	460	250	3-17-1778	10-28-1782	Canoe Cr.
Waightstill Avery	461	100	2-3-1778	10-28-1782	Catawba R. N. side
Waightstill Avery	499	80	7-12-1778	10-28-1782	Catawba Is., N. side, fish trap
Waightstill Avery	711	100	3-17-1778	10-11-1783	Catawba R., S. side
Waightstill Avery	747	640	3-10-1783	10-11-1783	Catawba R., N.side, Swann Pond
Waightstill Avery	834	150	7-27-1778	11-9-1784	Towe R., Mtn. Cr.
Waightstill Avery	836	320	7-12-1778	11-9-1784	Catawba R., N. fork
Waightstill Avery	880	180	9-19-1778	11-9-1784	Towe R., Sugartree Cr.
Waightstill Avery	881	600	3-17-1778	11-9-1784	Towe R., Sugartree bottom
Waightstill Avery	882	150	n/a	11-9-1784	Towe R., Grassy Meadow
Waightstill Avery	883	100	7-27-1778	11-9-1784	Towe R., Great Crabtree orchard
Waightstill Avery	884	100	3-17-1778	n/a	Towe R., Great Crabtree orchard
Waightstill Avery	885	300	9-3-1778	11-9-1784	Tow R. head, Grassey meadow
Waightstill Avery	886	600	3-17-1778	11-9-1784	Towe R., Big Crab orchard
Waightstill Avery	887	150	5-7-1783	11-9-1784	Grassey Meadow, N. side
Waightstill Avery	888	300	5-7-1783	11-9-1784	Towe R.
Waightstill Avery	967	100	9-19-1778	8-7-1787	Rock Cr., E. fork
Waightstill Avery	997	100	9-19-1778	8-7-1787	Toe R., Cain Cr.
Waightstill Avery	1007	100	9-19-1778	8-7-1787	Rock Cr., E. fork
Waightstill Avery	1008	180	n/a	8-7-1787	Rock Cr., E. fork
Waightstill Avery	1010	350	1-4-1784	8-7-1787	FB River, 3 mi. above War Path
Waightstill Avery	1058	350	1-14-1784	8-7-1787	FB River, Cain Cr. W. side
Waightstill Avery	1067	250	1-14-1784	8-7-1787	FB River, 3 mi. below Cany Cr.
Waightstill Avery	1068	150	n/a	8-7-1787	Toe R., Cane Cr., E. fork
Waightstill Avery	1069	640	8-1-1783	8-7-1787	FB River, W. side, opp. Cane Cr.
Waightstill Avery (3)	1091	640	8-1-1783	12-13-1787	Cane Cr.
Waightstill Avery	1149	100	9-3-1778	5-18-1789	Three Mile Br.
Waightstill Avery	1153	180	7-27-1778	5-18-1789	Three Mile Br., head
Waightstill Avery	1166	80	9-3-1778	5-18-1789	Toe R., Three Mile Br.
Waightstill Avery	1300	200	10-7-1779	11-16-1790	Canew Cr., Jumping Br.
Waightstill Avery	1397	100	8-24-1778	12-15-1791	Lenville Cove, Meadow Cr.
Waightstill Avery	1398	180	8-12-1778	12-15-1791	S. Toe R., Big Cr.
Waightstill Avery	1408	180	8-12-1778	12-15-1791	Big Cr.
Waightstill Avery	1409	640	8-24-1778	12-15-1791	S. Toe R., Great Cove
Waightstill Avery	1410	320	5-23-1790	12-15-1791	FB River, W. side, Warm Springs
Waightstill Avery	1411	320	5-23-1790	12-15-1791	FB River, W. side, Warm Springs

Avery Family NC Land Grants

Waightstill Avery	1682	50	9-24-1792	12-16-1793	Cranberry Cr.
Waightstill Avery	1683	100	9-24-1792	12-16-1793	Cranberry Cr.
Waightstill Avery	1684	100	n/a	12-16-1793	S. Toe R., Round Bottom Hill
Waightstill Avery	1685	50	n/a	12-16-1793	Cranberry Cr., E. side
Waightstill Avery (4)	1889	100	7-27-1778	7-7-1794	Read Sale Br.
Waightstill Avery	2126	100	3-17-1778	6-60-1796	Toe R.
Waightstill Avery	2127	60	9-3-1778	6-6-1796	Rich Mtn., Rich Cove
Waightstill Avery	2128	150	9-3-1778	6-6-1796	Linville R.
Waightstill Avery	2129	50	9-24-1792	6-6-1796	Cranberry Cr.
Waightstill Avery	2130	100	n/a	6-6-1796	Plumbtree Cr., adj own land
Waightstill Avery	2131	80	9-3-1778	6-6-1796	Linville R.
Waightstill Avery	2133	100	n/a	1-6-1796	Linville R.
Waightstill Avery	2134	60	9-3-1778	6-6-1796	Rich Mtn.
Waightstill Avery	2135	100	9-3-1778	6-6-1796	Toe R.
Waightstill Avery	2136	100	7-27-1778	6-6-1796	W. Yallow Mtn.
Waightstill Avery	2137	60	n/a	6-6-1796	Toe R.
Waightstill Avery	2138	50	9-3-1778	6-6-1796	Toe R., Old Field
Waightstill Avery	2139	200	9-3-1778	6-6-1796	Beaverdam Cr., head
Waightstill Avery	2140	100	n/a	6--6-1796	Linville R., Big Cr.
Waightstill Avery	2141	100	n/a	6-6-1796	Sugartree Cr.
Waightstill Avery	2142	80	9-3-1778	6-6-1796	Linville R.
Waightstill Avery	2143	100	7-27-1778	6-6-1796	Toe R.
Waightstill Avery	2157	100	9-3-1778	11-23-1796	Sugar Tree Cr.
Waightstill Avery	2158	100	9-3-1778	11-23-1796	Tow R.
Waightstill Avery	2159	100	n/a	11-23-1796	Plum Tree crossing, above falls
Waightstill Avery	2160	100	n/a	11-23-1796	Tow R., Three forks
Waightstill Avery	2161	180	8-12-1778	11-23-1796	S. Tow, Cove
Waightstill Avery	2162	180	8-12-1778	11-23-1796	S. Tow, Cove
Waightstill Avery	2163	70	n/a	11-23-1796	Big Crab Tree
Waightstill Avery	2164	180	7-27-1778	11-23-1796	Plumb Tree Cr., N. fork
Waightstill Avery	2165	80	9-3-1778	11-23-1796	Tow R., Roaring fork,Yellow Mtn.
Waightstill Avery	2166	320	8-24-1778	11-23-1796	S. Tow Cove
Waightstill Avery	2167	100	n/a	11-23-1796	Caney R., E. side
Waightstill Avery	2168	150	9-3-1778	11-23-1796	Toe R.
Waightstill Avery	2169	60	9-3-1778	11-23-1796	Squirrel Cr., W. side
Waightstill Avery	2170	190	9-3-1778	11-23-1796	Toe R., Rich Mtn.
Waightstill Avery	2171	200	n/a	11-23-1794	Toe R., W. fork
Waightstill Avery	2172	70	6-22-1790	11-23-1796	Big Crabtree, Seven Mile Ridge
Waightstill Avery	2174	320	8-24-1788	11-23-1796	S. Toe R., E. Side
Waightstill Avery	2175	150	5-31-1791	11-23-1796	Cranberry Cr.
Waightstill Avery	2176	100	7-27-1778	11-23-1796	Toe R., below three forks

Avery Family NC Land Grants

Waightstill Avery	2177	200	5-23-1790	11-23-1796	Toe R., Big Br.
Waightstill Avery	2178	50	9-9-1792	11-23-1796	Ainsworth land, W. side
Waightstill Avery	2179	100	7-27-1778	11-23-1796	Toe R., E. fork
Waightstill Avery	2423	50	4-9-1793	12-24-1798	Little Silver Cr.
Waightstill Avery	2424	50	5-22-1790	12-24-1798	Catawba R., N. fork, Pepers Cr.
Waightstill Avery	2425	160	5-22-1790	12-24-1798	Linville R., E. side
Waightstill Avery	2427	100	8-10-1783	12-24-1798	Honeycutt' sCr., head
Waightstill Avery	2428	200	10-31-1797	12-24-1798	Lenville Cove
Waightstill Avery	2429	150	9-3-1778	12-24-1798	Toe R., Cain Cr.
Waightstill Avery	2430	200	9-19-1778	12-24-1798	Toe R., N. side, Little Rock Cr.
Waightstill Avery	2431	50	3-31-1790	12-24-1798	Toe R., Caney Cr.
Waightstill Avery	2432	50	11-17-1790	12-24-1798	Toe R., E. side
Waightstill Avery	2433	200	7-3-1788	12-24-1798	Linville R., Grandfather Mtn.
Waightstill Avery	2434	200	8-19-1778	12-24-1798	Linville R.
Waightstill Avery	2744	700	5-2-1799	12-23-1799	Catawba R., N. side
Waightstill Avery	2751	100	2-2-1778	12-24-1799	Cane Cr.., adj. David Baker
Waightstill Avery	2882	320	8-1-1800	12-16-1800	FB River, S. side Painted Rock
Waightstill Avery	2955	400	12-1-1783	11-14-1801	Little Rock Cr.
Waightstill Avery	2956	100	9-3-1801	11-12-1801	Towe R., E. fork
Waightstill Avery	3439	100	1-29-1795	9-13-1808	Little Rock, Sugar Cove fork
Waightstill Avery	3440	100	1-29-1795	9-13-1808	Linville R., Great Falls
Waightstill Avery	3441	100	3-5-1794	9-13-1808	Adj. Pointers
Waightstill Avery	3442	150	1-7-1784	9-13-1808	Toe R.
Waightstill Avery	3443	100	9-3-1778	9-13-1808	Honeycutts Br.
Waightstill Avery	3444	60	2-22-1804	9-13-1808	Catawba R., S. side
Waightstill Avery	3476	140	8-27-1808	9-16-1808	Toe R., three Mile Cr.
Waightstill Avery	3514	100	6-17-1810	11-30-1810	Toe R., Cain Cr.
Waightstill Avery	3569	250	12-21-1810	9-30-1812	Linvill R., Keebys Cr.
Waightstill Avery (5)	3476	100	8-30-1814	11-27-1816	Catawba R., N. Cove fork
Waightstill Avery	3771	100	2-22-1816	12-12-1816	Catawba R., N. fork,Phillips Cr.
Waightstill Avery	3814	150	9-9-1812	11-26-1817	Linville R., N. side
Waightstill Avery	3815	640	1-4-1814	11-26-1817	Ridge Rd.
Waightstill Avery	3816	100	1-4-1815	11-26-1817	Catawba R., S. side
Waightstill Avery	3839	100	1-17-1810	12-13-1817	Canoe Cr., adj. own land
Waightstill Avery	3840	100	1-17-1810	12-13-1817	Canoe Cr., adj. own land
Waightstill Avery	3930	100	6-30-1817	12-5-1818	Catawba R., S. side
Waightstill Avery	3949	100	12-17-1818	12-25-1818	Adj. own land
Waightstill Avery	3966	800	4-29-1817	11-16-1819	Toe R., Roaring Cr.

Footnotes - Burke

(1) also E. E. Greenlee & J. C. Tate

Avery Family NC Land Grants

(2) also Laura Avery & James Colton, listed 1st

(3) also James Miller

(4) also John Headley

(5) also Josiah Askew

Waightstill Avery was an obsessive accumulator of land in Burke and Buncombe Counties. From 1778 to 1818, he entered 21,170 acres in 117 NC grants in Burke Co. and 9,165 acres in 34 blocks in Buncombe Co. Many small blocks from the Burke Co. entries were located in what later was to become Mitchell and Avery Counties, along the Toe and Linville Rivers. Some Burke Co. blocks later became Buncombe and Madison Cos., i.e., along the French Broad River. Avery also entered 3 blocks in Washington Co., TN, and 1 block in Carter Co. TN, in 1784 and 1801. The Tennessee acreage totaled 660 acres.

His son, Isaac Thomas Avery reportedly either inherited or acquired 50,000 acres in Mitchell and Avery Counties. By 1850, Isaac had 140 slaves, but in 1860 he had only 103 slaves at which time his real estate was valued at $45,000 and personal property was valued at $73,450.

On the other hand, Alphonso Calhoun Avery inherited the same passion as his grandfather and entered 18,323 acres in 38 NC grants in Western North Carolina from 1872 to 1873. Most blocks were in the mountainous area, along the Burke/McDowell Co. line, near Linville.

Baird Family NC Land Grants

Buncombe Co.

Registered Name	Grant	Acres	Entered	Patent	Location
Adolphus E. Baird	3686	50	11-23-1837	12-20-1838	FBR, Bailey Br.
Bedent Beard (1)	1186	150	10-7-1794	12-16-1803	adj. Joseph Hughey
Beden Baird	1937	50	4-17-1804	12-11-1811	Whitsons Cr., headwaters
Beden Baird	1938	200	4-17-1804	12-11-1811	Beaverdam Cr.
Bedent Baird	2570	250	5-13-1818	11-28-1823	Beaverdam Cr., S. side
Israel Baird	2466	640	4-4-1816	12-1-1823	Beaverdam Cr., S. side
Israel Baird (2)	2623	40	11-9-1824	12-9-1825	Rims Cr.
Israel Baird	2864	151	4-8-1829	12-4-1830	Beaverdam Cr., Bull Mill Cr.
Israel Baird	3148	100	1-7-1831	12-5-1833	Beaverdam Cr., S. side
James Baird	1516	320	10-9-1804	11-29-1806	Locah Br.
Joseph C. Baird	3637	50	10-27-1836	11-5-1838	FB River, Case Botts Cr.
Joseph C. Baird	3688	25	5-19-1838	12-20-1838	Glenns Br., S. fork
J(ames) S. T. Baird	13278	x 0.9	n/a	n/a	Beaverdam Cr.
William R. Baird	3016	100	10-13-1829	12-22-1831	Beaverdam Cr.
William R. Baird	3306	200	1-12-1833	11-18-1835	FB River, E. side
William R. Baird	3307	35	2-9-1833	11-18-1835	Reams Cr., E. side
Zebulon Beard (3)	745	400	3-19-1794	12-6-1799	Glenns Cr.

Name	Grant	Acres	Entered	Patent	Location
Zebulon Baird (4)	1185	200	3-3-1794	12-16-1803	Bull Cr., Ivey
Zebulon Baird	1505	100	10-19-1803	6-27-1803	Flat Cr., adj. Silas Gillespie
Zebulon Baird	1564	350	1-23-1806	12-5-1806	Sweeten Cr., Swannanoa
Zebulon Beard	1743	400	11-2-1807	12-17-1808	FB River, W. side

Footnotes

(1) also Joseph Hughey - listed 1st

(2) also Henry Waggoner

(3) also Bedent Beard

(4) also Bedent Baird

Baird-Beard Family Land Grants

Burke Co.

Registered Name	Grant	Acres	Entered	Patent	Location
Andrew Baird (1)	2188	3000	n/a	12-26-1796	Gunpowder Cr., Ready Cr.
Andrew Baird	3006	50	7-21-1801	12-4-1801	Gunpowder Cr.
Andrew Baird	3894	100	12-28-1818	11-28-1818	Silver Cr.
Andrew Baird	4088	50	9-29-1818	12-18-1820	Catawba R.
Andrew Baird	4093	45	9-29-1818	12-19-1820	Catawba R.
Andrew Baird	4094	150	7-27-1818	12-19-1820	Catawba R., Silver Cr.
Andrew Baird	5051	30	6-4-1818	12-26-1821	Little Gunpowder Cr.
Andrew Baird	5197	70	11-7-1825	1-4-1827	Gunpowder Cr., N. side
John Baird	5100	100	12-10-1817	11-28-1823	Abingtons Cr., Lower Cr.
Mathew Baird	5196	80	11-7-1825	1-4-1827	Silver Cr., headwaters
Andrew Beard	1919	18500	n/a	5-11-1795	Catawba R., 2nd Little R.
Andrew Beard	1920	12160	n/a	5-11-1795	Gunpowder Cr., Clarkes
Andrew Beard	1921	640	9-25-1794	5-11-1795	Catawba R., Clarkes Little R.
Andrew Beard	1922	13640	n/a	5-11-1795	Little Gunpowder Cr.
Andrew Beard	1923	640	9-25-1794	5-11-1795	Lower Little R., N of springs
Andrew Beard	1924	640	9-25-1794	5-11-1795	Lower Little R., Min. springs
Andrew Beard	1925	640	9-25-1794	5-11-1795	Lower Little R.
Andrew Beard	1926	640	9-25-1794	5-11-1795	Lower Little R.
Andrew Beard (2)	2124	640	2-9-1792	5-30-1795	Catawba R., S. fork
Andrew Beard (3)	2125	640	2-9-1792	5-30-1795	Drowning Cr.
Andrew Beard (4)	2126	640	2-9-1792	5-30-1795	Catawba R., Drowning Cr.
Andrew Beard (5)	2145	25000	1-30-1795	n/a	Catawba R., S. fork
Andrew Beard (6)	2146	5130	n/a	7-8-1796	Henrys Cr., Jacobs Cr.
Andrew Beard (7)	2767	200	12-11-1792	3-12-1800	Gunpowder Cr., Silver Cr.
Lewis Beard	2275	200	9-6-1794	12-13-1798	Muddy Cr., E. fork
Lewis Beard	2276	50	12-3-1793	12-13-1798	Linvil Ridge, iron ore bank

Lewis Beard	2277	50	12-3-1792	12-13-1798	Muddy Cr.
Lewis Beard	2278	30	1-30-1793	12-13-1798	Muddy Cr., Bear Br.
Lewis Beard	2279	50	12-3-1792	12-13-1798	Grants Br.
Lewis Beard	2280	50	1-26-1793	12-13-1798	Muddy Cr.
Lewis Beard	2281	60	12-3-1792	12-13-1798	Muddy Cr.
William Beard	1235	60	6-15-1784	5-18-1789	Muddy Cr., Youngs fork

Footnotes

(1) also Clizby Cobb; Baird Iron Works

(2) also William Tate

(3) also William Tate

(4) also William Tate - listed 1st

(5) also William Tate - listed 1st

(6) also William Tate - listed 1st

(7) also Elizabeth Cobb (Clizby Cobb)

Editor's Notes:

The relationship of the Bairds of Buncombe Co. and the Bairds/Beards of Burke Co. is not clear.

Biffel/Eller/Weaver NC Land Grants

The Reems Creek Contingent

Buncombe Co.

Registered Name	Grant	Acres	Entered	Patent	Location
Adam Biffel	305	100	1795	7-17-1797	Rims Cr., N. side
Jacob Biffel (1)	307	100	n/a	n/a	Pole Cr.
Jacob Bufle	792	100	7-16-1797	9-1-1800	Pigion R., SW fork
John Beefle	119	100	7-17-1793	1-19-1795	FB River, E. side
John Beffee	346	100	n/a	12-2-1797	Newfound Cr., N. side
Jno. Bifle	723	200	4-16-1798	12-6-1799	Newfound Cr., both sides
John Biffle	856	60	1-22-1800	12-11-1800	Newfound Cr.
Jno. Biffel	925	100	6-22-1800	12-2-1801	Newfound Cr.
John Befel	1403	100			Dicks Cr.
John Biffil	1597	50	12-18-1804	12-20-1806	Newfound Cr., main
John Biffel	1605	100	9-13-1802	12-20-1806	Dicks Cr.

*****

Adam Eller	2756	50	8-2-1827	12-6-1828	Flatt Cr., S. fork
Adam Eller	2862	100	3-13-1828	12-4-1830	Flat Cr., adj own land
Joseph Eller	2293	30	7-4-1815	11-26-1817	Rims Cr., N. side
Joseph Eller	2626	50			Rims Cr.

Joseph Eller	2771	50	8-11-1826	1-26-1829	Flat Cr., adj. own land
Joseph Eller	3184	200	n/a	n/a	Mtn. between Ream & Flat C.
Jos. Eller	3701	50	8-19-1838	12-20-1838	Rims Cr.
Joseph Eller	3702	100	10-17-1835	12-28-1838	Rims Cr.

*****

Anno Weaver	3878	50	10-9-1837	12-9-1840	Turkey Cr., Glady fork
Chesley G. Weaver	3722	12	12-20-1836	12-20-1838	Flatt Cr., both forks
Jacob Weaver	1898	80	10-14-1808	12-11-1810	Hominy Cr., Thomas Cr.
Jacob Weaver	2010	23	1-7-1812	11-28-1812	Rims Cr., S. side
James Weaver	2879	22.5	n/a	n/a	Flat Cr., both sides
James Weaver	3305	46	3-1-1834	11-13-1835	Reaves Cr. (Reems Cr.)
James Weaver	3586	25	2-15-1837	11-9-1837	Reams Cr., S. side
John Weaver	29	200	9-2-1784	1-6-1794	Main Ivey, N. fork
John Weaver	307	100	8-11-1795	7-19-1797	Rims Cr., N. side
John Weaver	345	100	7-5-1795	12-2-1797	Rims Cr., S. side, now lives
John Weaver	516	50	7-1-1795	12-5-1798	Rims Cr., N. side
John Weaver	1678	50	1-21-1807	12-2-1807	Rims Cr., N. side
John Weaver	1990	150	9-28-1811	11-23-1812	Hominy Cr., Glady fork
Montraville Weaver	3683	100	n/a	n/a	Flatt Cr.
Zilpha Ann Weaver	3162	100	9-24-1832	12-5-1833	Hominy Cr., Glady fork

*****

Burke Co.

Jacob Biffle	792	100	7-18-1797	9-1-1800	Pigeon River
Jacob Weaver	287	265	12-11-1780	3-14-1780	Long Branch, N. fork
Jacob Weaver	547	100	4-1-1779	10-28-1782	Anthony Mill Cr.
Jacob Weaver	787	200	12-10-1778	11-9-1784	Bear Br., Jacobs fork

Brank Family NC Land Grants

Burke Co.

Registered Name	Grant	Acres	Entered	Patent	Location
Robert Brank, Sr.	48	200	7-20-1778	9-20-1779	Hunting Cr., Meadow Br.
Robert Brank	54	300	7-20-1778	9-20-1779	Catawba R., S. side
Robert Brank	812	73	n/a	n/a	Catawba R., S. side

Buncombe Co.

Robert Brank	2630	100	6-1-1824	12-9-1825	Rims Cr., E. side
Robert Brank	3408	50	1-24-1835	12-5-1836	Reams Cr., N. side
Robert Brank, Sr.	3689	50	6-4-1838	12-20-1838	Reams Cr., Wash br., head

Brevard Family NC Land Grants

Burke Co.

Registered Name	Grant	Acres	Entered	Patent	Location
Alexander Brevard	1669	200	1-10-1778	11-26-1793	Tow R.
Hugh Brevard	117	150	11-28-1778	3-15-1780	Balls Cr., adj. William Cole
Hugh Brevard	296	640	9-10-1778	3-14-1780	Catawba R., S. side
Hugh Brevard	314	300	9-10-1778	3-14-1780	Catawba R., S. side
Thomas Brevard	2686	44	7-23-1799	12-6-1799	Brevards Cr., adj own land
Thomas Brevard	3159	50	4-28-1802	12-8-1802	Brevards Cr., Cherry Cr.
Thomas Brevard	3174	90	4-28-1802	12-2-1802	Brevards Cr.
Zebulon Brevard	920	100	9-3-1778	8--7-1787	Beardons Cr., both sides

Buncombe Co.

D. L. Brevard	4335	13	7-16-1857	3-1-1860	FB River, E. side, Cane Cr.

Brittain Family NC Land Grants

Buncombe Co.

Registered Name	Grant	Acres	Entered	Patent	Location
Aaron Britton (1)	107	400	5-21-1794	1-19-1795	Pigeon R., Richland Cr.
James Brittain (2)	1304	600	11-13-1802	6-15-1804	Richland Cr., both sides
James Brittain	1536	200	1-23-1800	12-5-1806	FB River, Milser (Mills) R.
Col. James Brittain (3)	1886	n/a	4-5-1809	12-6-1810	Little R., High Shoal
James Brittain	1963	150	11-11-1809	12-18-1811	FB River, W. side, Israels Br.

James Brittain	1968	50	11-20-1809	12-18-1811	adj. Lenoirs
James Brittain	1969	100	11-20-1809	12-18-1811	McDowels Cr.
James Brittain, Jr	2772	100	9-22-1813	8-11-1829	McDowell Cr.
Joseph Brittain	2414	100	4-2-1817	12-17-1818	Flat Cr., head N&S forks
Joseph F. Brittain	2621	30	8-14-1823	12-9-1825	Big Branch
Joseph F. Britton	3324	21	12-25-1832	12-9-1834	Reams Cr.
Philip Britain (4)	2033	75	1-9-1811	12-10-1812	FB River, W. side, Fosters Cr.
Phillip Brittain (5)	2069	150	5-8-1812	11-24-1813	Millers R.
Phillip Brittain (6)	2070	100	n/a	11-24-1813	Millers R.
Philip Brittain	2460	50	2-8-1818	11-20-1820	FB River, Ballards Br.
Phillip Brittain	3276	100	4-15-1835	11-9-1835	Little Mud Cr.
P. Brittain (10)	3277	100	4-15-1833	11-13-1835	Mud Cr.
Phillip Brittain	3778	100	4-18-1834	11-13-1835	Bradleys Cr.
Philip Brittain	2919	50	6-19-1830	12-21-1830	Mills R., both sides
Phillip Brittain	3601	300	2-10-1836	1-29-1838	Boylstones Cr., both sides
Philip Brittain	3737	50	4-26-1837	12-24-1838	Big Mud Cr.
Robert Brittain	2865	30	4-7-1829	12-4-1830	Flat Cr., left fork
Robert Brittain	3279	30	3-16-1833	11-13-1835	Flat Cr., left fork
Robert Britain	3308	50	3-16-1823	11-18-1835	Flat Cr., S. fork
William Britain	339	50	4-19-1797	12-2-1797	Flat Cr., S. fork
William Brittain (7)	340	200	3-7-1794	12-2-1797	Hayns run, both sides
William Brittain	1246	50	n/a	12-16-1803	FB River, E. side
William Britton	1901	50	6-6-1808	12-11-1810	Rims Cr.
William Brittain	2863	80	1-5-1829	12-4-1830	Flatt Cr., S. fork
William Brittain	3224	70	3-3-1832	12-9-1834	Britains Lick Mtn.
William Brittain	3309	50	7-11-1834	11-18-1835	Linards Cr., Averys Cr.
Mary Edwards, et al (9)	3195	100	12-28-1821	1-6-1834	Crab Cr.

Footnotes - Buncombe Co.

(1) also Joseph Dobson - 1st

(2) also Jno. Strother - 1st

(3) also Epaphroditus Hightower

(4) also John Murray - 1st

(5) also John Murray

(6) also John Murray

(7) twelve jointly listed as follows - all probably related

Mary Edwards	Lorenzo D. Brittain
Amelia Edwards	Benj. S. Brittain
Joseph Brittain	Horatio M. Brittain
Phillip Brittain	Delia Pace
William Brittain	Kesida Pace
James Brittain	Nancy Stewart

Bryson Family NC Land Grants

Buncombe Co.

Registered Name	Grant	Acres	Entered	Patent	Location
John Bryson	2421	100	2-26-1816	11-24-1819	Mills R., S. fork, Work's bottom
John Bryson	2422	50	1-26-1816	11-24-1819	Mills R., S. fork, Cantrelle bott.
John Bryson	2685	50	6-21-1825	1-30-1827	Boydstons Cr.
John Bryson	2814	50	11-2-1829	5-12-1830	Boodstons Cr., adj. own land
William Bryson	997	100	n/a	n/a	Scotts Cr.
William Bryson	1023	150	n/a	n/a	Tuckasege R.
William Bryson	2892	25	4-9-1828	12-18-1830	Mills R., N. side
William Bryson	3238	50	1-7-1835	12-5-1835	Mills R., N. side
William Bryson, Jr.,	3531	50	4-21-1834	1-4-1837	Millses R., Bradleys Cr.
William Bryson	3532	50	4-21-1834	1-4-1837	Millses R., Bradleys Cr.
William Bryson (1)	3596	50	10-26-1835	1-29-1838	Mills R., Bradley Cr., Pea br.

Footnotes

(1) also L. Banning

Census Records

Hugh Bryson occurs on the 1790 NC Census, Mecklenburg Co., Salisbury District, with 6 males and 4 females.

James Bryson occurs on the 1800 NC Census, Buncombe Co. with 7 males and 3 females

John Bryson occurs on the 1800 NC Census, Buncombe Co. with 3 males and 1 female

Samuel Bryson occurs on the 1800 NC Census, BuncombeCo. with 6 males and 7 females

Burton Family NC Land Grants

Burke Co.

Registered Name	Grant	Acres	Entered	Patent	Location
Joseph Burton	3163	50	n/a	n/a	Sandy Run
Joseph Burton	3211	100	n/a	n/a	Sandy Run, head

Buncombe Co.

Registered Name	Grant	Acres	Entered	Patent	Location
David Burton	1840	150	n/a	n/a	Strains Cr.
John Burtain	53	50	7-22-1793	7-7-1794	FB River, adj. Nathan Smith
John Burton (1)	63	400	4-18-1792	7-7-1794	see notes 1 && 2 below
John Burtain (2)	64	200	4-18-1792	7-7-1794	ditto, adj. Gellehan
John Burtain	69	200	1-5-1791	7-9-1794	FB River, Glens Cr.
John Burton	459	250	7-12-1794	8-231-1798	Gap Cr., Wagon Rd.
Seth Burton	1051	100	10-28-1805	n/a	Ivey R., Sugar fork

Footnotes

(1) 2.5 mi. from Colo. Davidsons

(2) 2.5 mi. from Colo. Davidsons

Editor's Notes

(1) John Burton (n.d.) married Jane (Jean) Forster (1746-1824).

(2) Burton is widely credited with developing circa 1794 the town of Morrisville (later Asheville). This location probably is grant no. 63 whose location is vaguely described as "being 2.5 miles from Col. Davidsons, on the other side of the Swananoa."

(3) Three John Burtons are listed in the 1790 NC Census. The individual above possibly is identified with the one from Rockingham Co., Salisbury District.

Zachariah Candler NC Land Grants

Buncombe Co.

Registered Name	Grant	Acres	Entered	Patent	Location
Zachariah Candler	928	200	7-15-1800	12-2-1801	French Broad River, West Fork
as above	1027	500	9-23-1800	12-8-1802	FB River, Cherryfield Creek
	1028	640	8-15-1800	4-3-1804	French Broad River
	1116	640	4-20-1802	4-2-1804	French Broad River, J. Ierland Mill Cr.
	1117	600	4-20-1802	4-2-1804	French Broad River, West Fork
	1118	250	4-20-1802	3-17-1804	French Broad River, East Fork
	1119	100	4-20-1802	12-10-1803	French Broad River, Upper Cr.
	1120	450	4-20-1802	12-10-1803	French Broad River,East Fork
	1121	250	1-19-1802	12-28-1803	French Broad River, Middle Fork
	1122	300	12-7-1803	12-10-1803	Cherryfield Creek, Mid & N. forks
	1123	200	1-19-1802	12-11-1803	FB River, Cherry Field Cr.
	1407	200	7-21-1802	12-19-1804	French Broad River, Catheys Cr.
	1408	640	10-20-1803	12-19-1804	French Broad River
	1409	300	4-20-1803	12-19-1804	French Broad River, Catheys Cr.
	1410	640	10-20-1803	12-19-1804	French Broad River, Catheys Cr.
	1411	640	10-20-1803	12--19-1804	French Broad River
	1412	100	4-20-1802	12-19-1804	French Broad R., Cherryfield Crs.
	1416	300	10-21-1803	12-19-1804	French Broad River
	1478	400	10-20-1803	12-19-1805	Averys Cr.
	1479	200	10-20-1803	12-19-1804	Averys & Rogers Creeks
	1501	150	10-20-1803	12-21-1805	French Broad River, Walkers Cr.
	1596	100	10-20-1804	12-20-1806	French Broad R., E. fork, Walker Cr.
	1599	60	1-18-1804	12-20-1806	French Broad River, E. fork
	1600	100	1-18-1804	12-20-1806	French Broad River, E. fork
	1622	200	3-31-1807	11-27-1807	Big Ivy, Adkins Branch
	1654	150	1-29-1807	11-27-1808	Little Ivy, Big Br.
	1661	200	10-4-1806	11-27-1807	Flatt Creek, Rims Cr.
	1664	400	10-4-1806	11-27-1807	Big Ivey, Flatt Creek
	1738	200	1-21-1807	12-17-1808	Hominy Creek, Beaverdam Cr.
	1794	120	1-2-1809	11-30-1809	French Broad River, E. fork
	1795	200	10-2-1807	11-30-1809	South Fork Hominy, Reedy Br.
	1796	100	10-2-1807	11-20-1809	South Fork Rims Cr.
	1797	640	10-3-1807	11-30-1809	French Broad River, W. side, Lees Cr.
	1806	100	3-31-1807	11-30-1809	French Broad River
	1876	200	1-21-1807	12-3-1810	Hominy Creek, Beaverdam Cr.
	2029	150	8-21-1811	12-4-1812	McDowell & Avery Creeks
	2051	300	1-20-1808	11-24-1813	Grassy Cr.
	2076	200	1-11-1811	12-4-1813	French Broad, W. side, Newfound Cr.

2148	300	1-6-1813	12-7-1814	Dicks Cr., Newfound Cr.
2154	400	1-7-1811	12-7-1814	FB River, Beaverdam Cr. (fish trap)
2156	1000	1-7-1811	12-7-1813	Ragsdells Cr.
2157	300	1-7-1811	12-7-1814	Flatt Creek, Upper Camp Br.
2345	200	10-5-1813	11-25-1818	French Broad R., E. Fork, Eastofoa Cr.
2346	50	1-6-1813	11-15-1818	Flatt Creek, French Broad R.
2349	100	8-21-1811	11-25-1818	Mills River, Forrester Cr.
2350	50	3-31-1813	11-25-1818	Rims Creek, N. side, Bald Mtn. Rd.
2351	100	2-26-1813	11-25-1818	FB River, Beaverdam Cr.
2352	1000	1-6-1813	11-25-1818	FB River, E. side, Davies Cr.
2353	1000	10-13-1817	11-28-1818	Rims Creek, Beaverdam Cr.
2556	1000	1-7-1811	12-7-1814	Ragsdale Creek
2559	50	6-11-1821	12-10-1822	Hominy Creek, both sides
2767	640	4-19-1826	1-10-1829	FB River, Jenkins Br. (his ferry)
2768	640	4-19-1826	1-10-1828	Wm. Moore's Cr., Hominy Cr.
2769	640	4-19-1826	1-10-1829	FB River, Sandy Mush Cr. Mouth
2925	50	4-19-1826	12-29-1832	Big Ivy, Gabriels Cr.
2972	100	4-19-1826	12-12-1831	FB River, Cherry Field Cr., CatheyCr.
2995	50	4-19-1826	12-29-1830	William Moore's Cr., Hominy
3014	50	1-8-1830	12-22-1830	Turkey Branch, Little Ivy
3043	200	1-7-1830	11-19-1832	Little Ivy, Indian Camp Cr.
3044	100	1-4-1830	11-19-1832	Big Ivy, Gabriels Cr.
3045	640	1-4-1830	11-19-1832	FB River, Walnut Cr.
3119	100	1-4-1830	9-16-1833	Flatt Creek
3196	100	1-8-1830	1-6-1834	Little Ivy, Bald Mtn fork
3239	50	1-8-1830	12-5-1833	Thomas Moore's Cr., Pole Cr.
3240	50	1-5-1835	12-5-1835	Samuel Smith Mill Cr. (Hawkins Mill)
3371	20	1-3-1832	12-12-1835	Flatt Cr.
3373	200	4-11-1831	12-12-1831	Long Btr.
3375	200	2-5-1833	12-16-1835	French Broad near Walnut, Big Laurel
3378	150	6-26-1807	12-16-1835	French Broad R., Bare Cr.
3394	640	2-5-1833	11-22-1836	French Broad R., Pine Cr. mouth
3511	10	1-7-1834	12-17-1836	Catheys Cr.
3512	25	8-20-1834	12-17-1836	French Broad R., Doe Br.
3513	25	1-7-1834	12-17-1836	Glady Br.
3541	200	1-6-1835	6-15-1837	French Broad R., Baley Br.
3542	40	10-14-1835	6-15-1837	French Broad R., Glenns Cr.
3823	100	1-6-1835	12-9-1840	Pole Cr., Tomas Moore Cr.
3824	40	1-18-1836	12-9-1840	Hominy Cr. At N. & S. forks
3825	25	3-18-1836	12-9-1840	Pole Creek, Hominy cr.
3826	10	1-18-1836	12-9-1840	Hominy Cr. At N. & S. forks
3911	100	1-14-1839	12-21-1840	Ragsdale Creek, Dicks Cr.

3977	50	4-21-1841	1-10-1843	Hominy Cr., Newfound Cr.

Remarks

From 1800 to about 1820, Zachariah Candler paid 50 shillings per 100 acres;

from about 1820, he paid $10 per 100 acres, or $0.10 per acre.

The above costs were taken from a copy of the deeds at the Buncombe County courthouse;

about 25% of the records are missing; some obvious errors are in the handwritten copy.

Carland Family NC Land Grants

Buncombe Co.

Registered Name	Grant	Acres	Entered	Patent	Location
Armstead Carland	2913	50	1-6-1829	12-21-1830	FB River, W. side, adj. own land
Armstead Carland	3035	150	10-20-1830	12-26-1831	Averys Cr., FB River
Armstead B. Carland	3342	50	4-15-1834	12-5-1835	FB River, W. side, Bent Cr. Mtn.
Hiram Carlin	2860	100	10-8-1828	12-4-1830	Hominy Cr., S. fork
Hiram Carlen	2704	150	8-7-1826	12-29-1827	Hominy Cr., Wards Br.

Selected Reference

Haller, Charles R., 2005, Who were John & Marey Carland? Asheville, NC, *A Lot of Bunkum*
vol. 26, no. 3, p. 17-18.

Carson Family NC Land Grants

Burke Co.

Registered Name	Grant	Acres	Entered	Patent	Location
Alexander Carson	468	200	3-26-1778	10-22-1782	Gunpowder Cr.
Alexander Carson	625	250	10-1-1779	10-11-1783	Gunpowder Cr., Silver Cr.
Alexander Carson	626	100	1-21-1779	10-11-1783	Upper Little R.
Geo. M. Carson (1)	5567	8	n/a	n/a	2nd Broad R.
Geo. M. Carson	5981	100	1-28-1840	12-12-1840	S. Catawba
Geo. M. Carson (2)	6043	50	9-14-1840	12-13-1841	Buck Creek
Geo. M. Carson	6089	50	8-20-1841	1-21-1843	adj. J. D. Lackey
I. L. Carson	6110	40	56-10-1841	8-26-1843	above Concord Mtg. House

James Carson	1318	150	7-24-1793	8-22-1795	Tow River
James Carson	1370	100	n/a	8-22-1795	Grassey Cr.
		100	7-24-1793	8-22-1795	Grassy Cr.
James Carson	1373	100	n/a	8-22-1795	Grassey Br., W. fork
James Carson	1607	640	2-2-1778	11-27-1792	Grassy Cr., Toe R.
Jason Carson	3682	50	1-27-1815	12-5-1815	Catawba R., S. side
Jason Carson	3841	50	1-28-1817	12-22-1817	Hawkins Br., adj. John Carson
Jason Carson (3)	4002	240	4-28-1819	12-17-1819	Crooked Cr.
Jason Carson	5003	50	7-27-1818	12-22-1820	Wiggins Br.
Jason Carson	5007	33	3-23-1819	12-22-1820	Catawba R., S. side
Jason Carson	5008	50	9-7-1818	12-22-1820	Wiggins Br.
John Carson	96	447	10-9-1778	9-20-1779	Catawba R., Nicks Cr.
John Carson	435	500	8-24-1778	10-28-1782	Clarks Little R.
John Carson	731	250	1-15-1783	10-16-1783	Clarks Little R.
John Carson	1084	640	4-6-1784	12-8-1787	Richland Cr., E. fork
John Carson	1415	576	n/a	1-4-1792	Catawba R., Hawkins Br.
John Carson	1523	90	n/a	n/a	Catawba R.
John Carson	2422	640	12-21-1793	12-24-1798	Buck & Clear Cr.
John Carsons	2698	450	9-26-1798	12-18-1799	Catawba R., N. fork
John Carson	3170	100	8-12-1802	12-8-1802	Crooked Cr.
John Carson	3173	60	5-19-1801	12-8-1802	Catawba R., N. side
John Carson	3206	50	5-15-1802	9-24-1803	Hawkins Br.
John Carson	3333	100	5-7-1802	11-29-1804	Catawba R., NW side
Col. John Carson	3482	50	1-25-1809	12-6-1809	Buck Cr., adj. own land
John Carson	3523	100	9-23-1808	12-12-1810	Catawba R., N. side
John Crison	3986	100	9-11-1818	11-30-1819	Coxes Cr.
John Carson	4085	640	9-29-1818	12-14-1820	Pleasant Garden
John Carson	5009	50	10-26-1840	6-22-1841	North fork, Buck Cr.
John Carson., Jr. (4)	6030	50	10-26-1840	6-22-1841	Buck Cr.
John Carson	6092	7	11-5-1842	1-21-1843	Nicks Cr., aj. J. L. Carson
J. L. Carson	6083	100	10-26-1840	1-4-1843	Clear Cr.
Jonathan L. Carson	6090	100	5-31-1842	1-21-1843	Nicks Cr., Catawba R.
John W. Carson	5004	320	3-27-1819	12-22-1820	Long Br., head
Joseph McD. Carson (5)	5828	380	10-21-1835	7-29-1837	Silver Cr., S. fork
Sam'l Carson (6)	3935	100	7-30-1817	12-17-1818	S. Toe R., Still fork

Sam'l Carson (7)	3936	50	7-30-1817	12-17-1818	Towe R., Armstr. Cr.
Sam'l Carson (8)	3937	100	7-3-1817	12-17-1818	Armstrongs Cr.
Samuel Carson (9)	3938	50	9-30-1817	12-7-1818	S. Towe R.
Samuel Carson (10)	3939	50	7-30-1817	12-17-1818	S. Towe R .
Samuel Carson (11)	3940	50	7-3--1817	12-17-1818	Armstrongs Cr.
Samuel Carson (12)	3941	100	7-30-1817	12-17-1818	Blue Ridge Mtn., 7 Mile Ridge
Samuel Carson (13)	3942	100	7-30-1817	12-17-1818	Crabtree
Samuel Carson (14)	3943	100	9-8-1817	12-17-1818	Blue Ridge Mtn.
Samuel Carson (15)	3944	100	9-8-1817	12-17-1818	W. Blue Ridge
Samuel Carson	3945	100	9-8-1817	12-17-1818	Armstrongs Cr.
Samuel Carson	3946	100	10-4-1819	12-17-1818	Catawba R., S. side, adj. J.Carson
Samuel P. Carson (16)	5568	100	5-5-1829	1-12-1832	Tomes Cr.
Wm. L. Carson	6071	100	n/a	n/a	Catawba R.
Wm. L. Carson	6091	100	5031-1842	1-21-1843	Catawba R. , adj. J. L. Carson
Wm. M. Carson	5760	100	10-23-1836	11-23-1836	Colberts Cr.
Wm. M. Carson	5761	50	10-28-1833	11-23-1836	Middle Cr.
Wm. M. Carson (17)	5982	50	5-14-1839	12-12-1840	Buck Cr. , Burchfield Br.
Wm. M. Carson	6082	100	10-26-1840	1-4-1843	Buck Cr.
Wm. M. Carson	6087	100	4-27-1841	1-21-1843	Clear Cr.
Wm. M. Carson	6088	50	9-14-1840	1-21-1843	Clear Cr.

Footnotes - Burke Co.

(1) also John M. Carson

(2) adj. Col. John Carson & James McDowell

(3) also Thomas Green

(4) next to Col. John Carson

(5) also John Crawley

(6) also Wm. Shelton, listed 1st , & Jason Carson

(7) as above

(8) as above

(9) as above

(10) as above

(11) as above

(12) as above

(13) as above

(14) as above

(15) as above

(16) also Wm. Ainsworth

(17) adj. Col. John Carson

Buncombe Co.

Registered Name	Grant	Acres	Entered	Patent	Location
David G. M. Carson	4289	100	9-10-1853	7-24-1855	FB River, W. side
James Carson	1624	200	3-3-1806	11-27-1807	Big Ivey, Rye Cove Br.
James Carson	1627	100	1-3-1806	11-27-1807	Big Ivey., Rye Cove
James Carson	3283	50	7-31-1833	11-13-1835	Big Ivey, W. side
James Carson	3284	100	7-31-1833	11-13-1835	Big Ivey, Rye Cove
John Carson	466	200	6-17-1794	9-28-1798	FB River. W. side
John Carson	530	150	6-17-1794	12-5-1798	FB River, E. side
Wm. Carson	2172	100	10-5-1813	12-4-1815	Big Ivey, N. side
Wm. Carson	3647	200	4-28-1836	12-8-1838	Big Ivy, Haw Br.

Cathey Family NC Land Grants

Burke Co.

Registered Name	Grant	Acres	Entered	Patent	Location
Archibald Cathy	2391	60	7-2-1798	12-21-1799	Grassy Cr.
Archey Cathy	2395	150	7-2-1796	12-21-1798	Grasse Cr.
George Cathey, Jr. (1)	90	640	10-10-1779	9-20-1779	Catawba R., below Pl. Garden
William Cathey	45	640	10-19-1778	9-20-1779	Catawba R., N. fork, Turkey Co.
William Cathey	95	64	10-10-1778	9-20-1779	Catawba R., N. fork
William Cathey	1356	50	10-22-1792	8-22-1795	Gardian Cr., Hawkins br.

Buncombe Co.

George Cathey (2)	507	100	4-19-1796	12-5-1798	Pidgon R., First Cr.
George Cathey	1529	150	n/a	12-5-1806	Pigeon R.
George Cathey	1612	150	2-10-1806	7-2-1807	adj. own land & James Chambers
William Cathey	1363	100	1-2-1802	12-10-1804	Oconatufta Cr.

Footnotes

(1) also Joseph Henry; apparently Capt. George Cathey (c.1747-1840)

(2) apparently Capt. George Cathey (c.1747-1840)

Chunn NC Land Grants

Buncombe Co.

Registered Name	Grant	Acres	Entered	Patent	Location
Samuel Chunn	1786	50	10-15-1804	4-26-1809	Homney Cr., S. fork
Samuel Chunn	1788	50	10-17-1804	4-26-1809	Homney Cr., S. fork
Samuel Chunn	2468	50	11-9-1811	12-7-1820	Homney Cr., S. fork
Samuel Chunn	2469	50	11-9-1811	12-7-1820	Homney Cr., S. fork
Samuel Chunn	2589	300	2-10-1816	11-18-1824	Ridge NE of Asheville
Samuel Chunn	2590	100	11-9-1811	11-18-1824	Beaverdam Cr.
Samuel Chunn	3317	100	11-8-1834	11-25-1835	FB River, Little Pine Cr.

Census Records

Samuel Chunn is on the 1800 NC Census, Buncombe Co., with 2 males, 2 females, and 5 slaves.

Samuel Chunn is on the 1810 NC Census, Buncombe Co., with 6 males, 5 females, and 3 slaves.

Samuel Chunn is on the 1820 NC Census, Buncombe Co, with 5 males and 3 females.

Editor's Notes

In his 1922 book *Asheville and Buncombe County*, Foster A. Sondley printed a map of Asheville on page. 70. The map evidently dates from about 1798. On this map, Chunn holds town lot 11 and is a partner on town lot 13.

Samuel Chunn is mentioned in connection with the 1820s development of the Buncombe Turnpike; see for instance, *A Lot of Bunkum*, vol. 31, no. 3, p. 13.

The elaborately engraved marble for Samuel Chunn (1772-1855) in the Riverside Cemetery apparently was moved from the cemetery at First Presbyterian Church. Chunn joined the Church in 1833. Samuel Chunn m. Hannah last name unknown (1776-1846).

A daughter, Clara E. Chunn (1812-1858) m. Rev. Robert H. Chapman (1806-1858) who presided over the 1st Presbyterian Church in Asheville from 1855-1862. Chapman was temporarily associated with the church in 1829.

Selected Reference

A Lot of Bunkum, vol. 26, no. 3, p. 19 (2005)

Lambert Clayton NC Land Grants

Burke Co.

Registered Name	Grant	Acres	Entered	Patent	Location
Lambert Clayton	6038	100	8-25-1840	9-28-1841	Broad River, E. bank, Black's Knob

Buncombe Co.

Lambert Clayton	42	300	2-16-1793	1-7-1794	Sains Cr., Adj. Ben Davidson, et al
Lambert Clayton	85	340	7-12-1778	7-7-1794	French Broad R., town fork
Lambert Clayton	117	100	6-22-1794	1-19-1795	Adj. Plumley
Lambert Clayton	142	50	6-22-1794	1-19-1795	adj. own land
Lambert Clayton (1)	650	150	4-21-1797	11-26-1799	FB River, adj. Kings land
Lambert Clayton	651	400	8-23-1792	11-26-1799	FB River, mill shoal
Lambert Clayton	652	150	5-23-1792	11-26-1799	FBR, Hides Cr, big Willow
Lambert Clayton	653	200	8-28-1799	11-26-1799	Glade Cr. & FB River
Lambert Clayton (2)	665	100	4-27-1797	11-26-1799	Willow Cr., adj. Polly Bowman
Lambert Clayton	673	100	12-28-1793	11-26-1799	Little river
Lambert Clayton (3)	677	150	4-21-1797	11-26-1799	FBR, big Willow,Llittle r.
Lambert Clayton	1264	100	10-19-1801	12-20-1803	adj. Edward Johnston
Lambert Clayton	1397	100	2-4-1801	12-18-1804	Glade Cr., N. side
Lambert Clayton	1399	100	8-13-1800	12-18-1804	Crab Tree Cr., Little River
Lambert Clayton	1400	250	9-25-1800	12-18-1804	FB River., E. side, Little Willow
Lambert Clayton	1401	100	9-25-1800	12-18-1804	Fodderstack Cr. & FBR, W. side
Lambert Clayton	1402	100	7-21-1804	12-18-1814	French Broad R., E. side
Lambert Clayton (4)	1591	100	12-11-1804	12-20-1806	FBR headwaters, adj Davidsons Bdg.
Lambert Clayton (5)	1592	100	12-11-1804	12-20-1806	Ben Davidson Cr.
Lambert Clayton	3391	100	10-12-1835	9-19-1836	Turkey Cr.

Footnotes

(1) also Robert Orr - listed 1st

(2) also Robert Orr

(3) also Robert Orr

(4) also Joseph Henry

(5) also Joseph Henry

Other Clayton Family NC Land Grants

Buncombe Co.

Registered Name	Grant	Acres	Entered	Patent	Location
Ephraim Clayton	1860	300	1-16-1809	11-30-1810	Ben Davidson R., Turkey Cr.
Ephraim Clayton	4333	8	4-18-1858	12-13-1859	FB River, Beaver Cr., N. fork
George Clayton (1)	2710	100	10-11-1825	12-29-1827	Silver Cr.
George Clayton (2)	2830	50	8-15-1828	11-20-1830	Silver Cr.
George Clayton (3)	2835	50	8-15-1828	11-20-1830	Turkey Cr.
George Clayton (4)	3412	50	7-6-1831	12-5-1836	FB River, head Wagon Rd.

George Clayton (5)	3438	50	7-6-1831	12-5-1836	Black Snake Br., Turkey Cr.
George Clayton, Sr.	3736	50	10-16-1837	12-24-1838	FB River, head Turkey Cr.
George Clayton	3829	30	3-5-1838	12-9-1840	Glade Cr.
John Clayton	2136	200	8-22-1812	11-29-1814	Glade Cr., N. fork
John Clayton (6)	2139	50	8-22-1812	11-29-1814	Turkey Cr.
John Clayton (7)	2140	50	8-22-1812	11-29-1814	Turkey Cr.
John Clayton	2176	100	n/a	n/a	Glade Cr. (now lives)
John Clayton (8)	2255	200	5-13-1816	11-30-1816	Davidson R.
John Clayton (9)	2358	150	1-3-1816	12-5-1818	Glade Cr., N. fork
John Clayton	3315	20	4-23-1835	11-25-1835	Mills R., S. fork, Cantrels Cr.
John Clayton	3550	70	1-11-1834	9-15-1837	Lydia Haystack Br.
John Clayton	3827	50	3-5-1838	12-9-12840	Glade Cr.
T. L. Clayton	4392	25	2-15-1868	12-24-1870	FB River, W. side

(1) also Ephraim Clayton

(2) also Ephraim Clayton

(3) also Ephraim Clayton

(4) also Ephraim Clayton

(5) also Ephraim Clayton

(6) also George O'Neill - listed 1st

(7) also George O'Neill - listed 1st

(8) also Thomas D. Clayton

(9) also Ben O'Kelly - listed 1st

Craig Family NC Land Grants

Buncombe Co.

Registered Name	Grant	Acres	Entered	Patent	Location
Edward Craig (1)	696	n/a	7-2-1796	12-2-1799	Cain Cr.
Edward Craig	1662	20	5-22-1807	112-27-1807	Cain Cr., both sides
James Creag	721	100	n/a	n/a	Cane Cr., Gap Cr.
James Craig (2)	948	200	11-22-1799	12-15-1801	Cane Cr., adj. McDowell
James Craig	1625	2009	10-28-1806	11-27-1807	Bull Cr, both sides, adj own land
James Craig (3)	2928	38	n/a	n/a	Bull Cr., W. side
James Craig	2929	50	n/a	n/a	Grassey Cr., E. side
James Craig	3090	50	n/a	n/a	Grassy Br.
James Craig	3830	50	n/a	n/a	Bull Cr., Tanyard Br.

John Crig	72	50	10-25-1792	7-7-1794	Gap Br., FB River
John Creag (4)	78	136	5-16-1793	7-7-1794	Swannanoa, Cain Cr
John Creag	157	200	4-18-1792	1-31-1795	FB River
John Craig	178	200	4-18-1792	5-30-1795	FB River, Swannaoa, Cain Cr.
John Creag	404	100	7-12-1794	4-12-1798	Gillihams Cr.
John Creag	405	150	7-12-1794	4-12-1798	Gap Cr., both sides
John Creag	406	200	3-15-1794	4-12-1798	Shoal Cr.
John Creag	416	150	5-11-1794	8-31-1798	Gap Cr., both sides
John Craig	794	100	7-17-1794	9-1-1800	Pigeon R., W. side
John Craig	796	200	7-17-1794	9-1-1800	Pigeon R., Richland Cr.
John Craig	814	200	7-17-1794	9-1-1800	Pigeon R., W. side
John Craig	1369	200	n/a	n/a	Four Mile Br.
John Craig	2486	50	10-24-1818	12-19-1820	Swannanoa, Bee Tree
John Craig	2718	25	9-8-1825	12-29-1827	Swannanoa, Bee Tree, E. side
Robert Craig	1511	200	1-18-1792	9-26-1806	FB River, Flatt Cr.
William B. Craig	2511	100	10-4-1819	11-29-1821	Big Ivy, Haw Br.
William Craig (5)	2928	38	2-3-1828	1-4-1831	Bull Cr., W. side
William Craig	2929	50	2-2-1828	1-4-1831	Grassy Br., E. side
William Craig (6)	3830	50	6-6-1837	12-9-1840	Swannanoa, Bull Cr., Tanyard Br.
William Craig	3909	50	10-13-1838	12-31-184-	Grassy Br.

Footnotes

(1) assignee

(2) also John Craig - listed 1st

(3) also William Craig

(4) 5 miles to Col. Davidsons

(5) also James Craig

(6) also James Craig

Census Records

Robert Craige was on the 1790 NC Census, Burke Co., Morgan District, Thirteenth Company
 (now East & SE Burke Co.) with 3 males and 1 female

Jno. Craig was on the 1790 Census, Burke Co. ,Morgan District, Thirteenth Company
 with 3 males and 1 female

John Craig was on the 1800 Census, Buncombe Co., with 3 males and 4 females

In April, 1795, John Craig bought lot 20 in Morrisville (later Asheville) from John Burton.

Selected References

Benfield, Jean Boone, 2004, Putting Alfred in His Place. The Search for my Craig Ancestor
in Buncombe Co., NC: Asheville, NC, *A Lot of Bunkum*, vol. 24, no. 4, p. 15-19.

Felmet, L. Holt, Jr., 2011, Murder on Bull Creek in 1808 - Was the Victim John, or James Craig?
Asheville, NC, *A Lot of Bunkum,* vol. 32, no. 4, p. 17-20

Davidson Family NC Land Grants-A

Burke Co.

Registered Name	Grant	Acres	Entered	Patent	Location
Benjamin Davidson	33	200	8-3-1778	12-10-1788	Catawba R., Newberry Cr.
Ephraim Davidson (1)	1490	440	8-1-1783	11-27-1792	Swannanoa R., mostly N. side
Gen. Ephr. Davidson	3327	120	2-19-1804	11-29-1804	Catawba R.
Ephraim Davidson	3828	150	3-24-1817	11-29-1817	Catawba R., S. side
Ephraim Davidson	3829	50	12-11-1816	11-29-1817	Big Br., S. side, fort survey
Ephraim Davidson	3833	100	5-24-1817	11-25-1817	Brevard Cr.
Ephraim Davidson	3834	150	5-24-1817	11-29-1817	Catawba R., Brevard Cr.
George Davison (2)	130	100	6-18-1778	3-15-1780	Catawba R., N. fork
George Davison	186	500	7-29-1779	3-14-1780	Catawba R.
George Davidson	242	640	9-10-1778	3-14-1780	Catawba R., Mill fork
George Davidson (3)	250	250	7-29-1779	3-14-1780	Turkey Cove, Lime Kiln
George Davison (4)	299	217	1-2-1779	3-15-1780	Turkey Cove, Lime Kiln
George Davidson	305	200	9-10-1778	3-15-1780	Crooked Cr.
George Davidson	306	100	9-2-1778	3-15-1780	Catawba R., Mill fork
George Davidson	573	180	9-28-1779	10-11-1783	Catawba R.
Geo. Davidson, Sr. (5)	1562	50	n/a	11-27-1792	Catawba R., N. side
George Davidson, Jr.	1891	53	n/a	7-7-1794	Catawba R., W. side
George F. Davidson (6)	6097	100	11-6-1840	1-23-1843	Mill Cr, M. fork.
James Davidson	76	453	10-9-1778	9-20-1779	Catawba R., Buck Cr.
James Davidson	1183	250	8-13-1783	5-18-1789	Flat Cr., Swannanoa R.
James Davidson	1231	300	4-23-1787	5-18-1789	Flat Cr., Swannanoa R.
James Davidson, Jr.	1271	150	n/a	11-27-1789	Turkey Cr., W. fork
James Davidson	1370	200	7-?-1784	11-16-1793	Long Branch, Flat Cr.
James Davidson (7)	1628	640	7-1-1783	11-27-1792	Swananoa R., Flat Cr.
James Davidson	1662	100	7-?-1784	1-1-1793	Flat Cr., Swannanoa R.
James Davidson (8)	3207	100	4-9-1802	9-29-1803	2nd Broad

John Davidson	118	200	10-12-1778	3-15-1780	Crooked Cr., Hampton fork
John Davidson	131	100	8-24-1778	3-15-1780	Camp Cr., Crooked Cr.
John Davidson	174	200	12-12-1778	3-15-1780	Catawba R.
John Davidson	188	200	8-24-1778	3-14-1780	Catawba R., N. fork
John Davidson	238	520	11-17-1778	3--14-1780	Catawba R., N. side
John Davidson	370	200	12-27-1778	10-28-1782	Catawba R., Osburns Cr.
John Davidson	1214	100	8-4-1784	5-18-1789	Cane Cr.
John Davidson	1278	50	11-15-1778	11-16-1790	Hamptons Cr., E. fork
John Davidson (9)	1321	150	10-7-1778	11-16-1790	Haw Br., Crooked Cr.
John Davidson	1379	150	n/a	8-22-1795	Bridge Br.. Buck Cr.
John Davidson, Jr.	1489	200	7-15-1784	11-27-1792	Swannanoa, S. side
John Davidson	1493	75	8-11-1784	11-27-1792	Catawba R., Pleasant Gardens
John Davidson (10)	1898	150	11-12-1783	7-7-1794	Crooked Cr.
Samuel Davidson	156	400	5-12-1778	3-15-1781	Crook Cr., Boyers ford
William Davidson	72	100	10-9-1778	9-20-1779	Clear Cr.
William Davidson	80	300	10-9-1778	9-20-1779	Catawba R., Clear Cr., now lives
William Davidson	85	237	10-9-1778	9-20-1779	Catawba R., Clear Cr.
William Davidson (11)	141	200	12-29-1778	3-15-1780	Muddy Cr., N. fork , now lives
William Davidson (12)	912	640	8-1-1783	8-7-1787	Savanah R., both sides
William Davidson	1078	100	10-11-1785	8-7-1787	Cane Cr.
William Davidson	1141	150	8-13-1778	11-20-1783	Broad R., Crooked Cr.
Wm. Davidson, Jr. (13)	1142	100	8-13-1778	11-20-1788	Broad R., Crooked Cr.
William Davidson (14)	1201	125	7-26-1787	5-18-1789	Turkey Cr., NW. fork
William Davidson (15)	1207	150	4-23-1787	5-18-1789	Turkey Cr., W. fork
William Davidson	1208	300	11-15-1778	5-18-1789	Catawba R., Glade Cr.
William Davidson	1216	400	n/a	12-15-1791	Turkey Cr., S. fork
William Davidson (16)	1219	600	8-12-1783	5-18-1789	Sandy Mush Cr., FB River
William Davidson (17)	1221	250	4-23-1787	5-18-1789	Turkey Cr., NW fork
William Davidson (18)	1230	220	7-23-1787	5-18-1789	Turkey Cr.
William Davidson	1244	271	9-10-1778	5-18-1789	Mudy Cr., Morrison fork
William Davidson	1247	70	9-17-1778	8-22-1795	Bridge Br., Clear Cr.
William Davidson (19)	1259	200	8-15-1783	5-18-1789	Sandy Mush Cr., FB River
William Davidson (20)	1374	300	3-2-1788	10-5-1788	Homney Cr., FB River
William Davidson (21)	1407	400	n/a	12-15-1791	Turkey Cr., S. fork
William Davidson, Sr.	1492	50	n/a	11-27-1792	Pleasant Gard., Catawba
Wm. Davidson, Sr. (22)	1498	100	9-13-1787	11-27-1792	Swanano, both sides
W. Davidson heirs (23)	3188	640	8-1-1783	12-8-1802	Davidsons Cr., FB R.

Footnotes - Burke Co.:

(1) also John Davidson; includes improvements of (nephew & brother) Samuel Davidson

(2) below William Cathey

(3) at William Cathey's

(4) at William Cathey's

(5) opposite own land

(6) next to Buck Richard & Jonathan Bidicks

(7) Flat Creek now Sweeten Cr.

(8) next to Hodge Rabun

(9) also Charles McDowell

(10) path from Coll. Davidsons Mill

(11) next to James McKinney

(12) also James Davidson

(13) William Davidson, Jr., heir of G. Davidson

(14) also John Davidson

(15) also John Davidson, next to Neals

(16) also James Murphey

(17) also James Davidson

(18) also James Davidson

(19) also James Murphey

(20) also Samuel Forgay

(21) also David Vance

(22) near McNab

(23) Gen. William Lee Davidson heirs: Jean, George, Pamela, John, Margaret, Ephraim

  (23) cont'd: north of NW corner of James & Col. William Davidson

  (23) cont'd: survey map says Mills River (i.e, Henderson Co.)

Rutherford Co.

Name					
Alexander Davidson, Jr.	720	150	5-1-1788	11-28-1792	Wilsons Cr., Sandy Run
Benjamin Davidson (1)	545	640	n/a	11-16-1790	FB River, above James Davidson
James Davidson (2)	360	640	11-1-1783	5-9-1787	Davidsons Cr. (Mills R.)
James Davidson	531	640	8-1-1783	11-16-1790	FB River
James Davidson	566	200	6-1-1787	11-16-1790	Sandy River
John Davidson	578	100	6-15-1787	11-16-1790	Sandy Run
John Davidson	840	n/a	n/a	n/a	n/a
Samuel Davidson (3)	944	150	4-10-1782	7-9-1794	Pigeon R., Jonathan Cr.
William Davidson (4)	371	500	11-1-1783	8-9-1787	Davidsons Cr.

William Davidson (5)	526	200	10-22-1788	11-16-1790	Cane Cr. Mtn.
William Davidson (6)	527	250	3-1-1788	11-16-1790	Mills R., S. fork
William Davidson (7)	534	250	3-1-1788	11-16-1790	FB River, Henrys Cr.
William Davidson (8)	536	250	3-1-1788	11-16-1790	FB River, Jenkins Cabin
William Davidson (9)	539	250	n/a	11-16-1790	FB River, Town Cr.
William Davidson (10)	614	250	11-1-1778	1-4-1792	FB River, E. side
William Davidson	905	200	11-1-1789	7-9-1794	FB River, W. side

Footnotes - Rutherford Co.

(1) above James Davidson

(2) also William Davidson

(3) also Andrew Miller

(4) also James Davidson

(5) also Joseph Henry

(6) also Joseph Henry

(7) also Joseph Henry

(8) also Joseph Henry

(9) also Joseph Henry

(10) also Joseph Henry

Davidson Family NC Land Grants-B

Buncombe Co.

Registered Name	Grant	Acres	Entered	Patent	Location
Benjamin Davidson	768	100	10-17-1797	12-20-1799	nr. McCullocks cabin
Ben Davidson, Jr. (1)	1770	33	9-4-1807	12-17-1808	FB River, W side, Lains Cr.
Ephraim Davidson	868	50	4-23-1800	12-11-1800	Swannanoa/both sides
Ephraim Davidson	893	100	8-2-1799	12-19-1800	both sides McMahon Cr.
George Davidson (2)	45	300	4-25-1792	1-9-1794	Pigeon R., W. side, war ford
George Davidson	141	100	1-1-1790	1-19-1795	Cherryfield Cr.
George Davidson	146	50	7-25-1794	1-19-1795	Weavers Mill, W of old entry
George Davidson	204	200	4-10-1793	12-3-1795	Crabtree Cr., Rush fork
George Davidson	212	50	11-7-1794	12-9-1795	joins SW line
George Davidson	420	100	1-25-1794	8-31-1798	Double Br. (iron ore)
George Davidson	1105	100	1-19-1803	12-10-1803	Bee Tree, Double Br., Swannanoa
George Davidson	1292	100	n/a	n/a	McMahan Cr.
George Lee Davidson	1327	300	12-7-1802	11-22-1804	Boylstons Cr., Mills River
George L. Davidson	1394	150	9-7-1802	12-12-1804	Mills R.

George L. Davidson	1429	300	3-5-1804	11-22-1805	Mills R., Bolstons Cr.
Geo. Lee Davidson (3)	1652	82	9-7-1802	11-27-1807	Bolstens Cr., FB River, Mills R.
Hugh Davidson	413	200	11-10-1794	8-31-1798	Richland Cr., Gap Cr.. Pigeon R.
Hugh Davidson	427	100	11-10-1794	8-23-1798	Sugar Tree & Crabtree Cr.
Hugh Davidson	515	300	2-12-1794	12-5-1798	Jonathans Cr.
Hugh Davidson (4)	532	100	7-17-1794	12-5-1798	Pigeon R., Crabtree Cr.
Hugh Davidson (5)	1621	150	4-22-1806	11-11-1807	Big Creek
Hugh Davidson (6)	1622	100	4-22-1806	11-11-1807	Gnat Camp
Hugh Davidson (7)	1623	150	4-22-1806	11--11-1807	Mount Sterling
Hugh Davidson (8)	1624	150	1-23-1805	11-11-1807	Catalutchy Cr.
Hugh Davidson (9)	1625	50	4-22-1806	11-11-1807	Cove Cr., Jonathan Cr.
Hugh Davidson (10)	1626	150	7-26-1805	11-11-1807	below other entry
Hugh Davidson (11)	1627	150	7-16-1806	11-11-1807	Pigeon R., Jonathans Cr.
James Davidson (12)	94	150	2-15-1794	1-19-1795	South of Carson
James Davidson (13)	496	80	5-11-1794	9-28-1798	FB River
James Davidson (14)	561	150	n/a	12-13-1798	FB River, both sides
James Davidson (15)	640	50	11-20-1792	7-29-1799	Turkey Cr., both sides
James Davidson (16)	642	100	2-20-1793	8-29-1799	Sandy Mush Cr., S. side
James Davidson (17)	643	50	2-12-1795	8-29-1799	Sandy Mush Cr.
James Davidson (18)	644	50	11-20-1792	8-29-1799	Sandy Mush, Turkey Cr.
James Davidson	645	50	12-20-1792	8-29-1794	Sandy Mush, Turkey Cr.
James Davidson (19)	790	400	10-10-1790	9-1-1800	FB River, Hommany Cr
James Davidson	1183	250	n/a	8-9-1787	Flat Cr. (Sweeten Cr.)
James Davidson	1231	300	n/a	5-18-1789	Flat Cr., Swannanoa
James Davidson	1628	640	n/a	11-27-1792	Swannanoe, Flat Cr.
James Davidson	1662	100	n/a	1-1-1793	Swanoah, Flat Cr. (Sweeten Cr.)
Jean Davidson, etc (20)	1045	640	2-18-1778	12-8-1802	Mills R. (Davidsons Cr.)
Jean Davidson, etc (21)	1090	640	8-1-1783	9-7-1803	FB River, Davidsons Cr.
John Davidson (22)	44	300	1-19-1791	1-9-1794	FB River, Warm Springs
John Davidson	118	50	5-11-1794	1-19-1795	J. Davidsons Mill Dam
John Davidson (23)	215	25	6-15-1794	12-9-1795	Forges Cr., next to old grant
John Davidson	455	150	9-11-1793	8-31-1798	FB River, Jenkins Br.
John Davidson, Jr.	489	200	n/a	11-27-1792	Jonathans Cr.
John Davidson	613	150	9-11-1793	6-7-1799	Raccoon Cr., Richland Cr., Pigeon R.
John Davidson	616	150	9-1-1793	6-7-1799	Turkey Cr., W. fork, Sandy Mush
John Davidson (24)	716	150	8-17-1792	12-6-1799	Turkey Cr., N. fork
John Davidson	897	100	4-24-1799	12-20-1800	Elijah Lee's Mill Cr.
John Davidson (25)	898	150	4-17-1792	6-26-1801	Newfound Cr.

John Davidson (26)	968	300	3-21-1794	8-27-1802	Jonathans Cr., both sides
John Davidson (27)	969	300	5-4-1792	7-18-1802	Jonathans Cr., both sides
John Davidson (28)	970	200	3-21-1794	8-30-1802	Richland Cr., Pigeon R.
John Davidson (29)	980	150	1-22-1800	8-27-1802	Homeny, Gorges Br.
John Davidson (30)	981	100	1-22-1800	8-27-1802	Homeny Cr.
John Davidson (31)	982	100	1-11-1800	8-3-1802	Homeny, S. fork
John Davidson	1006	300	4-21-1802	12-8-1802	W. of old survey
John Davidson	1104	100	1-20-1803	12-11-1803	adj. Aaron Paton
John Davidson	1374	100	1-19-1803	12-16-1804	FB River, E. side
John Davidson (32)	1611	100	3-21-1794	7-2-1807	Pigeon R., W. side
John Davidson	1614	150	12-24-1806	7-2-1807	FB River, W. side
John Davidson	1615	150	12-24-1806	7-2-1807	Dicks Cr.
John Davidson	1719	150	4-17-1792	12-17-1808	Pigeon R., opp. McDowells gardens
John Davidson (33)	1723	400	n/a	n/a	Richlands Cr.
Josias Davidson (34)	887	200	4-22-1794	12-18-1800	Turkey Cr., S. fork
Samuel Davidson (35)	1567	500	1-25-1805	12-5-1806	Sandy Mush Cr., Pine fork
Samuel W. Davidson	2011	50	10-11-1811	11-28-1812	Swannanoa, N. side, Big Br.
Samuel W. Davidson	2267	50	1-14-1814	12-6-1816	Grassy Br.
Samuel W. Davidson	2474	50	3-31-1818	12-14-1820	Meeting House Cove
Samuel W. Davidson	2571	50	3-6-1823	12-8-1823	Swannanoa, S. side; adj.. R. Paton
Samuel W. Davidson	2572	50	9-30-1822	12-8-1823	Swannano, S. side
Samuel W. Davidson	2893	25	1-5-1830	12-18-1830	Swannano, N. side; Todius Cove
Samuel W. Davidson	2898	150	1-5-1820	12-18-1830	Swannano, S. side; adj. own land
Samuel W. Davidson	3011	182	4-12-1831	12-22-1831	Swannano, Ballards Cr.
Samuel W. Davidson	3113	16	n/a	n/a	Swannanoah R.
Samuel W. Davidson	3699	50	4-20-1837	12-20-1838	Swannanoah R., N. side
Samuel W. Davidson	3700	10	10-16-1837	12-20-1838	Swananoe, Grassy Br.
Samuel W. Davidson	3987	100	10-20-1840	1-21-1843	Rims Cr.
Samuel W. Davidson	3988	100	8-6-1841	1-21-1843	Swannano, N. fork
Samuel W. Davidson	4192	75	11-16-1850	1-13-1852	Averies Cr. (Owenies?)
Thomas Davidson (36)	56	400	4-20-1793	7-9-1794	Gashes Cr./Indian graves
Thomas Davidson (37)	175	50,000	9-10-1793	4-1-5-1795	FB River, S. side, Jenkins Cr.
Thomas Davidson (38)	461	300	2-11-1794	8-31-1798	Big Pigeon, Jonathans Cr.
William Davidson (39)	12	300	4-20-1793	1-6-1794	Swannanoa, FB River
William Davidson (40)	24	250	n/a	1-6-1794	FB River, NW side
William Davidson (41)	58	300	4-12-1792	7-7-1794	Swananoe, adj. Daniel Smith
William Davidson (42)	66	49	5-1-1791	7-4-1794	FB River, E. side, town fork

William Davidson (43)	84	150	9-5-1792	7-7-1794	Sandy Mush Cr., both sides
William Davidson (44)	92	100	5-11-1794	1-1-1795	FB River, W. side
William Davidson	130	100	6-28-1795	8-31-1798	Newfound Cr.
William Davidson	421	300	5-10-1794	8-31-1798	Jonathans Cr, Big Pigeon, W. side
William Davidson	422	400	7-17-1794	8-31-1798	Pigeon R., E. side, Crabtree Cr.
William Davidson	423	50	7-10-1793	7-31-1798	Cole pit, Meadow Br.
William Davidson	424	100	6-28-1794	8-31-1798	FB R., W. side, Hommeny
William Davidson	429	100	6-28-1794	8-31-1798	FB R., Newfound Cr.
William Davidson	430	100	6-28-1794	8-31-1798	FB R., Newfound Cr.
William Davidson	451	100	11-7-1794	7-31-1798	Racoon Cr., Richland Cr.
William Davidson	462	100	11-7-1794	8-31-1798	Beverdam Cr., Hominy
William Davidson	463	50	7-10-1793	8-31-1798	Swannanoa, N. side
William Davidson	563	100	1-1-1792	12-13-1798	Beverdam Cr., Hominy (Rutherford)
William Davidson (45)	807	200	10-26-1791	9-1-1800	FB River, Swannanoa
William Davidson (46)	960	960	n/a	1-2-1786	FB River, District of 96
William Davidson	994	400	9-8-1798	11-19-1802	?(Ivey, Beck Mtn.)

Footnotes:

(1) also David Haddon - listed 1st

(2) also Thomas Davidson

(3) also John Hightower

(4) adj. William Davidson

(5) also John Mahon - listed 1st

(6) also John Mahon

(7) also John Mahon - listed 1st

(8) also William Mitchel Davidson

(9) also William Mitchel Davidson

(10) also William Mitchel Davidson

(11) also William Mitchel Davidson

(12) also Ebenezar Fain

(13) between William Davidson and Benjamin Davidson's old survey

(14) also Ebenezar Fain

(15) also Joseph Henry

(16) also Joseph Henry

(17) also Joseph Henry

(18) also Joseph Henry

(19) also James Greenlee

(20) Gen. Wm. Lee Davidson heirs in order: Jean, George Lee, Pamela, Margaret, John, Ephraim

(21) heirs in order: Jean, George Lee, Pamela, Margaret, John, Ephraim; adj James & William D.

(22) also James Benson

(23) also Ephraim Davidson

(24) also John Hightower

(25) also John Hightower- listed 1st

(26) also Robert Love, assignee

(27) also Robert Love-assignee; adj. William & Thomas Davidson

(28) also Robert Love

(29) also Hardy Hightower

(30) also Hardy Hightower

(31) also Hardy Hightower

(32) also Robert Love

(33) also Lewis Smith, assignee

(34) also Joseph Sorrells

(35) also Samuel H. Williams - listed 1st

(36) also James McNab & (William Davidson - plat only)

(37) also Mark Mitchell

(38) also Joshua Davidson

(39) also Thomas Davidson

(40) also Joseph Henry - 1st; adj. Wm. & Thomas Davidson

(41) also Thomas Davidson; adj. David Smith & William Foster

(42) also Joseph Henry

(43) also Joseph Henry -listed 1st

(44) where Wm. Ingram now lives

(45) also Joseph Henry - listed 1st

(46) also Richard Hightower, tenants in common, not joint tenants

Deaver Family NC Land Grants

Buncombe Co.

Registered Name	Grant	Acres	Entered	Patent	Location
James Dever (1)	110	500	n/a	n/a	Severtons Rd. (Sweeten Cr.)
Nathan Dever (2)	1347	150	7-14-1794	123-10-1804	Pine Cr., S. fork
Reuben Deaver	3374	150	1-26-1833	12-14-1835	Hominy Cr., adj. own land
Reuben Deaver	3978	200	1-6-1840	1-10-1843	Sulphur Spr. Br., Mt. Yeadon
Reuben Deaver	3979	36	12-8-1841	1-10-1843	FB River, W. side, Sulphur Spr.
Reuben Deaver	4149	100	1-13-1843	10-28-1848	FB River, W. side
Richard Dever (3)	513	150	10-19-1796	12-5-1798	Flower Garden Cr., E. side
Richard Dever (4)	518	150	n/a	n/a	Pigeon R., McDowels garden
Thomas B. Dever	3290	115	n/a	n/a	Big Ivy, both sides

William Dever, Jr.	25	400	8-1-1793	1-6-1794	Rims Cr., right fork
William Dever	37	50	1-3-1793	1-7-1794	Rims Cr., both sides
William Dever	436	100	2-5-1796	8-31-1798	Rims Cr., adj. own land
William Dever, Sr.	545	50	4-19-1796	12-13-1798	Pigeon R., W. fork
William Deaver, Jr.	826	50	4-19-1797	12-4-1800	Pigeon R., both sides
William Dever	1307	90	4-19-1803	6-15-1800	Pigeon R., Davises Br.
William Dever	1613	320	3-25-1805	7-2-1808	Pigeon R., E. side
William Deaver (5)	3650	100	10-7-1836	12-8-1838	FB River, SE side

Footnotes

(1) also Joseph D. Gash

(2) also William Dever

(3) also Hamilton Kyle - listed 1st

(4) also Hamilton Kyle

(5) adj. Robert Henry

Census Records

William Deever is on the 1790 NC Census, Burke Co., Morgan District, Eleventh Company
(now Buncombe Co.) with 6 males and 4 females

William Dever is on the 1800 NC Census, Buncombe Co., with 2 males and 1 female

William Dever, Jr. is on the 1800 NC Census, Buncombe Co., with 4 males and 1 female

Fletcher Family NC Land Grants

Buncombe Co.

Registered Name	Grant	Acres	Entered	Patent	Location
Jno. Fletcher	1312	100	1-19-1803	11-14-1804	Mud Cr., adj. Wm. Fletcher
Reuben Fletcher	2364	100	3-9-1818	12-5-1818	Little Mud Cr.
Reuben Fletcher (1)	2372	100	1-6-1816	12-5-1818	Little Mud Cr.
William Fletcher	134	50	n/a	n/a	Mud Cr., adj. own land
William Fletcher	143	200	5-11-1794	1-19-1795	Cane Cr., S. side
William Fletcher	236	100	11-26-1794	10-17-1796	Mud Cr., both sides, assignee
William Fletcher (2)	464	100	4-24-1795	9-31-1798	Mossets Camp
William Fletcher	486	200	4-24-1795	9-28-1798	Cane Cr., Mud Cr.
William Fletcher	614	200	7-31-1792	7-7-1799	Cane Cr., both sides
William Fletcher (3)	675	100	3-15-1790	11-26-1799	Cane Cr., E. side
William Fletcher (4)	1422	200	3-27-1799	12-11-1804	Boydstons Cr.
William Fletcher	1846	300	4-7-1803	1-6-1810	FB River, E. side

Footnotes

(1) adj. Samuel King

(2) assignee, adj. Col. Avery

(3) assignee

(4) adj. James Boydston

Census Records

Wm. Fletcher is on the 1790 NC Census, Rutherford Co., Morgan District, Thirteenth Company
  with 7 males, 2 females, and 1 slave.

William Fletcher I on the 1800 NC Census, Buncombe Co., with 7 males, 3 females, & 4 slaves.

Emmett R. White's 1998 book *Revolutionary War Soldiers of Western North Carolina* shows a
  Reuben Fletcher, b. 1757 VA, d. c. 1833 in Buncombe Co.

Foster Family NC Land Grants

Buncombe Co.

Registered Name	Grant	Acres	Entered	Patent	Location
Barbary Foster	2662	100	9-24-1824	1-8-1827	Big Ivey R.
Benjamin Forister	3004	200	1-4-1831	12-22-1831	Little Mud Cr., head, Glassy Mtn.
Mark Foster, Sr. (1)	1331	200	9-31-1791	11-29-1804	Little Crabtree Cr.
Thomas Foster	103	640	11-12-1794	1-19-1795	Beaverdam Cr., FB river
Thomas Foster (2)	454	100	6-11-1794	8-31-1798	Mills R.., Fosters Br.
Thomas Foster	863	200	1-1-1799	12-11-1800	Sweetens Cr., S. fork
Thomas Foster (3)	899	50	4-18-1798	5-26-1801	Pigeon R., W. side
Thomas Foster	998	100	n/a	n/a	n/a
Thomas Foster	999	100	n/a	n/a	Swannanoa, Sweeten Cr.
Thomas Forster	2618	100	3-25-1822	12-9-1824	Bull Cr., right fork
Thomas Forster	2619	100	3-25-1822	12-9-1825	Longs Br., head
Thomas Forster	3143	30	1-12-1831	12-5-1833	Newfound Cr., Gooches Br.
T. Forster	3404	10	11-11-1835	12-10-1836	Sweetens Cr.
T. Forster	3473	10	11-11-1835	12-10-1836	Sweetens Cr., Swannanoa
Thomas Foster (4)	4097	600	11-1-1841	1-7-1845	Busbee Mtn.
Thomas Foster	4098	34	8-6-1841	1-7-1845	Sweetens Cr., Swannanoa
William Foster (5)	120	150	5-26-1794	1-19-1795	Ivey, N. side
William Foster (6)	121	150	n/a	n/a	Betree Cr.
William Foster (7)	145	150	5-26-1794	1-19-1795	Bull Cr., N. side
William Foster (8)	153	150	5-26-1794	1-19-1795	Lowell Br., Ivey, S. side

William Foster (9)	376	150	5-26-1794	1-19-1795	Betree Br.
William Foster (10)	478	200	2-26-?	9-28-1798	Ivey, S. side
William Forster	497	150	11-7-1794	9-29-1798	Rims Cr., S. side
William Foster	688	200	7-8-1794	12-2-1799	Beaver Dam, adj. B. Davis
William Forster, Jr.	2549	34	10-1-1817	12-11-1822	Swannanoa, Sweeten Cr., W. side
William Forster, Jr.	2550	26	10-30-1817	12-10-1822	Whitsons Cr., both sides
William Fortener	3656	100	9-8-1836	12-8-1838	FB River, N. side, Baileys Br.

Footnotes

(1) also Mark Forster, Jr.

(2) assignee

(3) also Joseph Sorrells - 1st; opp. flower gardens

(4) also Jeremiah West

(5) also Edward Palmer

(6) also Edward Palmer

(7) also Edward Palmer

(8) also Edward Palmer

(9) also Edward Palmer

(10) also Edward Palmer

Editor's Notes

In Oct., 1794, Thomas Foster bought lots 3, 7, & 11 in the village of Morrisville from John Burton.

In April, 1795, William Forster bought lot 12.

Gash, Gudger, Whitson NC Land Grants

Burke Co.

Registered Name	Grant	Acres	Entered	Patent	Location
Martin Gash	1479	78	10-1-1790	11-27-1792	Swannanoa R., both sides
			*****		
Benjamin Gudger (1)	1495	100	7-20-1787	11-27-1792	Swannanoa R., both sides
William Gudger	1499	640	n/a	11-27-1792	Bull Cr., Ivy R.
			*****		
Thomas Whitson	178	200	11-8-1778	3-14-1780	Husbands Br, Lower Cr.
Thomas Whitson	668	441	12-29-1778	10-11-1783	Lower Cr., Littles Br.
William Whitson	569	50	11-21-1778	10-11-1783	Garden Cr., adj. John McDowell
William Whitson	1040	400	8-1-1783	7-7-1787	Ivey R., S. fork
William Whitson	1076	200	8-1-1783	8-7-1787	FB R., E. side, Swannanoa
William Whitson	1128	500	3-12-1784	12-8-1787	Ivey R., S. fork
William Whitson	1129	100	8-1-1783	12-8-1787	Newfound Cr., FB River
William Whitson	1171	400	4-25-1784	5-18-1789	S. fork Turkey Cr., FB River

Buncombe Co.

B. S. Gash	4286	45	3-3-1854	6-21-1855	Swannanoa R., S. side, Little Mtn.

John Gash	10	400	6-1-1788	1-6-1794	S. fork Hominy
John Gash, Sr.	2365	100	2-3-1817	12-5-1818	Swannanoa R.
John Gash, Sr.	3568	100	10-25-1836	11-9-1837	Swannanoa R.. S. side, adj. own land
John Gash	3997	5	11-1-1841	8-14-1843	Whitsons Mill Cr.
Joseph Dennis Gash	8	200	4-24-1792	1-6-1794	Sandy Mush Cr., N side
Joseph Dennis Gash	9	200	7-17-1793	1-6-1794	Sandy Mush Cr., N. side
Joseph Dennis Gash (2)	110	500	7-17-1793	1-19-1795	Sweeten Cr.. N. fork
Leander S.Gash	3554	100	12-22-1836	12-15-1837	Fodder Stack Mtn, FBR, W. side
Martin Gash	211	100	8-8-1793	12-9-1795	Swannanoa R., S. side
Martin Gash	213	50	3-7-1794	12-9-1795	Gashes Cr.
Martin Gash	216	50	8-8-1793	12-9-1795	Swannanoa R., Bens Br.
Martin A. Gash	3537	100	10-25-1836	4-11-1837	FB River, N. side, adj.Gashes
William R. Gash	3706	100	3-8-1836	12-20-1838	Hoopers Cr., Burneys Mtn.

*****

Benjamin Gudger	1151	100	11-29-1800	12-14-1802	Newfound Cr., S. side
James Gudger	1983	100	7--29-1802	7-6-1812	Newfound Cr.
James Gudger	3659	100	9-6-1834	12-8-1838	Bear Cr., head
Joseph Gudger	3114	50	11-7-1829	1-1-1833	Rock House Cr., Swannanoa
Joseph Gudger	3115	100	11-9-1820	1-1-1833	as above
Joseph Gudger	3704	20	2-16-1837	12-20-1838	Gudgers Mill Cr., Swannanoa
Nehemiah Gudger	525	100	4-28-1794	12--5-1798	Rosses Cr.
William Gudger (3)	68	10	9-12-1793	7-7-1794	Swannanoa R., S. side
William Gudger (4)	217	100	5-11-1794	12-9-1795	Swannanoa R., S. side
William Gudger	472	99	n/a	10-13-1783	Indian Cr., Washington Co., TN
William Gudger	570	100	4-30-1792	12-24-1798	Swannanoa, adj. now lives
William Gudger	787	100	2-26-1796	9-1-1800	Ivey
William Gudger	1268	100	2-16-1812	12-20-1813	Swannanoa, near now lives
William Gudger (5)	1499	640	n/a	11-27-1792	Bull Cr., Ivey (Burke)
William Gudger	2020	150	11-3-1807	11-28-1813	Hominy Cr., S. side
William Gudger (6)	2094	400	7-29-1802	11-28-1814	Swananoi, below Gudgers mill
William Gudger	2208	50	1-4-1815	12-12-1815	Bull Cr.
William Gudger, Jr.	2366	100	1-10-1817	12-5-1818	Whitson Cr., adj. own land

*****

Reuben Johnston	2751	25	10-27-1826	12-6-1828	French BR, both sides
R. B. Johnston	4424	60	1-1-1880	10-8-1880	French BR, W. side

*****

Ann Whitson	2101	400	8-13-1811	11-29-1814	Turkey Cr., S. fork
Jason C. Whitson	3940	50	10-26-1840	6-4-1841	Spring Cr., Meadow F. (?Missouri)
Jason C. Whitson	4143	50	10-26-1840	11-9-1847	Spring Cr., Meadow F. (?Missouri)
Joseph Whitson(7)	2650	100	4-8-1808	1-12-1826	Grassy Branch
Joseph Whitson	3154	23	1-4-1831	12-4-1833	Sevannah R. (Swannanoa R.)
Joseph Whitson (8)	3185	50	2-17-1832	12-18-1833	Swannanoa R., N. side

Joseph Whitson	3370	20	7-22-1833	12-5-1835	Swannano R., both sides
William Whitson	214	100	5-11-1794	12-9-1795	Swannanoa R., adj. Wm. Gudger
William Whitson	218	100	5-11-1794	12-5-1795	Swannanoa R., N. side
William Whitson	1076	200	n/a	8-7-1787	FB River, E. side
William Whitson	1171	400	4-25-1784	5-18-1789	FB River, Turkey Cr., S fork
William Whitson	1504	320	3-14-1805	4-14-1806	FB River, W side, Newfound Cr.

Footnotes:

(1) adj. Geo. Cunningham

(2) also James Dever

(3) where he now lives

(4) also M. Gash, opp. Gudgers

(5) see above, Burke Co.

(6) also John Gash

(7) Above Martin Gash

(8) adj. Whitsons saw mill

Editor's Notes

Two daughters of William Gudger married two sons of Martin Gash, and two daughters of
   William Gudger married two son of William Whitson, thus a three family connection.

Reuben Johnston was the son of Ann Dennis by her 1st marriage. She later married
   Martin Gash.

In Oct., 1794, Ann Gash bought lot no. 2 in the village of Morrisville (later Asheville) from John Burton.

Gillaspie Family NC Land Grants

Buncombe Co.

Registered Name	Grant	Acres	Entered	Patent	Location
Jackson Gillaspie	2970	50	7-9-1829	12-12-1831	FB River, E. fork
Matthew Gillaspie	2823	50	10-8-1828	11-20-1830	Millses R.
Mathew Gillaspie	2824	50	10-8-1828	11-20-1830	Millses R., Slated fork
Matthew Gillaspie	2948	75	7-6-1829	12-5-1831	Millses R., Davies Br.
Robert Gillispey	229	100	9-2-1796	12-6-1799	Hominy, N. fork
Robert Gillispey	730	250	9-28-1796	12-6-1799	Pigeon R., Hominy, N. fork
Robert Gillispey	731	100	9-2-1796	12-6-1799	Pigeon R., Hominy, N. fork
Robert Gillispey	732	250	5-5-1796	12-6-1799	Pigeon R., Homony Cr.
Robert Galaspy (1)	897	100	7-22-1800	4-1-1801	Hominy Cr., N. side
Robert Gillispie (2)	1234	200	7-22-1800	12-16-1803	Pigeon R., W. side
Robert Galaspy (3)	1247	150	1-19-1803	12-16-1803	Pigeon R., W. side
Robert H. Gillaspie	2949	50	10-12-1829	12-5-1831	FB River, E. fork
Robert H. Gillaspie	2950	50	10-12-1829	12-5-1831	FB River, E. fork

Silas Gillaspie	358	100	5-20-1796	12-2-1797	Flat Creek
William Gillaspie (4)	2963	100	9-1-1829	12-12-1831	Beaverdam, Turkey Cr.
William Gillaspie	3406	100	2-13-1836	12-5-1836	FB River, E. fork

Footnotes

(1) adj. John Webb

(2) adj. George Cathey

(3) adj. George Davidson

(4) also John Reynolds - listed 1st

Census Records

Robert Gillaspie is on the 1800 NC Census, Buncombe Co., with 1 male and 2 females.

Silas Gillaspie is on the 1800 NC Census, Buncombe Co., with 1 male and 4 females.

Selected References

Brookshire, Greg, 2010, Fortuitous Meeting of Cousins at OBCGS: Asheville, NC, *A Lot of Bunkum*
   vol. 31, no. 1 p. 9-10

Felmet, L. Holt., 2009, More on the Gillespie Family: Asheville, NC, *A Lot of Bunkum*
   vol. 30, no. 3, p. 8-10.

Greenlee Family NC Land Grants

Burke Co.

Registered Name	Grant	Acres	Entered	Patent	Location
David Greenlee (1)	1261	262	8-1-1783	5-18-1789	Ivy R., N. fork
David Greenlee	1515	400	n/a	11-27-1792	Ivey R., Pant Fork
David W. Greenlee	3711	200	3-7-1814	12-5-1815	Catawba, adj. own
David W.Greenlee (2)	3889	100	3-25-1817	11-29-1818	Jacks Cr.,Osburns Cr.
David W. Greenlee	5010	50	3-28-1820	12-22-1820	Crib Cr. (Cub Cr.)
D. W. Greenlee	6062	100	10-22-1841	12-6-1842	Clear Cr.
David W. Greenlee	6166	60	10-18-1844	2-24-1845	Buck Cr.
E. M. Greenlee	6073	100	5-18-1841	12-19-1803	adj. Z. Hawkins
E. M. Greenlee	6074	78	3-6-1841	12-19-1842	adj. own land
E. M. Greenlee (3)	6075	65	5-18-1841	12-9-1842	adj. own land; adj. J. Carson
E. E. Greenlee (4)	6395	21	1-1-1859	3-7-1859	Silver Cr.

James Greenlee	58	570	11-11-1778	9-20-1779	Catawba R., S. side
James Greenlee	318	100	12-29-1779	10-28-1782	Jumping Cr.
James Greenlee	319	500	11-11-1778	10-28-1782	Canoe Cr.
James Greenlee	322	640	11-11-1778	10-28-1783	Linevells R.
James Greenlee	396	800	11-4-1778	10-28-1783	Silver Cr., Catawba R.
James Greenlee	399	473	11-11-1778	10-28-1782	Canoe Cr.
James Greenlee	474	640	11-4-1778	10-28-1782	Silver Cr.
James Greenlee (5)	943	540	8-1-1783	8-7-1787	Swannanoe R., both sides
James Greenlee (6)	1233	100	8-1-1783	5-18-1789	Ivy R., W. fork
James Greenlee (7)	1249	200	8-1-1783	5-18-1789	Ivey R., middle fork
James Greenlee	1291	490	1-2-1779	11-16-1790	Whites Mill Cr.
James Greenlee	1507	200	8-1-1783	11-27-1792	Bee Tree Cr., Swanona
James Greenlee	1638	100	3-17-1784	11-27-1798	Ivy R., Flat Cr., Nolechucky
James Greenlee	1861	200	12-29-1778	7-7-1794	E. Lower Cr.
James Greenlee (8)	2125	30,080	n/a	12-9-1795	Catawba, S. fork, Jacobs fork
James Greenlee	2603	200	8-31-1778	6-7-1799	Canoe Cr.
James Greenlee	2604	200	11-3-1778	6-7-1799	Dates Br.
James Greenlee (9)	2605	200	11-3-1778	6-7-1799	Hunting Cr., Sandy Run
James Greenlee	2606	200	9-16-1778	6-7-1799	Poneys Cr.
James Greenlee	2607	200	10-28-1778	6-7-1799	Catawba R., S. fork
James Greenlee	2608	200	10-28-1778	6-7-1799	Crooked Cr., McCaffertys Br.
James Greenlee	2768	50	7-15-1788	3-12-1800	Bailey's Mill Cr.
James Greenlee	2773	26	9-15-1791	3-12-1800	Cane Cr.
James Greenlee	3070	100	11-3-1778	12-28-1801	John's R., S. side
James Greenlee (10)	3992	200	5-2-1817	11-30-1818	Catawba R., N. fork
James H. Greenlee	6007	100	5-14-1839	12-23-1840	Turkey Cove Cr.
Jas. M. Greenlee	6081	49 3/4	7-25-1842	1-3-1842	Clear Cr.
John M. Greenlee	3772	640	4-26-1814	12-12-1816	Turkey Cove Cr., wagon rd.
John M. Greenlee	3773	50	5-29-1816	12-14-1816	Turkey Cove Cr., bridge br.
John M. Greenlee	3774	50	10-28-1814	12-17-1816	his Mill Cr.
John M. Greenlee	3843	100	9-14-1814	3-5-1818	Catawba R., N. fork
John M. Greenlee (11)	3920	50	12-5-1816	11-30-1818	Catawba R., S. side
John M. Greenlee	3979	300	12-8-1818	11-30-1818	Turkey Cove, Reedy Br.
Samuel Greenlee (12)	838	640	8-1-1783	11-9-1784	Swannanoa R., Bee Cr.
Samuel Greenlee	5015	380	7-29-1820	2-19-1821	Silver Cr., Hartly Pl.
Samuel Greenlee	5016	628	7-27-1820	2-19-1821	Silver Cr.

Footnotes - Burke Co.

(1) also James Greenlee, Mary Bowman - listed 1st

(2) adj. Col. John Carson

(3) adj. Col. John Carson

(4) also C. M. Avery - listed1st, J. C. Tate

(5) also Mary Bowman

(6) also Mary Bowman

(7) also Mary Bowman

(8) also James Erwin, William Erwin (overlaps blocks 1920,1922 of Andrew Beard & Wm. Tate)

(9) Killian old place

(10) also John McGee

(11) adj. Ephraim Greenlee

(12) also Jos. McDowell

Buncombe Co.

John Greenlee (1)	790	400	10-10-1783	9-1-1800	FB River, HominyCr.
James Greenlee	801	250	3-17-1784	9-1-1800	Ivey R., S. fork
John Greenlee	813	50	5-11-1794	9-1-1800	FB River, W. side (assignee)
James Greenlee (2)	966	400	8-1-1783	12-28-1801	Flat Cr. (Fourth Cr.)
James Greenlee (3)	967	200	n/a	n/a	FB River
James Greenlee (4)	1301	250	n/a	n/a	FB River
James Greenlee (5)	1302	640	2-13-1778	12-31-1803	FB River
James Greenlee	1340	320	1-19-1804	12-5-1804	Pigeon R., W. fork
James Greenlee (6)	1609	400	2-24-1778	12-22-1806	Cany R., W. fork
James Greenlee (7)	1610	400	2-24-1778	12-22-1806	Cany R., Crab Orchard
James Greenlee	2688	100	8-12-1827	2-9-1827	Shepherds Mills Cr.,Caney R.

Footnotes - Buncombe Co.

(1) also James Davidson - listed 1st

(2) also Mary Tate (M. Bowman; wife of Wm. Tate)

(3) also Mary Tate

(4) also Mary Tate; heir of John Bowman

(5) also John Bowman

(6) also Charles McDowell, Thomas Little, Wm. Cathey

(7) also Charles McDowell, Thomas Little, Wm. Cathey

Rutherford Co.

James Greenlee	496	300	6-23-1795	11-26-1789	FB River, Big Reedy Cr.
James Greenlee	497	200	3-10-1784	11-26-1789	FB River, adj. Gen. McDowell
Jas. Greenlee (1)	1001	6,400	5-1-1790	6-13-1796	Broad R., Sandy Run
Jas. Greenlee (2)	1002	3,840	1-26-1795	6-13-1796	Broad R., Sandy Run
Jas. Greenlee (3)	1003	2,560	1-26-1795	6-13-1796	Green R., Walnut Cr.
Jas. Greenlee (4)	1004	2,560	1-26-1795	6-13-1796	Grey Cr.
Jas. Greenlee (5)	1005	11,520	1-26-1795	6-13-1796	Cove Cr., Catheys Cr., Mtn. C.

Jas. Greenlee (6)	1006	1,280	1-26-1795	6-13-1796	Green R., Walnut Cr.
Jas. Greenlee (7)	1007	12,160	1-26-1795	6-13-1796	Broad R., Sandy Run
Jas. Greenlee (8)	1008	1,920	1-26-1795	6-13-1796	Webb Cr., Sandy R., Broad R.
Jas. Greenlee (9)	1009	2,460	1-26-1795	6-13-1796	Puzzle Cr., Broad R.
Jas. Greenlee (10)	1010	3,840	n/a	6-13-1796	White Oak, Green R.
Jas. Greenlee (11)	1011	2,560	1-26-1795	6-13-1796	Green R.
Jas. Greenlee (12)	1012	3,200	1-26-1795	6-13-1796	Cedar Cr.
Jas. Greenlee (13)	1013	16,640	n/a	6-13-1795	N. Pacolet
Jas. Greenlee (14)	1014	10,240	1-27-1795	6-13-1796	Sandy Run, Harpers Cr.
Jas. Greenlee (15)	1015	640	1-26-1795	6-13-1796	Sandy Run, Broad R.
Jas. Greenlee (16)	1016	1,920	n/a	6-13-1796	Sandy Run, Brushy Cr.
Jas. Greenlee (17)	1117	1,000	11-18-1794	12-20-1796	Mud Cr.

Footnotes - Rutherford Co.

notes 1-16, James Greenlee had as partners Lewis Bearda& William Erwin

(17) Greenlee had 6 other partners

Editor's Notes

James Greenlee, b. c. 1707 Ireland, d. 1757 PA, m. Mary Elizabeth McDowell (8 child.)

James Greenlee, Jr., b.1740 VA, d. 1813, Morganton, m. 1st Mary Mitchell (8 child.)

 James Greenlee, Jr. m. 2nd widow Ruth Howard

Selected References

Anthony, Margaret H., et al, 1981, *Hemphills in North Carolina*: Collegedale, TN
  College Press, 246 p.

Greenlee, Mary M., & Catherine C. Mann, 1976, *Hemphill-McEntire-Greenlee Families*
  and Connections: Cedar Bluff, AL., privately printed (Greenlee, p. 238)

White, Emmett R., 1984, *Revolutionary War Soldiers of Western North Carolina:*
  Vol. I, Burke Co., Easley, SC, Southern Historical Press, 318 p.

Hawkins Family NC Land Grants

Burke Co.

Registered name	Grant	Acre	Entered	Patent	Location
Augustine Hawkins	377	200	8-13-1778	10-28-1782	Sandy Br.
Augustin Hawkins	3017	42	2-23-1801	12-4-1801	Hunting Cr.
Brittain Hawkins	5614	25	2-17-1830	12-20-1832	Sandy Run

Charles Hawkins	3642	120	10-30-1813	12-2-1814	Gilford Br.
Charles Hawkins	5046	60	1-27-1820	12-19-1821	Guilford Br.
Charles Hawkins	5048	50	3-28-1820	12-19-1821	Guilford Br.
H. B. Hawkins (1)	6292	25	11-30-1852	6-15-1855	Hunting Cr.
Isaac Hawkins	3641	100	10-30-1813	12-2-1814	N. Muddy Cr.
John Hawkins	456	250	5-20-1779	10-28-1782	Beaverdam Br.
Samuel Hawkins	3495	50	9-26-1808	12-22-1809	Muddy Cr.
Zachariah Hawkins	4097	50	7-23-1816	12-19-1820	Muddy Cr.
Zachariah Hawkins	5813	50	10-29-1834	12-21-1836	N. Muddy Cr.
Zachariah Hawkins	6138	100	1-16-1843	12-6-1844	N. Muddy Cr.
Zachariah Hawkins	6165	100	1-16-1843	2-17-1845	N. Muddy Cr.

Footnotes - Burke Co.

(1) joins heirs of A.B. Hawkins

Buncombe Co.

Benjamin Hawkins	2266	164	4-25-1816	12-6-1816	FB River, E. side
Benj. Hawkins	3766	100	10-24-1834	1-2-1839	Turkey Cr.
James Hawkins	1579	50	4-7-1804	12-3-1806	Phillips Cr.
James Hawkins	1866	50	1-3-1810	11-30-1810	FB River, W. side
James Hawkins	1868	50	12-29-1808	11-30-1810	Pawpaw Cr.
James Hawkins	2038	50	10-2-1811	12-18-1812	Turkey Cr.
James Hawkins	2548	50	2-16-1820	12-10-1822	Pawpaw Cr.
Thomas Hawkins	3844	73	6-4-1838	12-9-1840	Turkey Cr.

Census Records

Ben Hawkins is on the 1790 NC Census, Rutherford Co., Morgan District, Thirteenth
  Company with 1 male and 2 females.

Benjamin Hawkins is on the 1800 NC Census, Buncombe Co., with 4 males, 4 females,
  and 3 slaves.

James Hawkins is on the 1800 NC Census, Buncombe Co. with 3 males and 4 females.

Selected References

Felmet, L. Holt, Jr., 2005, Pioneer Benjamin Hawkins: Asheville, NC, *A Lot of Bunkum*, vol. 26, no. 2, p. 4-7

Gowing, Audrey G., 2001, *All Roads Lead to Haywood Co., NC, Vol. 1: Waynesboro, VA*
Humphries Press, 447 p. (Benjamin Hawkins - p. 15-36)

White, Emmett R., 1998, *Revolutionary War Soldiers of Western North Carolina.*
Vol. II, Burke Co.*: Easley, SC, Southern Historical Press, 358 p.

Hemphill Family NC Land Grants

Burke Co.

Registered Name	Grant	Acres	Entered	Patent	Location
Andrew Hemphill	5423	25	12-29-1829	5-11-1830	Silver Cr., adj. own land
Andrew Hemphill	5491	50	12-29-1829	12-21-1830	Cove Cr. (Cane Cr.), Catawba R.
Andrew Hemphill	5493	100	12-29-1829	12-21-1830	Catawba R.
Andrew Hemphill	5803	50	9-22-1835	12-8-1836	Catawba R., Newberrys fork
Andrew Hemphill	5804	50	9-22-1835	12-8-1836	Catawba R., Newberrys fork
Andrew Hemphill	5928	50	5-28-1836	12-26-1836	Catawba R., Newberrys fork
Andrew M. Hemphill	5897	50	10-4-1836	12-10-1838	Catawba R.
Andrew M. Hemphill	5899	8.5	10-4-1836	12-10-1838	Catawba R.
Archibald Mc. Hemphill	6102	100	10-21-1841	1-23-1843	Newberrys fork
C. D. Hemphill (1)	17347	23	n/a	n/a	U. Turkey Twp.
Eliza Ann Hemphill (2)	6178	220	4-18-1845	12-2-1846	S. Muddy Cr.
James Hemphill	260	300	11-24-1778	3-15-1780	Silver Cr., Whites fork
James Hemphill	2309	40	4-8-1797	12-29-1798	Silver Cr.
James Hemphill	5422	50	7-28-1828	5-11-1830	Silver Cr., adj. Thomas Hemp.
James Hemphill	6101	27	1-25-1841	1-25-1843	Mill Cr.
James Hemphill	6241	50	5-11-1850	5-24-1851	Silver Cr., Shoal Br., Reedy Br.
Thomas Himphill	273	400	10-29-1778	3-14-1780	Silver Cr., Catawba R.
Thomas Hemphill	979	50	8-7-1778	8-7-1787	Catawba R., S. side
Thomas Hemphill	1001	50	12-28-1778	8-7-1787	Catawba R., Newberrys fork
Thomas Hemphill	1035	22.5	8-7-1778	8-7-1787	Catawba R., S. side
Thomas Hemphill	1186	640	1-28-1778	5-18-1789	Sandy Mush Cr., big cove
Thomas Hemphill	1243	100	9-6-1786	5-18-1789	Davidsons Mill Cr.
Thomas Hemphill	1321	50	4-23-1793	8-22-1795	Brevards Cr.
Thos. Hemphill	1329	100	n/a	8-22-1795	Davidsons Mill Cr., cane break
Thomas Hemphill	1396	150	n/a	1-4-1792	Jonathans Cr., Big Pigeon R.
Thomas Hemphill	1397	300	n/a	1-4-1792	Jonathans Cr., Big Pigeon R.

Thos. Hemphill (4)	1401	600	4-21-1790	1-4-1792	Jonathans Cr., Pigeon R.
Thos. Hemphill (5)	1405	600	n/a	1-4-1792	Big Pidgeon R., Jonathan Cr.
Thos. Hemphill	1551	50	n/a	11-27-1792	Davidsons Mill Cr.
Thos. Hemphill	1626	150	9-2-1791	11-27-1792	FB River, Newfound Cr.
Thos. Hemphill (6)	1642	50	n/a	11-27-1791	Davidsons Mill Cr.
Thos. Hempill	2946	150	9-4-1800	9-26-1801	Davidsons Mill Cr.
Thomas Hemphill, Jr.	3059	30	1-13-1801	12-17-1801	Silver Cr., adj. own land
Thos. Hemphill	3272	100	3-7-1803	12-19-1803	Davidsons Mill Cr.
Thos. Hemphill	3547	50	n/a	n/a	Catawba R., N. side, adj. own
Thos. M. Hemphill	5598	100	7-23-1839	12-17-1840	Catawba R., Newberrys fork
Thos. Hemphill	6017	100	7-22-1839	12-29-1840	Catawba R., Newberrys fork
Thos. M. Hemphill	6018	150	3-27-1838	12-29-1840	Catawba R., adj. Hemphill
Thomas L. Hemphill	6099	100	5-19-1840	1-23-1843	Catawba R., Newberrys fork
Thos. Hemphill	6100	100	1-25-1841	1-23-1843	Catawba R., Newberrys fork
Thomas Hemphill (7)	6401	100	1-1-1857	4-26-1859	Silver Cr., adj. Hugh A. Tate
Thomas Hemphill	6442	13	8-22-1859	7-12-1861	Silver Cr., adj. own land
William Hemphill	6076	42	11-12-1841	12-18-1842	Silver Cr., adj. R. McElrath

Footnotes - Burke Co.

(1) also J. H. Morrison

(2) also Wm. P., Thomas I., Lafayett, Sarah E., heirs of Wm. P. Hemphill

(3)also Eliza Ann Hemphill, Wm. P. Hemphill, Thomas I. Hemphill

(4) also James McDowell

(5) also James McDowell

(6) adj. Geo. Davidson

(7) also Bable Moore - listed 1st

Buncombe Co.

Andrew Hemphill (1)	2909	300	1-7-1829	12-21-1830	Flat Cr., Swannano R.
Thomas Hemphill	755	300	n/a	n/a	FB River
Thomas Hemphill (2)	821	300	2-6-1778	9-29-1800	FB River, Cane Cr.
Thomas Hemphill (3)	822	200	2-6-1778	9-29-1800	FB River, Cane Cr.
Thomas Hemphill (4)	823	300	2-6-1778	9-29-1800	FB River, Cane Cr.
Thomas Hemphill	906	200	1-9-1800	9-26-1801	FB River, adj. John Carson
Thomas Hemphill	1881	300	n/a	n/a	FB River
Thomas Hemphill	1939	150	8-9-1809	12-11-1811	Dunsmore Cr., wagon rd.

Footnotes - Buncombe Co.

(1)also Moses Whiteside - listed1st & John Young

(2) also Jason Willson, James Patton, Jno McKay, Wm. Morrison, Wm. Willson

(3) also (as above)

(4) also (as above)

Census Records

Thomas Hemphill is on the 1790 NC Census, Burke Co., Morgan District, 1st Company with
  4 males, 7 females, and 11 slaves. (Thomas was b. c.1746, d. 1826)

Selected References

Anthony, Margaret H., et al, 1981, *Hemphills in North Carolina*: Collegedale, TN College Press, 246 p.

Greenlee, Mary M., & Catherine C. Mann, 1976, *Hemphill-NcEntire-Greenlee Families
  and Connections*: CedarBluff, AL., privately printed

White, Emmett R., 1984, *Revolutionary War Soldiers in Western North Carolina,
  Vol. I, Burke Co.*: Easley, SC, Southern Historical Press, 318 p.

Henry Family NC Land Grants

Burke Co.

Registered Name	Grant	Acres	Entered	Patent	Location
Joseph Henry	1582	320	3-10-1784	11-27-1792	FB River, above John Davidson
Robert Henry	3009	200	1-29-1800	12-4-1801	Catawba R., Crib Creek

Buncombe Co.

Registered Name	Grant	Acres	Entered	Patent	Location
Reuben Deaver	3374	150	1-26-1833	12-14-1835	Hominy Cr.
Reuben Deaver	3978	200	1-6-1840	1-10-1843	Sulphur Spr. Br. Mt. Yeadon
Reuben Deaver	3979	36	12-8-1841	1-10-1843	FB River, W. side, Sulphur Spr.
Reuben Deaver	4149	100	1-13-1843	10-28-1848	FB River, W. side
			*****		
Alexander Henry	3204	100	11-29-1829	11-29-1834	Cane Cr., E. side
Ephraim Henry (1)	2734	320	10-11-1826	10-3-1828	Bridge Cr., Wolfpen Cr.
Francis Henry	827	320	3-28-1800	12-10-1800	Tuckysegy R., above Stechoa
Joseph Henry (2)	66	49	5-1-1791	7-7-1794	FB River, E. side
Joseph Henry (3)	84	150	9-5-1792	7-7-1794	Sandy Marsh Cr.
Joseph Henry (4)	206	100	n/a	n/a	New Found Cr.
Joseph Henry (5)	309	100	8-17-1794	10-17-1796	Crabtree Cr., Pigeon
Joseph Henry (6)	310	300	8-27-1794	10-17-1796	Richland Cr., Racoon Cr., E. fork

Joseph Henry (7)	311	100	8-27-1794	10-17-1796	Beaverdam, Hominy Cr.
Joseph Henry (8)	312	100	8-27-1794	10-17-1796	Pigeon R., Crabtree Cr., N. fork
Joseph Henry (9)	313	100	8-27-1794	10-17-1796	Beaverdam Cr., Hominy
Joseph Henry (10)	314	100	8-27-1794	10-17-1796	Crabtree Cr., Pigeon R.
Joseph Henry (11)	315	100	8-27-1794	10-17-1796	Crabtree Cr., Pigeon R.
Joseph Henry (12)	507	100	4-19-1796	12-5-1798	Pigeon R., W. side
Joseph Henry	617	20	3-19-1798	6-7-1799	Cane Cr., E side, adj. own land
Joseph Henry (13)	642	100	2-20-1793	8-29-1799	Sandy Mush Cr., S. side
Joseph Henry (14)	643	50	2-12-1795	8-29-1799	Sandy Mush Cr.
Joseph Henry (15)	644	50	10-20-1792	8-29-1799	Turkey Cr., both sides
Joseph Henry (16)	645	50	10-20-1792	7-29-1799	Turkey Cr., both sides
Joseph Henry	646	200	2-20-1793	8-29-1799	Phillips Cr., Indian Camp
Joseph Henry	746	400	1-17-1795	12-6-1799	Cane Cr., W. side, now lives
Joseph Henry (17)	807	200	10-26-1798	8-1-1800	FBR, Swananoa, Wagon Rd.
Joseph Henry (18)	844	250	10-17-1799	12-11-1800	Hoopers Cr., Kyles Cr.
Joseph Henry (19)	845	200	11-1-1799	12-11-1800	Hoopers Cr., Clear Cr.
Joseph Henry (20)	907	400	1-26-1801	98-26-1801	FB River, Little Willow Cr.
Joseph Henry (21)	943	50	n/a	n/a	Kyles Cr., Hoopers
Joseph Henry	1005	640	n/a	n/a	Pigeon R.
Joseph Henry	1029	50	n/a	n/a	Green R.
Joseph Henry (22)	1154	80	1-29-1801	12-14-1803	Kyles Cr., Hoopers
Joseph Henry (23)	1161	100	10-10-1801	12-14-1803	Hoopers Cr.
Joseph Henry	1169	170	10-16-1802	12-14-1803	FB River, E. side, N. fork
Joseph Henry (24)	1257	150	1-6-1801	12-16-1803	Big Bear Wallow, Clear Cr.
Joseph Henry (25)	1366	40	11-5-1802	12-10-1802	Hoopers Cr.
Joseph Henry (26)	1389	125	10-10-1801	12-10-1804	Hoopers Cr., Pigeon R., E. side
Joseph Henry	1486	130	n/a	n/a	N. fork
Joseph Henry (27)	1591	100	12-11-1804	12-20-1806	FB River, headwaters, Cedar Mtn.
Joseph Henry (28)	1592	100	12-11-1804	12-20-1806	head Ben Davidson Cr.
Joseph Henry (29)	1701	500	1-26-1801	9-24-1808	FB River, N & E, adj. own land
Joseph Henry (30)	1781	200	n/a	n/a	FB River
Joseph Henry (31)	1790	60	9-20-1804	9-16-1809	Clear Cr.
Joseph Henry, Sr.	1808	250	12-10-1804	9-9-1809	Mills Cr.
Joseph Henry, Sr.	2278	65	1-1-1810	12-12-1816	Cane Cr., W. side
Joseph Henry	2279	107	10-29-1808	12-12-1816	Cane Cr.
Joseph Henry, Jr.	2734	320	n/a	n/a	Bridge Cr.
Joseph Henry	2877	50	3-23-1801	12-12-1816	Cane Cr., SE side
Robert Henry (32)	593	300	n/a	n/a	Jonathans Cr.
Robert Henery (33)	761	200	1-27-1790	12-18-1799	Caney R., Bolins Cr.
Robert Henry	754	250	10-30-1794	12-18-1799	Pigeon R., Crystal Cr.
Robert Henry	811	200	2-11-1794	9-1-1800	Erwins Cr., Robinson Cr.

Robert Henry	1329	165	6-6-1803	11-29-1804	FB River, Davises Mill Cr.
Robert Henry	1448	150	6-6-1803	12-12-1805	FB River, Davises Mill Cr.
Robert M. Henry	4348	100	1-14-1854	4-4-1861	FB River, W. side, Dicks Cr.
William Henry	2158	150	1-6-1813	12-20-1814	Turkey Cr., S. fork
William L. Henry	4459	129.25	9-4-1883	1-9-1885	Ragsdale Cr.
William L. Henry	4422	537	12-4-1876	12-31-1878	Ragsdale Cr., Deavers View

Footnotes - Buncombe Co.

(1) also Joseph Henry, Jr.

(2) also William Davidson

(3) also William Davidson

(4) also Gabriel Ragsdale

(5) also Gabriel Ragsdale - 1st

(6) also Gabriel Ragsdale

(7) also Gabriel Ragsdale

(8) also Gabriel Ragsdale

(9) also Gabriel Ragsdale

(10) also Gabriel Ragsdale

(11) also Gabriel Ragsdale

(12) also George Cathey

(13) also James Davidson - 1st

(14) also James Davidson - 1st

(15) also James Davidson - 1st

(16) also James Davidson - 1st

(17) also William Davidson

(18) also William Mills - 1st

(19) also William Mills - 1st

(20) also Robert Henry

(21) also William Mills

(22) also William Mills - 1st

(23) also William Mills

(24) also William Mills - 1st

(25) also William Mills

(26) also Lambert Clayton - 1st

(27) also Lambert Clayton - 1st

(28) also Robert Henry

(29) also Ben Odell

(30) also William Mills

(31) also William Mills

(32) also Joseph Dobson

(33) also Joseph Dobson

Rutherford Co.

Joseph Henry	67	150	4-10-1780	12-16-1785	Cove Cr., Goodbreads Cr.
Joseph Henry	68	150	10-28-1779	12-16-1795	White Oak
Joseph Henry	69	50	4-10-1780	12-16-1785	Cove Cr., Darnels Cr.
Joseph Henry	70	100	11-25-1779	12-16-1785	Green R., Little Cove Cr.
Joseph Henry (1)	71	150	3-28-1780	12-16-1785	Reynolds Cr.
Joseph Henry	72	100	4-10-1780	12-16-1785	Cove Cr., Goodbread Cr.
Joseph Henry (2)	91	600	1-15-1780	10-27-1784	First Little Broad R., Wilkeys Cr.
Joseph Henry	207	200	2-10-1785	8-9-1787	Green R., S. fork, Salada path
Joseph Henry (3)	244	150	3-28-1780	8-9-1787	Brants Cr.
Joseph Henry	505	140	11-1-1787	11-29-1790	N. Pacolet, Skyuke. Big Bottom
Joseph Henry (4)	526	200	10-22-1788	11-16-1790	Green R. Road
Joseph Henry (5)	527	250	3-1-1788	11-16-1790	Mill R., S. fork (Davison Cr.)
Joseph Henry (6)	534	150	3-1-1786	11-16-1790	FB River, Henry Cr.
Joseph Henry (7)	536	250	3-1-1788	11-16-1790	FB River, Jenkins cabin
Joseph Henry (8)	539	250	11-1-1789	11-16-1790	FB River, Town Cr.

Joseph Henry (9)	606	640	10-24-1791	10-24-1791	Pidgeon R., Jonathan Cr.
Joseph Henry (10)	614	250	11-1-1788	1-4-1792	FB River
Joseph Henry	670	100	8-1-1789	1-4-1792	Green R.
Joseph Henry (11)	973	320	10-29-1791	1-31-1795	Pigeon R., W. side
William Henry	420	50	12-10-1785	11-26-1789	Green R.

Footnotes - Rutherford Co.

(1) also James Miller - 1st

(2) also Robert Alexander

(3) also James Miller - 1st

(4) also William Davidson - 1st

(5) also William Davidson - 1st

(6) also William Davidson - 1st

(7) also William Davidson - 1st

(8) also William Davidson - 1st

(9) also Joseph Cummin - 1st

(10) also William Davidson - 1st

(11) also John Cummin

Hoodenpile Family NC Land Grants

Burke Co.

Registered Name	Grant	Acres	Entered	Patent	Location
Philip Hoodenpyl	1255	50	2-2-1786	5-18-1789	Thoms Creek
Philip Hoodenpyl	1273	250	n/a	11-27-1789	FBR, adj. Carson & McDowell

Buncombe Co.

Philip Hoodingpyle (1)	288	50	n/a	4-5-1797	Elk fork
Philip Hoodingpyle	290	50	2-19-1796	4-5-1797	Hintons Cr.
Philip Hodenpile	1667	640	1-22-1806	12-2-1807	FB River, below Warm Spr.
Philip Hoodenpile	1674	400	1-22-1806	12-2-1807	FB River, below Warm Spr.
Philip Hoodenpile	1676	50	12-2-1805	12-2-1807	FB River, NE side, adj. Nelson
Philip Whotenpile (2)	1917	100	2-7-1809	12-12-1810	Warm Spring
Philip Whoodenpyle	1919	50	2-7-1809	3-4-1811	Warm Spr. Rd., adj. Boll
Philip Hoodenpyle	1926	50	10-5-1809	12-3-1811	Warm Spr., Big Laurel R.
Philip Hoodenpyle	1927	100	2-7-1809	12-9-1811	FB River, NE side, adj. own
Philip Hoodenpyle	1928	200	2-1-1808	12-3-1811	FB River, SW side, Shutin Cr.
Philip Hoodenpile	2109	100	3-13-1809	11-29-1814	Big Lorel, Middle fork
Philip Hoodenpile, Sr.	2110	100	3-13-1809	11-29-1814	Little Lorel, both sides

Footnotes

(1) also George Baker   (2) also John Marburg

Editor's Notes

Philip Hoodenpile was born in 1757 in Holland and went to Philadelphia in the early 1780s.
He went to Burke Co., NC about 1786.

On the 1790 NC census, he was living in the 12th Company, Morgan District, Burke Co. with 4 other males and 5 females. He served as a Buncombe Co. justice from 1792 to 1801, and as a state representative in 1796. In the 1800 census for Buncombe County, his family had 3 males and 5 females. In the 1810 census for Buncombe County, his family had 6 males, 2 females, and 4 slaves.

Bishop Asbury mentions Hoodenpile in his notes of Oct., 1809.

Phillip Hoodenpile married twice, first to Helena Key by whom he apparently had one son. His second marriage was to Jane Rounsavall and resulted in 10 children.

The first road from Asheville, NC to Greenville, TN was forged about 1794. In 1812, Philip Hoodenpile was in charge of the section from Warm Springs to Newport, TN. He was mentioned as a tavern keeper and conducted a ferry across the French broad River. According to the land records above, he had land at Warm Springs as early as 1807.

Philip Hoodenpile moved to Bledsoe Co., TN by 1813. Deeds record his land purchases there for the period 1817 to 1832. He died there about 1834.

Hughey Family NC Land Grants

Buncombe Co.

Registered Name	Grant	Acres	Entered	Patent	Location
David Hughey	2197	140	6-13-1814	12-5-1815	Big Ivey, Paint fork
James Hughey	428	100	4-4-1794	8-31-1798	Glens Cr.
Joseph Hughey	277	150	3-22-1794	11-21-1796	Glens Cr., both sides
Joseph Hughey	278	150	3-22-1794	11-21-1796	Nathan Smith Cr., S. fork
Joseph Hughey	431	100	9-5-1789	8-31-1798	Ivey, White Oak Br.
Joseph Hughey	432	200	9-5-1789	8-31-1798	White Oak Br. (Gilberts Cr.)
Joseph Hughey	452	200	9-5-1789	8-21-1798	Gilberts Cr.
Joseph Hughey	737	100	n/a	n/a	Newports Cr.
Joseph Hughey	802	200	9-5-1789	9-1-1800	Ivey, Gilberts Cr.
Joseph Hughey (1)	1186	150	n/a	n/a	adj. Joseph Hughey
Joseph Hughey	1545	50	n/a	n/a	Rims Cr.
Joseph Hughey	1688	200	10-23-1789	12-5-1807	Glens Cr., FB River
Joseph Hughey	1883	100	1-10-1810	12-3-1810	Mills R., W. fork
Joseph Hughey	1914	100	4-7-1808	12-14-1810	Mills R., both sides
Joseph Hughey	2239	50	4-3-1810	11-30-1816	Warm Spring Rd. (Green R.)
Samuel Hughey	537	250	n/a	n/a	Davidsons Cr.
Samuel Hughey, Jr.	2894	75	n/a	n/a	Rims Cr.
Samuel Hughey, Jr.	3028	50	4-9-1829	12-22-1831	Rd. Rims Cr. to Ivey
Samuel Hughey, Jr.	3273	50	1-27-1834	5-13-1835	Big Ivey, Harwoods Cr.
Samuel Hughey, Jr.	3275	50	1-7-1834	5-15-1835	Big Ivey, Harwoods Cr.
Samuel Hughey	3661	50	9-1-1834	12-8-1838	Rims Cr., Rich Cove

Footnotes

(1) also Bedent Baird

Israel Family NC Land Grants

Buncombe Co.

Registered Name	Grant	Acres	Entered	Patent	Location
Frederick Israel	3743	100	10-24-1836	12-24-1838	FB river, W. side, Averies Cr.
Isham Israel	1541	200	n/a	n/a	Averys Cr.
Jesse Israel	1003	100	n/a	n/a	FB river, W. side, Averies Cr.
Jesse Israel	1450	200	1-26-1802	12-13-1805	(Old War Trail)
Jesse T. Israel	10588	163.5	6-12-1890	1-12-1891	S. Hominy Cr., Curtis Cr.
John C. Israel	4328	4.5	1-8-1856	4-5-1859	FB River, W. side, Averys Cr.
Michael Israel	2554	100	10-6-1820	12-10-1822	FB River, W. side
Michael Israel	3742	100	10-20-1835	12-24-1838	Averies Cr.
P. J. Israel	4354	10.5	3-25-1861	4-13-1861	FB River, W. side, Averys Cr.
Philip J. Israel	4297	17	10-13-1853	12-3-1855	FB River, W. side, Averys Cr.
William Israel	2553	100	2-8-1821	12-10-1822	FB River, W. side

Census Records

Jesse Israel is on the 1790 NC Census, Wilkes Co., Morgan District, First Company, with
  1 male and 1 female.

Jesse Israel is on the 1800 NC Census, Buncombe Co., with 3 males and 3 females.

Michal Israel is on the 1790 NC Census , Wilkes Co., Morgan District, First Company
  with 5 males, 2 females, and 4 slaves.

Selected References

Israel, Kenneth D., 1981, *The Children of Israel*: Jacksonville, FL, privately printed, 606 p.

_____, & Evelyn P. Campbell, 2003, *Joshua Jones of the Misty Blue Mountains*: Greenville,
  SC, Southern Historical Press, 905 p.

Jarret Family NC Land Grants

Buncombe Co.

Registered Name	Grant	Acres	Entered	Patent	Location
Daniel Jarrat	362	300	6-28-1787	10-17-1797	FB River, W. side, Beaver Cr.
Daniel Jarret (1)	829	200	7-17-1799	12-10-1800	Hominy Cr.
Daniel Jarret (2)	830	200	4-18-1799	12-10-1800	FB River, W. side
Daniel Jarret	831	200	4-18-1799	12-10-1800	Beaver Cr., S. fork
Daniel Jarrett, Jr.	898	100	4-16-1799	12-20-1800	Beaver Cr., N. fork
David Jarratt, Sr.	1206	50	1-20-1800	12-16-1803	FB River, W. side, Beaver Cr.
Daniel Jarrat, Sr.	1233	150	7-13-1802	12-16-1803	FB River, W. side, Beaver Cr.
Daniel Jarret, Sr.	1356	80	8-13-1802	12-10-1804	FB River, W. side, Beaver Cr.
Daniel Jarrett, Sr.	1495	64	8-10-1804	12-20-1805	FB River, W. side, Beaver Cr.
Daniel Jarrett, Jr.	1779	100	4-22-1806	12-21-1808	FB River, W. side, Hominy Cr.
Daniel Jarrette	1880	37	1-3-1810	12-3-1810	FB River, W. side, Beaver Cr.
Daniel Jarrette (3)	1884	50	1-3-1810	12-6-1810	FB River, W. side
Daniel Jarratt, Sr.	2013	50	7-7-1812	12-18-1812	FB River, W. side, Beaver Cr.
Daniel Jarret, Sr.	2322	60	1-13-1815	11-28-1817	FB Rkiver, W. side, Grassy Br.
Daniel Jarrett	2555	18	1-4-1821	12-10-1822	FB River, W. side
Fanny Jarret	3491	23	8-18-1834	13-10-1836	Swannanoa
Jacob Jarrette	2791	50	3-10-1828	12-17-1829	Atkinson Br., head
James M. Jarret	4133	20	1-10-1846	1-5-1847	FB River, W. side
John Jarret	828	100	4-23-1800	12-10-1800	
John Jarrett	2229	86	4-4-1815	11-26-1817	FB River, W. side
John C. Jarret	4132	40	10-31-1845	1-5-1847	FB River, W. side
Moses Jarret	1742	220	11-23-1807	12-17-1808	Beaver Cr., S. fork, head
Moses Jarret (4)	1761	64	11-28-1807	12-17-1808	FB River, W. side
Moses Jarratt	2052	12	9-7-1812	11-24-1803	FB River, Beaver Cr., m. fork

Footnotes

(1) adj. Joseph Smith

(2) adj. Joseph Smith

(3) adj. own land

(4) adj. own land

Selected References:

Jarrett, Charles E. & Elizabeth J. Walton, 2006, *Jarrett. Pennsylvania to North* Carolina *and*

Beyond: Bountiful, UT, Family History Publ., 465 p.

Editor's Notes

Daniel Jarrett (1747-1822) was the youngestof 13 children. He died in Buncombe Co., NC.

Daniel Jarret is on the 1790 NC Census, Mecklenburg Co. , Salisbury District with 5 males and 5 females.

Daniel Jarrett is on the 1800 NC Census, Buncombe Co., with 5 males and 4 females.

Justice Family NC Land Grants

Buncombe Co.

Registered Name	Grant	Acres	Entered	Patent	Location
Amos Justice	681	200	1-3-1793	11-27-1799	Shaws Cr., head
Amos Justice	682	100	1-3-1793	11-27-1799	Timber Ridge, S. side
Amos Justice	683	100	3-17-1792	11-27-1799	Clear Cr., Wolf Br.
Amos Justice	684	100	7-17-1792	11-27-1799	FB River, W. side, Gap Camp
Amos Justice (1)	942	50	8-17-1799	12-15-1801	Mud Cr., Big Meadow
Amos Justus (2)	1824	300	7-3-1807	12-15-1807	FB River, N. fork, now lives
Isaac Justice	3212	50	11-13-1832	12-6-1834	Clear Cr., N. side, Big Mtn.
James D. Justice	2896	200	10-12-1825	12-18-1830	Bent Ridge, Watkins land
James M. Justice	2773	100	12-24-1827	9-10-1829	Mud Cr., Big Spring
John Justice	1266	70	10-6-1801	12-20-1803	Clear Cr., Mill Br., adj. own land
John Justice, Jr.	2395	50	2-3-1816	12-5-1818	Clear Cr., Blue Ridge
R. B. Justice (3)	7073	160	n/a	n/a	Swannanoa, Flat Cr.
Thomas Justice	680	150	2-1-1798	11-26-1799	Shaws Cr., now lives
Thomas Justice	979	100	n/a	n/a	Mud Cr.
William Justice	2696	250	5-20-1825	12-29-1827	Green R.
William Justice (4)	2777	250	10-19-1838	11-25-1829	Mud Cr., Bats fork
William Justice	2888	200	10-10-1828	12-7-1830	FB River, W. side, Sandy Bottom
William Justice	2903	100	1-4-1828	12-21-1830	Green R.
William Justis (5)	2954	50	9-12-1829	12-12-1831	Mud Cr.
William Justis	3638	137	2-8-1838	10-19-1838	Mud Cr., Bats fork

Footnotes

(1) also John Taber

(2) village of Gloster

(3) also John McDowell & J. L. Patton

(4) also Gilbert Pennell

(5) son of John Justis

Census Records

Amos Justice is on the 1790 NC Census, Rutherford Co., Morgan District, with 2 males and 2 females.

Amos Justice is on the 1800 NC Census, BuncombeCo., with 5 males and 5 females.

Tho. Justice, Sr. is on the 1790 NC Census, Rutherford Co., Morgan District with 5 males & 3 females

Thomas Justice is on the 1800 NC Census, Buncombe Co., with 4 males, 4 females, and 2 slaves.

Selected References

Parris, Joyce Justus, 1993, *Justis, Justus, Justice for All. A Compilation of An Early American Family.*
 Swannanoa, NC, privately publ., 223 p.

_____, 2006, *Justice Gone Astray: ibid*, 66 p.

Killian Family NC Land Grants

Burke Co.

Registered Name	Grant	Acres	Entered	Patented	Location
Abraham Killian	3139	150	8-14-1802	11-27-1802	Muddy Br.
George Killian	562	100	6-7-1778	9-20-1779	Catawba R., Hunting Br.
John Killian	504	141	10-27-1778	10-28-1782	Clarks Cr.
William Kelton	1671	40	10-5-1778	11-26-1793	Nicks Cr.

Buncombe Co.

Andrew Killian	184	200	n/a	5-30-1795	Pigeon R.
Andrew Killian	185	200	11-14-1791	5-30-1795	Pigeon R., adj. J. McDowells
Andrew Killian	607	100	10-4-1787	6-7-1799	Hominy Cr., Old War ford
Daniel Killian	337	200	1792	12-2-1797	Beaver Dam Cr.
Daniel Killian	815	100	2-13-1794	9-1-1800	Newfound Cr.
John Killian	2537	75	4-7-1808	12-19-1821	Beaverdam Cr., S. side
John Killian	2540	75	4-7-1808	12-19-1821	Beaverdam Cr., N. side
John Killiam	2880	100	10-13-1830	12-4-1830	Beaverdam Cr., N. fork
Joseph Killian	2484	100	3-9-1818	12-19-1820	Beaverdam Cr., S. side
Joseph Killian	2764	50	10-7-1826	12-27-1828	Beaverdam Cr., Bull fork
William W. Killian	2470	100	3-9-1818	12-14-1820	Beaverdam Cr., N. side
William W. Killian	2789	100	3-12-1828	12/11/1828	Beaverdam Cr., N. side

Selected References

Eaker, Lorena S., 1994, *German Speaking People West of the Catawba River in North Carolina, 1750-1800:* Franklin, NC, Genealogy Publ. Service, 578 p. (Killian, p. 255-260)

Eckard, Lucy J., 1996, *The Ancestors and Descendants of Floyd Glenn Killian and Elsie Viola Killian:* n.p., privately printed, irregular pages, ca. 200

Killian, Cheryl Mann (ed.), 2009, *The Family of North Carolina Pioneer Andreas Killian (1702-1788)* Alpharetta, GA, Apex Book Mfg., 235 p.

Killian, J. Yates, 1955, *The History of the Killian Family in North Carolina*: Lincolnton, NC Assoc. Descendants of Pioneer Andreas Killian, 20 p., + 9 p. index

McCreight, William R., 2011, *The Forefathers of North Carolina Andreas Killian:* Ellenwood, GA, privately publ., 268 p.

White, Emmett R., 1998, *Revolutionary War Soldiers of Western North Carolina. Vol. I, Burke Co.*: Easley, Sc, Southern Historical Press, 538 p.

Kuykendall Family NC Land Grants

Rutherford Co.

Registered Name	Grant	Acres	Entered	Patent	Location
Abraham Kuykendoll	595	400	12-20-1796	1-4-1792	FB River, Mud Cr.
Abraham Kuykendoll	761	900	7-1-1791	11-28-1792	FB River, Mudd Cr.
Abraham Kuykendall (1)	1093	600	7-28-1791	12-20-1796	Mud Cr., E. side
Abraham Kuykendoll (2)	1100	200	5-28-1791	12-20-1796	Mills R., Fosters Cr.
Abraham Kuykendoll (3)	1103	300	7-28-1791	12-20-1796	FB River, Mud Cr., Traff Cr.
Abraham Kuykendoll (4)	1117`	300	7-28-1791	12-20-1796	Mud Cr.
Abraham Kuykendoll (5)	1127	300	7-28-1791	12-20-1796	Mudd Cr., W. fork
Abraham Kuykendoll (6)	1128	300	12-10-1791	12-20-1796	Mud Cr.
Abraham Kuykendoll (7)	1129	150	5-28-1791	12-20-1796	Mud Cr.
Abraham Kuykendoll	1132	300	10-10-1779	12-20-1796	Mud Cr.
Abraham Kuykendoll	1524	100	10-11-1796	12-18-1797	Sandy Run
Abraham Kurkendoll	1557	100	5-1-1789	12-18-1797	Mill Cr., Sandy Run
Francis Kendoll	902	50	1-24-1793	7-9-1794	Green R., Big Cove
Mathew Kerkendall	469	200	6-10-1786	11-26-1789	Wagon Road
Simon Kerkendoll (8)	707	300	9-1-1791	11-27-1792	FB River, Mud Cr.

Footnotes - Rutherford Co.

(1) also David Miller

(2) also David Miller

(3) also David Miller

(4) also James Greenlee + 5 others

(5) also David Miller

(6) also Andrew Miller

(7) also David Miller

(8) also David Miller

Buncombe Co.

Abraham Keykendale, Sr.	1277	100	10-1-1800	12-20-1803	Big Mud Cr.
Abraham Keykendale, Jr.	1287	150	12-15-1801	12-20-1803	Bates Br.
Abraham Keykendale (1)	1457	240	12-21-1801	12-19-1805	Little Mud Cr.
Abraham Keykendale	1472	300	12-15-1801	12-19-1805	Earle Cr., Devils fork
Ann Kindall	1199	50	11-2-1801	12-16-1803	adj. Col. Earles
Jacob Keykendale	1358	50	1-18-1804	12-10-1804	Little Mud Cr.
James Keykendall	585	200	6-11-1798	12-24-1798	Mud Cr., W. side
James Keykendall	596	200	1-18-1798	12-24-1798	Mud Cr., W. side, adj. Abraham
James Keykindale	865	200	10-1-1799	12-11-1800	Poplar Camp Cr., adj. own
James Keykindale	1093	400	2-3-1801	12-11-1804	Little Mud Cr.
James Keykendale	1405	100	2-3-1801	12-18-1804	Little Mud Cr., Maple Swamp
Jno. Keykendoll	935	300	1-23-1799	12-15-1801	Earle Cr., E. side
Jno. Keykendall	950	300	10-13-1799	12-13-1800	Earles Cr., E. side
Peter Keykindale	1690	200	6-5-1800	12-16-1803	Mud Cr., Devils fork
Peter Keykendale	1382	200	2-3-1803	12-11-1804	Batewood Cr.
Simon Keykendall	939	300	1-23-1800	12-15-1801	Mud Cr., Camp Cr., adj. own
Simon Kuykendale	1267	150	2-3-1801	12-20-1803	Little Mud Cr.
Simon Keykendale	1286	200	4-13-1801	12-20-1803	Camp Cr., adj. Grant 939

Footnotes - Buncombe Co.

(1) also George B. Greer

Selected References

Eaker, Lorena S., 1994, *German Speaking Peoples West of the Catawba River in North Carolina*
  1750-1800: Church Hill, TN, SCK Publ.,578 p. (Abraham Kuykendall land grant entry 1751, Anson Co. NC)
Price, Betty K., 2005, The Revolutionary War Serviceof Captain Abraham Kuykendall:
  Asheville, NC., *A Lot of Bunkum*, vol. 26, no. 1, p. 9-13

Census Records

Abram Kinkindal, Jr. is listed in the 1790 NC Census, Rutherford Co., Morgan District, Sixth Company
  with 3 males, 4 females, and 7 slaves
Abraham Kuykindoll is listed on the 1800 Census, Buncombe Co. (now Henderson Co.) with
  2 males, 1 female, and 5 slaves

Simon Kikendal is listed on the 1790 Census, Rutherford Co., Morgan District, Fourteenth company
   with 2 males and 1 female

Simon Kuykendol is listed on the 1800 NC Census, Buncombe Co. (now Henderson Co.)
   with 5 males, 1 female, and 1 slave

Lance Family NC Land Grants

Buncombe Co.

Registered Name	Grant	Acres	Entered	Patented	Location
Benjamin Lance	4018	70	11-4-1842	11-30-1844	FB River, W. side
Charles H. Lance	2664	100	1-8-1824	1-8-1827	Cane Cr., E. side, Burneys Mtn.
Henry Lance	1126	100	2-24-1802	12-10-1803	Hoopers Cr., adj. own land
Henry Lance (1)	1465	200	7-16-1803	12-19-1805	Hoopers Cr., Gap Cr.
Henry Lance	3241	50	10-4-1831	12-5-1835	FB River, E. fork
John Lance	3967	5	3-15-1841	12-6-1842	FB River, E. side
Joseph Lance	4189	100	12-15-1848	3-21-1851	FB River. W. side, Averys Cr.
Martin Lance	2301	150	9-11-1815	11-26-1817	FB River, SW side
Martin B. Lance	2916	43	6-23-1826	12-29-1827	Kinseys Cr., both sides
Peter Lince	883	100	10-31-1799	12-18-1800	Shoal Cr.
Peter Lince	1376	50	9-21-1803	12-10-1804	Turkey Br., S. fork
Peter Lince (2)	3436	8	2-11-1835	12-5-1836	FB River, W. side
Samuel Lance	1209	160	11-30-1801	12-16-1803	Kane Cr.
Samuel Lance	1337	50	10-16-1802	12-5-1804	adj. own land
Samuel J. Lance	4204	134	10-11-1848	12-30-1852	Averys Cr., adj. M. B. Lance
Valentine Lance	1323	150	6-18-1802	11-14-1804	FB River, SW side
Valentine Lance	2616	50	11-15-1819	12-9-1825	Boydstons Cr.
Valentine Lance	3432	40	4-20-1835	12-?-1836	FB River, E. fork
W. E. Lance	12138	159	1-24-1891	3-22-1893	Averys Cr., head, adj. E. Lance
William B. Lance	4243	50	11-2-1852	7-15-1854	FB River, W. side, Ortons Br.
W. N. Lance	9865	41.5	10-26-1889	1-6-1890	Averys Cr., adj J. R. Lance

Footnotes

(1) also David Harden

(2) adj. own land, includes island

Census Records

Henry Lentz is on the 1790 NC Census, Rowan Co., Salisbury District, with 2 males and 5 females

Henry Lance is on the 1800 NC Census, Buncombe Co., with 3 males and 7 females.

Peter Lance is on the 1790 NC Census, Rowan Co., Salisbury District with 4 males and 5 females

Peter Lance is on the 1800 NC Census, Buncombe Co., with 3 males and 2 females.

Selected References

Lentz, John C., 1986, *Lentz Heritage*: Burlington, NC, privately publ., approx. 400 p.

 (note Peter Lentz, Sr., Chapt. VI - but not recognized in the following update)

Norris, Catherine B. & Jeff L. Norris, 2005, *Lentz Heritage Revisited. A Genealogy of Bastian and Doppelt Lentz:* Boone, NC, Minor's Printing Co., 402 p.

Lane/Swain Family NC land Grants

Buncombe Co.

Registered Name	Grant	Acres	Entered	Patent	Location
Charles Lane (1)	192	640	8-9-1793	8-27-1795	Gashes Cr., Bens Br.
Charles Lane (2)	435	100	4-29-1795	8-31-1798	FB River, Rims Cr.
Charles Lane	738	100	9-20-1791	12-6-1799	Rims Cr., below Befles Mill
Charles Lane (3)	837	300	9-37-1799	12-10-1800	Hominy Cr.
David L. Swain	3218	100	5-2-1834	12-6-1834	Beaver Dam Cr., Bull Cove
E. C. Swain	4393	8	10-18-1869	1-16-1871	Newfound Cr., Jones Br.
George Swain	1568	100	1-13-1806	12-5-1806	Beaverdam Cr., N. side
George Swain	1569	100	1-13-1806	12-5-1806	Beaverdam Cr., both sides

*****

Swain/Swaim?					
Andrew E. Swain	4219	65	11-26-1847	11-31-1853	Turkey Cr., S fork, adj. Reynolds
Enoch Swan	1666	100	5-9-1804	12-2-1807	Newfound Cr.
Enoch Swain	1825	60	11-7-1807	12-15-1809	Newfound Cr., both sides
Enoch Swain	2384	50	12-12-1816	12-5-1818	Newfound Cr., both sides

Enoch Swain	2397	150	12-13-1816	12-5-1818	Newfound Cr., head
James Swain	4157	43	n/a	n/a	Turkey Cr., adj . Enoch Swain
James Swain	4218	100	11-9-1849	11-9-1853	Turkey Cr., S. fork
James F. Swain	4220	74	1-1-1853	10-31-1853	Turkey Cr., S. fork
James Swain	4237	120	11-22-1853	5-24-1854	FR River, Turkey Cr., S. fork
James Swain	4350	193	11-3-1858	8-22-1859	FB River, W. side, S. Turkey Cr.
James Swain (4)	4331	66	3-20-1858	8-22-1859	S. Turkey Cr.
James Swain	4332	71	12-21-1857	9-9-1859	FB River, S. Turkey Cr.
Jas. Swain (5)	4290	100	11-22-1853	7-24-1855	FB River, Turkey Cr., adj. own
John Swain(e)	2083	100	12-26-1811	12-4-1813	Turkey Cr., Tomahauk Spr.
Levi Swain	1802	100	2-2-1808	11-30-1809	Newfound Cr., both sides

Footnotes

(1) also Henry West

(2) also John Lane

(3) also John Smith & Samuel Smith

(4) and 5 others

(5) and Elias Triplett

Love Family NC Land Grants

Burke Co.

Registered Name	Grant	Acres	Entered	Patented	Location
Samuel Love	3950	12	4-17-1817	9-9-1819	Zacks fork, lower Cr.

Buncombe Co.

James Love	139	100	2-11-1794	1-19-1795	Flatt Cr., Wolf Pitt Br.
James R. Love	3178	50	9-22-1828	12-18-1833	FB River, SW side, Spring Cr.
James R. Love	3179	50	9-22-1828	12-18-1833	FB River, Warm Springs Cr.
John Love	1892	150	11-11-1808	12-8-1810	Lee's Mill Cr., both sides
Robert Love	38	150	4-17-1792	1-7-1794	Swanano, above J. McNabb
Robert Love (1)	283	100	n/a	n/a	Jacks Cr.
Robert Love	776	200	2-19-1794	12-22-1799	Richland Cr., both sides
Robert Love (2)	963	300	5-11-1792	12-19-1801	Pigeon R., W. side
Robert Love (3)	968	300	3-21-1794	8-27-1802	Jonathans Cr.
Robert Love (4)	969	300	5-4-1792	7-18-1802	Jonathans Cr., both sides
Robert Love (5)	970	200	3-21-1794	8-30-1802	Richland Cr., Pigeon R.

Registered Name	Grant	Acres	Entered	Patented	Location
Robert Love (7)	1611	100	3-21-1794	7-2-1807	Pigeon R., W. side
Robert Love	1639	150	2-28-1806	11-27-1807	Richland Cr.
Robert Love	2678	60	8-30-1825	1-13-1827	Clear Cr., N. side
Samuel Love	2679	25	8-30-1825	1-13-1827	Clear Cr., N. side
Thomas Love	300	100	7-20-1795	7-10-1797	Ivey, Bald Mtn. fork
Thomas Love (6)	1521	100	n/a	n/a	Paint Fork, Little Ivey
Thomas Love	1959	100	3-21-1805	12-14-1811	Pawpaw Cr., Pine Cr.
Thomas Love (8)	1980	200	7-11-1804	7-6-1812	FB River, W. side, Bear Cr.

Footnotes

(1) also George Baker

(2) also Waightstill Avery

(3) also John Davidson

(4) also John Davidson

(5) also John Davidson

(6) also William Rogers

(7) also John Davidson

(8) also David Webb

Lytle Family NC Land Grants

Burke Co.

Registered Name	Grant	Acres	Entered	Patented	Location
Abraham Little	157	150	9-3-1789	3-15-1780	Catawba R., Littles Cr.
Elizabeth Little	3043	50	n/a	n/a	Little Cr.
George Lytle	1241	200	12-29-1778	5-18-1789	Toms Cr.
John Little	1561	200	n/a	n/a	Sealeys Cr.
Jno. Little	5724	50	4-23-1833	12-9-1835	Crooked Cr.
Jno. Lyttle	5901	50	7-25-1835	12-10-1838	Crooked Cr., Byers fork
Millington Lytle	5060	50	n/a	n/a	Crooked Cr., Cold Cove Br.
Thomas Little	509	440	12-11-1778	10-28-1782	Catawba, W. side, McCockles Cr.
Thomas Little	672	250	12-11-1783	10-11-1783	Halls Cr., Mountain Cr.
Thomas Little	1360	200	8-1-1783	11-16-1790	Bull Cr., both sides
Thos. Lytle	5902	50	10-25-1836	12-10-1838	Catawba R., Lower Cr.

Thomas Lytle	5913	50	3-24-1834	12-10-1838	Crooked Cr., Cove Cr.

Buncombe Co.

Thomas Little (1)	1609	400	2-24-1778	12-22-1806	Cany R., W. fork
Thomas Little (2)	1610	400	2-24-1778	12-23-1806	Cany River, W. fork

Footnotes - Buncombe Co.

(1) also James Greenlee, Charles McDowell, William Cathey - Jas. Greenlee listed 1st

(2) also James Greenlee, Charles McDowell, William Cathey - Jas. Greenlee listed 1st

Maney Family NC Land Grants

Buncombe Co.

Registered Name	Grant	Acres	Entered	Patented	Location
John Maney	2733	50	10-16-1826	1-3-1828	Little Ivy, Paint fork
John Many	2886	50	10-9-1828	7-10-1830	Piney Fork, Mill Post Br.
John Maney	2956	50	8-14-1829	12-18-1831	Little Ivy, Paint fork
Martin Maney	294	100	10-9-1793	7-10-1797	Ivy, Bald Mtn, assignee

Selected References

Maney, Milus B., 1999, *Martin Maney, 1752-1830, A Revolutionary War Soldier and Related Families*: n.p. (GA), privately printed, 536 p.

Anonymous, 2008, Grave Marker Dedication for Private Martin Maney: Asheville, NC, *A Lot of Bunkum*, vol. 29, no. 2, p. 26

Editor's Notes:

Martin Mainey is on the 1800 NC Census, Buncombe Co., with 5 males and 2 females.

In 2010, a military marble for Martin Maney, who served in the Revolutionary War, was erected in the Maney Cemetery, near Barnardsville. This action was taken on the basis of unmarked fieldstones.

McDowell Family NC Land Grants

Burke Co.

Registered Name	Grant	Acres	Entered	Patent	Location
Athan A. McDowell (1)	indent.	640	n/a	n/a	Rock Cr.
Athan A. McDowell (2)	indent.	16000	n/a	7-7-1815	Rock Cr.
Athan A. McDowell (3)	indent.	2760	n/a	7-7-1815	Rock Cr.

Athan A. McDowell (4)	indent.	2000	n/a	n/a	Rock Cr.
Charles McDowell	265	365	6-28-1778	3-14-1778	Mills Br., Miery Br.
Charles McDowell	275	376	3-25-1778	3-14-1781	Catawba R., N. side
Charles McDowell	291	1000	3-30-1779	8-29-1779	Catawba R., N. side
Charles McDowell (5)	524	400	12-12-1778	12-28-1782	Catawba R., Maiden Cr.
Charles McDowell	567	454	2-5-1778	10-11-1782	Johns R., Mulberry Fork
Charles McDowell	823	1000	3-30-1779	8-30-1779	FB River, Cane Cr.
Charles McDowell	875	330	2-22-1779	11-9-1784	Hunting Cr.
Charles McDowell	991	450	12-5-1778	8-7-1787	Henrys Fork, both sides
Charles McDowell	1165	320	10-22-1779	5-18-1789	Henrys Fork, Laurel fork
Charles McDowell	1133	45	12-25-1779	7-10-1788	Mulberry Cr., Johns R.
Charles McDowell	1195	120	8-1-1783	5-18-1789	Ivey R., middle fork
Charles McDowell	1211	164	2-2-1778	5-18-1789	Mills Br., adj. home survey
Charles McDowell (6)	1215	400	8-13-1783	5-18-1789	Richland Cr., Moores Cr.
Charles McDowell	1237	50	3-7-1780	5-18-1789	Mulberry Cr., John R.
McDowells, Chas. (7)	1246	400	6-2-1784	5-18-1789	Newfound Cr., main fork
Charles McDowell	1260	110	n/a	5-18-1789	Ivy R., Middle fork
Charles McDowell (8)	1311	640	12-12-1783	11-16-1790	Swanoe R.
Charles McDowell (9)	1321	150	10-7-1778	11-16-1790	Haw Br.
Charles McDowell	1403	100	1-10-1778	1-4-1792	Catawba R., N. fork, both sides
Charles McDowell (10)	1413	640	12-12-1783	12-15-1791	Swannanoa R.,
Charles McDowell (11)	1895	400	n/a	n/a	Big Pigeon, Racoon Cr.
Charles McDowell (12)	2522	300	10-28-1778	6-7-1799	Buck Cr.
Charles McDowell (13)	2536	300	10-16-1778	6-7-1799	Buck Cr.
Charles McDowell	2825	400	6-1-1799	12-11-1800	S. Toe R., Mine Cr.
Charles McDowell	2878	200	10-20-1799	12-11-1800	S. Towe R.
Charles McDowell	2981	300	1-1-1799	12-4-1801	Canoe Cr.
Charles McDowell	3074	100	8-13-1783	11-19-1802	Catawba R., Silver Cr.
Charles McDowell	3089	50	7-23-1799	11-26-1802	Mulberry Cr.
Charles McDowell (14)	3209	640	9-23-1778	11-23-1803	Linvil R.
Charles McDowell	3486	300	1-1-1799	12-4-1801	Canoe Cr.
James McDowell	1268	100	n/a	11-27-1789	Pigeon R., Richland Cr.
James McDowell	1269	244	5-19-1787	11-27-1789	Richland Cr.
James McDowell (15)	1401	600	4-21-1790	1-4-1792	Pigeon R., Jonathans Cr.
James McDowell (16)	1405	600	n/a	1-4-1792	Pigeon R., Jonathans Cr.
James McDowell	1858	200	8-6-1793	7-7-1794	FB River, W side
James McDowell	3678	150	2-17-1814	12-5-1815	Garden Cr., adj. own
James McDowell (17)	3947	320	3-25-1818	12-17-1818	Catawba R., S. side
James McDowell	5653	50	3-29-1822	12-30-1833	Catawba R., S. side
James McDowell	5954	100	5-23-1836	11-24-1840	Armstrongs Cr.

James McDowell	6198	150	2-17-1814	12-5-1815	Garden Cr.
John McDowell	41	160	10-10-1778	9-20-1779	Catawba R., Garden Cr.
John McDowell	47	640	10-10-1778	9-20-1779	Catawba R., Garden Cr.
John McDowell	93	640	10-3-1778	9-20-1779	Silver Cr.
John McDowel	198	640	5-28-1778	3-14-1780	Catawba R., N. side
John McDowell	328	100	12-10-1779	10-28-1782	Catawba R., N. side
John McDowell	401	640	10-10-1778	9-20-1779	Catawba, Pleasant Gardens
John McDowell	402	160	10-10-1778	9-20-1779	Catawba, both sides
John McDowell	500	300	12-29-1778	10-28-1782	Silver R., W. side
John McDowell Jr. (18)	1020	640	1-29-1778	8-7-1787	Caney R.
John McDowell	1059	320	9-4-1783	8-7-1787	Rims Cr., FB River
John McDowell Sr.	1082	640	12-1-1787	12-8-1787	Richland Cr., both sides
John McDowell	1087	50	4-26-1784	12-8-1787	Rims Cr.
John McDowell, Sr. (19)	1089	640	12-1-1783	12-8-1787	Richland Cr.
John McDowell	1145	120	12-1-1783	5-18-1789	Rims Cr.
John McDowell	1210	320	n/a	5-18-1789	Newfound Cr.
John McDowell, Sr. (20)	1215	400	8-13-1783	5-18-1789	First Large Cr.
Jno. McDowell (21)	1251	640	4-25-1784	3-22-1795	Pigeon R., both sides
John McDowell	1256	320	5-18-1784	5-18-1789	Ivy R., Middle fork
John McDowell	1257	320	5-30-1778	8-22-1795	Pigeon R., Crystal Cr.
John McDowell (22)	1260	320	4-26-1784	11-27-1789	Pigeon R.
John McDowell	1266	640	8-1-1783	11-26-1790	Swannanoa R., Green R.
John McDowall	1355	200	4-17-1792	8-22-1795	Pigeon R., Camp Cr.
John McDowell Sr.	1618	100	12-11-1783	11-27-1792	Pigeon R., both sides
John McDowell Sr.	1668	200	9-1-1791	11-26-1793	Pigeon R., Raccoon Cr.
John McDowell	1680	320	9-4-1787	11--26-1793	Pigeon R., 5 Mile Cr.
John McDowell, Sr.	1895	400	11-18-1778	7-7-1794	Pigeon R., Racoon Cr.
John McDowell (23)	1898	150	11-12-1783	7-7-1794	Crooked Cr.
John McDowell (24)	2522	300	10-28-1788	6-7-1799	Buck Cr.
John McDowell	2695	300	10-1-1790	12-18-1799	Silver Cr., Reed Br.
John McDowell	2740	50	3-4-1799	12-20-1799	Averytown Cr.
John McDowell	3054	100	9-27-1800	12-10-1801	Silver Cr.
John McDowell	3055	150	3--20-1801	12-10-1801	Silver Cr.
John McDowell	3883	50	7-28-1817	11-21-1818	Chestnut Br., Buck Cr.
John McDowell	3886	50	7-28-1817	11-21-1818	Moses Brown Br., Buck Cr.
John McDowell	3981	50	9-1-1818	11-30-1819	Moses Brown Br.
Joseph McDowel	134	600	5-5-1785	3-15-1780	Johns R.
Joseph McDowell	532	370	4-12-1779	12-28-1782	Franklin Cr., Johns R.
Joseph McDowell (25)	838	640	8-1-1783	11-9-1784	Swannanoa R., Bee Cr.
Joseph McDowell	1081	400	10-6-1787	12-8-1787	FB River, E. side, Swannanoa

Joseph McDowell	1266	378	2-8-1778	11-27-1789	FB River, adj. fathers survey
Joseph McDowell (26)	1274	525	10-20-1778	11-27-1789	FB River
Joseph McDowell	1390	26	9-1-1788	11-16-1790	Nicks Cr.
Joseph McDowell	1400	700	8-1-1783	1-4-1792	Pigeon R.
Joseph McDowell (27)	1681	200	8-1-1783	12-16-1793	FB River
Joseph McDowell	2692	30	9-8-1794	12-12-1799	Johns R.
Joseph McDowell	2885	1280	10-30-1799	12-18-1800	Johns R., E. side
Joseph McDowell	5953	100	5-23-1830	11-24-1840	Armstrongs Cr.
Margaret McDowell (28)	289	551	9-30-1778	3-14-1780	Canoe Cr.
William McDowell	195	553	10-3-1778	3-14-1780	Silver Cr.
William McDowell	1354	100	n/a	8-22-1795	Allens Cr.
William McDowell	2826	100	5-27-1799	12-11-1800	Catawba R., N. side
William McDowell	2827	98	6-17-1799	12-11-1800	Cane Cr.
William McDowell	5955	100	5-23-1836	11-24-1840	Blue Ridge, Armstrongs Cr.

Footnotes - Burke Co.

(1) Sheriff's deed

(2) Sheriff's deed

(3) Sheriff's deed

(4) Sheriff's deed, Wm. Cathcart Grant 2148

(5) also James Martin

(6) also John McDowell

(7) also Joseph McDowell

(8) also Jas. Miller & Robert Patto

(9) also John Davidson - listed 1st

(10) also James Miller - listed 1st, & Robert Patton

(11) assigned to John McDowell, Sr.

(12) also John McDowell - listed 1st

(13) also John McDowell - listed 1st

(14) also William McElroy

(15) also Thomas Hemphill - listed 1st

(14) also William McElroy

(15) also Thomas Hemphill - listed 1st

(16) also Thomas Hemphill - listed 1st

(17) Capt. James McDowell

(18) Capt. Winslow encampment

(19) also Joseph McDowell

(20) also Charles McDowell

(21) also Charles McDowell

(22) also Joseph McDowell

(23) near Col. Davidson's mill

(24) also Charles McDowell

(25) also Samuel Greenlee

(26) also James Glasgow; adj. Charles McDowell

(27) also James Miller

(28) also Hannah McDowell & Mary McDowell

Buncombe Co.

Charles McDowell (1)	203	300	2-10-1791	12-3-1796	Scotts Cr., Tuckasegee
Charles McDowell	514	500	7-25-1788	12-5-1790	Ben Davidsons Cr.
Charles McDowell (2)	946	200	n/a	n/a	FB River, E. side
Charles McDowell	993	911	8-1-1793	11-19-1802	FB River, E. side
Charles McDowell	1012	150	n/a	n/a	Little Ivey, Paint Fork
Charles McDowell (3)	1447	250	11-10-1787	12-12-1805	FB River, Cherry Fields

Charles McDowell (4)	1609	400	2-24-1778	12-22-1806	Cany R. W. fork
Charles McDowell (5)	1610	400	2-24-1778	12-22-1806	Cany R., W. fork
Daniel McDowell	1384	150	10-20-1802	12-10-1804	Pigeon R., W. side, Scots Cr.
John McDowall	1623	200	1-22-1807	11-27-1807	Richland Cr., W. fork
John McDowall	1721	237	12-29-1807	12-17-1808	Richland Cr.

Footnotes - Buncombe Co.

(1) also James Glasgow & David Miller

(2) also William Willowby

(3) also William Willowby

(4) also James Greenlee, Thomas Little & Wm. Cathey

(5) also James Greenlee, Thomas Little & Wm. Cathey

McLean Family NC Land Grants

Burke Co.

Registered Name	Grant	Acres	Entered	Patented	Location
Ephraim McLean	29	215	1-29-1778	12-10-1778	Catawba R., Newberrys fork
Ephraim McLean	56	200	n/a	9-20-1779	Reedy Cr.
Ephraim McLean	419	300	4-29-1778	10-28-1782	Catawba R., Newberrys fork
Ephraim McLean	426	640	12-31-1779	10-28-1782	Cainey Cr.
Ephraim McLean	462	640	12-31-1779	10-28-1282	McLeans fork
Ephraim McLean	528	640	12-31-1779	10-28-1782	McLeans fork

Editor's Notes:
The 1937 book *History of old Tryon and Rutherford Counties, NC, 1779-1934*, states that Ephraim McLean entered 3,000 acres in Tryon County, NC and York District, SC, evidently about 1770.
As noted above, in 1778-1779, Ephraim McLean entered 2,635 acres in Burke Co.

The Tryon County history remarks that, about 1782, Ephraim McLean entered "several thousand acres of land near Nashville and south of that town."
On the other hand, the 2000 book by Irene M. Griffey, *Earliest Tennessee Land Records*, more precisely shows that Ephraim McLean was granted 9,920 acres in Tennessee during the years 1783-1784. This was located in the Davidson area, the Middle District, and the Western District.

McPeters, et al Land Grants
(sons-in-law of Capt. Wm. Moore)

Burke Co.

Registered Name	Grant	Acres	Entered	Patented	Location
McPeters, Charles	130	150	9-27-1779	3-15-1780	N. side river,N. side own survey
McPeters, Charles	224	300	12-29-1778	3-14-1780	S. side Catawba R., adj. J. Montgm.
McPeters, Charles	293	500	12-29-1778	3-14-1780	Catawba R., Muddy Cr.
McPeters, Jonathan	1088	200	1-28-1779	12-8-1787	Richland Cr., both sides 1st Cr.

Buncombe Co.

McPeters, Charles (1)	782	640	2-16-1778	4-2-1800	FB River, below George Cathey
McPeters, Jonathan	144	200	3-7-1794	1-19-1795	Prices Cr., Caney R.
McPeters, Jonathan	783	640	2-16-1778	4-2-1800	FB River, Sugar Loaf Mtn.
McPeters, Jonathan	1446	100	11-17-1804	12-10-1805	Mills River

Burke Co.

Montgomery, John, Jr.	576	580	1-30-1778	10-11-1783	N. fork Catawba
Montgomery, John, Jr.	712	213	8-17-1778	10-11-1783	N. side Catawba, adj. Michael M.
Montgomery, John	1205	200	8-9-1780	5-18-1789	Catheys Cr., both sides
Montgomery, John	1308	361	n/a	n/a	N. side Catawba, Paddys Cr.
Rutherford, James	483	483	n/a	n/a	N. fork Homany, adj. Wm. Moore
Rutherford, James	1218	100	7-17-1787	5-18-1789	Homeny Cr., both sides
Rutherford, John (2)	2535	90	x-28-1779	6-7-1799	Muddy Cr., adj. George Hodges
Rutherford, John	2627	100	n/a	n/a	Muddy Cr., E. side
Rutherford, John, Sr.	3005	300	10-13-1801	12-4-1801	Catawba R., N. side
Rutherford, John, Sr.	3731	300	12-28-1813	9-7-1816	Muddy Cr., adj.own land
Rutherford, John	5054	200	n/a	n/a	Shadracks Cr., Muddy Cr.
Rutherford, John, Jr.	5128	100	n/a	n/a	S. fork Shadricks Cr.
Rutherford, John	5274	300	n/a	n/a	Old Tent
Rutherford, Jno., Jr.	5545	200	11-2-1827	12-12-1831	Humpback Mtn.
Rutherford, Jno., Jr.	5546	200	11-2-1827	12-12-1831	Humpback Mtn.
Rutherford, John Sr.	5564	1.5	1-28-1829	12-22-1831	Catawba R.
Rutherford, John	5657	50	10-19-1831	2-24-1834	Holl yBr., Toe R.
Rutherford, John	5658	100	10-19-1831	2-24-1834	Toe R., Holly Br.
Rutherford, John (3)	5659	150	10-23-1831	2-24-1834	Reeds Mtn.
Rutherford, John	6149	53	6-14-1843	12-9-1844	Catawba R.

Buncombe Co.

Registered Name	Grant	Acres	Entered	Patent	Location
Rutherford, James	847	200	8-23-1799	12-11-1800	Hominy Cr., Waters Pole Br.
Rutherford, James	850	100	8-23-1799	12-11-1800	Hominy Cr., adj. John Webb
Rutherford, James	867	100	8-23-1799	12-11-1800	Hominy Cr.
Rutherford, James	987	200	n/a	n/a	Hominy Cr.
Rutherford, James	1342	100	10-10-1800	12-5-1804	Pole Cr.
Rutherford, James	1343	100	10-10-1800	12-5-1804	Pole Cr., Beffel Mill path
Rutherford, James	1507	200	9-21-1801	6-27-1806	Hominy Cr., John Webb Br.
Rutherford, James	1671	100	3-14-1807	2-2-1807	Homney Cr., W. fork
Rutherford, James	1703	100	1-8-1806	11-11-1808	Poles Cr., head
Rutherford, James	1915	150	1-8-1806	12-17-1810	Hominy Cr., both sides
Rutherford, James	4229	100	11-24-1853	1-27-1854	Newfound Cr., Haywood Co. line
Rutherford, John (4)	14162	195	n/a	n/a	Newfound Cr., Pole Cr.

Footnotes

(1) Heirs of

(2) assignee

(3) also James Gibbs

(4) assignee

Merrill Family NC Land Grants

Buncombe Co.

Registered Name	Grant	Acres	Entered	Patent	Location
Benjamin Merrill	789	100	11-21-1793	9-1-1800	adj. William Wilson
Benjamin Merrell	1000	100	n/a	n/a	Kane Cr., Hoopers Cr., Mtn.
Benjamin Merrell	1182	150	6-25-1800	12-16-1803	Clear Cr., Hoopers Cr., Mtn.
Benjamin Merrill	1188	60	6-25-1800	12-16-1803	Hoopers Cr., S. fork, head
Benjamin Merrill	1458	50	n/a	n/a	FB River, W. side
Benjamin Merrell	1803	50	9-29-1808	11-30-1809	Bear Wallow Mtn., Clear Cr.
Benjamin Merrel, Jr.	2142	500	11-11-1813	11-29-1814	Clear Cr. (Walkers Cr.)
B. F. Merrell	13969	16.75	n/a	n/a	Cane Cr., W. side Blue Ridge
Jacob Merrell (1)	4023	50	1-17-1843	12-30-1844	Blue Ridge, Spring
Jessee Merrill (2)	2982	75	n/a	n/a	Crabtree Cr., Inlands Cove
John Merrel	1107	100	n/a	n/a	Brush Cr., Hoopers Cr.
John Mirrell (3)	1139	220	9-29-1800	12-10-1803	Cane Cr., E. side

John Merrell	1383	60	5-29-1804	12-10-1804	Cane Cr., adj. own land
John M. C. Merrell (4)	4213	25	7-11-1849	4-30-1853	Blue Ridge, W. side
John M. C. Merrell	4214	18	4-24-1852	4-30-1853	FB River, E. side, Cane Cr.
John Merrell, Sr. (5)	4258	48	10-28-1854	12-20-1854	Cane Cr., Wood's fork, FBR
Levi Merrell (6)	3084	63	6-6-1830	12-12-1832	Cane Cr., Maple Cr.
Margaret Merrell (7)	4360	8.75	1-8-1862	1-29-1862	FB River, E. side
Nimrod Merrell (8)	2779	50	3-1-1827	11-25-1829	Cane Cr., Gap Cr.
William Merrell	1745	120	9-18-1807	12-17-1808	Cane Cr., Big Springs Mtn.
William Merrel	2082	270	8-17-1811	12-4-1813	Crabtree Cr., both sides
William Merrell	2169	50	2-26-1825	1-13-1827	Crabtree Cr. N. side, Little R.
William Merrill (9)	2982	75	10-14-1829	12-15-1831	Crabtree Cr., Irelands Cove
William Merrell (10)	3103	150	n/a	n/a	Shoal Cr., James Cr.
William Merrell	3424	50	4-21-1835	12-5-1836	ShoaL Cr., adj. own land
W. A. Merrill	4443	16	8-14-1882	9-4-1882	Cane Cr., adj. own land

Footnotes

(1) adj. James Cooper

(2) also William Merrill

(3) includes Benjamin Merrill House

(4) near Henderson Co. line

(5) also Dempsey Sumner - listed 1st

(6) adj. David Merrell

(7) adj. own land, near Four Miles Bridge

(8) also Jonathan Merrell

(9) also Jessee Merrill

(10) also Epaphroditus Hightower

Census Records

Benjamin Merrill is on the 1790 NC Census, Randolph Co., Hillsborough District with

 4 males, 5 females, and 1 slave.

Benjn. Merril is on the 1800 NC Census, Buncombe Co., with 5 males, 8 females, and 1 slave.

John Merrill is on the 1790 NC Census, Randolph Co., Hillsborough District with

 5 males and3 females.

John Merril is on the 1800 NC Census, BuncombeCo., with 5 males and 6 females.

Benjamin and John Merrill are listed in the 1993 DAR Patriot Index. Contemporary markers

 for both exist in the Merrill-Patton cemetery in Fairview.

Selected References

Merrill, William E., 1935, Captain Benjamin Merrill and the Merrill Family of North Carolina: Brevard, NC,
 Transylvania Times, 109 p.

Styles, Marshall L., 2010a, *Western North Carolina's Revolutionary War Patriot Soldiers.*

  Benjamin Merrill Pension File S8891: Simpsonville, SC, privately publ., 78 p.

  _____, 2010b, *ibid, Vol. II, John Merrill Pension file S7220, ibid*, 78 p.

Mills Family NC Land Grants

Rutherford Co.

Registered Name	Grant	Acres	Entered	Patented	Location
Ambrose Mills	1615	50	11-18-1797	12-22-1798	Green R., Panthers Cr.
Ambros Mills	1932	50	10-18-1798	12-16-1799	Green R., S. side
Ambrose Mills	2225	150	10-17-1800	12-7-1802	Green R., adj own land
Ambrose Mills	2763	50	3-23-1809	12-11-1811	Green R., both sides
Ambrose Mills	2900	40	1-3-1814	12-15-1814	Green R., N. side
Jessee Mills	1554	100	5-1-1795	12-18-1797	Green R., Flat Br.
Jessee Mills	2007	100	10-178-1795	12-4-1800	Green R.
Jesse Mills	2314	50	2-26-1802	12-3-1803	Green R., both sides
Jesse Mills	2853	150	6-20-1811	11-24-1813	Green R., both sides
Jno. Mills	2908	30	5-22-1812	12-15-1814	N. Pacolate R.
Jno. Mills	2914	50	3-9-1812	12-15-1814	Green R., Silver Cr.
John Mills	2917	20	10-31-1812	12-15-1814	Alstons Cr.
Jno. Mills	2918	200	7-27-1812	12-15-1814	White Oak, S. side
Col. John Mills	3036	100	1-2-1815	11-29-1817	N. Pacolet, Little Cr.
Milley Mills	1616	50	11-18-1797	12-22-1798	Green R., Panthers Cr.
Thomas Mills (1)	1531	160	4-8-1786	12-18-1797	Green R., S. side
William Mills (2)	44	100	12-12-1785	11-26-1789	Broad R., Clear Cr.
William Mills	151	50	6-10-1785	8-9-1787	Green R., Panters Cr.
William Mills	254	100	n/a	8-9-1787	Green R., Rottens Cr.
William Mills	263	100	1-10-1785	8-9-1787	Green R., Panters Cr.
William Mills	278	100	1-20-1785	8-9-1787	Green R., Silver Cr.
William Mills (3)	461	300	12-10-1785	11-26-1789	Clear Cr., Little Mtn.
William Mills	569	100	4-10-1786	11-16-1790	Green R., Rottens Cr.
William Mills	827	50	11-1-1791	7-9-1794	Green R., three forks
William Mills (4)	845	500	5-10-1791	7-9-1794	Clear Cr.
William Mills (5)	846	200	11-1-1790	7-9-1794	Clear Cr., Buckhorn fork
William Mills (6)	936	300	3-10-1794	7-9-1794	Pidgeon R., Richland Cr.
William Mills (7)	951	200	4-10-1792	7-9-1794	Clear Cr.
William Mills	1220	50	1-10-1794	12-20-1796	Green R., Brights Cr.

Footnotes - Rutherford Co.

(1) assignee of Wm.Mills

(2) also James Miller

(3) also James Miller

(4) also James Miller

(5) also James Miller

(6) also Andrew Miller - 1st, & David Miller

(7) also Andrew Miller - 1st, & David Miller

Buncombe Co.

William Mills	444	150	7-13-1796	8-31-1798	Clear Cr., now lives
William Mills	714	150	2-13-1799	12-6-1799	Henderson Cr., both sides
William Mills	724	50	2-10-1798	12-6-1799	Green Mtn., adj. own land
William Mills (1)	1161	100	10-10-1801	12-14-1803	Hoopers Cr.
William Mills (2)	1366	40	11-5-1802	12-10-1804	Clear Cr., Hoopers Cr.
William Mills (3)	1389	125	10-10-1801	12-10-1804	Pigeon R., E. side, Hoopers
William Miles	1635	100	1-22-1807	11-27-1807	Cedar (Clear) Cr.
William Mills	1700	50	10-19-1807	6-30-1808	Hooper Cr., main road
William Mills	1748	200	11-7-1807	12-17-1808	Clear Cr., adj. own land
William Mills (4)	1790	60	9-20-1804	9-16-1809	Celear Cr.

Footnotes - Buncombe Co.

(1) also Joseph Henry - 1st

(2) also Joseph Henry

(3) also Joseph Henry - 1st

(4) also Joseph Henry - 1st

Moore Family NC Land Grants

Burke Co.

Registered Name	Grant	Acres	Entered	Patented	Location
William Moore	70	640	8-15-1778	9/20/1779	Catawba-Shadracks Cr.
William Moore	961	75	8-1-1783	8-7-1787	Hominy (Rutherfords) Cr.
William Moore (1)	1031	450	1-7-1783	8-7-1787	Hominy (Rutherfords) Cr.
William Moore	1032	420	8-10-1783	8-7-1787	Hominey (Rutherfords) Cr.
William Moore	1064	250	8-1-1783	8-7-1787	Homeny Cr., FBR, W. side
William Moore	1170	100	8-10-1783	8-7-1787	Hominy Cr., both sides
William More	1232	220	1778	12-8-1785	Mill Fork, Muddy Cr.
Willliam Moore	2308	100	1-23-1798	12-8-1798	Glade Br., Muddy Cr.
William Moore	3583	50	7-26-1811	11-28-1812	S. Muddy Cr.
William Moore, Jr.	3733	50	10-29-1814	11-23-1816	S. Muddy Cr.

| William Moore | 5512 | 50 | 8-5-1829 | 4-12-1831 | Dysart Cr. |
| William Moore | 5589 | 1 | 9-27-1831 | 12-12-1832 | S. Muddy Cr. |

Buncombe Co., Grant after 1791

William Moore	143	150	6-11-1794	n/a	Hominy Cr.
William Moore	144	150	6-11-1794	n/a	Hominy Cr.
William Moore	250	150	n/a	12-21-1796	Homony Cr.
William Moore	257	100	n/a	12-21-1796	N. side Homony Cr.
William Moore	258	150	10-25-1794	12-212-1796	N. side Hommony Cr.
William Moore, et al (2)	377	5,000	4-1-1784	11-19-1800	Elk River, Swan Cr.
William Moore	479	150	6-4-1798	9-28-1798	Homony Cr., S. side
William Moore	853	640	1-28-1778	12-11-1800	Homeny Cr. at ford
William Moore, Sr.	1231	100	5-20-1802	12-16-1803	N. side Hominy Cr.
William Moore, Jr.	1595	100	4-16-1805	12-20-1806	Moores Cr.
William Moore	2539	72	12-4-1816	12-19-1821	S. side Hominy Cr.
William Moore	2547	28	1-20-1816	12-10-1822	Moores & Hominy Cr.
Charles Moore	2792	50	11-11-1816	12-17-1829	S. side Homoney Cr.
Charles Moore	2798	10	1-10-1829	12-21-1829	Ragsdale & Homoney Cr.

*****

Grantee		Acres	Entered	Recorded	**Location/Grantor**
William Moore		100	7-22-1806	n/a	Bald Mtn./ John Strother
William Moore		100	1-22-1806	3-27-1807	Bald Mtn./ Roderick Shelton
William Moore		200	10-8-1808	11-17-1808	Hominy Cr./Sheriff
William Moore		40	4-17-1810	7-30-1810	Hominy Cr./Samuel Lusk
William Moore		180	7-4-1802	n/a	Hominy Cr./John Davidson
William Moore		200	7-23-1813	10-5-1819	John Strother

Footnotes:

(1) Grant 1031 is a typed version in Buncombe Co. Deed book 187/296, re-registered 11-3-1913

(2) Grant no. 377 included Daniel Vance, Wm. Moore, and Daniel Williams in that order

(2) Grant No. 377 is also in Buncombe Co. Deed book S2-6/26; this plot is in Tennessee

Murray Family NC Land Grants

Buncombe Co.

Registered Name	Grant	Acres	Entered	Patented	Location
James Murray	1873	7.25	11-6-1809	11-30-1810	Green R.
James Murray	2780	25	7-25-1829	11-25-1829	Green R.
James Murray	2846	100	9-15-1829	11-27-1830	Green R.
James Murray	2847	300	2-25-1829	11-17-1830	adj. own land

John Murry	1417	100	1-29-1803	12-14-1804	Indian Camp, Mud R.
John Murray (1)	2033	75	1-9-1811	12-10-1812	FB River, Fosters Cr.
John Murray (2)	2069	150	5-8-1812	11-24-1813	Millers R., adj. Keykendall
John Murray (3)	2070	100	n/a	11-24-1813	Millers R.
John Murray (4)	2970	100	n/a	n/a	n/a
John Murray	2201	100	1-22-1813	12-6-1815	Camp Br., Mill. Cr.
Robert Murray	1966	50	11-6-1809	12-18-1811	Green R.
RobertMurry	2280	640	4-29-1814	12-12-1816	Green R.
Robert Murray	2281	150	1-20-1814	12-12-1816	Green R.
Samuel Murrey	403	290	5-18-1796	4-12-1798	Gillihans Cr.
Samuel Murry	733	125	1-25-1799	12-6-1799	Big Mud Cr., now lives
Samuel Murry	734	100	3-30-1799	12-6-1799	Cane Cr., E. side
Samuel Murry, Sr.	951	50	11-8-1799	12-15-1801	adj. own land
Samuel Murry, Sr.	976	300	n/a	n/a	Cane Cr., adj. Col. Avery
Samuel Murry, Sr. (5)	1157	200	10-15-1801	12-14-1803	Cane Cr.
Samuel Murrey, Sr.	1202	100	12-15-1802	12-16-1803	Cane Cr.
Samuel Murray, Jr.	1242	100	2-2-1801	12-16-1803	adj. Daniel McCarson
Samuel Murray, Jr.	1291	650	4-8-1800	12-20-1803	Big Mud Cr., now lives
Samuel Murry, Sr.	1370	150	3-15-1804	12-10-1804	Mud Cr., W. side
Samuel Murry, Jr.	1388	640	3-19-1802	12-10-1804	Mud Cr., E. side
Samuel Murry, Sr.	1395	100	9-13-1800	12-11-1804	Kinzeys Cr.
Samuel Murry, Jr.	1398	100	2-2-1801	12-18-1804	Mud Cr.
Samuel Murry, Sr.	1406	50	12-18-1804	8-24-1801	Mud Cr.
Samuel Murry, Jr.	1477	68	6-16-1803	12-19-1805	Mud Cr.
Samuel Murray	1832	50	1-20-1808	12-19-1809	Cane Cr.
Samuel Murray, Sr.	1834	43	1-20-1804	12-19-1809	Cane Cr.
Samuel Murray, Sr.	1954	125	4-6-1809	12-11-1811	Cane Cr., Meadow Cr.
Samuel Murray, Jr.	2021	25	11-9-1811	11-28-1812	Saluda Rd.
Samuel Murray, Jr.	2047	50	11-21-1811	11-24-1813	Big Mud Cr.
Samuel Murray, Jr.	2271	50	7-23-1814	12-6-1816	Cane Cr.
Thomas Murry	1555	10	6-12-1806	12-5-1806	Wagon Rd., adj. Greenlee
Thomas Murray	1560	200	7-9-1804	12-5-1806	Penners Cr., Gap Cr.
Thomas Murray	1827	100	11-11-1808	12-19-1809	adj. Craig
Thomas Murray	1971	120	4-27-1807	12-18-1811	Kinzeys Cr.
Thomas Murray	2545	11	1-8-1822	12-10-1822	Hoopers Cr.
Thomas Murray	2614	25	10-27-1823	12-9-1825	Gap Cr.
Thomas Murray	2677	25	1-7-1825	1-13-1827	adj. own land, Phillips, etc.
Thomas Murray	2796	25	10-9-1827	12-21-1829	adj. Jesse Whitaker

William Murray	1833	54	5-23-1807	12-19-1809	adj. David Miller
William Murray	1966	100	4-12-1813	12-23-1814	Cane Cr.
William Murray	2159	100	4-12-1813	12-23-1814	Cane Cr.
William Murray	2316	65	11-10-1815	11-29-1817	Spring Cr.
William Murray	2797	50	7-30-1827	12-21-1829	Gap Cr., Limestone Cr.
William Murray	3175	25	10-20-1831	12-18-1833	Blue Ridge, W. side
Wm. L. Murray	3750	100	1-9-1838	12-24-1838	Barlstons Cr.
Wm. L. Murray	3756	5	1-9-1837	12-24-1838	Boylston Cr.
W. R. Murray	4414	19+	4-20-1875	2-22-1876	FB River, E. side
W. R. Murray	4415	5.75	4-20-1875	2-22-1876	E. side of road

Footnotes

(1) also Phillip Brittain

(2) also Phillip Brittain - listed 1st

(3) also Phillip Brittain - listed 1st

(4) also Phillip Brittain - listed 1st

(5) also Benjamin Kinley

Patten/Patton Family NC Land Grants

Cluster Analysis - below

Asheville Pattons = A

Biltmore Pattons = B

Swannanoa Pattons = C

Burke Co.

Registered Name	Grant	Acres	Entered	Patented	Location
A. E. Patten	6285	89	n/a	n/a	Silver Cr., adj. Mary Patten
Burke Paton	1200	100	2-22-1786	8-7-1799	*Swannanoa, S. side
Charity Patten	751	136.5	11-24-1778	10-11-1783	S. Muddy Cr.
Elijah Patten	102	347	10-9-1778	9-20-1779	Catawba R., Clear Cr.
Elijah Patton (1)	2154	640	10-30-1793	10-17-1796	Cataba R., Nicks Cr.
Francis Patten	325	148	1779	10-28-1782	S. Muddy Cr., Mill fork
Francis Patten	721	200	11-24-1778	10-11-1783	S. Muddy Cr.
Francis Patten	2630	80	3-3-1795	12-6-1799	S. Muddy Cr.
Francis Patton	2685	100	3-3-1795	12-6-1799	Muddy Cr., Mill fork

James Patton	764	300	12-18-1779	10-11-1783	S. Muddy Cr., adj. Elijah Patton
James Patton	4069	100	n/a	n/a	Cane Cr.
Joseph Patton	1015	195	1-13-1779	8-7-1787	Drowning Cr.
Mathew Patton	1491	50	1-6-1790	11-27-1792	*Bee Tree Cr.
Robert Patten - C	498	100	12-18-1779	10-28-1782	Muddy Cr., E. side, main
Robert Patton - C	1047	300	8-15-1787	8-7-1787	FB River, E. side
Robt. Paton	1200	100	n/a	n/a	Swannanoa R.
Robert Patten (2) - C	1311	640	12-12-1783	11-16-1790	*Swanaoe R., both sides
Robert Patten - C	1337	100	n/a	11-16-1790	*Swannanoa R., N. fork
Robert Pattin - C	1358	100	12-3-1787	11-16-1790	*Swannanoa R., N. fork
Robert Patton (3) - C	1413	640	12-12-1783	12-15-1791	*Swannanoa R.
Robert Patton	6608	11.5	4-18-1876	8-16-1876	Irish Cr., Upper Cr. Twp.
Samuel Patton	3184	50	5-9-1801	12-8-1802	N. Muddy Cr., adj own land
Samuel Patton	3312	70	4-21-1802	11-29-1804	N. Muddy Cr.
Samuel Patton	3501	50	9-9-1808	9-11-1810	Muddy Cr., Bobs fork
Samuel Patton	3657	22	6-15-1813	12-2-1814	Muddy Cr.
Samuel Patton	3769	50	1-17-1815	12-7-1816	Muddy Cr., Bobs fork
Thomas Patten	327	345	5-29-1778	10-28-1782	Silver Cr.
Thomas Patten	392	100	10-17-1778	10-28-1782	Silver Cr., E. br.
William Patten	575	100	12-27-1778	10-11-1783	N. Muddy Cr.
William Patten	622	100	12-24-1778	10-11-1783	Muddy Cr., Glady Br.
William Patten	993	150	12-17-1783	8-7-1787	Bobes Cr., both sides
William Patten	3681	50	6-15-1813	12-5-1815	Muddy Cr., adj.oown land
William B. Patton	6227	83	11-25-1848	12-20-1850	Silver Cr.. Adj. Mary Patton

Footnotes - Burke Co.

(1) also William Kilton - listed 1st

(2) also James Miller - 1st & Charles McDowel

(3) also Charles McDowel - 1st & James Miller

Editor's note - Burke Co.

* indicates locality now in Buncombe Co.

Most other locations above now in eastern McDowell Co.

Elijah Patten, Francis Patten, Robert Patten, and Thomas Patten are on the 1770 list of taxables along the Catawba River, above Horn Ford (Burke Co.)—thus probably closely related.

Buncombe Co.

Registered Name	Grant	Acres	Entered	Patent	Location
Aaron Patton -C	114	50	3-31-1794	1-19-1795	adj. former house
Fidelio Patton - B	2546	50	9-29-1821	12-10-1822	Little Mud Cr.
Fidelio Patton - B	2665	40	9-6-1822	1-13-1827	Little Mud Cr.
Fidelio Patton - B	3182	90	6-11-1831	12-18-1833	John Pattons (decd.)Mill Cr.
George Patton - C	2629	50	1-14-1825	12-9-1825	Swannanoa R., S. side
George N. Patton - C	3865	150	9-30-1837	12-9-1840	Beetree Cr, Longs br.
James (Jesse) Patton(1)	821	300	n/a	n/a	Cane Cr., French BR
as above	822	200	n/a	n/a	Mud Cr., Cane Cr., FBR
as above	823	300	n/a	n/a	unknown
James Patton (2) - A	2218	24	5-9-1809	11-28-1816	Swannanoa, N. side
James Patton - A	2219	100	5-9-1809	11-28-1816	as above
James Patton - A	2220	200	5-9-1809	11-28-1816	as above
James Patton, Sr. - A	2328	50	12-2-1816	11-29-1817	Swannao R., N. side
James Patton, Sr. - A	2719	100	4-29-1825	1-3-1828	Ridge, Asheville/Swannanoa
James Patton, Sr. - A	2720	100	3-24-1826	1-3-1828	Elk Wallow Mtn, Rims Cr.
James Patton, Sr. - A	2721	45	12-6-1826	1-3-1828	Rosses Cr. (Chunn's Cove)
James Patton, Sr. - A	2722	300	12-6-1826	1-3-1828	Rosses Cr. (Chunn's Cove)
James L. Patton	4155	25	1-1-1846	11-27-1848	Cain Cr., Shoal Cr.
James L. Patton (3)	4265	50	10-22-1853	12-20-1854	Cane Cr
James L. Patton	4266	357	10-11-1854	12-20-1854	Cane Cr., Woods fork
James L. Patton	4294	100	7-12-1853	11-3-1855	Cane Cr., W. side Blue Ridge
James L. Patton	4295	300	11-17-1853	11-3-1855	Cane Cr., FB River, E. side
Jno. Patton - B	777	200	10-11-1797	12-23-1799	Sweetens Cr., Holly Spring
Jno. Patton - B	786	100	8-20-1795	9-1-1800	FB River, E. side
John Patton - B	2617	300	1-27-1817	12-9-1825	Swannanoa R., S. side, adj.own
John Patton, Jr.	2873	91	11-29-1828	12-4-1830	FB River, W. side, Big br.
John Patton, Sr. - B	2955	100	12-12-1818	12-12-1831	Avery Cr., head, S. fork
John Patton (decd.) - B	2957	100	12-12-1818	12-22-1831	Averys Cr.
John Patton, Jr.	3310	n/a	n/a	n/a	French BR, E. side
Jno. Patton, Sr.	3380	30	4-15-1833	12-17-1835	FB River, E. side, Shoal Cr.
Jno. Patton	3392	50	11-22-1834	11-11-1836	FB River, E. side, adj Fid. Pattons
John Patton, Sr.	3862	50	2-13-1839	12-9-1840	Bull Cr., Tanyard Ridge
John Patton, Sr.	3863	50	12-1-1837	12-9-1840	Bull Cr., left fork
John Patton, Sr.	3864	50	12-1-1837	12-9-1840	Bull Cr., left fork

John E. Patton (4) - A	3573	150	2-11-1836	11-9-1837	Spring Cr.
Joseph Patton	2251	50	4-5-1816	11-30-1816	FB River
Joseph Patton	2334	100	n/a	n/a	French BR, SW side
Joseph E. Patton	3441	50	2-10-1836	12-5-1836	Stillhouse Br, adj. own land
Jos. E. Patton	3226	100	n/a	n/a	Williamson Cr.
J. L. Patton	4435	40	2-22-1881	3-2-1882	Cane Cr., Woods fork
J. L. Pateon (5)	7073	160	9-17-1883	2-17-1885	Flat Cr., Swannanoa
Mathew Patton, Sr.	296	50	5-14-1796	7-10-1797	Bee Tree Cr. ,Swannanoa
Mathew Patton	447	50	4-23-1796	8-31-1798	N. Swannore, adj. own land
Mathew Patton	1127	100	1-19-1803	12-10-1803	Swannanoa, N. side
Montraville Patton - B	3209	50	10-29-1832	12-6-1834	Boilstons Cr., Woody fork
Neely Patton (6)	1297	100	n/a	n/a	Whitsons Cr., W. side
Robert Patton - C	59	43	1-10-1793	7-7-1794	Swanannoa
Robert Patton - C	292	50	8-25-1795	7-10-1797	adj. own land
Robert Patton	992	100	n/a	n/a	French BR, NE side
Robert Patton (7) - C	1768	50	3-31-1807	12-17-1808	Swannanoa R.,
Robert Patton - C	2162	50	4-6-1814	11-4-1815	Flat Cr., Wallace Mtn.
R. L. Patton	7342	50	n/a	n/a	Cane Cr., adj. J. L. Patton (dec.)
Samuel Patton	3199	33	1-6-1833	3-1-1834	FB River, E. side, adj. Tanyard br.
Thomas Patton	929	50	1-22-1800	12-7-1801	FB River, SE side
Thomas Patton, Sr.	956	60	5-11-1794	12-7-1801	Swananoe, N. side, adj. Wm. Davidson

Footnotes - Buncombe Co.

(1) four others incl. Thomas Hemphill

(2) also Andrew Erwin

(3) also Joshua Whittaker

(4) also James W. Patton

(5) also John McMurrelly - listed 1st, & R. B. Justice

(6) also Jeremih Cleveland

(7) adj. Aaron Patton smith shop

Penland Family NC Land Grants

Burke Co.

Registered Name	Grant	Acres	Entered	Patented	Location
George Pentland	666	200	9-3-1778	10-11-1783	Upper Cr., middle fork
George Pentland	697	200	1-31-1780	10-11-1783	Upper Cr., middle fork
George Penland	710	n/a	n/a	n/a	n/a
George Penland	1864	50	n/a	7-7-1794	Upper Cr., Schoolhouse br.
John Penland	1360	50	3-29-1793	8-22-1795	Shadracks Cr.
Jno. Penland	3687	100	9-25-1810	12-5-1815	Shadracks Cr., adj. I. Bradshaw
Robert Penland	52	150	6-3-1778	9-20-1779	Catawba R., Canoe Cr.
Robert Penland	612	100	5-19-1778	9-11-1783	Upper Cr., N. fork, Canoe Cr.
Robert Penland	734	175	1-25-1779	10-11-1783	Canoe Cr., Falling br.
Robert Penland	1367	150	6-15-1789	11-16-1790	*FB River, New Found Cr.
Robert Penland	2564	100	1-25-1795	6-7-1799	Canoe Cr., Jumping Br.
Robert Penland	3587	50	11-29-1811	11-28-1812	Canoe Cr., adj. own land
Robert Penland	3999	50	8-8-1818	12-17-1819	Falling br.
William Pendland	138	300	9-24-1778	3-15-1780	Upper Cr., S. fork
William Penley	656	50	2-1-1779	10-11-1783	Upper Cr., N. fork
William Pentland	710	200	12-20-1778	10-11-1783	Upper Cr., Warrior fork
William Penland	1177	100	7-6-1779	5-18-1789	Linvill R., big br.
Willian Penley	1365	100	3-2-1793	8-22-1795	Canoe Cr.
William Penland	1838	160	12-2-1778	7-7-1794	Upper Cr., S. fork
William Penley	2593	100	n/a	n/a	James Mill Cr.
William Penland	2935	100	6-3-1789	12-19-1800	Steeds Cr., Little fork
William Pinland	3347	100	11-19-1800	12-18-1804	Canoe Cr., N. fork, Paddies Br.
William Penland	3462	50	1-25-1799	12-17-1808	Upper Cr., S. side, Line Br.
William Penland	3463	60	1-25-1799	12-17-1808	Big Cabbin Br.
William Penland, Sr.	3753	100	7-26-1814	12-7-1816	Canoe Cr.
William Penland, Sr.	3754	300	12-13-1813	12-7-1816	Upper Cr.

****

Demaris Pendly	5862	50	9-26-1836	12-6-1838	Wilsons Cr.
Jessee Penley	5484	50	4-22-1830	12-21-1830	Wilsons Cr.
Jonathan Pendley	6119	25	5-20-1842	9-25-1843	Upper Cr., Timbered Br.
Jonathan Penley	6254	25	5-10-1852	12-15-1852	Upper Cr., N. fork

Joshua Perley	1180	100	12-10-1778	5-18-1789	Lower Cr.
Joshua Penley	1567	100	12-10-1778	11-27-1792	Upper Cr.
Joshua Penley	1768	50	1-29-1793	7-7-1794	Caubauba R., Smoekey Cr.
William Pinland	3070	100	9-13-1794	9-23-1802	Jumping Br.
William Penley	3151	100	7-29-1802	11-27-1802	Jumping Br.

Footnote

* now in Buncombe Co.

Buncombe Co.

Abraham D. Penland	2286	200	3-31-1813	11-21-1817	FB River,W. side, Hominy Cr.
Abraham Penland (1)	3211	100	1-9-1833	12-6-1834	FB River, W. side, Wildcat Br.
Alex. Penland	3099	50	10-29-1830	12-12-1832	Rims Cr., adj. A. Penland
George Penland	133	100	5-11-1794	6-19-1795	Rims Cr., N. side
Geo. Penland	736	x100	4-17-1798	12-6-1799	Sandy Mush Cr.
George Penland	1510	100	8-13-1802	6-27-1806	Bee Tree Cr., Swannanoa
George Penland	2268	50	5-24-1815	12-6-1816	Wolf Pen Br.
George N. Penland (2)	4060	100	11-11-1853	1-27-1854	FB River, Ragsdale Cr.
Hugh H. Penland	3954	100	9-7-1839	12-20-1841	Rims Cr., Penlands Br.
J. D. Penland	15110	1.5	7/30/1902	2/17/1903	FB River, W. side, Youngs Br.
J. D. Penland	15111	10	7/30/1903	2/17/1903	FB River, W. side, Averys Cr.
J. D. Penland	15112	161	7/30/1902	2/17/1903	FB River, W. side, Bent Cr.
Noble Penland	3902	50	8-31-1837	12-17-1840	Rims Cr., S. side, Sugar Cove
N. A. Penland	9946	n/a	n/a	n/a	FB River, Buncombe Turnpike
Marcus L. Pendland (3)	3529	100	7-22-1834	1-3-1837	Big & Little Ivey
Peter Pendland (4)	2150	50	1-4-1814	12-7-1814	FB River, W. side
Peter Penland	2320	30	11-4-1816	11-29-1817	Bull Cr., right fork
William Pendland	1668	100	12-18-1806	12-2-1807	Rims Cr., N. side, adj. Samuel Chunn
Willliam Pendland	1690	100	12-18-1806	12-15-1807	Rims Cr., both sides
William Pendland	1692	100	1-21-1807	12-17-1807	Rims Cr., N. side
William S. Penland	3222	15	8-19-1833	12-9-1834	Rims Cr., right br., adj. Geo. P.
William S. Penland	3226	50	10-27-1832	12-9-1834	Rims Cr., right br., adj. Geo. P.

Footnotes - Buncombe Co.

(1) also William B. Westall

(2) also Joshua Jones - listed 1st

(3) at Wild Cat Trap br.

(4) at Elijah Lees Mill Cr.

Ragsdale NC Land Grants

Buncombe Co.

Registered Name	Grant	Acres	Entered	Patent	Location
Gabrel Ragsdale	1	200	4-27-1792	12-5-1793	Sandy Mush Cr., N. side
Gabrel Ragsdale	3	640	8-2-1792	12-5-1792	Richland Cr., W. fork
Gabrel Ragsdale	4	200	n/a	n/a	Sandy Mush Cr.
Gabriel Ragsdale	200	100	3-19-1794	11--27-1795	Newfound Cr., Big Branch
Gabriel Ragsdale (1)	201	50	3-19-1794	11-27-1795	Newfound Cr., Big Branch
Gabriel Ragsdale (2)	205	200	7-27-1794	12-3-1795	Newfound Cr., S. fork
Gabriel Ragsdale (3)	206	100	7-27-1794	12-4-1795	Newfound Cr., S. fork
Gabriel Ragsdale	207	200	8-1-1790	12-4-1795	Mills R., FB River
Gabriel Ragsdale (4)	309	100	8-27-1794	10-17-1796	Pigeon R., Crabtree Cr.
Gabriel Ragsdale (5)	310	300	8-27-1794	10-17-1796	Richland Cr., Raccoon Cr.
Gabriel Ragsdale (6)	311	100	8-27-1794	10-17-1796	Hominy Cr.
Gabriel Ragsdale (7)	312	100	8-27-1794	10-17-1796	Pigeon R., Crabtree Cr.
Gabriel Ragsdale (8)	313	100	8-27-1794	10-17-1796	Beaverdam Cr.
Gabriel Ragsdale (9)	314	100	2-27-1794	10-17-1796	Pigeon R., Crabtree Cr.
Gabriel Ragsdale (10)	315	100	8-7-1794	10-17-1796	Pigeon R., Crabtree Cr.
Gabriel Ragsdale	372	100	n/a	n/a	Crabtree Cr.
Gabriel Ragsdale	415	150	n/a	n/a	Newfound Cr., Big Branch
Gabriel Ragsdale	803	200	7-3-1794	9-1-1800	Hominy, S. fork

Footnotes

(1) assignee William Gilleham

(2) als Joseph Henry

(3) also Joseph Henry

(4) also Joseph Henry

(5) also Joseph Henry - listed 1st

(6) also Joseph Henry - listed 1st

(7) also Joseph Henry

(8) also Joseph Henry

(9) also Joseph Henry - listed 1st

(10) also Joseph Henry - listed 1st

Editor's Notes

Gabrl. Ragsdil is on the 1790 NC Census, Burke Co., Morgan district, Eleventh Company

(now Buncombe Co.), with 3 males, 1 female, and 3 slaves.

Gabriel Ragsdale was in the North Carolina House of Commons from 1792 to 1796.

Mary Ragsdale is on the 1800 NC Census, Buncombe Co., with 4 males, 2 females, and 1 slave.

 (evidently Gabriel Ragsdale died between 1796 and 1800)

Reynolds Family NC Land Grants

Buncombe Co.

Registered Name	Grant	Acres	Entered	Patented	Location
Abraham Randels	824	200	2-25-1800	12-25-1800	Bent Cr., west side FB River
Abraham Runnels	1137	200	10-7-1800	12-10-1803	Bent Cr.
Abraham Reynolds	1791	200	10-10-1807	9-16-1809	Bent Cr., west side FB River
Abraham Runnels	1811	200	11-7-1807	12-9-1809	Bent Cr.
Abraham Runnels	1838	640	11-7-1807	12-19-1809	Bent Cr.
Abraham Reynolds	2452	100	2-9-1820	10-2-1820	Bent Cr., west side FB River
Abraham Runnels	2604	100	12-26-1822	11-30-1824	Bent Cr., Walnut Cove Br.
Abraham Reynolds	3961	100	7-25-1838	12-5-1842	Bent Cr., head
total acres		1740			
John Reynolds (1)	2963	100	9-1-1829	12-12-1831	Beaverdam Cr.
John Reynolds	3868	100	5-1-1840	12-9-1840	S. Turkey Cr.
Daniel Reynolds	3923	200	7-25-1838	12-35-1840	Bent Cr.
Daniel Raynolds	4139	82	12-7-1844	1-18-1847	Bent Cr.
Daniel Reynolds	4140	200	9-5-1846	1-18-1847	Bent Cr., west side FB River
Daniel Reynolds	4145	50	5-16-1843	12-29-1847	Bent Cr.
Daniel Reynolds	4146	50	5-16-1843	12-29-1847	Bent Cr.
Daniel Reynolds (2)	4388	33	4-10-1869	2-14-1870	Bent Cr., west side BR River

Footnotes

(1) also Wm. Gallaspie

(2) Grant 4338 = 33 acres + 112 poles

Rice Family NC Land Grants

Burke Co.

Registered Name	Grant	Acres	Entered	Patented	Location
Joseph Rice	1414	200	n/a	n/a	Bull Cr., Swannanoa

Buncombe Co.

Isaac Rice	2612	50	10-9-1822	12-20-1824	Big Laurel, both sides

Jeremiah Rice	3757	50	2-31-1837	12-24-1838	Crabtree Cr., Dismal Cr.
John Rice	2427	150	12-23-1817	11-24-1819	Laurel Cr., both sides
John Rice	3164	22	3-13-1832	12-5-1833	Little Ivey, Bald Mtn. fork
John Rice	3165	50	1-3-1831	12-5-1833	Turkey Cr.
Joseph Rice	99	15	2-11-1794	1-19-1795	* Bull Cr.
Joseph Rice	130	50	2-11-1794	1-19-1795	Bull Cr.
Joseph Rice	1099	100	n/a	n/a	Bull Cr., left fork
Joseph Rice	1138	33	1-19-1802	12-10-1802	Bull Cr.
Joseph Rice	1424	50	7-19-1803	12-11-1804	Bull Cr., left fork, Craven Gap
Joseph Rice	2168	50	6-13-1814	12-4-1815	Bull Cr., left fork
Joseph Rice, Sr.	2574	40	1-14-1822	12-8-1823	Bull Cr., left fork
Joseph Rice	2611	100	10-5-1822	12-20-1824	Walnut Cr., head
Joseph Rice, Sr.	3024	40	8-9-1829	12-22-1831	Bull Cr., left fork
Joseph Rice, Sr.	3578	25	3-14-1836	9-9-1837	Bull Cr.
Joseph M. Rice, Jr.	2711	50	1-3-1826	12-29-1827	Bull Cr., left fork
Joseph M. Rice.	3716	100	3-25-1838	12-20-1838	Beaverdam, N. fork
Larkin Rice	3440	100	4-20-1835	12-5-1836	Crabtree Cr., Blythes Cr.
Samuel Rice	1212	133	7-4-1800	12-16-1803	Pigeon R., E. side
William Rice (1)	568	100	n/a	n/a	Little Ivey
William Rice	2428	100	12-23-1817	11-24-1819	Pawpaw Cr.
William Rice	2478	40	n/a	n/a	Walnut Cr., middle fork
William Rice	2580	35	1-8-1822	12-18-1823	Bull Cr., left fork
William Rice	2583	15	2-12-1823	12-18-1823	Bull Cr.
William Rice	2584	14	1-14-1822	12-18-1823	Bull Cr., left fork
William Rice (2)	2837	60	9-6-1828	11-20-1830	Bull Cr., left fork
William Rice (3)	3589	100	6-9-1834	11-9-1837	Reams Cr., head

Footnotes
(1) assignee
(2) also Joseph M. Rice
(3) also Joseph M. Rice

Sams Family NC Land Grants

Burke Co.

Registered Name	Grant	Acres	Entered	Patented	Location
Edm. Sams	1636	150	n/a	n/a	Cold Mtn. Cr. Assignee
James Sams	27	200	5-2-1790	1-6-1794	Little Ivey, below forks
Reuben Sams	3619	50	1-27-1813	11-24-1813	Lower Cr., Zacks fork
Reuben Sams	3620	50	1-27-1813	11-24-1813	Lower Cr,. Zacks fork
William Sams	1587	144.5	10-24-1789	11-27-1792	Ivy R., Bold Mtn. fork

Buncombe Co.

Burdit Sames	546	50	2-6--1798	12-13-1798	Haw Br., adj. J. McDowell
Burdit Sams (1)	1033	200	n/a	n/a	Thomas Moor's Cr
Burdit Sams	1167	85	6-10-1801	12-14-1803	FB River, W. side
Bardit Sams (2)	1178	100	2-19-1801	12-16-1803	Pole Cr., N. fork
Bardit Sams (3)	1181	100	2-19-1801	12-16-1803	Pole Cr., N. fork
Burdit Sams (4)	1222	100	2-19-1801	12-16-1803	Pole Cr., N. fork
Burdit Sams (5)	1252	200	7-13-1802	12-16-1803	Pole Cr., N. fork
Burdit Sams (6)	1254	200	2-19-1801	12-16-1803	Thomas Moore's Cr.
Burdit Sams (7)	1368	200	2-19-1801	12-10-1804	Thomas Moore's Cr.
Burdit Sams	1656	12	9-13-1806	11-27-1807	FB River, W. side
David Sams	4021	23	8-5-1842	11-30-1804	Newfound Cr., Stillhouse
Edmund Sams	1262	100	1-2-1812	12-20-1803	Big Ivey
Edmond Sams	1776	300	9-13-1806	12-21-1808	FB River, W. side
Larkin Sams	3874	100	n/a	n/a	Little Ivey
Larkin Sams	4215	2	5-8-1853	6-7-1853	Swedens Cr., W. side
Warren Sams	2398	100	6-9-1817	12-5-1818	Little Ivey
Warren Sams	3054	200	11-7-1829	12-4-1832	Big Ivey
William Sams	569	100	n/a	n/a	Little Ivy, assignee

Footnotes:

(1) thru (7) also William Young - listed 1st

Census Records

Edmund Sams is on the 1800 NC Census, Buncombe Co. with 5 males and 5 females.

James Sams is on the 1800 NC Census, Buncombe Co. with 4 males and 2 females.

William Sams is on the 1800 NC Census, Buncombe Co. with 6 males and 2 females.

Smith Family NC Land Grants

(Selected Smiths only)

Buncombe Co.

Registered Name	Grant	Acres	Entered	Patent	Location
Daniel Smith (1)	510	200	n/a	12-5-1798	Homeny Cr.
Daniel Smith (2)	511	100	8-28-1778	12-5-1798	Homeny Cr.
Daniel Smith (3)	1957	118	1-3-1810	12-11-1811	FB River, W. side
Daniel Smith	2996	50	5-3-1830	12-22-1831	Swannanoa, N. fork, Buckeye
Daniel Smith	2997	50	5-8-1830	12-22-1831	Swannanoa, N. fork
Daniel Smith	3718	50	3-10-1835	12-20-1838	Swannanoa, Balards Cove
Daniel Smith	3720	28	9-13-1838	12-20-1838	Joseph Gudgers Mill Cr.
James Smith	3131	150	4-12-1831	12-5-1833	S. Hominy Cr.
James M. Smith	2308	118	7-15-1817	11-26-1817	Gashes Cr.
James M. Smith (4)	2569	100	5-14-1823	11-11-1823	FB River, W. side
James M. Smith (5)	2812	250	1-13-1829	2-30-1830	FB River, NE side
James M. Smith (6)	2991	640	1-13-1829	12-15-1831	FB River, W. side
James M. Smith	3369	100	2-17-1834	12-5-1835	Rims Cr., Bee Br.
James M. Smith	3584	300	6-8-1835	11-9-1837	Reams Cr., head
James M. Smith	3585	150	6-8-1835	11-9-1837	Mtn. - Big Ivy & Reams Cr.
James M. Smith	4138	20	1-17-1844	7-18-1844	FB River, SW side
Jno. Smith	654	250	11-1-1796	11-26-1799	Clear Cr., Lorrell fork
John Smith	1709	50	8-28-1806	11-11-1808	Fryles Cr., Gap Cr.
Joseph Smith	726	150	6-22-1799	12-6-1799	adj. own land
Joseph Smith	1189	40	8-14-1801	12-16-1803	Philips Cr.
Nathan Smith	709	100	4-15-1799	12-6-1799	Elijah Lees Mill Cr.
Nathan Smith	936	250	5-28-197	12-15-1799	Elijah Lees Mill Cr., Phillips Br.
Nathan Smith	1230	100	7-21-1801	12-16-1803	Dicks Cr., S. fork
Nathan Smith	1260	100	1-21-1801	12-16-1803	adj. own land
Nathan Smith (7)	1434	80	1-22-1805	11/30/1905	FB River, W. side
Nathan Smith (8)	1435	50	4-21-1801	11-30-1805	FB River, W. side

Nathan Smith	1773	100	1-21-1801	12-21-1808	Dicks Cr., S. fork
Nathan Smith (9)	1897	100	7-21-1801	12-11-1810	FB River, W. side
Philip Smith (10)	23	100	6-31-1790	6-6-1794	Swannanoa R., E. side
Philip Smith	335	200	10-10-1793	1-2-1797	Beaver Dam Cr.
Samuel Smith	197	100	7-23-1794	11-13-1795	FB River, W. side
Samuel Smith (11)	435	100	4-29-1795	8-31-1798	FB River, NE side
Samuel Smith	456	150	9-11-1793	8-31-17698	Hominy Cr.
Samuel Smith	836	150	9-22-1800	12-10-1800	adj. own land
Samuel Smith	1733	170	11-28-1807	12-17-1808	FB River, adj. own land
William Smith	527	300	5-2-1795	12-5-1798	Walnut Cr.
William D. Smith	2008	250	4-3-1810	11-28-1812	Catheys Cr.
William Smith	2116	93	5-9-1812	11-29-1814	Mud Cr.
William D. Smith	2633	50	1-8-1824	12-17-1825	adj. Gaise
William D. Smith	2634	100	1-9-1824	12-7-1825	Little Mud Cr.
William D. Smith (12)	2533	600	2-5-1819	11-29-1821	FB River, both sides

Footnotes

(1) also David Vance

(2) also David Vance

(3) adj. Edmund Sams

(4) headwaters Samuel Smiths mill Cr., (Reams Cr.)

(5) opp. Newfound Cr.

(6) opp. Newfound Cr.

(7) Elijah Lees Mill Cr.

(8) Elijah Lees Mill Cr.

(9) adj. own land

(10) Rosses Cr.

(11) Rims Cr., Betree Cr.

(12) adj. Underwood

Stroup Family NC Land Grants

Buncombe Co.

Registered Name	Grant	Acres	Entered	Patented	Location
David Stroup	3582	100	2-15-1836	11-9-1837	Swannanoa, Rock House Cr.
Joseph Stroup	2833	92	12-10-1829	11-20-1830	Grassy Br., adj. own land
Joseph Stroup	2834	25	8-14-1829	11-20-1830	Beaver Dam Cr. ,Bull Cr.
Joseph Stroup	2838	50	8-14-1829	11-20-1830	Bull Cr., head, Rich cove
Joseph Stroup	2839	30	12-10-1829	11-20-1830	Bull Cr., right fork, adj. own
Joseph Stroup	3494	50	6-21-1835	12-10-1836	Bull Cr., Swannanoa
Joseph Stroup	3515	150	6-21-1834	12-18-1836	Bull Cr., Swannanoa, left fork
Joseph Stroup	3719	50	10-26-1836	12-20-1838	Bull Cr., adj. Nicholas Shope
Joseph Stroup	3872	50	6-6-1837	12-9-1840	Bull Cr., Tanyard Br.
Joseph Stroup	3873	50	12-26-1837	12-9-1840	Bull Cr., Bull Mtn. Gap

Solomon Stroup	3581	100	11-8-1836	11-9-1837	Rock House Cr.,head

*****

Joseph Stopp	3094	100	10-11-1830	12-12-1832	North Flatt Cr., both sides
Joseph Stepp	3583	100	4-22-1835	11-9-1837	N. Flat Cr., W. side
Joseph Stepp	3992	100	6-13-1841	1-21-1843	N. Flatt Cr.
William Stapp	4095	50	7-4-1837	1-4-1845	Swannanoa, Stillhouse Br.
William Stopp	4118	10	5-13-1842	12-31-1846	Swannoa, N. fork
William Stepp	4147	30	5-30-1841	4-17-1848	Flat Cr.

*****

John Shroat	3454	50	10-17-1835	12-8-1836	Swannanoa, Gashes Cr.
William Shoap	2831	50	8-14-1829	11-30-1830	Bee Tree, High Water falls

Selected Reference

Haller, Charles R., 2005, Riceville Road Churches and Cemeteries: Asheville, NC
 A Lot of Bunkum, Vol. 26, No. 1, p. 23-26

Editor's Notes:

The names Stroup, Stepp, and similar spellings do not occur in the 1790 NC Census nor in the 1800
 NC Census, Buncombe Co. Three families: James, Rebecka, and William Step do occur
 in the 1800 NC Census, Buncombe Co. Stroup and Stepp do not appear to be related.

Joseph Stroup was the leader of a tiny German Lutheran communal group settling in the Riceville
 area about 1807. His first land purchase dates from 1822, being along Bull Creek.
 The Lutheran group included Joseph Stroup, Abraham & Adam Creasman, and John Shope, Sr.

Thrash Family NC Land Grants

Buncombe Co.

Registered Name	Grant	Acres	Entered	Patented	Location
A. B. Thrash	4303	100	9-7-1853	2-12-1856	FB River, W. side, Kellys Mill Br.
A. B. Thrash	4419	33.25	10-25-1876	12-31-18778	adj. J. M. Thrash
A. B. Thrash (1)	4268	100	9-24-1853	12-27-1854	FB River, Dicks Cr.
Augustus B. Thrash	4161	51	1-5-1847	11-27-1848	New Found Cr.
George H. Thrash	4302	90	10-7-1852	2-12-1856	Pole Cr., E. fork

Henry P. Thrash	4206	50	12-18-1849	12-30-1852	Newfound Cr.
Henry P. Thrash	4226	100	9-27-1853	1-27-1854	FB River, W. side, Kellys Mill Br.
Henry P. Thrash	4306	30	6-12-1854	6-6-1856	S. Turkey Cr.
John Thrash	2821	10	10-8-1828	11-20-1830	Newfound Cr., Round Hill Br.
J. L. Thrash	4391	15	3-1-1869	11-26-1870	Newfound Cr.
John M. Thrash	4407	150	10-20-1873	12-31-1874	Dicks Cr., adj. John Thrash
R. L. Thrash (2)	4406	39	10-13-1873	12-31-1874	FB River, W. side, Dicks Cr.
Valentine Thrash	1224	45	1-22-1800	12-16-1803	Turkey Cr., S. fork, adj. own land
Valentine Thrash	2004	50	1-19-1808	11-28-1812	Turkey Cr., S. fork, adj. own land

Footnotes

(1) also Willliam Herren - 1st

(2) also A. P. Thrash

Editor's Notes

"Volentine" Thrash is on the 1800 NC Census, Buncombe Co. with 2 males and 4 females.

Valentine Thrash (1749-1835) was a native of Germany. He m. Barbara Yountz and fought in the Revolutionary War. Thrash is buried in the Newfound Baptist Church cemetery.

Vance Family NC Land Grants

Burke Co.

Registered Name	Grant	Acres	Entered	Patented	Location
David Vance	144	100	9-10-1778	3-15-1780	Catawba R., Crooked Cr., Johns Cr.
David Vance	1027	320	8-5-1783	7-7-1787	Tims Cr. (Reems Cr.), N. fork
David Vance	1033	20	9-1-1783	8-7-1787	Catawba R., Muddy Cr.
David Vance (1)	1407	400	n/a	12-15-1791	Turkey Cr., S. fork
David Vance (2)	3332	100	12-31-1778	11-29-1804	S. Muddy Cr.
David Vance	5677	50	9-23-1833	11-29-1834	Beaver Cr.
William Vance	5611	50	7-27-1829	12-20-1833	Toe River
William Vance	6305	100	11-13-1853	10-29-1855	Linville
Buncombe Co.					
David Vance (3)	284	100	4-5-1797	4-5-1797	Quarter Camp Br.
David Vance (4)	285	100	5-20-1796	4-5-1797	Jacks Cr.
David Vance (5)	286	100	4-5-1797	4-5-1797	Crabtree

David Vance(6)	377	5000	4-1-1784	11-19-1800	Elk River, Swan Cr.
David Vance (7)	510	200	n/a	12-5-1798	Homeny Cr.
David Vance (8)	511	100	7-28-1778	12-5-1798	Hominy Cr.
David Vance (9)	749	100	3-7-1796	12-6-1799	Jacks Cr.
David Vance	1237	250	1-20-1803	12-16-1803	Rims Cr.
David Vance	3198	100	9-11-1831	2-20-1834	Reems Cr., S. side
David Vance	3303	25	4-18-1834	11-13-1835	Reems Cr.
David Vance	3721	100	3-23-1837	12-20-1838	Sandy Mush Cr., Trail Br.
Robert B. Vance	3636	50	10-27-1836	11-5-1838	Case Botts Br., FB River

Foot Notes

(1) also William Davidson

(2) also Andrew Woods

(3) also George Baker

(4) also George Baker -listed 1st

(5) also George Baker

(6) also William Moore & Daniel Williams; Tennessee - Bedford Co.

(7) also Daniel Smith - listed 1st

(8) also Daniel Smith - listed 1st

(9) also Hickman Hensley

Editor's Notes

David Vance, Sr. b. 1745, d. 1813; David Vance, Jr. b. 1792, d.1844

Webb Family NC Land Grants (see also Young)

Buncombe Co.

Registered Name	Grant	Acres	Entered	Patented	Location
David Webb	1063	100	n/a	n/a	Wm. Moores Cr., adj. own land
David Webb	1093	400	n/a	n/a	Pole Cr.
David Webb (1)	1299	100	12-9-1800	12-21-1803	Hominy Cr., N. side
David Webb	1321	150	5-13-1802	11-14-1804	Pole Cr.
David Webb	1403	200	5-13-1802	12-11-1804	Homany Cr.
David Webb	1410	100	9-23-1800	12-11-1804	S. fork Hominy, W. side
David Webb	1464	150	3-23-1801	12-19-1805	adj. Rutherford
David Webb	1509	200	12-2-1801	6-27-1806	Wm. Moores Cr., head
David Webb (2)	1980	200	7-11-1804	7-6-1812	FB River, W. side, Bear Cr.
Henry Webb (3)	542	100	7-1-1795	12-13-1798	Ivey, Spring Br.
Henry Webb	1643	150	1-3-1806	11-27-1807	Pole Cr., now lives
Henry Webb	1830	400	1-2-1806	12-19-1809	Hominy Cr.

John Webb	297	100	7-20-1797	7-10-1797	Big Ivey R., adj. own land
John Webb	1147	100	11-14-1801	12-10-1803	Wm. Moores Cr.
John Webb	1225	100	9-6-1800	12-16-1803	Hominy Cr.
John Webb	1249	200	9-6-1800	12-16-1803	adj. own land, now lives
John Webb	1250	50	9-9-1800	12-16-1803	Hominy Cr.
John Webb	1385	100	6-29-1802	12-10-1804	Indian Br.
John Webb	1588	200	3-22-1806	12-20-1806	Pole Cr.
John Webb	2163	100	11-1-1814	11-29-1815	Indian Br., head
Stacy Webb (4)	2783	20	3-7-1829	11-25-1829	Hominy Cr., N. side

Footnotes

(1) adj.William Young
(3) also Mary Webb; adj. Mary Webb
(2) also Thomas Love
(4) adj. own land

Editor's Notes

Stacy Young (1748-1844) married John Webb (1765-c.1826). See Young family.

Census Records

Jno. Webb is on the 1790 NC Census, Rutherford Co., Morgan District, Eleventh Company

with 4 males and 4 females.

John Webb is on the 1800 NC Census, Buncombe Co., with 1 male, 2 females, and 3 slaves.
John Webb is on the 1800 NC Census, Buncombe Co., with 3 males and 5 females.

Selected References

Haller, Charles R., 2009, The Strange Case of Stacy Webb: Asheville, NC, *A Lot of Bunkum,*

Vol. 30, no. 1, p. 15-20

Israel, Kenneth D., 2009, James Young, Sr. and his wife Ann, and Their Family: Asheville, NC

A Lot of Bunkum, vol. 30, no. 2, p. 6-14

Westall Family NC Land Grants

Buncombe Co.

Registered Name	Grant	Acres	Entered	Patent	Location
Thomas Westall	1955	100	3-3-1810	12-11-1811	Whitson Cr.
Thomas Westall	1956	100	9-10-1808	12-11-1811	Whitsons Cr.
Wm. B. Westall	2985	200	n/a	n/a	Rims Cr., adj. John Hyatt
Wm. B. Westall	3587	50	10-21-1834	11-9-1837	Reams Cr., Laurel fork
Wm. B. Westall (1)	3529	100	7-22-1834	1-3-1837	Big & Little Ivy

Footnotes

(1) also Marcus L. Penland -listed 1st

Selected References

Haller, Charles R., 2005, Thomas Wolfe's Father: Asheville, NC, *A Lot of Bunkum*,

   Vol. 26, no. 4, p. 13-17 (2005).

Editor's Notes:

The Westall family names occurs neither in the 1790 NC Buncombe Co. Census nor in the 1800 NC Census, Buncombe Co. The above circumstantial evidence indicates that William B. Westall was the son of Thomas Westall.

Whitaker Family NC Land Grants

Buncombe Co.

Registered Name	Grant	Acres	Entered	Patented	Location
Henry Whitaker (1)	4245	95	4-11-1854	9-12-1854	Cane Cr., S. side
Henry Whitaker	4263	17	9-2-1854	12-20-1854	Cane Cr., adj. own land
James Whitaker	1133	40	3-6-1802	12-10-1803	Cane Cr., Fullers Cr.
James Whiteker	1680	100	5-16-1804	12-2-1807	Ashworths Cr.
James Whitaker	2600	200	4-7-1823	11-30-1824	Swannanoa R., Jumping Br.
Jessee Whitaker	2702	100	1-1-1825	12-29-1827	Cane Cr., adj. own land
John Whitaker (2)	1430	100	11-2-1801	11-23-1805	Cane Cr., N. fork
John Whitaker	1935	75	12-23-1809	12-16-1811	Cain Cr., Gap Cr.
J. Whitaker, Jr.	3498	50	11-11-1836	12-10-1836	Swannanoa, Gashes Cr., head
J. L. Whitaker (3)	11930	3+	10-1-1892	12-16-1892	Fairview Twnshp.
Joshua Whitaker	2843	50	3-31-1828	11-27-1830	Cane Cr.
Joshua Whitaker (4)	4265	50	10-22-1853	12-20-1854	Cane Cr., adj. own land
Joshua Whitaker, Jr.	3269	10	6-7-1833	2-24-1835	Cain Cr., Woodses fork
William Whitaker	2637	150	4-8-1823	12-17-1825	McCrarys Mill Cr.
William Whitaker	2683	100	4-12-1825	1-13-1827	Cane Cr., (Poseys Cabin)
Wm. Noah Whitaker	13534	47.6	12-11-1896	2-24-1898	Cane Cr.

Footnotes

(1) also Joshua Whitaker

(2) also William Whitaker: adj. own land

(3) adj. Laning Clayton

(4) also J. L. Patton - listed 1st

Selected References

Whitaker, C. Bruce, 1989, *The Whitaker Family of Buncombe Co., NC*: Asheville, NC
  Ward Publ. Co., c. 400 p.

Census Records

John Whitteker is on the 1800 NC Census, Buncombe Co., with 1 male and 2 females.

William Whitteker is on the 1800 NC Census, Buncombe Co., with 2 males and 3 females.

Woodfin Family NC Land Grants

Buncombe Co.

Registered Name	Grant	Acres	Entered	Patented	Location
John Woodfin	1688	400	1-11-1806	12-11-1807	Boidstons Cr., both sides
John Woodfin	1689	300	1-11-1806	12-11-1807	Boidstons Cr., S. side
John Woodfin	1960	70	4-3-1811	12-14-1811	Boidstons Cr.
John Woodfin	1961	200	8-5-1809	12-14-1811	Boidstons Cr.
John Woodfin	2264	100	1-5-1814	12-6-1835	Boilstons Cr.
Jno. Woodfin	3082	100	7-8-1829	12-12-1832	FB River, Boilstons Cr.
Jno. Woodfin	3311	50	6-18-1830	11-25-1835	Mills R., N. fork
Jno. Woodfin	3112	50	6-18-1838	11-25-1835	Mills Cr., adj. own land
Jno. Woodfin	3113	50	4-25-1835	11-25-1835	Boylestones Cr.
Nicholas Woodfin	443	200	2-20-1797	8-31-1798	Jonathan Osburns Cr.
Nicholas Woodfin	552	50	4-23-1794	12-13-1798	FB River, E. side, Jonathans Cr.
Nicholas Woodfin	771	200	12-12-1798	12-20-1799	Own booring mill Cr.
Nicholas Woodfin (1)	1142	310	8-1-1801	12-14-1803	Mud Cr.
Nicholas Woodfin	3543	100	2-24-1836	5-15-1837	Little Pine Cr., both sides
Nicholas Woodfin	4272	400	2-21-1844	2-15-1855	Cain Cr., Shoal Cr., Road Br.

Footnotes

(1) also Jessee Laxton

Worley Family NC Land Grants

Buncombe Co.

Registered Name	Grant	Acres	Entered	Patented	Location
Francis Worley	547	300	6-7-1796	12-13-1798	Worleys Cr.
Nathan Worley	2100	200	8-12-1811	11-29-1814	Sandy Mush, N. fork
William M. G. Worley	3000	75	12-7-1829	12-22-1831	Beaverdam-Rims Cr.

Census Records

Frank Worley is on the 1790 NC Census, Burke Co., Morgan district, Sixth Company
 with 4 males and 2 females.

Francis Wordley is on the 1800 NC Census, Buncombe Co.with 4 males and 4 females.

Young Family NC Land Grants

Buncombe Co.

Registered Name	Grant	Acres	Entered	Patent	Locality
Elijah Young (1)	3448	50	7-11-1835	12-5-1836	Davidson R.
Harvey Young	2315	50	2-3-1816	11-29-1817	S. Hominy Cr., Glady Br.
Harvey Young (2)	4395	90	2-10-1871	11-21-1871	N. Hominy Cr., Welches Br.
James Young	2317	100	5-21-1816	11-29-1817	Hominey Cr.
James Young	2326	50	2-3-1816	11-29-1817	Hominey Cr., N. fork
James L. Young	3026	8	11-18-1830	12-22-1831	Whitons Cr.
J. C Young	12489	32	6-15-1893	5-8-1894	U. Hominy Twshp.
J. C. Young	13552	49	n/a	n/a	Cane Cr.
John Young	1253	200	10-21-1803	12-16-1803	Mud Cr.
John Young (3)	1720	150	7-21-1807	12-17-1808	FB River
John Young	2816	50	10-7-1828	11-20-1830	Swannanoa R., Mill cove
John Young (4)	2820	100	1-7-1830	11-20-1830	Swannanoa R., S. side
John Young	2836	50	10-7-1828	11-20-1830	Swannanoa R., Cane Cr.
John Young (5)	2909	300	n/a	n/a	Swannanoa R.
Joseph Young (6)	1179	400	2-2-1802	12-16-1803	FB River, both sides
Joseph Young (7)	1320	100	11-23-1801	11-14-1804	Rines Cr.
Joseph Young	1427		n/a	n/a	Whitsons Cr.
Joseph Young	2092	100	12-17-1803	1-28-1814	Whitsons Cr., head

T. C. Young (8)	13552	49	n/a	n/a	Cane Cr.
Washington Young	2318	58	2-3-1816	11-29-1817	Hominey Cr., Glady Br.
William Young	248	71	1-25-1795	10-17-1796	Jumping Br., Flatt Br.
William Young (9)	805	150	7-22-1794	9-1-1800	FB River, S. side
William Young (10)	1033	200	n/a	n/a	Thomas Moors Cr.
William Young (11)	1178	100	2-19-1801	12-16-1803	Pole Cr., N. fork
William Young (12)	1181	100	2-19-1801	12-15-1803	Pole Cr., W, Br.
William Young (13)	1222	100	2-19-1801	12-16-1803	Pole Cr., N. fork
William Young	1226	100	9-6-1800	12-16-1803	Pole Cr.
William Young	1227	100	9-16-1800	12-16-1803	Hominy Cr., S. fork
William Young	1229	50	12-9-1800	12-16-1803	Homony Cr., N. side
William Young	1251	100	12-6-1800	12-16-1803	Hominy Cr., S. fork
William Young (14)	1252	200	7-13-1802	12-16-1803	Pole Cr.
William Young (15)	1254	200	2-19-1801	12-16-1803	Thomas Moores Cr.
William Young (16)	1368	200	2-19-1801	12-10-1804	Thomas Moores Cr.
William Young	2379	100	1-17-1798	11-14-1800	FB River, SE side
William Young (17)	2735	50	n/a	n/a	Swannanoa R., Flatt Cr.
W. M. Young	4403	32	3-8-1873	12-8-1874	Hominy Cr.

Footnotes

(1) adj. William Young

(2) also James Young

(3) adj.Benjamin Murrit

(4) adj. own land

(5) also Moses Whiteside & Andrew Hemphill

(6) near Averys

(7) adj. John Weaver

(8) also J. B. Young

(9) adj. J. McDonald

(10) also Burdit Sams

(11) also Burdit Sams

(12) also Burdit Sams

(13) also Burdit Sams

(14) also Burdit Sams

(15) also Burdit Sams

(16) also Burdit Sams

(17) also Moses Whitesides

Appendix: Revolutionary War Patriots Buried in Western North Carolina
Updated June 2012
Compiled by Charles R. Haller, Asheville, NC

Name	Born	Born	Died	Burial Cemetery	Location
Thomas Henry Abel	1759	VA	1822	Locust Field Cem.	Canton
William Addington	1759	SC	1845	First Methodist Ch.	Franklin
James Alexander	1756	NC	1844	Piney Grove	Swannanoa
John Allen	c.1756	NC	1853	X	Price Creek
William Allen	X	X	X	Green Hill	Waynesville
Birch Allison	1763	MD	1848	X	x
James Anderson	1740		1814	Gabriels Cr. Baptist	X
Waightstill Avery	1741	x	1821	Avery	Morganton
Zebulon Baird	1764	NJ	1824	1st Presbyterian Ch.	Asheville
Daniel Ball	1763	NC	1844	Town Branch	Ivy
Benoni Banning	1744	x	1827	Ebenezer	Marion
Joel Blackwell	1755	x	1839	Jones Cemetery	Upward
John Blaylock	c.1762	VA	1846	X	x
Robert Brank, Sr.	c.1724	x	1785	x	x
James Brittain, Sr.	c.1740	NC	c.1823	x	x
James Brittain II	c.1760	VA	1833	Mills River Presbyt.	Mills River
William Brittain, Sr.	1762	NC	1846	Dula Springs	Weaverville
Samuel Broadway	1758	x	x	x	x
Amos Brown	1766	GA	x	x	x
Andrew Bryson	1750	PA	1835	Caney Fork	x
Daniel Bryson	1756	PA	1844	Sugar Fork Baptist	Franklin
James H. Bryson, Sr.	1745	PA	1833	Sugar Fork Baptist	Franklin
John W. Bryson	c.1760	PA	1851	Sugar Fork Baptist	Franklin
William H.Bryson	c.1758	PA	1817	Bryson Farm	Mills River
William Capps	1764	NC	1847	Fortune-Kuykendall	Hendersonville
John Carson	1752	IR	1841	?Round Hill	Marion
John Cathey	x	x	c.1788	x	x
William Cathey	1741	VA	1812	x	Richland Cr.
John Clarke	x	x	x	x	x
Lambert Clayton	1755	DE	1828	Davidson River Cem.	Brevard
George Clontz	1760	NC	1838	x	x
Joseph Cole	1746	NJ	c.1842	Newfound Bapt.	x
Adam Cooper, Sr.	1760	PA	1830	Cane Creek Bapt.	Fairview
John Peter Corn	1752	VA	1843	Ebenezer Baptist	Hendersonville
Joseph Cowan	1758	x	1835	x	x
James Cowden	x	VA	1810	Greenlee Hill	Marion

Co.	Rank	Wife
Hay.	Pvt	Mrs. Elizabeth Woodfin
Mac.	?Lt	Delila Duncan
Bun.	Pvt	Rhoda Cunningham
Yan.	Pvt	Patty (Molly) Turner
Hay.	Pvt	
Bur.	Pvt.	
Mad.	X	
Bur.	?Col	Leah Probart Franck
Bun.	X	Hannah Erwin
Bun.	Sgt	Ann _____
McD.	Pvt	Ann Clark
Hen.	X	
?Yan.		Polly Blalock
Bur.	X	Jean _____
?Bun.	X	
Hen.	Pvt	Delilah Stringfield
Bun.	Sgt	Rachel Brank
?Mac.	Pvt	
?Mac.	Pvt	Elizabeth _____
Jac.	X	Agnes Nancy Naill
Mac.	?Maj	1st Lucinda Jones 2nd Martha Morrow
Mac.	X	Sarah Countryman
Mac.	X	
Hen.	X	Susannah Bogle
Hen.	Pvt	Nancy Cocksey
McD.	?Col	1st Rachel M. McDowell 2nd Mary Moffitt McDowell
x	x	Mary Henry
Hay.	x	Rebecca Holeman
?Hen.	x	? Catherine Ransom
Tran.	Sgt	Sarah Davidson
?Bun.	Sgt	Chloe Cline
Bun.	Pvt	
Bun.	Pvt	Elizabeth Foybeson
Hen.	Pvt	Elizabeth Parr
Jac.	x	Nancy Buchanan
McD.	?Capt	Sarah Hawkins

Name	Born	Born	Died	Burial Cemetery	Location
Joseph Cross	1747	VA	1842	x	x
George Cunningham	1753	NC	1837	Cullowhee Baptist	Cullowhee
Benjamin Davidson	1743	VA	1825	Davidson River Cem	Brevard
John Davidson	c.1750	NC	1780	x	x
Samuel Davidson	x	x	1784	Hilltop Skyview Mem.	Swannanoa
William Davidson	1736	x	1814	?Piney Grove	Swannanoa
Clement Davis	1756	x	x	x	x
Isham Davis	1759	x	1835	Old Baptist Ch,	Franklin
Thomas Davis	1760	VA	x	x	x
Edward Decoine	1755	VA	x	x	x
Joseph Dobson, Jr.	1756	VA	1836	Dobson Cem.	x
Jacob Duckett, Jr.	1748	x	1809	Brick Church	Leicester
John Duckworth	1759	VA	1843	1st Presbyterian Ch.	Morganton
Alexander Erwin (Irwin)	1750	PA	c.1830	Quaker Meadows	Morganton
William Erwin (Irwin)	c 1740	PA	1812	x	x
William Erwin	c.1754	x	c.1842	x	x
William W. Erwin	1764	x	1837	Erwin Cem.	Belvedere
Michael Fannin	1758	x	x	x	x
Theodorus Felmott	c. 1754	x	1837	x	x
James W. Fisher	1753	x	1832	Toxaway Lakeside	x
Reubin Fletcher	1757	VA	x	x	x
Thomas Forster	1751	PA	1839	Newton Academy	Asheville
William Fortune, Sr.	1756	VA	c.1838	x	x
William Foster II	1748	IR	1830	Newton Academy	Asheville
John Franklin, Sr.	c.1728	x	c.1828	x	x
John Franklin, Jr.	c.1760	VA	1837	x	x
Alexander Fuller	1766	x	x	x	x
David Fulton	1751	x	x	Sugarfork Baptist	Franklin
Jesse Fulton	x	x	x	Sugarfork Baptist	Franklin
Alfred Gaither	x	x	1829	Presbyt. Ch.	Morganton
William Garrett	1754	x	x	x	x
William Garrison	x	x	x	x	Flat Creek
John Gillespie	x	x	x	East Fork	Brevard
Hugh Gourley	1747	x	1832	Shepherd Park	Naples
Jeremiah Green	1755	NC	1839	x	x
James Greenlee	1740	VA	1813	Quaker Meadows	Morganton
John Greenlee	1738	Va	1802	Quaker Meadows	Morganton
William Gudger, Sr.	1752	VA	1833	Piney Groove	Swannanoa
John Guthrie	1756	x	1822	Jupiter Baptist	Jupiter

Co.	Rank	Wife
Bun.	x	Sarah Cogdill
Jac.	Pvt	1st (unknown) 2nd Mary McCarthy
Tran.	x	
McD.		Nancy Brevard
Bun.	x	Mary Smith
Bun.	?Maj	Margaret McConnell
Bun.	Pvt	
Mac.	Pvt	
?Hay.	x	
Hen.	Sgt	Elizabeth Scoles
McD.	Pvt	Mary Mackey
Bun.	Pvt	Sara Odell
Bur.	Pvt	Mary Robertson
Bur.	?Col	1st Sarah Anne Robinson 2nd Mrs. Cynthia M. C. Patton
Bun.	Pvt	
Hen.	x	
Bur.	?Col	
Bun.	Pvt	
Hay.	Pvt.	Martha Swearingen
Tran.	x	
Bun.	Pvt	
Bun.	Pvt	Mary Robertson
Mac.	Pvt	
Bun.	Pvt	Elizabeth Heath
Bur.	x	
?Bur.	x	
?Bun.	Pvt	
Mac.	Pvt	
Mac.	x	
Bur.	?Col	
?Mac.	Pvt	
Bun.	x	
Tran.	x	
Hen.	x	1st (unknown) 2nd Nancy A. _____
Bun.	Pvt	1st (unknown) 2nd Polly Wiseman
Bur.	x	1st Mary Mitchell 2nd Ruth Howard
Bur.	x	1st (unknown) 2nd Hannah McClendon
Bun.	Pvt	Martha Young
Bun.	Pvt	

Name	Born	Born	Died	Burial Cemetery	Location
George Hall	x	x	x	Locust Field Cem.	Canton
Isham Harris	1759	VA	1846	x	x
Isham Harris, Sr.	c.1730	NC	1816	x	x
Joseph Harrison, Rev.	1735	VA	1811	Newfound Bapt.	Leicester
John Hays	1755	x	1830	Newfound Bapt.	Leicester
Thomas Hemphill	1750	PA	1826	Old Siloam Cem.	Old Fort/Marion
John Henry	1757	NC	1833	John Henry	Maggie Valley
Joseph Henry, Sr.	1765	x	1816	?Old Salem Bapt.	Fletcher
Joseph Henry	1763	NC	1840	Beulah Bapt.	?Etowah
Robert Henry	1765	x	1863	x	Tusquittee
Leonard Higdon	c.1754	NC	1837	x	x
Daniel Hinson (Henson)	1764	VA	1843	x	x
Elijah Hinson (Henson)	1761	VA	1845	x	x
Walter Hogsed	1764	x	1854	Hogsed Cem.	Brevard
John Hood	x	x	x	x	x
Absalom Hooper	c.1763	SC	1845	East La Porte Bap.	East La Porte
Zephaniah Horton	1760	NJ	1844	x	x
Edward Hyatt	1740	x	1817	Hyatt Cemetery	Qualla
Michael Israel, Sr.	c 1736	x	c.1820	Israel Cem.	Averys Creek
Edward James	x	x	x	private property	French Broad
Daniel Jarrett	1747	PA	1822	x	x
Jabez Jarvis	1730	x	c.1800	x	x
James Jennings	1757	DE	1837	George Cemetery	x
James Jester	1763	x	1837	x	x
James Johntson	1761	IR	1852	Shaws Creek Meth..	Hendersonville
Noble Johnson	c.1758	IR	1800	Shaws Creek Meth..	Hendersonville
Reuben Johnson	x	x	1843	x	x
Joshua Jones	c.1748	x	c.1839	Joshua Jones Cem.	Asheville
Thomas P. Jordan	c 1761	NC	1841	x	x
John Justus	1720	x	1794	x	x
Daniel Killian, Sr.	c.1750	NC	1836	Asbury Methodist	Asheville
Samuel King	1748	IR	1828	x	Flatrock
Abraham Kuykendall	c 1719	NY	1812	?Mud Creek Bapt.	Flatrock
John Lanning	1757	NJ	1839	Cane Creek Baptist	Fairview
Peter Ledford, Jr.	1758	NC	?1848	x	x
Robert Love	1760	VA	1845	Greenhill	Waynesville
Stephen Low(e)	c.1750	x	1797	x	x
Thomas Lytle, Sr.	1750	NC	1835	Bethel Cem.	Old Fort
Martin Maney	1752	x	1830	Maney Cemetery	Barnardsville
Jacob Martin	1763	x	1845	x	x

Co.	Rank	Wife
Hay.	Pvt	
Bun.		Ann Campbell
	?Capt	Martha _____
Bun.	Pvt	Margaret Hill
Bun.	Pvt	Mary _____
McD.	?Capt	Mary Ann Mackie
Hay.	?Capt	Nancy Newman
Hen.	Pvt	Mary McClaslin
Hen.	Pvt	2nd ElizabethPorter 3rd Charlotte Blythe
Clay	X	Dorcas Bell Love
Mac.	Pvt	Susannah Harris
?Hay.	Pvt	Fanba Pool
Hay.	Pvt	Fanny West
Tran.	X	
?Hay.	X	
Jac.	Pvt	Sarah Saters
Yan.	Pvt	Jean McCourry
Jac.	X	
Bun.	X	Sarah Graves
Bun.	X	
?Bu.	X	Mary Catherine Moyer
?Bun.	?Capt	Kesiah Ridge
Mad.	Pvt	Hannah Martin
Bun.	Pvt	
Hen.	Pvt	Ann Cole
Hen.	Pvt	Sara _____
Tran.		
Bun.	X	Elender Medley?
?Bun.	Pvt	Tabritha Wortham
?Bun.	X	Elizabeth _____
Bun.	Pvt	1st Osly Baker 2nd ?Polly _____
Hen.	X	Mrs. Eliz. U. Davenport
Hen.	?Capt	1st Elizabeth _____ 2nd Bathsheba _____
Bun.	Pvt	Sarah Whitaker
Clay	Pvt	
Hay.	?Lt	Mary Ann Dillard
?Bun.	X	Elizabeth _____
McD.	?Capt	Susannah Perkins
Bun.	X	Keziah Vann
Bun.	X	Polly Flemmons

Name	Born	Born	Died	Burial Cemetery	Location
John Massey	1758	VA	1835	x	x
Andrew Maxwell	x	x	x	Mud Creek Bapt.	Edneyville
Matthew Maybin	1756	IR	1845	Green River Cove	Tuxedo
John McClain	1750	PA	1795	x	x
William McLeod	1762	x	x	x	x
Malcolm McCourry	1742	NJ	1829	McCourry	Jacks Cr.
Charles McDowell	1743	VA	1815	Quaker Meadows	Morganton
John McDowell	1751	VA	1822	McDowell Presby.	Morganton
Joseph McDowell, Sr.	1756	VA	1801	x	Morganton
Joseph McDowell	1758	NC	1795	x	Marion
James McEntire	x	x	1820	1st Presbyterian Ch.	Morganton
Jonathan McPeters	1756	NC	1846	x	Yancey
Andrew Merrell	1757	x	1833	Mud Creek Bapt.	Edneyville
Benjamin Merrill	1752	NJ	1836	Merrill-Patton Cem.	Fairview
John Merrill	1757	NJ	1834	Merrill-Patton Cem.	Fairview
Christian S. Messer	1761	NC	1850	Panther Creek	
John Messer	x	x	x	Locust Field Cem.	Canton
David Miller	1753	NC	1845	x	x
George Miller	x	x	x	x	?Asheville
James Andrew Miller	1750	x	1808	Old French Broad B.	Horse Shoe
Samuel Monteith	1756	PA	1840	Old Love Cemetery	Sylva
David Moore	1764	VA	x	(Moore Cem.)	x
Jesse Moore, Sr.	1743	VA	1827	(Moore Cem.)	x
William Moore	?1726	x	?1812	Capt. Moore Cem.	Candler
James Murphy, Sr.	1759	NC	1831	Quaker Meadows	Morganton
Samuel Murray, Sr.	1739	PA	1817	Murray	Fairview
Robert Orr	1748	x	1808	Orr Cemetery	Little River
James Owenby	1761	VA	1850	Kran Family Cem.	Upper Mills
Edmund Palmer	1747	NJ	1835	Gabriells Cr. Baptist	Gabriele Cr.
Jesse Palmer, Sr.	1763	VA	1850	Big Sandy Meth.	Sandy Mush
Samuel Parks	1757	VA	1844	x	x
Aaron Patton	x	x	x	Patton Fam. Cem.	Swannanoa
Elijah Patton	x	x	x	x	x
Robert Patton	1747	x	1813	Druscilla Ch. Cem.	Dysartsville
Samuel Patton	c.1761	NC	1851	?Riverside Cem.	Asheville
Thomas Patton	1726	x	1808	Davidson River Cem.	Brevard
William Patton	1742	x	1818	Newton Academy	Asheville
Thomas Payne	1763	VA	x	x	x
George Penland	c.1753	x	1829	Vance Cem.	Reems Creek
John Penland	1764	PA	1855	Penland Family	Enka

Co.	Rank	Wife
?Hay.	Pvt	Lydia Sandlin
Hen.	Pvt	
Hen.	Pvt	
Hen.	X	
Mac.	Pvt	
Yan.		
Bur.	?Col	Mrs. Grace G. Bowman
Bur.	?Maj	Hannah Keller
Bur.	Maj	Margaretta Moffit
McD.	Capt	Mary Moffitt
Bur.	X	Nancy _____
Bun.	Pvt	?Nancy Moore
Hen.	X	
Bun.	Pvt	Penelope Merrill
Bun.	Pvt	Catherine Rhodes
Hay.	Pvt	Jane Barnet Freeman
Hay.	Pvt	
Bun.	X	
Bun.	X	
Hen.	X	
Jac.	Pvt	Margaret _____
Bur.	X	1st Rachel Stone 2nd Rachel Carroll
Bur.	X	Alley Johnson
Bun.	X	1st Margaret Patton 2nd Ann Cathy
Bur.	Pvt	1st Margaret McDowell 2nd Jane Fleming
Bun.		Elizabeth Rees
Tran.	X	Ann Hogsed
Rut.	Pvt	Johanna Sims
Mad.	Pvt	Mary Brittain
Bun.	Pvt	Elizabeth Hoffman
?Bur.	Pvt	
Bun.	X	
McD.	X	
McD.	?Capt	Elizabeth Dysart
Bun.	?Lt	Mary Alexander Johnston
Tran.	X	1st Mrs. Abigail Chambers 2nd Margaret Erwin
Bun.	X	
Bun.	Pvt	
?Bun.	X	Ann Alexander
Bun.	Pvt	Alice Moore

Name	Born	Born	Died	Burial Cemetery	Location
Robert Penland	c.1742	x	1826	x	x
Adam Phillips	1763	MD	1858	Bethesda Meth.	Haw Creek
Joseph Pyatt, Sr.(Piatt)	1756	ENG	1838	Old Nebo	Nebo
Peter Plemon	1755	x	1838	?Newfound Bapt.	?Leicester
Ephraim Powers	1757	NC	1835	x	x
Jonathan Prestwood	1758	x	1839	x	x
James Rector	1765	x	x	x	x
Samuel Reid (Reed)	1750	x	1851	x	x
Thomas Reid	c.1750	NC	1826	x	x
Joseph M. Rice	c.1761	VA	1850	Hughey Family Cem.	Riceville
William H. Rice	1761	VA	1847	?Big Ivy Cem.	Barnardsville
Jesse Rickman	1770	VA	1860	Rickman Fam. Cem.	Mills River
Frederick Rider	1750	x	1825	Moore Farm Cem.	x
George Roberts	1758	NC	1864	x	x
John Roberts	1758	x	x	x	x
William Roberts	1760	VA?	1845	Billy Roberts Cem.	x
William Robison	1760	PA	1837	Big Sandy Methodist	x
Thomas Robinson	1758	x	x	x	x
John Rockett	1764	VA	1848	Hudson-Corbe Cem.	Lo9velady
Hugh Rogers	1761	x	1848	Thad Rogers Cem.	Fines Creek
Samuel Rose	1755	x	1837	x	x
John Rutherford	1755	VA	1841	Rutherford	Bridgewater
Edmund Sams	1750	x	1845	Newton Academy	Asheville
William Sentell	1756	VA	c.1836	Sentell Family Cem.	Big Willow
Thomas Sharp	1755	PA	1830	X	X
Edward Shipman	c.1755	VA	c.1810	Little River Bapt.	Flat Rock
Jacob Shipman	1746	NC	1795	Ebenezer Baptist	Edneyville
Andrew Shook	1755	PA	x	x	x
Jacob Shook	1749	PA	1839	Pleasant Hill	Clyde
Uriah (Ute) Sherrill	x	x	1839	x	x
Weimer Siler	1755	x	1831	First Methodist Ch.	Franklin
Daniel Smith	1757	NJ	1824	Newton Academy	Asheville
Louis Smith	x	x	x	X	x
James Stepp, Jr	1754	VA	1821	Red Hill	Flat Rock
John Stiles	1757	x	1833	Dills Cemetery	Fisher Creek
Daniel Sullivan	1763	PA	1842	x	x
John Sutton	1732	x	1832	Old Savannah Bap.	Savannah
Michael Tanner	1761	VA	x	x	x
Samuel Tate	1730	IRE	1815	Tate	Bridgewater
Aaron Thomas	1765	x	x	x	x

Co.	Rank	Wife
?Bun.		Elizabeth Brank
Bun.	Pvt	Hannah Bailey
Bur.	Pvt	Sarah Jane Still
Bun.	Pvt	
Bun.	X	Sarah _____
Bun.	Sgt	
Bun.	X	
Cher.	X	
Bun.	Pvt	Ann Margaret Fletcher
Bun.	x	Margaret Young
Bun.	?Lt	1st Elizabeth M. Bowman 2nd Sarah Reid
Hen.	Pvt	1st Mary Trantham 2nd Rhoda Taylor Gadd
Bur.		
Bun.	Pvt	Polly Hines King
Bun.	x	
Mad.	x	
Bun.	Pvt	Sarah Duckworth
Bun.	Pvt	
Bur.	Sgt	Sarah Abernethy
Hay.	x	Nancy Thornton
Mac.	x	Mary Weist
Bur.	x	Susiane Ballew
Bun.	?Capt	
Hen.	Pvt	Elizabeth Stevens
Bun. Hen.	Pvt	Rhoda _____ 1st Sarah W. Osteen 2nd. Elizabeth Merrill
Hen.	Pvt	Sarah _____
?Hay.	Pvt	
Hay.	Pvt	Isabella Weitzell
Mac.	x	1st F. Dobson 2nd Elizabeth Thompson
Mac.	x	Margaret Rafferty
Bun.	?Capt	Mary M. Davidson
?Hay.	x	
Hen.		Mary (Polly) Mills
Jac.	Pvt	Lucy Beasley
?Bur.	Pvt	Margaret _____
Jac.	x	
Bun.	Pvt	
Bur.	Pvt	Elizabeth Caldwell
Mac.	Pvt	

Name	Born	Born	Died	Burial Cemetery	Location
Valentine Thrash	1749	GR	1835	Newfound Baptist	Leicester
William Trammell	c.1752	SC	1843	First Methodist Ch.	Franklin
Daniel T. Treadway	x	x	1824	?Ebenezer Baptist	?Hendersonville
David Vance	1748	VA	1813	Vance-Reems Cr.	Weaverville
Samuel Vermillian	1755	MD	1837	x	x
Edward Waldrop	1758	NC	1844	x	x
William Walton, Sr.	1736	VA	1806	1st Presbyterian Ch.	Morganton
John Weaver	1763	x	1830	Old Weaverville	Weaverville
John Webb	1765	x	1826	Hominy Baptist	Candler
Henry West	x	x	x	x	? Haw Creek
Jacob Wetzel	c.1751	x	c.1724	x	x
Charles White	1728	DE	1782	x	Cullasaia
James White	1760	VA	1811	x	x
Steven White	1725	DE	1818		Franklin
William Whitson	1750	x	1806	x	?Swannanoa
Thomas Williams	1757	x	x	Jennings Cem.	Holly Springs
Elijah Williamson	1755	NC	1837	Patton Fam. Cem.	Naples
Robert Williamson	x	x	x	Brank Fam. Cem.	Weaverville
William Wilson	1751	x	1832	1st Presbyterian Ch.	Morganton
James Withrow	1746	VA	1838	x	x
Henry Woods	1753	x	c.1844	x	x

Selected References

Anonymous, n.d., *Buncombe County, NC 1800 Census*

White, Emmett,1984, *Revolutionary War Soldiers, Burke Co., I*

White, Emmett, 1998, *Revolutionary War Soldiers, Burke Co., II*

Anonymous, (NSDAR), 2003, *DAR Patriot Index*

Moss, Bobby G., 1985, *Patriots at the Cowpens*

Moss, Bobby G., 1990, *Patriots at Kings Mountain*

White, Virgil, 1990, *Genealogical Abstracts-Pension Files*

Some pioneer resident veterans of Buncombe Co. lived their finals days in the following states:

AL: James Dunmore

GA: William Lewis Queen, Michael Tanner

KY: John Harper, James Stringfield

MO: Alexander Fuller

MS: Samuel Lusk

SC: Clement Davis, Isham Davis, Thomas Gladney, Matthew Maybin, John Prestwood, Charles Williamson

TN: Samuel Bryson, Daniel McPeters, John Sexton, Col. William Davidson

Unknown: Joseph Cross, William Deaver

Notes: Jesse Moore, Daniel Moore, & Frederick Rider were buried in the Moore Cemetery, Johns River, Burke Co.

Co.	Rank	Wife
Bun.	Pvt	Barbara Yountz
Mac.	x	1st (unknown) 2nd Sarah _____
?Hen.	x	
Bun.	Capt	Priscilla Brank
Mac.	Pvt	
Yan.	x	Frances Roberts
Bur.	?Lt.	Elizabeth Tilman
Bun.	x	Elizabeth Biffle
Bun.	x	Stacy Webb
Bun.	x	
Tran.	x	
Mac.	Cpl	
Bun.	x	Elizabeth Daves
Mac.	?Sgt.	Ann Ross
Bun.	Pvt	Ann McDowell
Mac.	Pvt	
Hen.	Pvt	Sarah Byrd
Bun.	x	
Bur.	x	
?Bun.	Capt	Mary Bronson
Bur.	Pvt	

Subject Index - Introductory Part

Arkansas Territory, 28
Board of Trade, 13
Boone's Barony, 32
Black Slaves, 11, 18-20, 24, 27-28, 31-32, 42,
    45, 60
Buncombe County Register of Deeds, 6, 7, 56
Cemeteries
    Ashworth, 5
    Capt. William Moore, 4, 5
    Central Methodist, 4
    Episcopalian, 4
    1st Presbyterian, 4
    Quaker Meadows, 3, 12, 38, 60
    Riverside, 4
    Thomas Jones, 57
Charlotte Mint, 42
Communities,
    Asheville, NC, 3-4, 6-7, 30, 37, 39, 42, 46
    Bath, NC, 20
    Chapel Hill, NC, 30
    Charleston, SC, 32, 51
    Charlotte, NC, 30
    Dahlonega, GA, 42
    Echoe, NC, 26
    Edenton, NC, 30, 36
    Enka, NC, 5
    Fairview, NC, 5
    Forest City, NC, 11-12, 65
    Greenville, SC, 40
    Greeneville, TN, 40
    Hillsborough, NC, 32, 36, 48
    Joara, NC, 41
    Jonesborough, TN, 7
    Morganton, NC, 7, 25, 41
    Nashville, TN, 28, 32, 51
    New Berne, NC, 20, 27, 30
    Pleasant Gardens, NC, 12, 60
    Raleigh, NC, 6, 25, 30, 38
    Salisbury, NC, 27
    Savannah, GA, 32
    Statesville, NC, 24, 27
    Tallahassee, FL, 33
    Wilmington, NC, 30

Continental Currency, 53
Cumberland Compact, 31
DAR, 59
Debtor's Prisons, 38, 44-45
    Prune Street Jail, 44
Deed Mapping
    Deed Mapper, 51
    Maptech Terrain Navigator, 51
Depreciation Lands, 17
Donation Lands, 17
Dutch East Indies Company, 22
Dutch West Indies Company, 22
Excessive Grants, 38
Forts,
    Fort Dobbs, 24, 27
    Fort Long Cane Creek, 26
    Fort Loudon, 26
    Fort Ninety-Six, 26
    Fort Prince George, 26
Genealogy Societies,
    Burke County G. S., 6, 11, 56-57
    Old Buncombe Co. G. S., 1, 57
    Old Tryon Co. G. S., 11, 57
Geographic Features
    Allegheny Mtns., 18
    Appalachian Mtns, 3, 23-24, 27, 36,
    40- 42
    Blue Ridge Province, 3, 39
    Cape Hatteras, 22
    Carolana, 13, 20
    Carolina, 13, 22-23, 35
    Cumberland Gap, 31
    Cumberland Valley, 16, 31-32
    Currituck Is., 36
    Delaware River Valley, 16
    Grandfather Mtn., 42
    Inner Coastal Plain, 21
    Mt. Mitchell, 45
    Outer Coastal Plain, 21
    Piedmont Province, 3, 21, 36, 42
    Watauga, 31-32
    Western Reserve, 17
    Wyoming Valley, 17

Indians,
    Catawba, 21
    Cherokee, 23-24, 26-28, 31, 41, 46, 50, 54
        Lower Towns, 27
        Middle Towns, 23, 27
        Overhill Towns, 23, 27
    Choctaw, 28
    Chickasaw, 26, 28
    Creek, 26, 28, 50
    Delaware, 16
    Five Civilized Tribes, 28
    Mississippian Mound Builders, 41
    Qualla Reservation, 46
    Seminole, 28
    Shawnee, 16
    Tuscarora, 23-24
    Walking Purchase, 17
    Yamasee, 23
Joint Boundary Commission, 36
Land Companies,
    Georgia Land Co., 49
    Georgia Mississippi Co., 49
    North American Land Co., 44
    Rutherford Land Co., 14, 15
    Speculation Land Co., 14
    Tennessee Co., 49
    Transylvania Land Co., 28, 31
    Upper Mississippi Co., 49
    Virginia Yazoo Co., 49
Land Frauds,
    Glasgow Land Fraud, 49-50
    Mussel Shoals Land Fraud, 49
    Yazoo Land Fraud, 49
Land Grants, 6-8, 13, 16, 18, 20, 29-33, 43-51
    Colonial, 8, 29
    Crown, 13, 16-17, 18, 20, 29
    Proprietary, 20-21, 29
Land Offices,
    Edenton, 36
    Hillsboro, 32, 48
    NC State, 29
    Ninety-Six District, 49
Land Ordinance of 1785, 34
Lawyers ,

Avery, Waightstill, 7, 30, 41-43, 59
    Benton, Thomas Hart, 45, 49, 58
    Calhoun, John C. , 28, 42
    Jackson, Andrew, 32, 36, 48, 58
    Sondley, Foster A., 7, 41, 56
    Swain, David L., 30, 43, 46
    Woodfin, Nicholas W., 45-46, 60
Louisiana Purchase, 45, 49-50
Maps & Mapping,
    Mason-Dixon Line, 17, 37
    NC/SC Line, 36-37
    MD/PA Line, see Mason-Dixon
    VA/NC Line, 20, 36-37
Migration, 6, 54-55
Military,
    Continental Army, 58-59
    Militia, 11-12, 23, 26-28, 32, 58-59
    Military Bounty Warrants, 17-18, 31-32, 50
    Military Reservation, 28, 31-32
Minerals
    Anthracite, 15
    Charlotte Mint, 42
    Gold, 41-42
    Gold Land Lottery, 42, 45
    Mica, 41
Mulberry Grove Plantation, 32
Nationalities,
    Dutch, 10, 16, 22
    English, 16, 21, 22-24, 54
    French, 22-24
    Germans, 9-10. 22-23
    Highland Scots, 10, 21, 54
    Scots-Irish, 9-10, 21, 54
    Spanish, 22-23, 41
NC State Archives,
    MARS Program, 6-8, 14, 46, 56
Northwest Ordinance of 1787, 24
Paris Peace Conference, 24
Pennsylvania Land Office, 15
Political Groups,
    Federalists, 14
    North Carolina Assembly, 21
    Patriots, 14, 58-59
    Pennsylvania Assembly, 17
    Republican, 14

Tories, 14, 58

Population, 11, 16-17, 21, 24, 26-28, 37, 54, 58, 65

Preempters, 17, 31, 39, 49, 54-55

Principals - American,

Alexander, John McKnitt, 34, 38

Allison, David, 45, 47-48

Armstrong, Martin, 32, 47-48

Avery, Waightstill, 7, 30, 41-43, 59

Baird, Zebulon, 4, 43

Benton, Thomas Hart, 45, 49, 58

Blount, John Gray, 8, 32, 39, 45, 49

Blount, William, 32, 45, 47-49

Calhoun, John C. , 28, 42

Candler, Zachariah, 6, 7, 43, 46,

Caswell, Richard, 31, 49, 59

Coxe, Tench, 13-15

Davidson, William Lee, 29, 32, 59

Donaldson, Stockley, 31, 39, 47-49, 50, 53

Greene, Nathanael, 32, 59

Gudger, William, 6

Henry, Robert, 30, 35

Jackson, Andrew, 32, 36, 48, 58

Kuykendall, Abraham, 59

Love, Robert, 6, 35-46, 50, 59

McDowell, Joseph, 27, 37, 59

Mills, William, 58

Morris, Robert, 19, 38, 44

Morgan, Daniel, 11

Newton, George, 30

Patton, James, 4

Reynolds, Abraham, 6, 9, 53

Rutherford, Griffith, 27-28, 32, 59

Sevier, John , 39, 48-49, 50, 59

Swain, David L., 30, 43, 46

Vance, David, 32, 45

Vanderbilt, George W., 7

Washington, George, 18-19

Principals - English,

Churton, William, 36

Coxe, Daniel, 13

Dobbs, Arthur, 21, 27, 36

Lord Granville, 20-21, 24, 29, 36

King Charles I, 13

King Charles II, 16, 20

King George I, 13

King George II, 24, 26

King George III, 54

McCulloch, Henry, 36

Penn, William, 13, 16-17

Tryon, William, 21, 27

Proprietors, 17, 20, 29, 36

First Proprietor's Map, 23

Second Proprietor's Map, 23

Religions,

Anglicans, 30

German Reformed, 10

Lutherans, 10

Moravians, 36

Pietists, 16, 21

Presbyterians, 10, 30

Quakers, 16, 21

Rivers & Waterways,

Albemarle Sound, 20-21

Ashley River, 23

Broad River, 14, 39, 54

Cape Fear River, 21, 36

Catawba River, 10, 12, 25, 27, 34, 38-39

Cumberland River, 31

Delaware River, 16

Dismal Swamp, 18-19, 24, 36

Duck River, 32

Flat Creek, 10

French Broad River, 10, 12, 25, 39

Green River, 14

Kanawa River, 18

Mississippi River, 13,18, 20, 23-24

Mills River, 12

Neuse River, 21, 23, 36

North Hominy Creek, 43

North Pacolet River, 14

Ohio River, 18, 34, 41

Pamlico River, 21

Pee Dee River, 36

Swannanoa River, 10, 12, 45, 65

Sweeten Creek, 10

Tennessee River, 49

Tuckasegee River, 39

Watauga River, 37

Yadkin River, 21, 51

Roads & Trails,
     Buncombe Turnpike, 40
     Great Wagon Road, 21, 54
     Hickory Nut Gap Turnpike, 39
     Oconaluftee Valley Turnpike, 39
     Philadelphia & Lancaster Turnpike, 15
     Rutherfords War Trace, 27
     Watauga Trail, 7
Royal Governors, 21, 27, 36
Schools,
     College of New Jersey, 30
     Liberty Hall Academy, 30
     Morgan Academy, 30
     Princeton College, 30
     Queens College, 30
     Union Hill Academy, 30
     UNC, Chapel Hill, 30, 32
1775 Mecklenburg Declaration of
Independence, 34
1790 U.S. Census, 11-12, 24, 65
Southern Army, 32
Squatters, see Preempters
Surveying
     Base Lines, 34
     Magnetic Declination, 35, 51
     Magnetic Pole, 35
     New England Survey System, 34
     North Pole, 35
     NOAA, 35, 51
     Principal Meridian, 34
     Southern Survey System, 34-36
     Surveyors, 34-37
     Surveying Instruments, 35
Tennessee, 28, 31-32, 37, 47-51
     Eastern District, 47-48, 50
     Mero District, 50
     Middle District, 47-48, 50
     State of Franklin, 50
     Western District, 47-38
Treaty of Sycamore Shoals, 31
UNCA Special Collections, 14, 57
U.S. Forestry Service, 6, 46, 56
     Pisgah National Forest, 7
Wars,
     Cherokee Wars, 26-28

Civil War, 4, 42, 46, 60
French & Indian War, 18, 26
Revolutionary War, 11-12, 14, 17-18,
37-38, 50, 58-60
     Battle of Cowpens, 11
     Battle of Kings Mountain, 50
     Battle of Moore's C. Bridge, 21
WPA, 4, 6, 56

www.ingramcontent.com/pod-product-compliance
Lightning Source LLC
Chambersburg PA
CBHW080402270326
41927CB00015B/3318